MILLEDULCIA:

A THOUSAND PLEASANT THINGS.

Selected from Notes and Queries.

What song the Syrens sang, or what name Achilles assumed when he hid himself among women, though puzzling questions, are not beyond all conjecture.

URN-BURIAL, chap. 5.

NEW YORK:
D. APPLETON AND COMPANY,
346 & 348 BROADWAY.
1857.

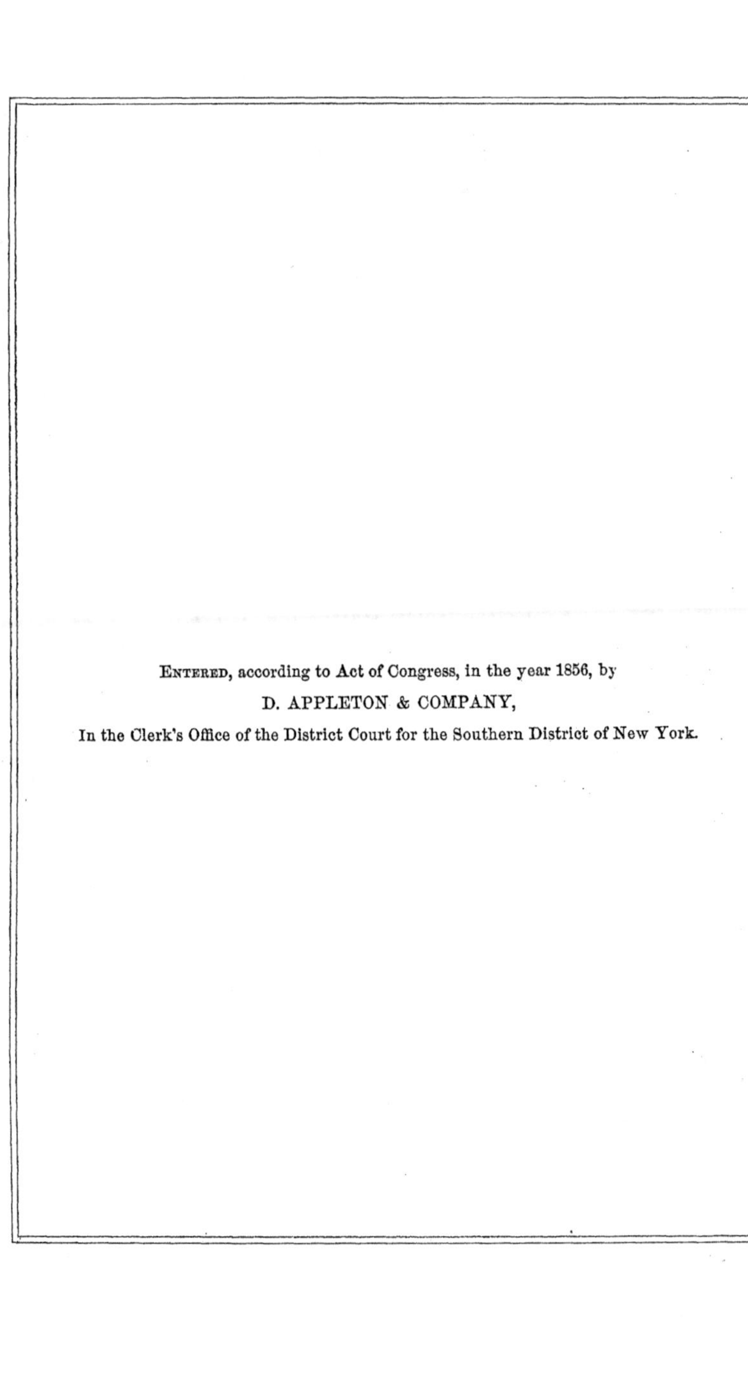

PREFACE.

Notes and Queries* may be called a literary exchange, where "all who know something—have something to ask—or who can solve something," may meet upon common ground.

This excellent idea has in its execution proved of real service to literature, by throwing light on many obscure and debated points, and by bringing out much valuable and pleasant knowledge, which, for want of such a publication, has lain hid in old crypts, in dust-incrusted pigeon-holes, and in the dark, unfrequented nooks of libraries, where, but for this work, it might have slumbered for ages, or have been altogether lost.

Southey, in The Doctor, characterizes the Gentleman's Magazine as a "great lumber-room, wherein small ware of all kinds has been laid up higgledy-piggledy, by half-pennyworths or farthingworths at a time, till, like broken

* Notes and Queries, a medium of intercommunication for literary men, Artists, Antiquaries, Genealogists, etc. London, published weekly, November, 1849, December, 1855. 1st series, 12 vols..

glass, rags, or rubbish, it has acquired value by mere accumulation."

NOTES AND QUERIES with higher aims, has a much greater value. In this "lumber-room," amid the "rubbish" inherent from the very nature of the work, gleam, so to speak, old gems, richly-chased bronzes, rare old china, or other objects of curiosity and interest.

Though occasionally some greedy *helluo librorum*, some "first cousin of the moth," some enthusiastic explorer who, in perambulating the fields of learning, has stumbled over a mare's nest of extraordinary magnitude and hastens to display his treasure; or two testy knights of the pen run foul of each other on some such subject (so *very* trying to temper) as Shakspearian emendation—though these may occupy much time and type, yet there is still a great deal in the work entertaining and valuable. This it has been our object to arrange and gather together. It has not been thought necessary to preserve the temporary form of queries and answers. Some additions have been made by the compiler whenever it seemed to him they might illustrate a subject, but they are few and trivial.

CONTENTS.

A.

C.

MILLEDULCIA.

THE BURIAL OF SIR JOHN MOORE.

THE undoubted author of the monody on the Burial of Sir John Moore, is the late Rev. Charles Wolfe, a young Irishman, curate of Donoughmore, diocese of Armagh, who died 1823, in the 32d year of his age. His *Life and Remains* were edited by the Archdeacon of Clogher; and a *fifth* edition of the volume, which is an 8vo, was published in 1832 by Hamilton, Adams & Co., Paternoster Row. At the twenty-fifth page of the Memoir there is the narration of an interesting discussion between Lord Byron, Shelley, and others, as to the most perfect ode that had ever been produced. Shelley contended for Coleridge's on Switzerland; others named Campbell's Hohenlinden and Lord Byron's Invocation in Manfred. But Lord Byron left the dinner-table before the cloth was removed, and returned with a magazine, from which he read this monody, which just then appeared anonymously. After he had read it, he repeated the third stanza, and pronounced it perfect, and especially the lines—

> But he lay like a warrior taking his rest,
> With his martial cloak around him.

"I should have taken the whole," said Shelley, "for a rough sketch of Campbell's."

"No," replied Lord Byron, "Campbell would have claimed it, had it been his."

The Memoir contains the fullest details on the subject of the authorship, Mr. Wolfe's claim to which was also fully established by the Rev. Dr. Miller, late Fellow of Trinity, Dublin, and author of *Lectures on the Philosophy of Modern History.*

It was stated in an English paper, published in France some few years back, that Wolfe had taken the lines from a poem at the end of the *Memoirs of Lally Tollendal*, the French governor of Pondicherry, in 1756, and subsequently executed in 1766. In this paper the French poem was given, professing to be a monody on Lally Tollendal, and to be found in the Appendix to his Memoirs. It was only a clever hoax from the ready pen of Father Prout, and first appeared in Bentley's *Miscellany.* No greater proof of the inconvenience of facetiæ of this peculiar nature can be required than the circumstance that the *fiction*, after a time, gets mistaken for a fact: as, in the present case, a statement having been made in the *Morning Chronicle* that Wolfe was the author of the poem. There shortly afterwards appeared the following letter in *The Courier*, Wednesday, Nov. 3, 1824.

ODE ON THE BURIAL OF SIR JOHN MOORE.

To the Editor of the Courier:

Sir,—Permit me, through the medium of your highly respectable journal (which I have chosen as the channel of this communication, from my having been a subscriber to it for the last fifteen years), to observe, that the statement lately published in the *Morning Chronicle*, the writer of which ascribes the lines on the Burial of Sir John Moore to Woolf, is *false*, and as barefaced a *fabrication* as ever was foisted on the public. The lines in question were not written by Woolf, nor by Hailey, nor is Deacoll the author, but they were composed by *me*. I published them originally some years ago in the *Durham County Advertiser*, a journal in which I have at different times inserted several poetical trifles, as the "Prisoner's Prayer to Sleep," "Lines on the lamented Death of Benjamin Galley, Esq.," and some other little effusions.

I should not, sir, have thought the lines on Sir John Moore's funeral worth owning, had not the false statement of the *Chronicle* met my eye. I can prove, by the most incontestable evidence, the truth of what I have asserted. The first copy of my lines was given by me to my friend and relation Captain Bell, and it is in his possession at present. It agrees perfectly with the copy now in circulation, with this exception, it does not contain the stanzas commencing with "Few and Short," which I added afterwards at the suggestion of the Rev. Dr. Alderson of Butterby.

I am, sir, yours, &c.,

South Street, Durham, Nov. 1, 1824. H. MARSHALL, M. D.

This letter was a mere hoax, and was so shown to be two or three days after its publication, by an authenticated statement that "Dr. Marshall, of South street, Durham," was a horse-doctor of dissipated rather than literary habits, and not even a graduate of the Veterinary College. He had of course nothing to do with the letter. Benjamin Galley, who is termed esquire in the letter, was a poor Durham idiot; and by the Rev. Dr. Alderson, of Butterby, was meant Hutchinson Alderson, the bellman of Durham.

The paragraph in the *Morning Chronicle*, to which Dr. Marshall's letter refers, had been inserted by John Sidney Taylor, a bosom-friend of the Rev. Charles Wolfe, the author of the monody. Mr. Taylor replied to the Doctor's letter in an angry philippic; wherein, after allusions to Celsus and Galen, he informs the Doctor he is not ambitious of taking his medicine, and advises him, instead of claiming verses which do not belong to him, to content himself with writing verses on the tombstones of his patients. Mr. Taylor evidently thought he was dealing with the genuine letter of a real M. D., though he insinuates that he was a quack.

It will be seen by the Doctor's letter, that he not only claimed the authorship of the "Monody on the Death of Sir John Moore," but also of "The Prisoner's Prayer to Sleep." Professor Wilson, of Edinburgh, thereupon avowed himself the author of the latter poem, and was probably as much deceived by the Doctor's letter as Mr. Taylor had been.

These particulars are derived from an amusing article entitled "The Wags of Durham," in Richardson's *Borderer's Table Book*, vii. 199–205; but in that article the Doctor's letter is stated to have appeared in the *Courier*, of December 30th, 1824. It is probable, however, that the date, November 3d, 1824, is correct.

In and about 1824, many hoaxing letters (some displaying much humor), appeared. The late Dr. Chaffy, master of Sidney College, and Mr. Coulburn, were the subjects of some of these letters. One of the ablest was from Dr. Chaffey to *The Times*, followed by another declaring it to be a forgery which could hardly require denial, as "everybody must be aware that the Chaffys of Lincolnshire spell their name without the *e*." Notwithstanding this exquisite piece of internal evidence, the second letter was as fictitious as the first.

Shortly after the publication of "Dr. Marshall's" letter, and its exposure, appeared a parody on the monody, which was ascribed to Praed and others until the Rev. Richard Harris Barham, the author of the Ingoldsby Legends, acknowledged them, in the first volume of that work, in the following manner :—

In the autumn of 1824, Captain Medwin having hinted that certain beautiful lines on the burial of this gallant officer might have been the production of Lord Byron's muse, the late Mr. Sidney Taylor, somewhat indignantly, claimed them for their rightful owner, the late Rev. Charles Wolfe. During the controversy a third claimant started up in the person of a soi-disant Doctor Marshall, who turned out to be a Durham blacksmith, and his pretensions a hoax. It was then that a certain Doctor Peppercorn put forth *his* pretensions to what he averred was the only "true and original" version, viz. :—

Not a *sous* had he got—not a guinea or note;
And he look'd most confoundedly flurried,
As he bolted away without paying his shot,
And the landlady after him hurried.

We saw him again at dead of night,
When home from the club returning;
We *twigg'd* the Doctor beneath the light
Of the gas-lamps brilliantly burning.

All bare and exposed to the midnight dews,
Reclin'd in the gutter we found him;
And he look'd like a gentleman taking a snooze,
With his *Marshall* cloak around him.

'The Doctor was drunk as the devil,' we said,
And we managed a shutter to borrow;
We rais'd him, and sigh'd at the thought that his head
Would consumedly ache on the morrow.

We bore him home, and we put him to bed,
And we told his wife and his daughter
To give him next morning a couple of red—
Herrings and soda-water.

Loudly they talk of his money that's gone,
And his lady began to upbraid him;
But little he reck'd, so they let him snore on,
'Neath the counterpane just as we laid him.

We tuck'd him in, and had hardly done,
When under the window calling,
We heard the rough voice of a son of a gun
Of a watchman 'one o'clock' bawling.

Slowly and sadly we all walked down
From his room in the uppermost story;
A rush-light we placed on the cold hearth-stone,
And we left him alone in his glory.

"Hos ego versiculos feci, tulit alter honores."—*Virgil.*

"I wrote the lines—M———l owned them—he told stories!"—*Thomas Ingoldsby.*

The clergyman who officiated on the occasion of Moore's burial was the Rev. H. J. Symons, at present vicar of St. Martin's, Hereford, who gives the following account of the ceremony in answer to some inquiries:

I am the clergyman alluded to, who officiated on that memorable occasion. I was chaplain to the brigade of Guards attached to the army under the command of the late Sir John Moore, and it fell to my lot to attend him in his last moments. During the battle he was conveyed from the field by a sergeant of the 42d, and some soldiers of that regiment and of the Guards, and I followed them into the quarters of the general, on the quay at Corunna, where he was laid on a mattress on the floor; and I remained with him till his death, when I was kneeling by his side. After which, it was the subject of deliberation whether his corpse should be conveyed to England, or be buried on the spot; which was not determined before I left the general's quarters. I determined, therefore, not to embark with the troops, but remained on shore till the morning, when, on going to his quarters, I found that his body had been removed during the night to the quarters of Col. Graham, in the citadel, by the officers of his staff, from whence it was borne by them, assisted by myself, to the grave which had been prepared for it, on one of the bastions of the citadel. It now being daylight, the enemy discovered that the troops had been withdrawn and embarked during the night. A fire was opened by them shortly after upon the ships which were still in the harbor. The funeral service was therefore performed without delay, as we were exposed to the fire of the enemy's guns; and after having shed a tear over the remains of the departed general, whose body was wrapt

With his martial cloak around him,—

there having been no means to provide a coffin,—the earth closed upon him, and

We left him alone in his glory!

A full and *authenticated* account of this interesting event will be found in *The Narrative of the Campaign of the British army in Spain commanded by His Excellency Sir John Moore, K. B., &c., authenticated by Official Papers and Original Letters.* By James Moore, Esq.

I trust that I have satisfactorily answered the inquiries of your correspondent, and shall be happy to reply to any farther inquiries which he may wish to make relating to that interesting event. H. J. SYMONS,

Vicar of St. Martin's, Hereford.

Hereford, Sept., 1852.

SMOLLETT'S HUGH STRAP

The following is an extract from an old newspaper of April, 1809:

SMOLLETT'S CELEBRATED HUGH STRAP.

On Sunday was interred, in the burial-ground of St. Martin's-in-the-Fields, the remains of Hugh Hewson, who died at the age of eighty-five. The deceased was a man of no mean celebrity. He had passed more than forty years in the parish of St. Martin's, and kept a hair-dresser's shop, being no less a personage than the identical *Hugh Strap*, whom Dr. Smollett rendered so conspicuously interesting in his life and adventures of Roderick Random. The deceased was a very intelligent man, and took delight in recounting the scenes of his early life. He spoke with pleasure of the time he passed in the service of the Doctor, and it was his pride as well as boast to say that he had been educated at the same seminary with so learned and distinguished a character. His shop was hung round with Latin quotations, and he would frequently point out to his acquaintance the several scenes in Roderick Random pertaining to himself, which had their foundation, not in the Doctor's inventive fancy, but in truth and reality. The Doctor's meeting with him at a barber's shop at Newcastle-upon-Tyne, the subsequent mistake at the Inn, their arrival together in London, and the assistance they experienced from *Strap's* friend, were all of that description. The deceased, to the last, obtained a comfortable subsistence by his industry, and of late years had been paid a weekly salary by the inhabitants of the Adelphi, for keeping the entrances to Villier's-walk, and securing the promenade from the intrusion of strangers.

There is another claimant for this honor mentioned by Mr. Faulkner, in his *History of Chelsea*, vol. i. p. 171, who states that Mr. W. Lewis, of Lombard Street, Chelsea, was the original of this character. He established himself in Chelsea by Smollett's advice, and died there about 1785. Faulkner states that he resided with his widow for seven years, and thus had opportunities of being acquainted with the facts.

COLERIDGE'S OPINION OF DEFOE.

Wilson, in his *Memoirs of the Life and Times of Defoe*, vol. ii. p. 205, having quoted the opinion of the editor of Cadell's edition of *Robinson Crusoe*—"that Defoe wanted many of those qualities, both of mind and manner, which fitted Steele and Addison to be the inimitable *arbitri elegantiarum* of English society, there can be no doubt,"—Coleridge wrote in the margin of his copy, "I doubt this, particularly in respect to Addison, and think I could select from Defoe's writings a volume equal in size to Addison's collected papers, little inferior in wit and humor, and greatly superior in vigor of style and thought."

BURNET'S OWN TIMES.

"Did you ever read that garrulous, pleasant history? He tells his story like an old man past political service, bragging to his sons on winter evenings of the part he took in public transactions when his 'old cap was new.' Full of scandal, which all true history is. So palliative; but all the stark wickedness that actually gives the *momentum* to national actors. Quite the prattle of age and outlived importance. Truth and sincerity staring out upon you perpetually *in alto relievo.* Himself a party-man, he makes you a party-man. None of the cursed philosophical Humeian indifference, 'so cold and unnatural and inhuman.' None of the cursed Gibbonian fine writing, so fine and composite. None of Dr. Robertson's periods with three members. None of Mr. Roscoe's sage remarks, all so apposite and coming in so clever, lest the reader should have had the trouble of drawing an inference. Burnet's good old prattle I can bring present to my mind; I can make the Revolution present to me."—*Charles Lamb: Letters.*

An Epigram on the Reverend Mr. Lawrence Eachard's and Bishop Gilbert Burnet's Histories. By Mr. Matthew Green, of the Custom-House.

Gil's History appears to me
Political anatomy—
A case of skeletons well done,
And malefactors every one.
His sharp and strong incision pen,
Historically cuts up men,
And does with lucid skill impart
Their inward ails of head and heart.
Lawrence proceeds another way,
And well-dressed figures does display;
His characters are all in flesh,
Their hands are fair, their faces fresh;

And from his sweet'ning art derive
A better scent than when alive;
He wax-work made to please the sons,
Whose fathers were Gil's skeletons.

From a *Collection of Poems by several hands.* London: Dodsley, 1748.

THE LAST OF THE PALEOLOGI.

About two centuries ago, lived and died in England, Theodore Paleologus, the immediate descendant of the Constantine family. He is buried in the church of St. Landulph, near Saltash, in the county of Cornwall. The following is his epitaph:

Here lyeth the body of Theodoro Paleologus
Of Pesaro in Italye, descended from ye Imperyail
Lyne of ye last Christian Emperors of Greece
Being the sonne of Camilio, ye soñe of Prosper
the sonne of Theodoro the sonne of Iohn, ye sonne
of Thomas, second brother to Constantine
Paleologus, the 8th of that name and last of
y^t^ lyne y^t^ raygned in Constantinople, untill sub-
dewed by the Turkes, who married with Mary
Y^e^ daughter of William Balls of Hadlye in
Souffolke Gent, & had issue 5 children, Theodoro, Iohn, Ferdinando, Maria & Dorothy, and departed this life at Clyfton ye 21th of January, 1636.

WORDS AND EXPRESSIONS.

Ennui.—"Cleland (voc. 165) has, with his usual sagacity, and with a great deal of trouble, as he himself acknowledges, traced out the true meaning and derivation of this word; for after he had long despaired of discovering the origin of it, mere chance, he says, offered to him what he took to be the genuine one. "In an old French book I met," says he, "with a passage where the author, speaking of a company that had sat up late, makes use of this expression, 'l'ennuit les avoit gagnés,' by the context of which it was plain he meant that the common influence of *the night*, in bringing on *heaviness* and *yawning*, had come upon them. The proper sense is totally antiquated, but the figurative remains in full currency to this day."—*Lemon's Etymological Dictionary.*

Tandem.—A practical pun is now naturalized in our language in the word "Tandem" (at length).

Brown Study.—Surely a corruption of brow-study, brow being derived from the old German, *braun*, in its compound form *aug-braun*, an eyebrow.

Scamp.—The word means literally a fugitive from the field, one *qui ex campo exit.*

Luncheon.—Our familiar name of *luncheon* is derived from the daily meal of the Spaniards at eleven o'clock, termed *once* or *l'once* (pronounced *l'onchey*).—*From Ford's Gatherings in Spain.*

Geho!—A learned friend, whose communications I have frequently had occasion to acknowledge in the course of this work, says the exclamation "*Geho! Geho!*" which carmen use to their horses, is probably of great antiquity. It is not peculiar to this country, as I have heard it used in France. In the story of the Milkmaid, who kicked down her pail, and with it all her hopes of getting rich, as related in a very ancient collection of apologues, entitled *Dialogus Creaturarum*, printed at Gonda in 1480, is the following passage: "Et cum sic gloriaretur, et cogitaret cum quantâ gloriâ duceretur ad illum virum super equum dicendo *gio gio*, cepit percutere terram quasi pungeret equum calcaribus."—*Brand's Popular Antiq.*

Hip, Hip, Hurrah!—Originally a war-cry, adopted by the stormers of a German town, wherein a great many Jews had taken their refuge. The place being sacked, they were all put to the sword, under the shouts of *Hierosolyma est perdita!* From the first letter of those words (*H. e. p.*) an exclamation was contrived.

There are two English words, in pronouncing which not a single letter of them is sounded; namely, *ewe* (yo), and *aye* (I).

Runic Names.—Sir William Temple, in his *Essay on Poetry*, says, speaking of the old Runic:

> The remainders are woven into our very language. *Mara*, in old Runic, was a goblin that seized upon men asleep in their beds, and took from them all speech and motion. Old *Nicka* was a spirit that came to strangle people who fell into the water. *Bo* was a fierce Gothic captain, son of Odin, whose name was used by his soldiers when they would fight or surprise their enemies.

Lack-a-daisy.—In Todd's *Johnson* it is explained as "a frequent colloquial term implying *alas;* most probably from the forgotten verb *lack*, to blame. The expression, therefore, may be considered as *blaming, finding fault with, the day* on which the event mentioned happened."

Banyan Day.—A marine term for those days in which the sailors have no flesh meat; and is probably derived from the practice of the Banians, a caste of Hindoos, who entirely abstained from all animal food.

Snooks.—This name, so generally associated with vulgarity, is only a corruption, or rather a contraction, of the more dignified name of *Sevenoaks*. This town is generally called *Se'noaks* in Kent; and the further contraction, coupled with the phonetic spelling of former days, easily passed into *S'nooks.* This is no imaginary conclusion, for Messrs. Sharp and Harrison, solicitors, Southampton, have recently had in their possession a series of deeds, in which all the modes of spelling occur from *Sevenokes* down to *S'nokes*, in connection with a family now known as *Snooks.*

VIOLIN INSCRIPTION.

This distich is said to have been inscribed on the violin of Palestrina, the "Musicæ Princeps" of the sixteenth century:—

Viva fui in sylvis; sum dura occisa securi;
Dum vixi tacui; mortua dulce sona.

Thus translated into French:

La hache m'arracha mourant du fond des bois;
Vivant, j'étais muet; mort, on vante ma voix.

Palestrina's violin was made by a great musical instrument-maker at Bologna, who had the same lines graven on his lutes, bass-viols, &c.

STORY OF A RELIC.

The following curious story is in a rare little Portuguese book. The work was printed at Vienna in 1717, and is an account of the embassy of Fernando Telles da Sylva, Conde de Ville Mayor, from the Court of Lisbon to that of Vienna, to demand in marriage, for the eldest son of King Pedro II., of Portugal, the hand of the Archduchess Maria Anna, of Austria. It was written by Father Francisco da Fonseca, a Jesuit priest, who accompanied the ambassador in quality of almoner and confessor, and is full of amusing matter, particularly in reference to the strange opinions concerning our laws, government, and religion, which the worthy padre appears to have picked up during his short stay in England.

The original of the annexed translation is to be found at pp. 318, 319, 320, § 268, of Fonseca's Narrative.

As we are now upon the subject of miracles wrought by Relics in Vienna, I shall proceed to relate another prodigy which happened in the said city, and which will greatly serve to confirm in us those feelings of piety with which we are wont to venerate such sacred objects. The Count Harrach, who was greatly favored by the Duke of Saxony, begged of him, as a present, a few of the many relics which the duke preserved in his treasury, assuredly less out of devotion than for the sake of their rarity and value. The duke, with his usual benignity, acceded to this request, and gave orders that sundry vials should be dispatched to the count, filled with most indubitable relics of Our Lord, of the Blessed Virgin, of the Apostles, of the Innocents, and of other holy persons. He directed two Lutheran ministers to pack these vials securely in a precious casket, which the duke himself sealed up with his own signet, and set off to Vienna. On its arrival there, it was deposited in the chapel of the count, which is situated in the street called Preiner. The count immediately informed the bishop of the arrival of this treasure, and invited him to witness the opening of the casket, and to attend for the purpose of verifying its contents. Accordingly the bishop came, and on opening the casket, there proceeded from it such an abominable stench that no man could endure it, infecting, as it did, the whole of the chapel. The bishop thereupon ordered all the vials to be taken out, and carefully examined one by one, hoping to ascertain the cause of this strange incident, which did not long remain a mystery, for they soon found the very vial from which this pestilent odor was issuing. It contained a small fragment of cloth, which was thus labelled: "*Ex caligis Divi Martini Lutheri*," that is to say, "*A bit of the breeches of Saint Martin Luther*," which the aforesaid two Lutheran ministers, by way of mockery of our piety, had slily packed up with the holy relics in the casket. The bishop instantly gave orders to burn this abominable rag of the great heresiarch, and forthwith not only the stench ceased, but there proceeded from the true relics such a delicious and heavenly odor as perfumed the entire building.

YANKEE.

The word *Yankee* is believed to have been derived from the manner in which the Indians endeavored to pronounce the word *English*, which they rendered *Yenghees*, whence the word *Yankee*. The statement in Irving's *Knickerbocker's History of New York*, concerning the tribe of *Yankoos*, is a mere joke. The word Yankee undoubtedly had the *Yenghees* origin referred to above, but it does not seem to have been very common until the time of the Revolutionary war. I have not met with it in any writings previous to that time; and in letters in which the word occurs, written in 1775, it is referred to in a manner which shows that the writer considered it something new, and intended to be contemptuous, used as it was by their then enemies, the British soldiers. Noah Webster, in his *Dictionary*, gives the *Yenghees* origin of the word, upon the authority of Heckewelder; and that fact may account for its being looked upon in New England as something novel. Heckewelder is excellent authority upon Indian subjects; but he spent his time principally among the Delawares and the Six Nations, and was not likely to be well acquainted with the Massachusetts Indians, who spoke a different dialect. Several of the regiments of British regulars who were transferred to Boston after the beginning of the troubles, had been stationed in the middle colonies, and had considerable experience in Indian warfare, and may have thus acquired a knowledge of the word. The 18th, or Royal Irish, for instance, had been engaged in nearly all the battles which had taken place in the colonies during two French wars, and they had acquired much familiarity with American affairs. That the word was rather uncommon in New England, is shown by various letters written from thence. One from the Rev. Wm. Gordon, published in the *Penna Gazette*, May 10, 1775, giving an account of the skirmishes at Concord and Lexington, says, "They (the British troops) were roughly handled by the *Yankees*, a term of reproach for the New Englanders, when applied by the regulars." Another letter, published in the same paper a few weeks afterward, dated "Hartford, Connecticut," gives an account of the capture of several letters from English officers in Boston to their friends in England, and says, "some of them are full of invectives against the poor Yankees, as they call us." From these facts it seems probable that the word was so unusual in New England that the writers thought themselves obliged to explain it. It was soon adopted, however. In a few months thereafter the citizens of Newbury fitted out a privateer called the *Yankee Hero*, and the name was used when speaking of the New Englanders, being spelt at times Yankie, Yanko, Yankoo, Yanku, and Yankee. At this day it is only applied in the United States to the inhabitants of New England, but foreigners use it to denote all the Americans.

In the *Poetical Works of John Trumbull, LL.D.*, published at Hartford, 1820, in two volumes, in the Appendix appears the following Note :

Yankies.—The first settlers of New England were mostly emigrants from London and its vicinity, and exclusively styled themselves the English. The Indians, in attempting to utter the word *English*, with their broad guttural accent, gave it a sound which would be nearly represented in this way, *Yaunghees;* the letter *g* being pronounced hard, and approaching to the sound of *k* joined with a strong aspirate, like the Hebrew *cheth*, or the Greek *chi*, and the *l* suppressed, as almost impossible to be distinctly heard in that combination. The Dutch settlers on the river Hudson and the adjacent country, during their long contest concerning the right of territory, adopted the name, and applied it in contempt to the inhabitants of New England. The British of the lower class have since extended it to all the people of the United States. This seems the most probable origin of the term. The pretended Indian tribe of Yankoos does not appear to have ever had an existence; as little can we believe in an etymological derivation of the word from ancient Scythia or Siberia, or that it was ever the name of a horde of savages in any part of the world.

In a curious book on the Round Towers of Ireland, the origin of the term Yankee-doodle was traced to the Persian phrase, "Yanki dooniah," or "Inhabitants of the New World." Layard, in his book on *Nineveh and its Remains*, also mentions "Yanghi-dunia" as the Persian name of America.

DEATH'S PAINTER.

Most persons have heard of the story of an Italian painter who embodied the idea of Death on the canvas so truthfully that the contemplation of it caused his own death. I always thought it was fabulous till I met with it in the translation of Vasari's *Lives of the Painters*, vol. ii. p. 305, now being published in Bohn's *Standard Library*. The name of Fivizzano is there given to the painter, and the following epigram is said to have been inscribed beneath the picture:

Me veram pictor divinus mente recepit.
Admota est operi deinde perita manus.
Dumque opere in facto defigit lumina pictor,
Intentus nimium, palluit et moritur.
Viva igitur sum mors, non mortua mortis imago
Si fungor, quo mors fungitur officio.

Which may be thus translated:

Me with such truth the painter's mind discerned,
While with such skilful hand the work he plied,
That when to view his finished work he turned,
With horror stricken, he grew pale, and died.
Sure I am living Death, not Death's dead shade,
That do Death's work, and am like Death obeyed.

STEAMBOATS.

In the Grenville Library in the British Museum is the following work, to the name of which, in the catalogue, is appended the accompanying note:

GRENVILLE CATALOGUE (Vol. i. p. 351).

Hulls, Jonathan. A Description and Draught of a new-invented Machine for carrying vessels or ships out of, or into any harbour, port, or river, against wind and tide, or in a calm. For which his Majesty has granted letters patent, for the sole benefit of the Author, for the space of Fourteen years. London, 1737. folding plate.* 8vo. R.†

This new-invented machine is a steam-boat. It entirely puts an end to the claims of America to the invention of steam navigation, and establishes for this country the honor of that important discovery.

The following doggerel is the burden of a common street-ditty, among the boys of Campden, in Gloucestershire:

Jonathan Hulls,
With his paper skulls,
Invented a machine
To go against wind and stream;
But he, being an ass,
Couldn't bring it to pass,
And so was asham'd to be seen.

WELSH WEDDINGS.

The practice of "making a bidding" and sending "bidding letters," of which the following is a specimen, is so general in most parts of Wales, that printers usually keep the form in type, and make alteration in it as occasion requires. The custom is confined to servants and mechanics in towns; but in the country, farmers of the humbler sort make biddings. Of late years tea parties have in Carmarthen been substituted for the bidding; but persons attending pay for what they get, and so incur no obligation; but givers at a bidding are expected and generally do return "all gifts of the above nature whenever called for on a similar occasion." When a bidding is made, it is usual for a large procession to accompany the young couple to church, and thence to the house where the bidding is held. Accompanying is considered an addition to the obligation conferred by the gift. I have seen, I dare say, six hundred persons in a wedding procession, and have been in one or two myself (when a child). The men walk together and the women together to church; but in returning they walk in pairs, or often in trios, one man between two women. The last time I was at such a wedding I had three strapping wenches attached to my person. In the country they ride, and generally there is a desperate race home to the bidding, where you would be surprised to see a comely lass, with Welsh hat on head and ordinary dress, often take the lead of fifty or a hundred smart fellows over rough roads that would shake your Astley riders out of their seats and propriety.

CARMARTHEN, *October* 2, 1850.

As we intend to enter the Matrimonial State, on Tuesday, the 22nd of October instant, we are encouraged by our Friends to make a Bidding on the occasion the same day, at the New Market House, near the Market Place; when and where the favour of your good and agreeable company is respectfully solicited, and whatever donation you may be pleased to confer on us then, will be thankfully received, warmly acknowledged, and cheerfully repaid whenever called for on a similar occasion,

By your most obedient Servants,
HENRY JONES,
(Shoemaker),
ELIZA DAVIES.

The Young Man, his Father (John Jones, Shoemaker), his Sister (Mary Jones), his Grandmother (Nurse Jones), his Uncle and Aunt (George Jones, Painter, and Mary, his wife), and his Aunt (Elizabeth Rees), desire that all gifts due to them be returned to the Young Man on the above day, and will be thankful for all additional favours.

The Young Woman, her Father and Mother (Evan Davies, Pig-drover, and Margaret, his wife), and her Brother and Sisters (John, Hannah, Jane, and Anne Davies), desire that all gifts of the above nature due to them be returned to the Young Woman on the above day, and will be thankful for all additional favours conferred.

VERSES TO LORD BACON.

On the fly-leaf of an old music-book is the following little poem. I do not remember to have seen it in print.

TO THE LORD BACON WHEN FALLING FROM FAVOUR.

Dazel'd thus with height of place,
Whilst our hopes our wits beguile;
No man marks the narrow space
'Twixt a prison and a smile.

Then since fortune's favours fade,
  You that in her arms do sleep,
Learn to swim, and not to wade,
  For the hearts of kings are deep.

But if greatness be so blind,
  As to burst in towers of air;
Let it be with goodness lin'd,
  That at least the fall be fair.

Then, though dark'ned you shall say,
  When friends fail and princes frown;
Virtue is the roughest way,
  But proves at night a bed of down.

It is in the handwriting of "Johs. Rasbrick vic. de Kirkton," but whether he was the author, or only the transcriber, is uncertain.

SPENSERIAN NOTES.

Spenser gives us a hint of the annoyances to which Shakspeare and Burbage may have been subject:

All suddenly they heard a troublous noise,
  That seemed some perilous tumult to design,
Confused with women's cries and shouts of boys,
  Such as the troubled theatres oft-times annoys.

B. IV. iii. 37.

Spenser's solitary pun occurs in book iv. canto viii. verse 31:

But when the world wox old, it wox *war-old*,
Whereof it hight.

Cleanliness does not appear to have been a virtue much in vogue in the "glorious days of good Queen Bess." Spenser (book iv. canto xi. verse 47) speaks of

Her silver feet, fair washed against this day,

i. e. for a special day of rejoicing.

An instance of the compound epithets, so much used by Chapman in his translation of Homer, is found in Spenser's description of the sea-nymphs, book iv. canto xi. verse 50:

> Eione well-in-age,
> And seeming-still-to-smile Glauconome.

GUTTA PERCHA.

In the *Musæum Tradescantianum, or a Collection of Rarities preserved at South Lambeth, near London*, by John Tradescant, 1656, is, amongst "other variety of rarities," "the pliable Mazer wood, which, being warmed in water, will work to any form;" and a little farther on, in the list of "utensils and household stuffe," is "Mazer dishes." It is more than a coincidence that Doctor Montgomery, who, in 1843, received the gold medal of the Society of Arts for bringing gutta percha and its useful properties under the notice of that body, describes it in almost the same words that Tradescant uses when speaking of the pliable Mazer wood. The Doctor says, "it could be moulded into any form by merely dipping it into boiling water." It is worthy of remark that Tradescant, who was the first botanist of his day, seems to have been uncertain of the true nature of the "Mazer wood," for he does not class it with his "gums, rootes, woods;" but, as before observed, in a heterogeneous collection which he styles "other variety of rarities." Presuming that this Mazer wood was what we now term gutta percha, the question may be propounded, How could Tradescant have procured it from its remote *locale?* The answer is easy. In another part of the *Musæum Tradescantianum* may be found a list of the "benefactors" to the collection; and amongst their names occurs that of William Curteen, Esq. Now this William Curteen and his father Sir William, of Flemish descent, were the most extensive British merchants of the time, and had not only ships trading to, but also possessed forts and factories on, some of the islands of the Eastern Archipelago, the native *habitat* of the sapotaceous tree that yields the gutta percha. Curteen was a collector of curiosities himself, and no doubt his captains and agents were instructed to procure such: in short, a specimen of gutta percha was just as likely to attract the attention of an intelligent Englishman at Amboyna in the fifteenth century, as it did at Singapore in the nineteenth.

If there are still any remains of Tradescant's collection in the Ashmolean Museum at Oxford, the question, whether the Mazer wood was gutta percha or not, might be soon set at rest; but it is highly probable that the men who ordered the relics of the Dodo to be thrown out, showed but little ceremony to the Mazer wood or dishes.

LINES ON THE TEMPLE.

The following lines are said to be the impromptu production of some passer-by, struck with the Horse and Lamb over the Temple gates. They are printed (probably for the first time) in the sixth number of *The Foundling Hospital for Wit*, 8vo.: Printed for W. Webb, near St. Paul's, 1749 (p. 73). The learned author of *Heraldic Anomalies* (2d edit. vol. i. p. 310), says they were *chalked* upon one of the public gates of the Temple; but from the following note, preceding the lines in question, in *The Foundling Hospital for Wit*, this statement is probably erroneous:—

> The Inner Temple Gate, London, being lately repaired, and curiously decorated, the following inscription, in honour of both the Temples, is *intended* to be put over it.

A MS. note, in a Cotemporary hand, in my copy in *The Foundling Hospital for Wit*, states the author of the original lines to have been the "Rev. William Dunkin, D. D." The answer which follows it, is said to be by "Sir Charles Hanbury Williams."

As by the Templars holds you go,
The Horse and Lamb display'd,
In emblematic figures show,
The merits of their trade.

That travellers may infer from hence
How just is their profession;
The lamb sets forth their innocence,
The horse their expedition.

Oh! happy Britons! happy isle,
May wondering nations say,
Where you get justice without guile,
And law without delay.

ANSWER.

Deluded men, these holds forego,
Nor trust such cunning elves;
These artful emblems tend to show
Their clients, not themselves.

'Tis all a trick; these are but shams,
By which they mean to cheat you;
For have a care, you are the LAMBS,
And they the wolves that eat you.

Nor let the thought of no "delay,"
To these their courts misguide you;
You are the showy HORSE, and they
Are jockeys that will ride you.

GIVING THE LIE.

The great affront of giving the lie arose from the phrase "Thou liest," in the oath taken by the defendant in judicial combats before engaging, when charged with any crime by the plaintiff; and Francis I. of France, to make current his giving the lie to the Emperor Charles V., first stamped it with infamy by saying, in a solemn assembly, that "he was no honest man that would bear the lie."

JOHN STOWE.

John Stowe the chronicler in his old age was reduced to poverty, or rather to actual beggary. Shortly before his death, when fourscore years old, he was permitted, by royal letters patent, to become a mendicant. This curious document is printed in Mr. Bolton Corney's *Curiosities of Literature Illustrated*, and sets forth, that

Whereas our louing Subiect, John Stowe, this fiue & forty yeers hath to his great charge, & with neglect of his ordinary meanes of maintenance (for the generall good as well of posteritie, as of the present age) compiled & published diuerse necessary bookes & Chronicles; and therefore we, in recompense of these his painfull laboures, & for the encouragement to the like, haue in our royall inclination ben pleased to graunt our Letters Patents &c. &c.; thereby authorizing him and his deputies to collect amongst our louing subiects, theyr voluntary contributions and kinde gratuities.

"YOUNG LEVITE."

Macaulay has been often assailed for the account which he has given in his History of the former condition and rank of the clergy. He says they frequently married domestics and retainers of great houses—a statement which has grievously excited the wrath of Mr. Babington and other champions. In a little book, once very popular, first published in 1628, with the title, *Micro-cosmographie, or a Piece of the World discovered*, and which is known to have been written by John Earle, after the Restoration Bishop of Worcester and then of Salisbury, is the following passage. It occurs in what the author calls a character of "a young raw preacher."

You shall know him by his narrow velvet cape and serge facing, and his ruffe, next his hire, the shortest thing about him. . . . His friends, and much painefulnesse, may preferre him to thirtie pounds a yeere, and this meanes, to a chamber-maide: with whom we leave him now in the bonds of wedlocke. Next Sunday you shall have him againe.

The following is an additional illustration of Macaulay's sketch, from Bishop Hall's *Byting Satyres*, 1599 :—

A gentle squire would gladly entertaine
Into his house some *Trencher-chapelaine ;*
Some willing man, that might instruct his sons,
And that would stand to good conditions.
First, that he lie upon the truckle-bed,
While his young maister lieth o'er his head ;
Second, that he do, upon no default,
Never to sit above the salt ;
Third, that he never change his trencher twise ;
Fourth, that he use all common courtesies,
Sit bare at meales, and one half rise and wait ;
Last, that he never his yong maister beat,
But he must aske his mother to define
How manie jerks she would his breech should line ;
All these observ'd, he could contented be,
To give five markes, and winter liverie.

In a satire addressed to a friend about to leave the University, by Oldham, the condition of a chaplain in the times of Charles II. is thus pictured :

Some think themselves exalted to the sky,
If they light in some noble Family :
Diet, an Horse, and thirty pounds a year,
Besides th' advantage of his Lordship's ear,
The credit of the business, and the State,
Are things that in a Youngster's sense sound great.
Little the unexperienc'd Wretch does know,
What slavery he oft must undergo :
Who, though in Silken Scarf and Cassock drest,
Wears but a gayer Livery at best :
When Dinner calls, the Implement must wait
With holy words to consecrate the Meat :
But hold it for a Favour seldom known,
If he be deign'd the Honour to sit down.
Soon as the Tarts appear, Sir Crape, withdraw!
Those Dainties are not for a spiritual Maw :

Observe your distance, and be sure to stand
Hard by the Cistern with your Cap in hand:
There for diversion you may pick your Teeth
Till the kind voider comes for your Relief:
For meer Boardwages such their Freedom sell
Slaves to an Hour, and vassals to a Bell:
And if th' enjoyment of one day be stole,
They are but Pris'ners out upon Parole:
Always the marks of slavery remain,
And they, tho' loose, still drag about their Chain.
And where's the mighty Prospect after all,
A Chaplainship serv'd up, and seven years' Thrall?
The menial things perhaps for a Reward
Is to some slender Benefice preferr'd,
With this Proviso bound, that he must wed
My Lady's antiquated Waiting-Maid,
In dressing only skill'd and Marmalade.

The following are additional evidences of the truth of Macaulay's picture. The first describes the life at Wrest in Bedfordshire, where Carew wrote, the seat of Selden's Countess of Kent:—

The Lord and Lady of this place delight
Rather to be in act than seem in sight;
Instead of statues to adorn their wall,
They throng with living men their merry hall,
Where at large tables filled with wholesome meats,
The servant tenant and kind neighbor eats.
Some of that rank, spun of a finer thread,
Are with the women, steward and chaplain fed
With daintier cates; others of better note,
Whom wealth, parts, office, or the herald's coat,
Have severed from the common, freely sit
At the Lord's table.

Carew. *To my friend G. N., from Wrest.*

The instances from Gay and Pope, or rather Swift, need no comment:—

Cheese that the table's closing rites denies,
And bids me with th' unwilling chaplain rise.
Gay, *Trivia*, 1716.

No sooner said, but from the hall
Rush chaplain, butler, dogs and all,
"A rat, a rat, clap to the door."
Pope and Swift, *Sixth Satire of Second Book of Horace.*

NAMES.

"Polly" is one of those "hypocorisms," or pet-names, in which our language abounds. Most are mere abbreviations, as Will, Nat, Pat, Bell, &c., taken usually from the beginning, sometimes from the end of the name. The ending *y* or *ie* is often added, as a more endearing form: as Annie, Willy, Amy, Charlie, &c. Many have letter-changes, most of which imitate the pronunciation of infants. *L* is lisped for *r*. A central consonant is doubled. *O* between *m* and *l* is more easily sounded than *a*. An infant forms *p* with its lips sooner than *m:* papa before mamma. The order of change is: Mary, Maly, Mally, Molly, Polly. *L* for *r* appears in Sally, Dolly, Hal; *P* for *m* in Patty, Peggy; vowel-change in Harry, Jim, Meg, Kitty, &c.; and in several of these the double consonant. To pursue the subject: reduplication is used; as in Nannie, Nell, Dandie; and (by substitution) in Bob. Ded would be of ill omen: therefore we have, for Edward, Ned or Ted, *n* and *t* being coheir to *d;* for Rick, Dick, perhaps on account of the final *d* in Richard. Letters are dropped for softness; as Fanny for Franny, Bab for Barb, Wat for Walt. Maud is Norman for Mald, from Mathild, as Bauduin for Baldwin. Argidius becomes Giles, our nursery friend Gill, who accompanied Jack in his disastrous expedition "up the hill." Elizabeth gives birth to Elspeth, Eliza (Eloisa?), Lisa, Lizzie, Bet, Betty, Betsy, Bessie, Bess; Alexander (x=cs) to Allick and Sandie. What are we to say of Jack for John? It seems to be from

Jacques, which is the French for our James. How came the confusion? I do not remember to have met with the name James in early English history, and it seems to have reached us from Scotland. Perhaps, as Jean and Jaques were among the commonest French names, John came into use as a baptismal name, and Jaques or Jack entered by its side as a familiar term. John answers to the German Johann or Jehann, the Sclavonic Ivan, the Italian Giovanni (all these languages using a strengthening consonant to begin the second syllable): the French Jean, the Spanish Juan, James to the German Jacob, the Italian Giacomo, the French Jacques, the Spanish Jago. It is observable that of these, James and Giacomo alone have the *m*. Most of our softened words are due to the smooth-tongued Normans. The harsh Saxon Schrobbesbyrigschire, or Shropshire, was by them softened into le Comté de Salop, and both names are still used.

BLOODY BAKER.

I one day was looking over the different monuments in Cranbrook Church in Kent, when in the chancel my attention was arrested by one erected to the memory of Sir Richard Baker. The gauntlet, gloves, helmet, and spurs were (as is often the case in monumental erections of Elizabethan date) suspended over the tomb. What chiefly attracted my attention was the color of the gloves, which was red. The old woman who acted as my cicerone, seeing me look at them, said, "Aye, miss, those are Bloody Baker's gloves; their red color comes from the blood he shed." This speech awakened my curiosity to hear more, and with very little pressing I induced my old guide to tell me the following strange tale:

The Baker family had formerly large possessions in Cranbrook, but in the reign of Edward VI. great misfortunes fell on them; by extravagance and dissipation they gradually lost all their lands, until an old house in the village (now used as the poor-house) was all that remained to them. The sole representative of the family remaining at the accession of Queen Mary was Sir Richard Baker. He had spent some years abroad in consequence of a duel; but when, said my informant, Bloody Queen Mary reigned, he thought he might safely return, as he was a Papist. When he came to Cranbrook he took up his abode in his old house. He only brought one foreign servant with him, and these two lived alone. Very soon strange stories began to be whispered respecting unearthly shrieks having been heard frequently to issue at nightfall from his house. Many people of importance were stopped and robbed in the Glastonbury woods, and many unfortunate travellers were missed and never heard of more. Richard Baker still continued to live in seclusion, but he gradually repurchased his alienated property, although he was known to have spent all he possessed before he left England. But wickedness was not always to prosper. He formed an apparent attachment to a young lady in the neighborhood, remarkable for always wearing a great many jewels. He often pressed her to come and see his old house, telling her he had many curious things he wished to show her. She had always resisted fixing a day for her visit, but happening to walk within a short distance of his house, she determined to surprise him with a visit; her companion, a lady older than herself, endeavored to dissuade her from doing so, but she would not be turned from her purpose. They knocked at the door, but no one answered them; they, however, discovered it was not locked, and determined to enter. At the head of the stairs hung a parrot, which, on their passing, cried out,—

"Peepoh, pretty lady, be not too bold,
Or your red blood will soon run cold."

And cold did run the blood of the adventurous damsel when, on opening one of the room doors, she found it filled with the dead bodies of murdered persons, chiefly women. Just then they heard a noise, and on looking out of the window saw Bloody Baker and his servant bringing in the murdered body of a lady. Nearly dead with fear, they concealed themselves in a recess under the staircase.

As the murderers with their dead burden passed by them, the hand of the unfortunate murdered lady hung in the baluster of the stairs; with an oath Bloody Baker chopped it off, and it fell into the lap of one of the concealed ladies. As soon as the murderers had passed by, the ladies ran away, having the presence of mind to carry with them the dead hand, on one of the fingers of which was a ring. On reaching home they told their story, and in confirmation of it displayed the ring. All the families who had lost relatives mysteriously were then told of what had been found out, and they determined to ask Baker to a large party, apparently in a friendly manner, but to have constables concealed ready to take him into custody. He came, suspecting nothing, and then the lady told him all she had seen, pretending it was a dream. "Fair lady," said he, "dreams are nothing; they are but fables." "They may be fables," said she; "but is this a fable?" and she produced the hand and ring. Upon this the constables rushed in and took him; and the tradition further says, he was burnt, notwithstanding Queen Mary tried to save him, on account of the religion he professed.

POEMS OF COLERIDGE.

Coleridge, in his *Biographia Literaria*, 1st edit., vol. i. p. 28, relates a story of some one who desired to be introduced to him, but hesitated because he asserted that he had written an epigram on "The Ancient Mariner," which Coleridge had himself written and inserted in *The Morning Post*, to this effect :—

Your poem must eternal be,
  Dear sir! it cannot fail:
For 'tis incomprehensible,
  And without head or tail.

This was, however, only a Gadshill robbery,—stealing stolen goods. The following epigram is said to be by Mr. Hole, in a MS. collection made by Spence, and it appeared first in print in *Terræ Filius*, from whence Dr. Salter copied it in his *Confusion worse Confounded*, p. 88:—

Thy verses are eternal, O my friend!
For he who reads them, reads them to no end.

In *The Crypt*, a periodical published by the late Rev. P. Hall, vol. i. p. 30, is the following poem by Coleridge:—

JOB'S LUCK. BY S. T. COLERIDGE, ESQ.

  Sly Beelzebub took all occasions
  To try Job's constancy and patience;
  He took his honors, took his health,
  He took his children, took his wealth,
  His camels, horses, asses, cows,—
Still the sly devil did not take his spouse.

  But Heav'n, that brings out good from evil,
  And likes to disappoint the devil,
  Had predetermined to restore
  Two-fold of all Job had before,
  His children, camels, asses, cows,—
Short-sighted devil, not to take his spouse.

This is merely an amplified version of the 199th epigram of the 3d Book of Owen.

Divitias Jobo, sobolemque, ipsamque salutem
  Abstulit (hoc Domino non prohibens) Satan.
Omnibus ablatis, miserò, tamen una superstes,
  Quæ magis afflictum redderet, uxor erat.

Of this there are several imitations in French, three of which are given in the *Epigrammes Choisies d'Owen*, par M. de Kerivalant, published by Labouisse, at Lyons, in 1819.

There is also another version of Job's luck :—

The devil engaged with Job's patience to battle,
  Tooth and nail strove to worry him out of his life ;
He robb'd him of children, slaves, houses, and cattle,
  But, mark me, he ne'er thought of taking his wife.

But heaven at length Job's forbearance rewards,
  At length double wealth, double honor arrives,
He doubles his children, slaves, houses, and herds,
  But we don't hear a word of a couple of wives.

TOUCHSTONE'S DIAL.

Mr. Knight, in a note on *As You Like It*, gives us the description of a dial presented to him by a friend who had picked it "out of a deal of old iron," and which he supposes to be such a one as the "fool i' the forest" drew from his poke, and looked on with lack-lustre eye. It is very probable that this species of chronometer is still in common use in the sister kingdom. Mr. Carleton, in his amusing *Traits and Stories of the Irish Peasantry*, thus describes them :—

The ring-dial was the hedge-schoolmaster's next best substitute for a watch. As it is possible that a great number of our readers may never have heard of, much less seen one, we shall in a word or two describe it—nothing, indeed, could be more simple. It was a bright brass ring, about three quarters of an inch broad, and two inches and a half in diameter. There was a small hole in it, which, when held opposite the sun, admitted the light against the inside of the ring behind. On this were marked the hours and the quarters, and the time was known by observing the hour or the quarter on which the slender ray, that came in from the hole in front, fell.

INFAMOUS FAME.

Marmoreo Licinus tumulo jacet, at Cato nullo,
Pompeius parvo. Quis putet, esse Deos?
Saxa premunt Licinum, levat altum Fama Catonem,
Pompeium Tituli. Credimus esse Deos?

O'er base Licinus costliest marbles rise;
Unburied Cato, meanly Pompey, lies.
Is there a God?
His tomb Licinus damns to endless fame,
Cato's and Pompey's monument their name.
There is a God.

A NOTE FOR LITTLE BOYS.

In order that all good little boys may know how much more lucky it is for them to be little boys now, than it was in the ancient times, be informed of the cruel manner in which even good little boys were liable to be treated by the law of the Ripuarians. When a sale of land took place, it was required that there should be twelve witnesses, and with these as many boys, in whose presence the price of the land should be paid, and its formal surrender take place; and then the boys were beaten, and their ears pulled, so that the pain thus inflicted upon them should make an impression upon their memory, and that they might, if necessary, be afterwards witnesses as to the sale and delivery of the land. (*Lex Ripuarium LX.*, *de Traditionibus et Testibus.*) In a note of Balucius upon this passage, he states :—

A practice somewhat similar to this prevails in our own times, for in some of the provinces, whenever a notorious criminal is condemned to death, parents bring their sons with them to the place of execution, and, at the moment that he is put to death, they whip their children with rods, so that being thus excited by their own sufferings, and by seeing the punishment inflicted on another for his sins, they may ever bear in mind how necessary it is for them, in their progress through life, to be prudent and virtuous.—*Rer. Gall. et Franc. Script.*, vol. iv. p. 277.

MRS. PARTINGTON.

The "original Mrs. Partington" was a respectable old lady, living at Sidmouth, in Devonshire. Her cottage was on the beach, and during an awful storm (that, I think, of November, 1824, when some fifty or sixty ships were wrecked at Plymouth) the sea rose to such a height as every now and then to invade the old lady's place of domicile; in fact, almost every wave dashed in at the door. Mrs. Partington, with such help as she could command, with mops and brooms, as fast as the water entered the house, mopped it out again; until at length the waves had the mastery, and the dame was compelled to retire to an upper story of the house. The first allusion to the circumstance was made by Sidney Smith, in a speech on the Reform Bill, in which he compared the Conservative opposition to the bill to be like the opposition of "Dame Partington and her mop, who endeavored to mop out the waves of the Atlantic."

MATRIMONIAL ADVERTISEMENT.

Mr. Burke, in his *Anecdotes of the Aristocracy*, furnishes the following specimen of an advertisement of Sir John Dinely for a partner :—

> To the angelic fair of true English breed,—Sir John Dinely, of Windsor Castle, recommends himself and his ample fortune to any angelic beauty of good breed, fit to become and willing to be a mother of a noble heir, and keep up the name of an ancient family, ennobled by deeds of arms and ancestral renown. Ladies at a certain period of life need not apply, as heirship is the object of the ladies' sincere admirer, Sir John Dinely. Fortune favors the bold. Such ladies as this advertisement may induce to apply or send their agents (but not servants or matrons), may direct to me at the Castle, Windsor. Happiness and pleasure are agreeable objects, and should be regarded as well as honor. The lady who thus becomes my wife will be a baronetess, and rank accordingly as Lady Dinely of Windsor. Good and favor to all ladies of Great Britain. Pull no caps on his account, but favor him with your smiles, and pæans of pleasure await your steps.

AMERICAN SURNAMES.

The changes that have taken place in family names during the short period that has elapsed since the settlement of America by Europeans, lead us to believe in the greater changes that are reported to have occurred in surnames in the Old World.

Whenever William Penn could translate a German name into a corresponding English one, he did so, in issuing patents for land in Pennsylvania: thus, the respectable Carpenter family in Lancaster are the descendants of a Zimmerman.

Many Swedish and German names have suffered change: from Soupli has come Supplee; from Up der Graeff, Graeff and Updegrove; from Hendrick's son, Henderson. The district of Southwark, in this county, covers ground once owned by a Swede named Swen. His son was called Swen's son, from whom the Swanson family derived their name. The Vastine family came from a Van de Vorstein.

A person whose family name was Sturdevant, Englished it into Treadaway a few years ago; and a family which during the Revolution spelt their name Boehm have since *softened* it into Bumm.

Occasionally a French name is translated. One of two brothers living near Philadelphia, is known as Mr. La Rue, his brother as Mr. Street. Several New England names are corrupted from those of the French Acadians: thus, Bumpus comes from Bon pas, Bunker from Bon cœur, and Peabody from Picbaudier.

Buckalew is evidently a corruption of Buccleugh, and Chism of Chisholm.

A large family in Virginia and other southern States spell their name Taliaferro, and pronounce it Toliver. Have they any connection with the Norman Taillefer?

SACK.

This is the same wine which is now named sherry. Falstaff calls it *sherris sack*, and also *sherris* only, using in fact both names indiscriminately (2 *Henry IV.*, Act IV. Sc. 3). For various commentaries regarding it, see Blount's *Glossographia;* Dr. Venner's *Via recta ad Vitam longam*, published in 1637; Nare's *Glossary*, &c. Cotgrave, in his *Dictionary*, makes sack to be derived from *vin sec*, French. In a MS. account of the disbursements by the chamberlain of the city of Worcester for 1592, Dr. Percy found the ancient mode of spelling to be *seck*, and thence concluded that sack is a corruption of *sec*, signifying a dry wine. Moreover, in the French version of a proclamation for regulating the prices of wines, issued by the Privy Council in 1633, the expression *vins secs* corresponds with the word *sacks* in the original. The term *sec* is still used as a substantive by the French to denote a Spanish wine; and the dry wine of Xeres is known at the place of its growth by the name of *vino seco*. The foregoing account is abridged from *The History of Ancient and Modern Wines*, by Alex. Henderson, Lond. 1824. The following is taken from Cyrus Redding's *History of Modern Wines*, Lond. 1833:

> In the early voyages to these islands (the Canaries), quoted in Ashley's collection, there is a passage relative to sack, which will puzzle wise heads about that wine. It is under the head of "Nicols' Voyage." Nicols lived eight years in the islands. The island of Teneriffe produces three sorts of wine, Canary, Malvasia, and Verdona, "which may all go under the denomination of sack." The term then was applied neither to sweet nor dry wines exclusively, but to Canary, Xeres (*i. e.* sherry), or Malaga generally. In Anglo-Spanish dictionaries of a century and a quarter old, sack is given as *Vino de Canarias*. Hence it was Canary sack, Xeres sack, or Malaga sack.

It may not be amiss here to quote the praises of sack as sounded by Falstaff (2 *Henry IV.* Act IV. Sc. 3):—

"It ascends me into the brain; dries me there all the foolish, and dull, and crudy vapours which environ it; makes it apprehensive, quick, forgetive, full of nimble, fiery, and delectable shapes, which, delivered o'er to the voice (the tongue), which is the frith, becomes excellent wit. * * * * * * If I had a thousand sons, the first human principle I would teach them should be,—to forswear their potations, and addict themselves to sack."

THOMSON'S HOUSE AND CELLAR.

None of the biographers of Thomson seem to have fallen in with a copy of the catalogue of his effects, disposed of by auction after his death in 1749. Thomson's residence for several years preceding his death was a snug cottage in Kewfoot Lane, near Richmond. The situation is one of the finest in that fine district. The cottage was embowered in trees and shrubbery, and behind it was a garden, in which the lazy good-humored poet took his ease of an afternoon, and muttered his verses throughout the moonlight nights. His garden-seat and writing-table are still preserved; but the cottage has been enlarged into a handsome villa, and the garden has been extended and improved so as to become one of the most exquisite and richly ornamented in that patrician neighborhood. Yet even in Thomson's time the cottage at Kewfoot Lane was a desirable residence; and the poet, after weathering many difficulties, had succeeded in gathering around him at least a moderate share of the comforts and elegancies of life. If his little Castle of Indolence could not boast its costly tapestry, huge covered tables and couches, "the pride of Turkey and of Persia land," there was no lack of respectable bachelor accommodation, with an assortment of valuable prints and books, and a cellar that could have supplied a dozen of jovial banquets to Quin, Armstrong, Lyttelton, Mitchell, and those other select friends whom he delighted to entertain, and by whom he was so tenderly beloved. But let us look at the different items in the sale catalogue, which consists of eight pages octavo.

The first division, marked "No. 1, right hand, two pair of stairs," seems to be the furniture of an inferior bedroom, the whole of which is valued at *4l.* *2s.* *6d.*, including what the auctioneer calls "a piece of ruins in a carved frame." No. 2 is a closet, containing feather-bed and portmanteau, valued at 17*s.* No. 3, left hand, two pair of stairs, was a better bedroom, containing a four-post bedstead, with blue harrateen furniture, four walnut-tree arm-chairs with black leather seats, a chimney glass, and mahogany table; the contents of this room are valued at *8l.* *7s.* No. 4, one pair of stairs, was evidently the best bedroom. It had a bed with moreen furniture and other accessories, valued at *8l.* *2s.* *6d.*; festoon window curtains, bottle cistern, walnut dressing-table and mirror, four walnut chairs, steel stove, &c.; the whole being valued at 13*l.* 12*s.* 6*d.* No 5, one pair of stairs, had a Turkey carpet valued at 1*l.* 11*s.* 6*d.*; a mahogany chest of drawers, 1*l.* 10*s.*; a sofa, 2*l.* 2*s.*; a mahogany writing-table, 1*l.* 3*s.*; four mahogany elbow chairs with yellow worsted damask seats, 2*l.* 10*s.*; a walnut-tree easy chair with matted seat and back, 12*s.*; mahogany pillar and claw, carved needlework fire-screen, with quilted case, 2*l.* 2*s.*; dining table, 12*s.*; with sconce for candles, yellow damask window curtains, &c.; the whole valued at 18*l.* 15*s.* No. 6, back parlor, possessed a steel stove, two walnut and three smoking chairs, dumb waiter, book shelves, a Scotch carpet (set down at 10*s.* 6*d.*), &c.; the whole valued at 5*l.* 6*s.* 6*d.* No. 7, left-hand parlor, had its writing-table, claw table, window curtains, &c., valued at 3*l.* 11*s.* 6*d.* No. 8, right-hand parlor, was evidently the principal sitting-room. It was decorated with a Scotch carpet, 10*s.* 6*d.*; a dining table, 1*l.* 11*s.* 6*d.*; a sconce, 1*l.* 5*s.*; six mahogany elbow chairs, with green worsted damask seats, 3*l.* 12*s.*; a backgammon table complete, with chessmen, 10*s.* 6*d.*; and other articles, the whole valued at 11*l.* 19*s.*

The next classification is plate, china, &c.; but here the enumeration is not extensive, and no prices are affixed. Besides cups, saucers, plates, and mugs, there are "Shagreen case, with twelve silver-handled knives and forks; a silver watch with a cornelian seal, box and case in one, by Graham; one silver-hilted sword; one mourning sword; an Alicant tea-chest, with silvered ornaments." The kitchen apparatus and furniture are valued at 5*l.* 11*s.*; and the wash-house, garden, and yard articles at 2*l.* 12*s.* 6*d.*

The contents of the cellar, to which no prices are affixed, are set down as follows: 30 bottles of Burgundy, 30 bottles of red port, 4 bottles of old hock, 7 bottles of mountain and Madeira, 10 bottles of Rhenish, 66 bottles of Edinburgh ale, 90 bottles of Dunbar ale. There is no mention of ardent spirits.

The library consisted of 260 lots, the greater part of the books foreign and classical. Editions of Dante, Tasso, and Ariosto are among the number. The English works include Milton, Theobald's *Shakspeare*, Harrington's *Oceana*, Raleigh's *History of the World*, Cowley, &c., Pope's *Works*, 1717, and his *Prose Works*, stitched, 1737, *The Dunciad*, stitched, and the *Ethic Epistles* in vellum, large paper, most likely a present from Pope. The library cannot be considered valuable, but it was fully equal to that of Johnson or Goldsmith. Authors resident in London, with public libraries at command, have little inducement to accumulate books at home, even if their worldly circumstances were such as to permit of the expensive luxury.

Thomson, it is well known, had a taste for the fine arts, and during his tour in Italy with Mr. Talbot, collected some drawings and prints from the old masters. He seems to have had no less than eighty-three pictures hung up in his different rooms, and "a large portfolio with maps, prints, and drawings, to be sold together or separate." The "antique drawings" are nine in number, all stated to be by Castelli. They consist of the Venus de Medici, the Fighting and Dying Gladiator, Perseus and Andromeda, Apollo Antinous, Meleager, Laocoon, Hercules Farnese, and "A Man and a Woman." The seventy-four engravings are all from the old masters, engraved by Frezza, Claudie, Stelle, J. Frey, Bandet, Dorigny, Duchange, Poilly, Hansart, Edlinck, and Picart. It is indicative of Thomson's taste that none of the engravings are from pictures of the Dutch school, but from those of Raphael, Guido, Correggio, Carlo Maratti, Poussin, Julio Romano, and other masters of the poetical and romantic.

It appears, then, that the furniture of Thomson was valued at 66*l.* 11*s.*, exclusive of his plate, china, wine, books, and pictures, which formed by far the most costly and valuable portion of his effects. The sale is stated to be "by order of the executrix," his sister, Mrs. Craig of Edinburgh, and it was to take place on Monday, May 15, 1749, and two following days. The poet's friends, who had been so sincere and so active in their sympathy on the occasion of his death, would no doubt come forward at the sale to promote its success, and to possess themselves of some relic of their departed associate. John Forbes of Culloden, the "joyous youth" of the *Castle of Indolence* (canto i. st. 62), bought the *Shakspeare*, Raleigh's *History*, Harrington's *Oceana*, &c., and they still remain in the library at Culloden House.

FOREIGN ENGLISH.

The accompanying specimens of foreign English are perhaps worth a corner among the minor curiosities of literature :—

Basle.—

Bains ordinaires et artificiels, tenu par B. Siegmund, Dr. in medicine Basle. In this new erected establishment, which the Owner recommends best to all foreigners are to have,—Ordinary and artful baths, russia and sulphury bagnios, pumpings, artful mineral waters, gauze lemonads, fournished apartments for patients.

Cologne. Title-page in lithograph.

Remembrance on the Cathedral of Cologne.—A collection of his most semarkable monumens, so as of the most artful ornamons and precious hilts of his renaconed tresory. Draconed and lithographed by Gerhardt Levy Elkan and Hallersch, collected by Gerhd. Emans.

Augsburg, Drei Mohren Hotel. Entry in travellers' book.

January 28, 1815.—His Grace Arthur Wellesley, Duke of Wellington, &c. &c. &c. Great honour arrived at the beginning of this year to the three Moors : this illustrious warrior, whose glorious atchievements, which, cradled in Asia, have filled Europe with his renown, descended in it.

Mount Sinai. (On the fly-leaf of the travellers' book.)

Here in too were inscribed as in one legend, all whose in the rule of the year come from different parts, different cities and countries, pilgrims and travellers of any different rank and religion or profession, for advise and notice thereof to their posterity, and even also in owr own of memory acknowledging. 1845, Mount Sinai.

RESTORATIVE HOTEL, FINE HOK.
KEPT BY FRANK PROSPERI,
FACING THE MILITARY QUARTER
AT POMPEII.

That hotel open since a very few days, is renowned for the cleanness of the apartments and linen; for the exactness of the service, and for the eccelence of the true french cookery. Being situated at proximity of that regeneration, it will be propitius to receive families, whatever, which will desire to reside alternatively into that town, to visit the monuments new found, and to breathe thither the salubrity of the air.

That establishment will avoid to all the travellers, visitors, of that sepult city, and to the artists, (willing draw the antiquities) a great disorder, occasioned by the tardy and expensive contour of the iron-whay. People will find equally thither, a complete sortment of stranger wines, and of the kingdom, hot and cold baths, stables and coach houses, the whole with very moderated prices. Now, all the applications, and endeavours of the hoste, will tend always to correspond to the tastes and desires, of their customers, which will acquire without doubt, to him, in to that town, the reputation whome, he is ambitious.

The above is a literal copy of a card.

The following wholesale assassination of the English language was perpetrated in the form of a circular, and distributed among the British residents at Naples in 1832 :—

Joseph the Cook, he offer to one illuminated public and most particular for British knowing men in general one remarkable, pretty, famous, and splendid collection of old goods, all quite new, excavated from private personal diggings. He sells cooked clays, old marble stones, with basso-relievos, with stewing-pots, brass sacrificing pots, and antik lamps. Here is a stocking of calves heads and feets for single ladies and amateurs travelling. Also old coppers and candlesticks; with Nola jugs, Etruscan saucers, and much more intellectual minds articles; all entitling him to learned man's inspection to examine him, and supply it with illustrious protection, of which he hope full and valorous satisfaction.

N. B.—He make all the old thing brand new for gentlemans who has collections, and wishes to change him. He have also one manner quite original for make join two sides of different monies; producing one medallion, all indeed unique, and advantage him to sell by exportation for strange cabinets and museums of the exterior potentates.

Southey says (*Omniana*, vol. ii. p. 131) :—

It is curious to observe how the English Catholics of the seventeenth century wrote English like men who habitually spoke French. Corps is sometimes used for the living body . . . and when they attempt to versify, their rhymes are only rhymes according to a French pronunciation.

The inscription placed by M. Girardin to the memory of Shenstone, at Ermenonville, is a rich specimen of French-English verse.

This plain stone
To William Shenstone;
In his writings he display'd
A mind natural
At Leasowes he laid,
Arcadian greens rural.

But the choicest philological curiosity in this way that I have met with, is the circular of an Italian hotel-keeper. This unique document, by which mine host of the "Torre di Londra," at Verona, seeks to make the advantages of his establishment known to tourists of various nations, is printed in parallel columns, in four different languages: first, the "Circolare," in his vernacular; next, a German "Bekanntmachung;" thirdly, a French "Circulaire;" and lastly, the *English* "Circulatory," which I copy *verb. et lit.*, interpolating the obscurer passages with a few words of explanatory Italian. It is as follows:—

CIRCULATORY.

The old Inn of London's Tower, placed among the more agreeable situation of Verona's course (*del corso di Verona*), belonging at Sir Theodosius Zignoni, restor'd by the decorum most indulgent to good things, of life's eases; (*del Sig. Teodosio Zignoni restaurato con la decenza la piu compatibilè al buon gusto, delli agi della vita*) which are favoured from every arts liable at Inn same (*che vengono favoriti da tutte le arti sottoporste all' albergo stesso*), with all object that is concerned conveniency of stage coaches (*unitamente a ciò che interesse il comodo delle vetture*) proper horses, but good forages, and coach-house; Do offers at Innkeeper the constant hope, to be honoured from a great concourse, where politeness, good genius of meats (*il buon gusto di cucina*), to delight of nations (*a genio delle Nazioni*), round table, Coffee-house, hackney-coach, men-servant of place (*servi di piazza*), swiftness of service, and moderation of prices, shall arrive to accomplish in Him all satisfaction, and at Sirs, who will do the favour honouring him a very assur'd kindness.

Surely than this, the force of foreign-English can no farther go: the German and the French are equally rich.

WHIPPING A LADY.

The following is from a MS. diary of the Rev. John Lewis, Rector of Chalfield, and Curate of Tilbury:—

August 1719. Sir Christopher Hales being jilted by a lady who promised him marriage, and put him off on the day set for their marriage, gave her a good whipping at parting. Remember the story.

THE IMPOSSIBILITIES OF HISTORY—CRANMER.

I am not aware that the fact of Cranmer's holding his right hand in the flames till it was consumed has been questioned. Fox says:—

> He stretched forth his right hand into the flames, and there held it so stedfast that all the people might see it burnt to a coal before his body was touched.—P. 927: ed. Milner, London, 1837, 8vo.

Or, as the passage is given in the last edition,–

> And when the wood was kindled, and the fire began to burn near him, he put his right hand into the flame, which he held so stedfast and immovable (saving that once with the same hand he wiped his face), that all men might see his hand burned before his body was touched.—*Acts and Monuments*, ed. 1839, vol. viii. p. 90.

Burnet is more circumstantial.

> When he came to the stake he prayed, and then undressed himself: and being tied to it, as the fire was kindling, he stretched forth his right hand towards the flame, never moving it, save that once he wiped his face with it, till it was burnt away, which was consumed before the fire reached his body. He expressed no disorder from the pain he was in; sometimes saying, "That unworthy hand;" and oft crying out, "Lord Jesus, receive my spirit." He was soon after quite burnt.—*Hist. of the Reformation*, vol. iii. p. 429, ed. 1825.

Hume says:—

> He stretched out his hand, and without betraying, either by his countenance or motions, the least sign of weakness, or even feeling, he held it in the flames till it was entirely consumed.—*Hume*, vol. iv. p. 476.

It is probable that Hume believed this, for while Burnet states positively as a fact, though only inferentially as a miracle, that "the heart was found entire and unconsumed among the ashes," Hume says, "it was pretended that his heart," &c.

I am not about to discuss the character of Cranmer: a timid man might have been roused under such circumstances into attempting to do what it is said he did. The laws of physiology and combustion show that he could not have gone beyond the attempt. If a furnace were so constructed, that a man might hold his hand in the flame without burning his body, the shock to the nervous system would deprive him of all command over muscular action before the skin could be "entirely consumed." If the hand were chained over the fire, the shock would produce death.

In this case the fire was unconfined. Whoever has seen the effect of flame in the open air, must know that the vast quantity sufficient entirely to consume a human hand, must have destroyed the life of its owner; though, from a peculiar disposition of the wood, the vital parts might have been protected.

The entire story is utterly impossible. May we, guided by the words "as the fire was kindling," believe that he *then* thrust his right hand into the flame—a practice, I believe, not unusual with our martyrs, and peculiarly suitable to him—and class the "holding it till consumed" with the whole and unconsumed heart?

In the accounts of martyrdoms, little investigation was made as to what was possible. Burnet, describing Hooper's execution, says, "one of his hands fell off before he died, with the other he continued to knock on his breast some time after." This, there is high medical authority for saying, could not be.

INVITATION BY BEN JONSON.

IMITATED FROM MARTIAL.

INVITING A FRIEND TO SUPPER.

To-night, grave sir, both my poor house and I
Do equally desire your company:
Not that we think us worthy such a guest,
But that your worth will dignify our feast,
With those that come; whose grace may make that seem
Something, which else could hope for no esteem.

It is the fair acceptance, Sir, creates
The entertainment perfect, not the cates.
Yet shall you have, to rectify your palate,
An olive, capers, or some better salad,
Ushering the mutton; with a short-legged hen,
If we can get her, full of eggs, and then,
Limons, and wine for sauce: to these, a coney
Is not to be despair'd of for our money;
And though fowl now be scarce, yet there are clerks,
The sky not falling, think we may have larks.
I'll tell you of more, and lie, so you will come:
Of partridge, pheasant, woodcock, of which some
May yet be there; and godwit if we can;
Knat, rail, and ruff too. Howsoe'er my man
Shall read a piece of Virgil, Tacitus,
Livy, or of some better book to us,
Of which we'll speak our minds, amidst our meat;
And I'll profess no verses to repeat;
To this if aught appear, which I not know of,
That will the pastry, not my paper, show of.
Digestive cheese, and fruit there sure will be;
But that which most doth take my muse and me,
Is a pure cup of rich Canary wine,
Which is the Mermaid's now, but shall be mine:
Of which had Horace or Anacreon tasted,
Their lives, as do their lines, till now had lasted.
Tobacco, nectar, or the Thespian spring,
Are all but Luther's beer, to this I sing.
Of this we will sup free, but moderately,
And we will have no Pooly', or Parrot by;
Nor shall our cups make any guilty men:
But at our parting, we will be, as when
We innocently met. No simple word,
That shall be utter'd at our mirthful board,
Shall make us sad next morning: or affright
The liberty, that we'll enjoy to-night.

INSCRIPTION AT PERSEPOLIS.

It is said that the following puzzling inscription was found by Captain Barth, graven on marble, among the ruins of Persepolis, and by him translated from the Arabic into Latin and English:

dicas	scis	dicit	scit	dicit	scit
facias	potes	facit	potest	facit	credit
credas	audis	credit	audit	credit	fieri potest
expendas	habes	expendit	habet	petit	habet
judices	vides	judicat	videt	judicat	est
non	quoddamque	nam qui	quodcunque	sæpe	quod non

The spirit of the thing (a sort of *verbal* magic square) seems to require the repetition of the same words in all three pairs of parallel columns. Therefore the last two columns might have consisted of precisely *the same* words as the two middle ones (excepting, of course, the bottom row), without injury to the sense: a circumstance that appears to have been lost sight of by whoever framed the Latin version.

The key consists in taking the words of the bottom row alternately with any of those of the upper rows in the same pair of columns. Thus, the first sentence is, " Non dicas quoddamque *scis*, nam qui *dicit* quodcunque scit, sæpe *dicit* quod non *scit*."

The following English version—in which the bottom line is transposed to the top, for the sake of clearness—will give some idea of the arrangement. The last word *sees*, in the last column, must be understood as *sees into* or *comprehends*.

never	all	for he who	everything	often	more than
tell	you may know	tells	he knows	tells	he knows
attempt	you can do	attempts	he can do	attempts	he can do
believe	you may hear	believes	he hears	believes	he hears
lay out	you can afford	lays out	he can afford	lays out	he can afford
decide upon	you may see	decides upon	he sees	decides upon	he sees

LONG NAMES.

In an appeal to the Privy Council of Madras, are the two following words, which appear to be names of estates: *Aradema-ravasadeloovaradooyou*; *Kaminagadeyathooroosoomokanoogo-nagira*. In the island of Mull, Scotland, is a locality called *Drimtaidhvrickhillichattan*. *Llanvairpwllgwyngyll*, a living in the diocese of Bangor, became vacant in March, 1850, by the death of its incumbent, the Rev. Richard Prichard, æt. ninety-three. The labor of writing the name on his benefice does not seem to have shortened his days.

The following are the names of two *employés* in the finance department at Madrid: *Don Epifanio Mirurzururdundua y Zéngotita*; *Don Juan Nepomuceno de Burionagonatotorecago-geazcoecha*.

There was, until 1851, a major in the British army named *Teyoninhokarawen* (one single name).

FOX AND GIBBON.

The following is taken from the fly-leaves of a copy of Gibbon's *Rome*, 1st vol. 1779, 8vo.:

The following anecdote and verses were written by the late Charles James Fox in the first volume of *his* Gibbon's *Decline and Fall of the Roman Empire.*

The author of this work declared publicly at Brookes's (a gaming-house in St. James' Street), upon the delivery of the Spanish Rescript in June, 1779, that there was no salvation for this country unless six of the heads of the cabinet council were cut off and laid upon the tables of both houses of parliament as examples; and in less than a fortnight he accepted a place under the same cabinet council.

ON THE AUTHOR'S PROMOTION TO THE BOARD OF TRADE IN 1779.

BY THE RIGHT HON. C. J. FOX.

King George in a fright
Lest Gibbon should write
The story of Britain's disgrace,
Thought no means more sure
His pen to secure
Than to give the historian a place.

But his caution is vain,
'Tis the curse of his reign,
That his projects should never succeed;
Tho' he wrote not a line,
Yet a cause of decline
In our author's example we read.

His book well describes
How corruption and bribes
O'erthrew the great empire of Rome;
And his writings declare
A degeneracy there,
Which his conduct exhibits at home.

SARDONIC SMILES.

A few words on the Γέλως σαρδάνιος, or Sardonius Risus, so celebrated in antiquity, may not be amiss, especially as the expression, "a Sardonic smile" is a common one in our language.

We find this epithet used by several Greek writers; it is even as old as Homer's time, for we read in the *Odyssey*, μείδησε δὲ θυμῷ σαρδάνιον μάλα τοῖον, "but he laughed in his soul a very bitter laugh." The word was written indifferently σαρδάνιος and σαρδόνιος; and some lexicographers derive it from the verb σαίρω, of σέσηρα, "to show the teeth, grin like a dog:" especially in scorn or malice. The more usual derivation is from σαρδόνιον, a plant of Sardinia (Σαρδώ), which was said to distort the face of the eater. In the English of the present day, a Sardonic laugh means a derisive, fiendish laugh, full of bitterness and mocking; stinging with insult and rancor. Lord Byron has hit it off in his portraiture of the Corsair, Conrad:—

> There was a laughing devil in his sneer,
> That rais'd emotions both of *rage* and *fear*.

In Izaak Walton's ever delightful *Complete Angler*, Venator, on coming to Tottenham High Cross, repeats his promised verse: "it is a copy printed among some of Sir Henry Wotton's, and doubtless made either by him or by a lover of angling." Here is the first stanza:—

> Quivering fears, heart-tearing cares,
> Anxious sighs, untimely tears,
>   Fly, fly to courts,
>   Fly to fond worldling's sports,
> Where strained *Sardonic* smiles are glossing still,
> And Grief is forced to laugh against her will;
>   Where mirth's but mummery,
>   And sorrows only real be.

In Sir J. Hawkins's edition is the following note on the word "Sardonic" in these lines:—

Feigned or forced smiles, from the word *Sardon*, the name of an herb resembling smallage, and growing in Sardinia, which, being eaten by men, contracts the muscles, and excites laughter even to death. Vide *Erasmi Adagia*, tit. Risus.

Sardonic, in this passage, means "forced, strained, unusual, artificial;" and is not taken in the worst sense. These lines of Sir H. Wotton's brings to mind some of Lorenzo de Medici's, in a platonic poem of his, when he contrasts the court and country. I quote Mr. Roscoe's translation:—

What the heart thinks, the tongue may here disclose,
Nor inward grief with outward smiles is drest;
Not like the world—where wisest he who knows
To hide the secret closest in his breast.

The *Edinburgh Review*, July, 1849, in an article on Tyndale's *Sardinia*, says:—

The *Sardonic smile*, so celebrated in antiquity, baffles research much more than the *intemperie;* nor have modern physiologists thrown any light on the nature of the deleterious plant which produces it. The tradition at least seems still to survive in the country, and Mr. Tyndale adduces some evidence to show that the *Ranunculus sceleratus* was the herb to which these exaggerated qualities were ascribed. Some insular antiquaries have found a different solution of the ancient proverb. The ancient Sardinians, they say, like many barbarous tribes, used to get rid of their relations in extreme old age, by throwing them alive into deep pits; which attention it was the fashion for the venerable objects of it to receive with great expressions of *delight;* whence the saying of a Sardinian laugh (vulgo), laughing on the wrong side of one's mouth. It seems not impossible that the phenomenon may have been a result of the effects of "Intemperie" working on weak constitutions, and in circumstances favorable to physical depression—like the epidemic chorea, and similar complaints, of which such strange accounts are read in medical books.

TRAVELLING OF OLD IN ENGLAND.

The history of travelling in this country, from the Creation to the present time, may be divided into four periods—those of no coaches, slow coaches, fast coaches, railways. Whether balloons, or rockets, or some new mode which as yet has no name, because it has no existence, may come next, one cannot tell, and it is hardly worth while to think about it; for, no doubt, it will be something quite inconceivable.

The third, or fast-coach period was brief, though brilliant. I doubt whether fifty years have elapsed since the newest news in the world of locomotive fashion was, that—to the utter confusion and defacement of the "Sick, Lame, and Lazy," a sober vehicle, so called from the nature of its cargo, which was nightly disbanded into comfortable beds at Newbury—a new post-coach had been set up which performed the journey to Bath in a single day. Perhaps the day extended from about five o'clock in the morning to midnight, but still the coach was, as it called itself, a "*Day*-coach," for it travelled all day; and if it did somewhat "add the night unto the day, and so make up the measure," the passengers had all the more for their money, and were incomparably better off as to time than they had ever been before. But after this many years elapsed before "Old Quicksilver" made good its ten miles an hour, in one unbroken trot to Exeter, and was rivalled by "Young Quicksilver" on the road to Bristol, and beaten by the light-winged Hirondelle, that flew from Liverpool to Cheltenham, and troops of others, each faster than the foregoing, each trumpeting its own fame on its own improved bugle, and beating time (all to nothing) with sixteen hoofs of invisible swiftness.

I do not know anywhere a more distinct account of the commencement and progress of a journey in England, two centuries ago, than is given in Taylor's (the Water-poet) narrative, in prose and verse, of his travels from London to the Isle of Wight, while

Charles I. was there. It is short as well as clear, and the stages, and the time it took to perform them, are one after another pointed out. Moreover, he states that the journey was performed in a public coach drawn by four horses, and conducted by two coachmen. There were four passengers besides Taylor, and they started from the Rose, near Holborn Bridge, in the Southampton coach (which came weekly to that inn), on Thursday, 19th October, 1647, and arrived on the same evening, at 5 o'clock, at Staines. They remained all night at the Bush, and next morning proceeded by Bagshot to Alton, where they put up at the White Hart, and again slept. On Saturday they again set off early, and by dint of "fiery speed" and "foaming bits," they reached the Dolphin at Southampton that day. The Rose, at the foot of Holborn Hill, which I can remember forty years ago, and from which the party set out, has disappeared; but the Bush, at Staines, and the Dolphin, at Southampton, still remain. A small part of Taylor's information is given in marginal notes, but his text, which in fact contains all that illustrates the point at issue, is the following:—

We took one coach, two coachmen, and four horses,
And merrily from London made our courses,
We wheel'd the top of the heavy hill call'd Holborn,
(Up which hath been full many a sinful soul borne,)
And so along we jolted past St. Giles's,
Which place from Brentford six, or near seven miles is,
To Staines that night at five o'clock we coasted,
Where, at the Bush, we had bak'd, boil'd, and roasted,
Bright Sol's illustrious rays the day adorning,
We past Bagshot and Bawwaw Friday morning.
That night we lodg'd at the White Hart at Alton,
And had good meat—a table with a salt on.
Next morn we rose with blushing-cheek'd Aurora;
The ways were fair, but not so fair as Flora,
For Flora was a goddess and a woman,
And, like the highways, to all men was common.

Our horses, with the coach which we went into,
Did hurry us amain, through thick and thin too,
With fiery speed, the foaming bits they champ'd on,
And brought us to the Dolphin at Southampton.

The tract from which I quote was printed in 1648, for the author, who was paid for it, as appeared by his title-page, in the following manner:—

When John Taylor hath been from London to the Isle of Wight and returned again, and at his return he do give, or cause to be given, to me a book or pamphlet of true news, and relations of passages, at the island, and to and fro in his journey, I do promise to give him, or his assignes, the sum of what I please in lawful money of England, provided that the said sum be not under six pence.

This, as many are aware, was a usual mode with Taylor and some others to pay themselves for their expeditions: the Water-poet made many journeys of the kind, as may be seen by the list of his works in the folio of 1630, in which, of course, his *Travels from London to the Isle of Wight*, in 1647, and various others subsequently printed, could not be included. There is no English author who gives us such minute and curious information respecting old customs, edifices, and peculiarities, as Taylor, the Water-poet, the contemporary and friend of Shakespeare, Ben Jonson, and of nearly all our poets and dramatists from the clôse of the reign of Elizabeth to the Restoration.

The two following handbills are copied from an original news-book almost two centuries old. They are interesting, as showing not only the snail-like pace at which our ancestors were content to travel, but also how much they were willing to give for the tardy infliction.

AN ADVERTISEMENT.

From the 26th day of April, 1658, there will continue to go stage coaches from the George Inn without Aldersgate, London, unto the several cities and towns, for the rates, and at the times, hereafter mentioned and declared.

Every Monday, Wednesday, and Friday.

To Salisbury in two days for xx*s*. To Blandford and Dorchester in two days and half for xxx*s*. To Burput in three days for xxx*s*. To Exmaster, Hunnington, and Exeter, in four days for xl*s*. To Stamford in two days for xx*s*. To Newark in two days and a half for xxv*s*. To Bawtrey in three days for xxx*s*. To Doncaster and Ferribridge for xxxv*s*. To York in four days for xl*s*.

Mondays and Wednesdays to Ockington and Plimouth for l*s*. Every Monday to Helperby and Northallerton for xlv*s*. To Darneton Ferryhil for l*s*. To Durham for lv*s*. To Newcastle for iii*l*. Once every fortnight to Edinburgh for iv*l*. a peece, Mondays. Every Friday to Wakefield in four days for xl*s*.

All persons who desire to travel unto the cities, towns, and roads, herein hereafter mentioned and expressed, namely, to Coventry, Litchfield, Stone, Namptwich, Chester, Warrington, Wiggan, Chorley, Preston, Gastang, Lancaster, and Kendal; and also to Stamford, Grantham, Newark, Tuxford, Bawtrey, Doncaster, Ferribridge, York, Helperby, Northallerton, Darneton, Ferryhill, Durham and Newcastle, Wakefield, Leeds, and Halifax; and also to Salisbury, Blandford, Dorchester, Barput, Exmaster, Hunnington and Exeter, Ockington, Plimouth and Cornwall; let them repair to the George Inn at Holborn Bridge, London, and thence they shall be in good coaches with good horses, upon every Monday, Wednesday, and Friday, at and for reasonable rates.—From *Mercurius Politicus* for Thursday, April 8th, 1658.

The post-masters on Chester road petitioning, have received orders, and do accordingly publish the following Advertisement:—

All gentlemen, merchants, and others, who have occasion to travel between London and Westchester, Manchester, and Warrington, or any other town upon the road, for the accommodation of trade, dispatch of business, and ease of purse, upon every Monday, Wednesday, and Friday morning, betwixt six and ten of the clock at the house of Mr. Christopher Charteris, at the sign of the Harts Horns in West Smithfield, and post-master there, and at the post-master of Chester, at the post-master of Manchester, and at the post-master of Warrington, may have a good and able single horse, or more, furnished, at threepence the mile, without charge of a guide; and so likewise at the house of Mr. Thomas Challenor, post-master at Stone in Staffordshire upon every Tuesday, and Thursday, and Saturday mornings to go into London; and so likewise at all the several post-masters upon the road, who will have all such set days so many horses with furniture in readiness to furnish the riders without any stay, to carry them to or from any the places aforesaid in four days, as well to London, as from thence, and to places nearer in less time, according as their occasions shall require, they ingaging at first stage where they take horse, for the safe delivery of the same to the next intermediate stage, and not to ride that horse any further, without consent of the post-master by whom he rides, and so from stage to stage on their journey's end.

All those who intend to ride this way, are desired to give a little notice beforehand, if conveniently they can, to the several post-masters where they first take horse, whereby they may be furnished with so many horses as the riders shall require with expedition.

This undertaking began the 28th of June, 1658, at all the places abovesaid, and so continues by the several post-masters.—From *Mercurius Politicus* for Thursday, 24th June, 1658.

This note is from a very quaintly-written *History of England*, without title-page, but apparently written in the early part of the reign of George the First. It is among the remarkable events of the reign of James the First :—

A. D. 1621, July the 17th, Bernart Calvart of Andover, rode from St. George's Church in Southwark to Dover, from thence passed by Barge to Callais in France, and from thence returned back to Saint George's Church the same day. This his journey he performed betwixt the hours of three in the morning and eight in the afternoon.

This appears a surprising feat.

The following copies of advertisements, which appear in some old newspapers, in some degree illustrate the history of travelling, and in themselves show the advance made between 1739 and 1767.

In the Sherborne paper all public stage conveyances are designated as *machines.*

Copies of advertisements in *The Daily Advertiser* of the 9th April, 1739 :—

For Bath.

A good Coach and able Horses will set out from the Black Swan Inn, in Holborn, on Wednesday or Thursday.

Enquire of William Maud.

Exeter Flying Stage Coach in Three Days, and
Dorchester and Blandford in Two Days.

Go from the Saracen's Head Inn, in Friday Street, London, every Monday, Wednesday, and Friday, and from the New Inn, in Exeter, every Tuesday and Thursday, perform'd by

JOAN PAYNE,
JOHN SANDERSON,
THOMAS BURY.

Note.—Once a week there is an entire Dorchester and Blandford Coach from Dorchester on Mondays, and from London on Fridays.

The Stage begins *Flying* on Monday next, the 16th instant.

The old standing constant Froom Flying Waggon
in Three days

Sets out with Goods and Passengers from Froom for London, every Monday, by One o'clock in the Morning, and will be at the King's Arms Inn, at Holborn Bridge, the Wednesday following by Twelve o'clock at Noon; from whence it will set out on Thursday morning, by One o'clock, for Amesbury, Shrewton, Chittern, Heytesbury, Warminster, Froom, and all other places adjacent, and will continue allowing each passenger fourteen pounds, and be at Froom, on Saturday by Twelve at noon.

If any Passengers have occasion to go from either of the aforesaid Places they shall be supplied with able Horses and a Guide by Joseph Clavey; the Proprietor of the said Flying Waggon. The Waggon calls at the White Bear in Picadilly coming in and going out.

Note—Attendance is constantly given at the King's Arms, Holborn Bridge aforesaid, to take in Goods and Passengers' names; but no Money, Plate, Bank Notes, or Jewels will be insured unless delivered as such, perform'd by

JOSEPH CLAVEY.

N. B. His other Waggons keep their Stages as usual.

From Cruttwell's *Sherborne*, *Shaftesbury*, *and Dorchester Journal*, or *Yeovil*, *Taunton*, *and Bridgewater Chronicle*, of Friday, February 6th, 12th, and 20th, 1767.

Taunton Flying Machine,
Hung on Steel Springs, in Two Days.

Sets out from the Saracen's Head Inn in Friday Street, London, and Taunton, every Monday, Wednesday and Friday, at Three o'clock in the morning;

and returns every Tuesday, Thursday, and Saturday, lays at the Antelope in Salisbury, going Up and Down: To carry Six inside Passengers, each to pay

	£	s.	d.
To Taunton - -	1	16	0
Ilminster - -	1	14	0
Yeovil - -	1	8	0
Sherborne - -	1	6	0
Shaftesbury -	1	4	0

Outside Passengers and Children in the Lap, Half Fare as above; each Inside Passenger allowed Fourteen Pounds Luggage; all above, to Taunton Two pence per Pound, and so in Proportion to any part of the Road.

☞ No Money, Plate, Jewels, or Writings, will be accounted for if Lost, unless Entered as such, and Paid for accordingly.

Performed by { JOHN WHITMASH. THOMAS LILEY.

The following is a copy of an original handbill:—

YORK Four Dayes

Stage Coach

Begins on Monday the 18 of March 1678.

All that are desirous to pass from London to York, or return from York to London or any other Place on that Road; Let them repair to the Black Swan in Holborn in London and the Black Swan in Cony-Street in York

At both which places they may be received in a Stage-Coach every Monday, Wednesday and Friday, which performs the whole journey in Four days (if God permit) and sets forth by Six in the Morning

And returns from York to Doncaster in a Forenoon, to Newark in a day and a half, to Stamford in Two days, and from Stamford to London in Two days more.

Performed by { Henry Moulen
Margaret Gardner
Francis Gardner

In the *Hereford Journal* of January, 1775, are two advertisements from which it appears that stages were then known as *machines*, which did not *ply*, but *fly* on their journeys. If we consider the state of the roads, the size of the vehicles, and the pace at which they travelled, the word flying (*lucus a non lucendo*) seems singularly inappropriate. When travelling by coaches had reached a state of perfection, proprietors modestly announced their vehicles to *run*.

1775, Jan. 12:—

HEREFORD MACHINE,

In a day and a half, twice a week, continues flying from the Swan and Falcon in Hereford, Monday and Thursday mornings, and from the Bolt in Tun, Monday and Thursday evenings.—Fare 19 shillings: outsides, half.

1775, Jan. 5:—

For the conveniency of sending presents at this season of the year, and for the quick conveyance of Passengers to and from London,

PRUEN'S MACHINE
will begin flying as follows:
HEREFORD MACHINE,

In a day and a half, twice a week, sets out from the Redstreak-tree Inn in Hereford, Tuesday and Thursday mornings at 7 o'clock; and from the Swan with Two Necks, Lad Lane, London, every Monday and Wednesday evenings. Insides, £1; outsides, half price.

In 1778 a similar vehicle is styled the *diligence*:—

HEREFORD DILIGENCE
3 times a week,
Leaves at 7 in the morning; reaches London next day to dinner time.
Fares: £1 12*s*., with 10 lbs. of luggage.

The following extract from Chamberlayne's *State of England* for 1692 gives an *official* statement of the expense and mode of travelling in those days, by those who did not use their own horses:—

Moreover, if any gentleman desire to ride post to any principal town in England, post-horses are always in readiness (taking no horse without the consent of his owner), which in other kings' reigns was not duly observed; and only 3*d*. is demanded for every English mile, and for every stage to the post-boy 4*d*. for conducting. Besides this excellent convenience of conveying letters and men on horse-back, there is of late such an admirable commodiousness, both for men and women of better rank, to travel from London to almost any town of England, and to almost all the villages near this great city, that the like has not been known in the world, and that is by stage coaches, wherein one may be transported to any place, sheltered from foul weather and foul ways, free from endamaging one's health or body by hard jogging or over-violent motion; and this not only at a low price, as about a shilling for every five miles, but with velocity and speed, as that the posts in some foreign countries make not more miles in a day; for the stage-coaches called "Flying-coaches" make forty or fifty miles in a day; as from London to Oxford or Cambridge, and that in the spaee of twelve hours, not counting the time for dining, setting forth not too early nor coming in too late.—Chamberlayne's *Present State*, 1692, Part ii. p. 206.

And I find this same notice continued in all the editions of the work down to 1748, the last I happen to have. The later editions add, that these coaches "now perform sometimes 70, 80, or 100 miles, to Southampton, Bury, Cirencester, and Norwich."

The following is a transcript of a MS. entry on a fly-leaf at the end of a Jewish calendar for the year 5458. The book is a thin 12mo., printed "at the Theater, Oxford," A.D. "1698," with which year the Jewish date corresponds, and it contains the Christian and Jewish calendars in parallel pages. It appears from the autograph of "Wm. Stukely, M. D., 1736," which is written on the inside of the cover of the book, that it once belonged to that antiquary. The handwriting of the entries resembles that of Thomas Hearne.

A. D. 1698.	£	s.	d.
Post-chaise from Oxford to London - - - - - -	0	7	6
Post-boy - - - - - - - - - - - -	0	0	1
Expences at the Red Lion: Dinner, Wine, one bottle of old Port, and fruit - - - - - - - - - -	0	1	9
Waiter - - - - - - - - - - - -	0	0	1
Expences at Half Moon Tavern: Salmon, lobster sauce, a bottle of Port - - - - - - - - - -	0	1	6
Bed and Chamberlain - - - - - - - -	0	0	3½
Post-chaise to Oxford, and Dinner—Shoulder and leg of House Lamb, and two bottles of Wine, with asparagrass -	0	11	2
	1	2	4½
Play House Exps. - - - - -	0	0	9
	£1	3	1½

RIDDLES FOR THE POST OFFICE.

The following ludicrous direction to a letter was copied verbatim from the original and interesting document:—

too dad Tomas
hat the ole oke
otchut
I O Bary pade
Sur plees to let ole feather have this sefe.

The letter found the gentleman at "The Old Oak Orchard, Tenbury." In another letter, the writer, after a severe struggle to express "Scotland," succeeded at length to his satisfaction, and wrote it thus: "stockling." A third letter was sent by a woman to a son who had settled in Tennessee, which the old lady had thus expressed with all phonetic simplicity, "10 S C."

The following is an exact copy of the direction of a letter mailed a few years ago by a German living in Lancaster County, Pa.:—

Tis is fur old Mr. Willy wot brinds de Baber in Lang Kaster ware ti gal is gist rede him assume as it cums to ti Pushtufous.

meaning:—

This is for old Mr. Willy, what prints the paper in Lancaster, where the jail is. Just read him as soon as it comes to the Post Office.

Inclosed was an essay *against public schools.*

JOE MILLER'S TOMB.

Joe Miller was buried in St. Clement's burial ground, Portugal street, Clare Market, London, with an epitaph over him by Stephen Duck. The epitaph and the stone itself were, about the beginning of the present century, in jeopardy of obliteration, but for the compassion of Mr. Bulger, the grave-digger; and being still in a very bad condition, Mr. Buck a few years afterwards repaired it. The following is the inscription:—

Here Lye the Remains of
honest Jo. Miller,
who was
a tender Husband,
a sincere Friend,
a facetious Companion,
and an excellent Comedian.
He departed this Life the 15th day of
August, 1738, aged 54 years.

If humour, wit, and honesty could save
The humorous, witty, honest from the grave,
The grave had not so soon this tenant found,
Whom honesty, and wit, and humour crowned;
Could but esteem and love preserve our breath,
And guard us longer from this stroke of death,
The stroke of death on him had later fell,
Whom all mankind esteemed and loved so well.

S. Duck.

From respect to social worth,
mirthful qualities, and histrionic excellence,
commemorated by poetic talent, humble life,
the above inscription, which Time
had nearly obliterated, has been restored
and transferred to this stone by order of
Mr. Jarvis Buck, Churchwarden.
A.D. 1816.

In consequence of some alterations his grave is likely to be disturbed; but surely "Old Joe" ought not to be carted away, and *shot* as rubbish. Some plain memorial of him might soon be raised, if an appeal were made to the public; and if every one whose conscience told him he had ever been indebted to Miller would subscribe only a penny to the memorial fund, the requisite sum would soon be collected.

SLAVES IN ENGLAND.

When was the date of the last public slave sale in England? Till the establishment of Granville Sharpe's great principle, in 1772, announcements of these are by no means uncommon. The following, from the *Public Ledger* of Dec. 31, 1761, grates harshly upon the feelings of the present generation:—

FOR SALE:

A healthy negro girl, aged about fifteen years; speaks good English, works at her needle, washes well, does household work, and has had the small-pox.

The Dublin Mercury, No. 283, Aug. 16, 1768, contains the following matter-of-fact advertisement:—

A neat beautiful black Negro girl, just brought from Carolina, aged eleven or twelve years, who understands and speaks English, very fit to wait on a lady, to be disposed of. Application to be made to James Carolan, Carrickmacross, or to Mr. Gavan in Bridge Street, Dublin.

There is a curious announcement in the *Critical Memoirs of the Times* for January, 1769, under the date of Tuesday, January 3, one, indeed, which is calculated to shock our present notions of what is right:—

There is an agent in town, we hear, purchasing a number of the finest, best-made black boys, in order to be sent to Petersburgh, as attendants on her Russian Majesty.

From the *Daily Post*, Thursday, August 4, 1720:

Went away the 22d of July last, from the house of William Webb in Limehouse Hole, a negro man, about twenty years old, call'd Dick, yellow complection, wool hair, about five foot six inches high, having on his right breast the word HARE burnt. Whoever brings him to the said Mr. Webb's shall have half a guinea reward, and reasonable charges.

A THAMES FERRY A CENTURY AND A QUARTER AGO.

DEFOE.

While so much has been said of coaches, very little notice has been taken of another mode of conveyance which has now become very important—that class mentioned by Defoe in the following sketch, taken from his *Great Land of Subordination*, 1724. We are not bound to suppose that this is a plain relation of matter of fact, any more than the *History of Robinson Crusoe;* but it is a graphic sketch of life and manners worth the notice of those who study such things. It forms at least a little contribution to the history of travelling in England. A passenger who had just landed from a Gravesend boat, to pursue his journey by land, might well be thankful to "be received in a coach" like that which had been started at York near half a century before.

After describing the malpractices of hackney coachmen, he proceeds:—

The next are the watermen; and, indeed, the insolence of these, though they are under some limitations too, is yet such at this time, that it stands in greater need than any other, of severe laws, and those laws being put in speedy execution.

Some years ago, one of these very people being steersman of a passage-boat between London and Gravesend, drown'd three-and-fifty people at one time. The boat was bound from Gravesend to London, was very full of passengers and goods, and deep loaden. The wind blew very hard at south-west, which being against them, obliged them to turn to windward, so the seamen call it, when they tack from side to side, to make their voyage against the wind by the help of the tide.

The passengers were exceedingly frighted when, in one tack stretching over the stream, in a place call'd Long-Reach, where the river is very broad, the waves broke in upon the boat, and not only wetted them all, but threw a great deal of water into the boat, and they all begg'd of the steersman or master not to venture again. He, sawcy and impudent, mock'd them, ask'd some of the poor frighted women if they were afraid of going to the Devil; bid them say their prayers and the like, and then stood over again, as it were, in a jest. The storm continuing, he shipp'd a great deal of water that time also. By this time the rest of the watermen begun to perswade him, and told him, in short, that if he stood over again the boat would founder, for that she was a great deal the deeper for the water she had taken in, and one of them begg'd of him not to venture; he swore at the fellow, call'd him fool, bade him let him alone to his business, and he would warrant him; then used a vulgar sea-proverb, which such fellows have in their mouths, "Blow Devil, the more wind, the better boat."

The fellow told him in so many words he would drown all the passengers, and before his face began to strip, and so did two more, that they might be in condition to swim for their lives. This extremely terrify'd the passengers, who, having a cloth or tilt over them, were in no condition to save their lives, so that there was a dreadful cry among them, and some of the men were making way to come at the steersman to make him by force let fly the sail and stand back for the shore; but before they could get to him the waves broke in upon the boat and carried them all to the bottom, none escaping but the three watermen that were prepar'd to swim.

It was but poor satisfaction for the loss of so many lives, to say the steersman was drown'd with them, who ought, indeed, to have died at the gallows, or on the wheel, for he was certainly the murtherer of all the rest.

I have many times pass'd between London and Gravesend with these fellows in their smaller boats, when I have seen them, in spite of the shrieks and cries of the women and the perswasions of the men passengers, and, indeed, as if they were the more bold by how much the passengers were the more afraid; I say, I have seen them run needless hazards, and go, as it were, within an inch of death, when they have been under no necessity of it, and, if not in contempt of the passengers, it has been in meer laziness to avoid their rowing; and I have been sometimes oblig'd, especially when there has been more men in the boat of the same mind, so that we have been strong enough for them, to threaten to cut their throats, to make them hand their sails and keep under shore, not to fright as well as hazard the passengers when there was no need of it.

One time, being in one of these boats all alone, coming from London to Gravesend, the wind freshen'd, and it begun to blow very hard after I was come about three or four mile of the way; and as I said above, that I always thought those fellows were the more venturous when their passengers were the most fearful, I resolved I would let this fellow alone to himself; so I lay down in the boat as if I was asleep, as is usual.

Just when I lay down, I called to the waterman, "It blows hard, waterman," said I; "can you swim?" "No, Sir," says he. "Nor can't your man swim neither?" said I. "No, Sir," says the servant. "Well, then," says I, "take care of yourselves, I shall shift as well as you, I suppose:" and so down I lay. However, I was not much disposed to sleep; I kept the tilt which they cover their passengers with open in one place, so that I could see how things went.

The wind was fair, but overblow'd so much, that in those reaches of the river which turn'd crossway, and where the wind by consequence was thwart the stream, the water went very high, and we took so much into the boat, that I began to feel the straw which lay under me at the bottom was wet, so I call'd to the waterman, and jesting told him, they must go all hands to the pump; he answered, he hoped I should not be wet; "But it's bad weather, master," says he, "we can't help it." "No, no," says I, "'tis pretty well yet, go on."

By and by I heard him say to himself, "It blows very hard," and every now and then he repeated it, and sometimes thus: "'Twill be a dirty night, twill be a terrible night," and the like; still I lay still and said nothing.

After some time, and his bringing out several such speeches as above, I rous'd as if I had but just wak'd; "Well, waterman," says I, "how d'ye go on?" "Very indifferently," says he; "it blows very hard." "Ay, so it does," says I; "where are we?" A little above Erith," says he: so down I lay again, and said no more for that time.

By and by he was at it again, "It blows a frett of wind," and "It blows very hard," and the like; but still I said nothing. At last we ship'd a dash of water over the boat's head, and the spry of it wetted me a little, and I started up again as if I had been asleep; "Waterman," says I, "what are you doing? what, did you ship a sea?" "Ay," says the waterman, "and a great one too; why it blows a frett of wind." "Well, well," says I, "come, have a good heart; where are we now?" "Almost in Gallions," says he, that's a reach below Woolwich.

Well, when we got into the Gallions reach, there the water was very rough, and I heard him say to his man, "Jack, we'll keep the weather-shore aboard, for it grows dark and it blows a storm." Ay, thought I, had I desir'd you to stand in under shore, you would have kept off in meer bravado, but I said nothing. By and by his mast broke, and gave a great crack, and the fellow cry'd out, "Lord have mercy upon us!" I started up again, but still spoke cheerfully; "What's the matter now?" says I. "L—d, Sir," says he, "how can you sleep? why my mast is come by the board." "Well, well," says I, "then you must take a goose-wing." "A goose-wing! why," says he, "I can't carry a knot of sail, it blows a storm." "Well," says I, "if you can't carry any sail, you must drive up under shore then, you have the tide under foot:" and with that I lay down again. The man did as I said. A piece of his mast being yet standing, he made what they call a goose-wing sail, that is, a little piece of the sail out, just to keep the boat steddy, and with this we got up as high as Blackwall: the night being then come on and very dark, and the storm increasing, I suffer'd myself to be perswaded to put in there, though five or six miles short of London; whereas, indeed, I was resolv'd to venture no further if the waterman would have done it.

When I was on shore, the man said to me, "Master, you have been us'd to the sea, I don't doubt; why you can sleep in a storm without any concern, as if you did not value your life; I never carry'd one in my life that did so; why, 'twas a wonder we had not founder'd." "Why," says I, "friend, for that you know I left it all to you; I did not doubt but you would take care of yourself;" but after that I told him my other reason for it, the fellow smil'd, but own'd the thing was true, and that he was the more cautious a great deal, for that I took no thought about it; and I am still of opinion, that the less frighted and timorous their passengers are, the more cautious and careful the watermen are, and the least apt to run into danger; whereas, if their passengers appear frighted, then the watermen grow sawcy and audacious, show themselves vent'rous, and contemn the dangers which they are really exposed to.—p. 130.

Defoe was engaged in the business of brick and tile making near Tilbury, and must consequently have had frequent occasion to make the trip from Gravesend to London. That Defoe was so engaged at Tilbury we learn from the following proclamation for his apprehension, taken from the *London Gazette*, dated St. James's, January 10, 1702–'3 :—

Whereas Daniel Defoe, alias Fooe, is charged with writing a scandalous and seditious pamphlet entitled *The Shortest Way with the Dissenters*. He is a middle sized spare man about forty years old, of a brown complexion, and dark brown-coloured hair, but wears a wig; a hooked nose, a sharp chin, grey eyes, and a large mole near his mouth; was born in London, and for many years an hose-factor in Freeman's Yard, Cornhill, and is now the owner of the brick and pantile works near Tilbury Fort, in Essex. Whoever shall discover the said Daniel Defoe to one of Her Majesty's principal secretaries of state, or any one of Her Majesty's justices of the peace, so as he may be apprehended, shall have a reward of fifty pounds, which Her Majesty has ordered immediately to be paid on such discovery.

He soon gave himself up; and having been tried, he stood in the pillory with great fortitude: for soon after he published his poem, entitled *A Hymn to the Pillory*, in which are the following singular lines:—

Men that are men, in thee can feel no pain,
And all thy insignificants disdain;
Contempt, that false new word for shame,
Is, without crime, an empty name;
A shadow to amuse mankind,
But never frights the wise or well-fix'd mind—
Virtue despises human scorn,
And scandals innocence adorn.

Referring to a design of putting the learned Selden into the pillory for his *History of Tithes*, he says smartly:—

Even the learned Selden saw
A prospect of thee thro' the law;
He had thy lofty pinnacles in view,
But so much honor never was thy due.
Had the great Selden triumph'd on thy stage,
Selden, the honor of his age,
No man would ever shun thee more,
Or grudge to stand where Selden stood before.

This original poem ends with these remarkable lines, referring to himself:—

Tell them, the men that placed him here,
Are scandals to the times,
Are at a loss to find his guilt,
And can't commit his crimes.

De Foe, however, was afterwards received into favor without any concessions on his part, and proceeded straight onwards in the discharge of what he deemed to be his duty to mankind. He certainly was an extraordinary man for disinterestedness, perseverance, and industry.

CLUBS.

Club is defined by Johnson to be "an assembly of good fellows, meeting under certain conditions." The present system of clubs may be traced in its progressive steps from those small associations, meeting (as clubs of a lower grade still do) at a house of public entertainment; then we come to a time when the club took exclusive possession of the house, and strangers could be only introduced, under regulations, by the members; in the third stage, the clubs build houses, or rather palaces, for themselves. The club at the Mermaid Tavern in Friday Street, owed its origin to Sir Walter Raleigh, who had here instituted a meeting of men of wit and genius, previously to his engagement with the unfortunate Cobham. This society comprised all that the age held most distinguished for learning and talent, numbering among its members Shakespeare, Ben Jonson, Beaumont and Fletcher, Selden, Sir Walter Raleigh, Donne, Cotton, Carew, Martin, and many others. There it was that the "wit-combats" took place between Shakespeare and Ben Jonson, to which, probably, Beaumont alludes with so much affection in his letter to the old poet, written from the country:—

What things have we seen
Done at the Mermaid! heard words that have been
So nimble and so full of subtle flame,
As if that every one from whom they came
Had meant to put his whole wit in a jest.

Ben Jonson had another club, of which he appears to have been the founder, held in a room of the old Devil Tavern, distinguished by the name of the "Apollo." It stood between the

Temple Gates and Temple Bar. It was for this club that Jonson wrote the "Leges Convivales," printed among his works.

In the reign of Henry IV. there was a club called "La Court de bone Compagnie," of which Occleve was a member, and probably Chaucer. In the works of the former are two ballads, written about 1413, one a congratulation from the brethren to Henry Somer, on his appointment as Sub-Treasurer of the Exchequer; and the other a reminder to the same person, that the "styward" had warned him that he was—

. . . for the dyner arraye
Ageyn Thirsday next, and nat it delaye.

That there were certain conditions to be observed by this Society, appears from the latter epistle, which commences with an answer to a letter of remonstrance the "Court" has received from Henry Somer against some undue extravagance, and a breach of their rules. They were evidently a jovial company; and such a history as could be collected of these Societies would be both interesting and curious. We have proof that Henry Somer received Chaucer's pension for him.

BANQUO'S GHOST.

It is said that John Kemble attempted to play the banquet scene in *Macbeth* without the visible appearance of the ghost of Banquo; but the galleries took offence, and roared "Ghost! ghost!" till Banquo was obliged to come on and take the chair. The late "Thomas Ingoldsby" praises Kemble highly for the improvement, and regrets that he was not allowed to free the stage from Banquo's ghost, as Garrick did from those of Jaffier and Pierre. In his own tale of *Hamilton Tighe*, "Ingoldsby" made the ghost a phantom of the mind, with good effect:—

'Tis ever the same, in hall or bower,
Wherever the place, whatever the hour,

The lady mutters, and *talks to the air*,
And her eye is fixed on *an empty chair*,
And the *mealy-faced* boy still whispers with dread,
"She talks to a man with never a head."

Robert Lloyd has, too, the same idea.

When chilling horrors shake th' affrighted king,
And guilt torments him with her scorpion's sting;
When keenest feelings at his bosom pull,
And fancy tells him that the seat is full;
Why need the ghost usurp the monarch's place,
To frighten children with his *mealy face?*
The king alone should form the phantom there,
And *talk and tremble at the vacant chair.*

The Poetical Works of Robert Lloyd, A.M.
London, 1774.

CHRONOGRAMS.

In the second paper by Addison on the different species of false wit (*Spectator*, No. 60), is noticed the medal that was struck of Gustavus Adolphus, with the motto—

ChrIstVs DuX ergo trIVMphVs.

"If you take the pains," continues the author, "to pick the figures out of the several words, and range them in their proper order, you will find they amount to MDCXVVVII, or 1627; the year in which the medal was stamped."

Perhaps the most extraordinary instance to be found in reference to chronograms, is the following:—

Chronographica Gratulatio in Felicissimum adventum Serenissimi Cardinalis Ferdinandi, Hispaniarum Infantis, a Collegio Soc. Jesu. Bruxellæ publico Belgarum Gaudio exhibita.

This title is followed by a dedication to S. Michael and an address to Ferdinand; after which come one hundred hexameters, *every one of which is a chronogram*, and each chronogram gives the same result, viz.: 1634. The first three verses are—

AngeLe CæLIVogI MIChaëL LUX UnICa CætUs.
Pro nUtU sUCCInCta tUo CUI CUnCta MInIstrant.
SIDera qUIqUe poLo gaUDentIa sIDera VoLVUnt.

The last two are—

Vota Cano: hæC LeVIbus qUamVIs nUnC InCLyte prInCeps.
VersICULIs InCLUsa, fLUent in sæCULa CentUm.

All the numeral letters are printed in capitals, and the whole is to be found in the *Parnassus Poeticus Societatis Jesu* (Francofurti, 1654,) at pp. 445–448 of part i. In the same volume there is another example of the chronogram, at p. 261, in the "Septem Mariæ Mysteria" of Antonius Chanut. It occurs at the close of an inscription:

StatUaM hanC—eX Voto ponIt
FernanDUs TertIUs AUgUstUs.

The date is 1647.

Here is another chronogram "by Godard, upon the birth of Louis XIV. in 1638, on a day when the eagle was in conjunction with the lion's heart:"

EXorIens DeLphIn AqUILa CorDIsqUe LeonIs
CongressU GaLLos spe LætItIaqUe refeCIt.

The banks of the Rhine furnish abundant examples of this literary pleasantry: chronograms are as thick as blackberries. Here are a dozen, gathered during a recent tour.

1. Cologne Cathedral, 1722; on a beam in a chapel, on the south side of the choir:—

pIa VIrgInIs MarIæ soDaLItas annos sæCVLarI renoVat.

2. Popplesdorf Church, near Bonn. 1812:—

paroChIaLIs teMpLI rVInIs æDIfICabar.

3. Bonn; on the base of a crucifix outside the minster, on the north side. 1711:

GLORIFICATE
ET
PORTATE DEVM
IN CORPORE VESTRO.
1 Cor. 6.

4. Bonn; within the minster. 1770:—

CAPITVLVM
PATRONIS PIE
DICAVIT.

5. Aix-la-Chapelle; on the baptistery. 1660:—

SACRVM
PAROCHIALE DIVI JOHANNIS
BAPTISTÆ.

6. Aix-la-Chapelle.—St. Michael; front of west gallery. 1821:—

SVM PIA CIVITATIS
LIBERALITATE RENOVATA DECORATA.

7. Aix-la-Chapelle, under the above. 1852:—

ECCE
MICHAELIS
AEDES.

8. Konigswinter; on the base of a crucifix at the northern end of the village. 1726:—

INVNIVS VERI AC IN
CARNATI DEI HONOREM
POSVERE.

JOANNES PETRUS MUMBER ET
MARIA GENGERS CONJUGES
2 DA SEPTEMBRIS.

9. Konigswinter; over the principal door of the church. 1828:

es Ist seInes MenCher WohnUng sonDem eIn
herrLIChes haUsz Unseres gottes, i. b. d. ker.
er. 29. c. v. i.

10. Konigswinter; under the last. 1778:

VnI sanCtIssIMo Deo, patrI atqVe
fiLIo spIrItVIqVe sanCto.

11. Konigswinter; under the last. 1779:

erIgor sVb MaX. frIDerICo konIgsegg antIstIte CoLonIensI
pIe gVbernante.

12. Coblenz.—S. Castor; round the arch of the west door. 1765:

DIro MarIa IVngfraV reIn
Las CobLenz aubefohLen seIn.

Of these, Nos. 9, 10, and 11 are incised on one stone, the letters indicating the chronogram being rubricated capitals; but in No. 10, the second I in "filio," and the first I in "spirituique," though capitals, are not in red.

Hugo Grotius, his *Sophompaneas.*
By FranCIs GoLDsMIth.

has no date on the title-page, the real date of 1652 being supplied by the chronogram, which is a better one than most of those quoted in "N. & Q.," inasmuch as all the numerical letters are employed, and it is consequently not dependent on the typography.

James Howell concludes his *Parly of Beasts* as follows:—

Gloria lausque Deo sæClorVM in sæcVla sunto.

A chronogrammaticall verse which includes not onely this year, 1660, but hath numericall letters enow [an illustration, by the way, of *enow* as expressive of number] to reach above a thousand years farther, untill the year 2867.

Query, How is this made out? And are there any other letters employed as numerical than the M, D, C, L, V, and I? If not, Howell's chronogram is equivalent to 1927 only.

The same author, in his *German Diet*, after narrating the death of Charles, son of Philip II. of Spain, says:—

> If you desire to know the yeer, this chronogram will tell you:
>
> fILIVs ante DIeM patrIos InqVIrIt In annos,

which would represent the date of 1568.

The same work contains an anagram on "Frere Jacques Clement," the murderer of Henry III. of France: "Cest l'enfer qui m'a créé."

VOLTAIRE.

Extract from the MS. journal of the late Major W. Broome, 5th Royal Irish Dragoons, for upwards of fifty years the most intimate friend of Sir Henry Grattan, Speaker of the House of Commons. He died in 1826, aged eighty-nine years.

> *March 16th*, 1765 (Geneva).—Dined with Mons. Voltaire, who behaved very politely. He is very old, was dressed in a robe-de chambre of blue sattan and gold spots in it, with a sort of sattan cap and blue tassle of gold. He spoke all the time English. . . . His house is not very fine, but genteel, and stands upon a mount close to the mountains. He is tall and very thin, has a very piercing eye, and a look singularly vivacious. He told me of his acquaintance with Pope, Swift (with whom he lived for three months at Lord Peterborough's), and Gay, who first showed him the *Beggars Oppora* before it was acted. He says he admires Swift, and loved Gay vastly. He said that Swift had a great deal of the "ridiculum acre." . . . He told me of his being present at the ceremony of Lord Kinsale's first wearing his hat before the king. . . . At the house of Mons. Voltaire there is a handsome new church, with this inscription on the upper part of the front to the west:—
>
> DEO
> EREXIT
> VOLTAIRE,
> MDCCLXI.

MEDICAL SUPERSTITIONS.

Il Medico Poeta (the Physician a Poet) is the title of a folio by Dr. Cammillo Brunori, published at Fabriano in 1726. The leading object of his work is to prove that there is nothing in the nature of things to forbid the banns of marriage between poetry and medicine; that an excellent physician may be an excellent poet, and *vice versa;* and the subject-matter they are to deal with the same in either capacity. And I know no reason why it should not be so—there are the examples of Lucretius, Redi, and Fracastoro in its favor—except the existence of worthy Dr. Brunori's attempt to demonstrate the affirmative of the proposition. The work consists of a poem in twelve cantos, or "Capitoli," as from the fifteenth century downwards it was the Italian fashion to call them, on the physical poet—a sort of medical *ars poetica;* and followed by a hundred and seventy-two sonnets on all diseases, drugs, parts of the body, functions of them, and curative means. Each sonnet is printed on one page, while that opposite is occupied by a compendious account in prose of the subject in hand. We have a sonnet on the stomach-ache, a sonnet on apoplexy, a sonnet on purges, another on blisters, and many others on far less mentionable subjects. The author's poetical view of the action of a black-dose compares it to that of a tidy and active housemaid, who, having swept together all the dirt in the house, throws it out of the window.

Mystic virtues are attributed to a variety of substances, animal, vegetable, and mineral. But the page of this strange farrago which specially induced me to introduce Dr. Cammillo Brunori to the readers of "N. & Q.," is that which details the medical uses of the human skull. It is easy to conceive the nature of the associations of idea, and more or less poetical imaginings, which generated such superstitions in the minds of men accustomed to seek facts in fancies as philosophers, rather than fancies in facts as poets. And in this, as in other similar instances, we may safely conclude that the simple unsupported superstition was antecedent to the laborious attempts at finding some rationale for it. Of course, the would-be reasoner supposes and represents the process to have been the reverse. But the truth is, that such essays belong to a time when the nascent ideas of inductive philosophy had obtained sufficient strength and currency to convince students of nature that something of the sort was needful; but when they were not yet strong enough to sweep away the whole baseless fabric.

All skulls, Dr. Brunori informs us, are not of equal value. Indeed, those of persons who have died a natural death, are good for little or nothing. The *reason* of this is, that the disease of which they died has consumed or dissipated the essential spirit! The skulls of murderers and bandits are particularly efficacious. And this is clearly because not only is the essential spirit of the cranium concentrated therein by the nature of their violent death, but also the force of it is increased by the long exposure to the atmosphere, occasioned by the heads of such persons being ordinarily placed on spikes over the gates of cities! Such skulls are used in various manners. Preparations of volatile salt, spirit, gelatine, essence, &c. are made from them, and are very useful in epilepsy and hæmorrhage. The notion soldiers have, that drinking out of a skull renders them invulnerable in battle, is a mere superstition; though respectable writers do maintain that such a practice is a proved preventive against scrofula!

These, and many other no less absurdities, may no doubt be met with in writers more known to fame than poor Cammillo Brunori. But it is curious to find science at this point in Italy, at the time when Mead and Freind were writing in England, and Boerhaave in Holland.

A GRUB-STREET POET.

Is there any thing known respecting a strange "madcap," one Robert Innes, who, according to a printed broadside, was a pauper in St. Peter's Hospital, 1787? He was in the habit of penning doggrel ballads and hawking them about for sale. Some of them have a degree of humor, and are, to a certain extent, valuable at the present time for their notices of passing events. In one of these now rare effusions, he styles himself "R. Innes, O.P.," and in explanation gives the following lines:—

Some put unto their name A. M.,
And others put a D. and D.,
If 'tis no harm to mimick them,
I adds unto my name O. P.

Master of Arts, sure I am not,
No Doctor, no Divine I be;
But OAKUM PICKING is my lot,
Of the same clay are we all three.

LONDON STREET CHARACTERS.

Dickens's graphic description of the Court of Chancery, in his *Bleak House*, contains the following sketch:—

Standing on a seat at the side of the hall, . . . is a little mad old woman in a squeezed bonnet, who is always in court . . . expecting some incomprehensible judgment to be given in her favor. Some say she really is, or was, a party to a suit; but no one knows for certain, because no one cares. She carries some small litter in a reticule, which she calls her documents: principally consisting of paper matches and dry lavender.

Was there any particular original for this character? More than twenty years ago, a female of about fifty was a constant attendant on the Court of Queen's Bench in Banco. She was meanly but tidily dressed, quiet and unobtrusive in manners, but much gratified by notice from any barrister. It was said she had been ruined by a suit. Her thoughts seemed fixed upon the business of the day. "Will they take motions? Will *it* come on next? I hope he will bring it on to-day!" but who was "he," or what was "it," could not be learnt; and when asked, she would pause as if to think, and, pointing to the bench, say, "That's Lord Tenterden." She would rise as if about to address the court, when the judges were going out, and look mortified, as if she felt neglected.

An old woman frequented Doctors' Commons about seven years ago. She appeared to listen to the arguments, but was reserved and mopish if spoken to. She often threw herself in the way of one of the leading advocates, and always addressed him in the same words: "Dr. ——, I am *virgo intacta.*"

A poor female lunatic, who was called *Rouge et noir*, from her crape sables and painted cheeks, used to loiter every day about the Royal Exchange at four o'clock, and seemed to depend for subsistence upon the stray bounty of the "money-changers." It was said that she had a brother who was hanged for forgery, and that this drove her mad.

Charles Lamb describes a character, whom it is also impossible to forget:—

> A well-known figure, or part of the figure of a man, who used to guide his upper half over the pavements of London, wheeling along with most ingenious celerity upon a machine of wood. . . . He was of a robust make, with a florid sailor-like complexion, and his head was bare to the storm and sunshine. . . . The accident which brought him low, took place during the riots of 1780.

His portrait is in Kirby's *Wonderful and Eccentric Museum*, vol. i. p. 331. Below it is "Samuel Horsey, aged fifty-five, a singular beggar in the streets of London." The date of the engraving is August 30, 1803. The accompanying letter-press is as follows:—

This person, who has so long past, that is to say, during nineteen years, attracted the notice of the public, by the severity of his misfortunes, in the loss of both his legs, and the singular means by which he removes himself from place to place, by the help of a wooden seat, constructed in the manner of a rocking-horse, and assisted by a pair of crutches, first met with his calamity by the falling of a piece of timber from a house at the lower end of Bow Lane, Cheapside. He is now fifty-five years of age, and commonly called the King of the Beggars: and as he is very corpulent, the facility he moves with is very singular. From his general appearance and complexion, he seems to enjoy a state of health remarkably good. The frequent obtrusion of a man naturally stout and well made, but now so miserably mutilated as he is, having excited the curiosity of great numbers of people daily passing through the most crowded thoroughfares of the metropolis, has been the leading motive of this account, and the striking representation of his person here given.

The likeness is very good. Among the stories told of him, one was that his ample earnings enabled him to keep two wives, and, what is more, to keep them from quarrelling. He presided in the evenings at a "cadgers' club," planted at the head of the table, with a wife on each side. This burly beggar had two daughters, to each of whom he is said to have given £500 on her wedding; and it was also said he left a handsome sum of money at his death.

About thirty years ago, there might be heard any morning in the smaller streets of "the city," a cry of "dolls' bedsteads," from a lean, lame man, on a crutch, who wore an apron, and carried miniature bedsteads for sale. Of this man it was generally reported, that he was implicated in the Cato street conspiracy, and turned king's evidence.

What becomes of these street heroes? Do they die the death of common men—in bed, and with friends near them; or do they generally find their fate at last in the workhouse or the jail; and get buried no one knows when, or by whom, or where?

We cannot agree with Dickens, that "no one knows for certain" about such persons, "*because* no one cares." Indeed, his philosophy and practice are at variance in this matter. He makes his own sketch of "the little mad old woman," because he feels that it will interest. How much more would the original, could we get at it! But the truth is, these people are as mysterious as the fireman's dog. They "come like shadows, so depart;" leaving behind them on many minds ineffaceable impressions, and often survive the memory of a thousand things of real importance: which could hardly be, were there not some psychological force in these street characters—an inexplicable interest and attraction.

JEWS-HARP.

The "Jews-harp," or "Jews-trump," is said by several authors to derive its name from the nation of the Jews, and is vulgarly believed to be one of their instruments of music. Dr. Littleton renders Jews-trump by *Sistrum Judaicum.* But no such musical instrument is spoken of by any of the old authors that treat of the Jewish music. In fact, the Jews-harp is a mere boy's plaything, and incapable in itself of being joined either with a voice or any other instrument: and its present orthography is nothing more than a corruption of the French *Jeu-trompe*, literally, a toy trumpet. It is called *jeu-trompe* by Bacon, *Jew-trump* by Beaumont and Fletcher, and *Jews-harp* by Hackluyt. In a rare black-letter volume, entitled *Newes from Scotland*, 1591, there is a curious story of one Geilles Duncan, a noted performer on the "Jews-harp," whose performance seems not only to have met with the approval of a numerous audience of witches, but to have been repeated in the presence of royalty, and by command of no less a personage than the "Scottish Solomon," King James VI. Agnes Sampson being brought before the king's majesty and his council, confessed that—

Upon the night of All-hallow-even last, shee was accompanied as well with the persons aforesaid, as also with a great many other witches, to the number of two hundredth; and that all they together went to sea, each one in a riddle or sive, and went into the same very substantially, with flaggons of wine, making merrie, and drinking by the way, in the same riddle or sives, to the Kirk of North Barrick in Lowthian; and that after they had landed, tooke handes on the lande and daunced this reill or short daunce, singing all with one voice—

Commer goe ye before, commer goe ye:
Gif ye will not goe before, commer let me.

At which time, she confessed that this Geilles Duncan (a servant girl) did goe before them, playing this reill or daunce uppon a small *trumpe* called a *Jews-trumpe*, until they entred into the Kirk of North Barrick. These confessions made the King in a wonderfull admiration, and sent for the said Geilles Duncan, who upon the like *trumpe* did play the saide daunce before the Kinge's Majestie; who in respect of the strangenes of these matters tooke great delight to be present at their examinations.

It may be as well to mention that in the Belgic or Low Dutch, from whence come many of our toys, a *tromp* is a rattle for children. Another etymon for *Jews-harp* is *Jaws-harp*, because the place where it is played upon is between the jaws.

HEXAMETERS IN THE BIBLE.

The following are examples of hexameter verses in the Psalms:—

Gōd cāme | ūp wīth ā | shōut: ōur—Lōrd wīth thē | sōund ōf ā trūmpēt. ||
Thēre ĭs ă | rīvĕr thĕ | flōwĭng whĕre|ōf shāll | glāddĕn thĕ cīty. ||
Hăllĕ|lūjăh thĕ | cīty ŏf | Gōd! Jēhōvāh hăth | blēst hĕr! ||

The following are two examples in the *New Testament*:—

Art thŏu hĕ | thāt shōuld | cōme ōr | dō wē | loōk fŏr ă|nōthēr. ||
Hūsbānds | lōve yoūr | wīves ānd—bē nōt—bīttĕr ă|gāinst thēm. ||

"THE DOCTOR."

The names of "*Doctor Dove, of Doncaster*," and his steed "*Nobbs*," must be familiar to all the admirers, in another word, to all the readers, of Southey's *Doctor*.

Many years ago there was published at Canterbury a periodical work called *The Kentish Register*. In the No. for September, 1793, there is a ludicrous letter, signed "Agricola," addressed to Sir John Sinclair, then President of the Royal Agricultural Society; and in that letter there is frequent mention made of "Doctor *Dobbs, of Doncaster*, and *his horse Nobbs.*"

In the *Parish Register*, of Doncaster, there is this entry:—

1723, Feb. 10. "Dorothy Dove, gentlewoman, bur."

Doctor Daniel Dove, of Doncaster, and his horse Nobbs, form the subjects of a paper in "The Nonpareil, or the Quintessence of Wit and Humour," published in 1757. There is a story told somewhere of "Doctor Dobbs and his horse Nobbs." The horse Nobbs was left, one cold night, outside a cottage, whilst the Doctor was within officiating as accoucheur (I believe); when he was ready to start, and came out, he found the horse apparently dead. The Doctor was miles from home, and, as the horse was dead, and the night dark, in place of walking home, he, with his host, dragged the horse into the kitchen and skinned him, by way of passing the time profitably. But, lo! when the skinning was finished, the horse gave signs of returning animation. What was to be done? Doctor Dobbs, fertile in resources, got sheepskins and sewed them on Nobbs, and completely clothed him therein; and—mirabile dictu!—the skins became attached to the flesh, Nobbs recovered, and from thenceforward carried a *woolly* coat, duly shorn every summer, to the profit of Doctor Dobbs, and to the wonder and admiration of the neighborhood.

It appears from the preface to the last edition of *The Doctor*, &c., that the story of Dr. Daniel Dove and his horse was one well known in Southey's domestic circle.

A letter is there quoted, written by Southey to Mrs. Southey (then Miss Caroline Bowles), in which he says:—

There is a story of Dr. D. D. of D. and of his horse Nobs, which has, I believe, been made into a Hawker's Book. Coleridge used to tell it, and the humor lay in making it as long-winded as possible; it suited, however, my long-windedness better than his, and I was frequently called upon for it by those who enjoyed it, and sometimes I volunteered it, when Coleridge protested against its being told.

DECEITFULNESS OF LOVE.

The following lines, written about 1600, have probably never been published, and are well worthy of preservation :—

DECEITFULNESS OF LOVE.

Go, sit by the summer sea,
  Thou, whom scorn wasteth,
And let thy musing be
  Where the flood hasteth.
Mark how o'er ocean's breast
Rolls the hoar billow's crest;
Such is his heart's unrest
  Who of love tasteth.

Griev'st thou that hearts should change?
  Lo! where life reigneth,
Or the free sight doth range,
  What long remaineth?
Spring with her flow'rs doth die;
Fast fades the gilded sky;
And the full moon on high
  Ceaselessly waneth.

Smile, then, ye sage and wise;
  And if love sever
Bonds which thy soul doth prize,
  Such does it ever!
Deep as the rolling seas,
Soft as the twilight breeze,
But of *more* than these
  Boast could it never!

DIVINATION BY, OR TOSSING OF, COFFEE GROUNDS.

The following curious advertisement is in the *Dublin Weekly Journal*, June 11, 1726. This species of divination is mentioned in a note to Ellis's edition of *Brand's Popular Antiquities*, vol. ii. p. 620, and reference made to the first volume of the *Gentleman's Magazine* (1731), p. 108, where an extract is made from the *Weekly Register*, March 20, No. 90, relating some occurrences the author met with in a visit he lately paid to a lady :—

> Whom he surprised and her company in close cabal over their coffee, the rest very intent upon one whom, by her address and intelligence, he guessed was a tire-woman [Mrs. Cherry ?], to which she added the secret of *divining by coffee grounds*. She was then in full inspiration, and with much solemnity observing the atoms round the cup; on the one hand sat a widow, on the other a maiden lady. . . . They assured him that every cast of the cup is a picture of all one's life to come, and every transaction and circumstance is delineated with the exactest certainty," &c.

The same practice is noticed in *The Connoisseur*, No. 56, where a girl is represented divining to find out of what rank her husband should be :—

> I have seen him several times in *coffee grounds* with a sword by his side; and he was once at the bottom of a tea-cup in a coach and six, with two footmen behind it.

In the following advertisement one cannot but be struck with the *piety* (?) of Mrs. Cherry, who declined business till prayers were over at St. Peter's Church (a proof of daily prayers, by the way, in 1726), as well as with the *economy* with which she exercised her profession :—

> Advice is hereby given that there is lately arrived in this city the famous Mrs. Cherry, the only gentlewoman truly learned in that occult science of *tossing of coffee grounds;* who has with uninterrupted success for some time past practised to the general satisfaction of her female visitants. She is to be heard of at Mrs. C—ks, or at Mrs. Q—ts, in Angier Street, Dublin. Her hours are

after prayers are done at St. Peter's Church, till dinner. N. B.—She never requires more than one ounce of coffee from a single gentlewoman, and so proportionable for a second or third person, but not to exceed that number at any one time.

KISSING.

Kissing would seem to have been the usual method of salutation in England in former times. According to Chalondylus,

Whenever an invited guest entered the house of his friend, he invariably saluted his wife and daughters, as a common act of courtesy.

Chaucer often alludes to it. Thus, the Frere in the Sompnour's Tale, upon the entrance of the mistress of the house into the room where her husband and he were together :—

ariseth up ful curtisly,
And hire embraceth in his armes narwe,
And kisseth hire swete, and chirketh as a sparwe
With his lippes.

Robert de Brunne says the custom formed part of the ceremony of drinking healths :—

That sais wasseille drinkis of the cup,
Kiss and his felow he gives it up.

On this subject, Collet's *Relics of Literature* contains the following passage :—

Dr. Pierius Winsemius, historiographer to their High Mightinesses the States of Friesland, in his *Chronijck van Frieslandt*, 1622, tells us that the pleasant practice of kissing was utterly "unpractised and unknown" in England, till the fair princess Rouix (Rowena), the daughter of King Hengist of Friezland, "pressed the beaker with her lipkens, and saluted the amorous Vortigern with a husjen (a little kiss)."

John Bunyan condemns the practice in his *Grace Abounding* :—

The common salutation of women I abhor; it is odious to me in whomsoever I see it. When I have seen good men salute those women that they have visited, or that have visited them, I have made my objection against it; and when they have answered that it was but a piece of civility, I have told them that it was not a comely sight. Some, indeed, have urged the holy kiss; but then I have asked them why they made balks? why they did salute the most handsome, and let the ill-favored ones go?

Before Bunyan, we find in Whytford's *Type of Perfection*, 1532, the following passage:—

It becometh not, therefore, the personnes religious to follow *the manere of secular persones*, that in theyr congresses or commune metynges, or departyngs, done use to *kysse*, take hands, or such other touchings that good religious persones shulde utterly avoyde.

The custom is thought to have gone out about the time of the Restoration. Peter Heylin says it had for some time before been unfashionable in France. Its abandonment in England might have formed part of that French code of politeness which Charles II. introduced on his return. Traces of it are to be found in the *Spectator*. Thus, Rustic Sprightly (No. 240) appeals for "judgment for or against kissing by way of civility or salutation," complaining that whereas, before, he "never came in public but he saluted them, though in great assemblies, all around." Now, since "the unhappy arrival of a courtier," who was content with "a profound bow," there is "no young gentlewoman has been kissed." The practice seems to have been regarded by foreigners as peculiarly English. Thus Cavendish, in his *Life of Wolsey*, says:—

I being in a fair great dining chamber (in a castle belonging to "M. Crequi, a nobleman born") I attended my Lady's coming; and after she came thither out of her own chamber, she received me most gently, like one of noble estate, having a train of twelve gentlewomen. And when she with her train came all out, she said to me, Forasmuch, quoth she, as ye be an Englishman, whose custom is in your country to kiss all ladies and gentlewomen without offence, and *although it be not so here in* this realm [France, t. Hen. VIII.] yet will I be so bold to kiss you, and so shall all my maidens. By means whereof, I kissed my Lady and all her women.

When Bulstrode Whitelock was at the court of Queen Christina of Sweden, as ambassador from Cromwell, he waited on her on May-day, to invite her to "take the air, and some little collation he had provided as her humble servant." She came with her ladies; and "both in supper-time and afterwards," being "full of pleasantness and gaiety of spirits, among other frolics, commanded him to teach her ladies *the English mode of salutation*, which, after some pretty defences, their lips obeyed, and Whitelock most readily."

The custom of salutation by *kissing* appears to have prevailed in Scotland about 1637. It is incidentally noticed in the following extract from *Memoirs of the Life of James Mitchell, of Dykes, in the Parish of Ardrossan (Ayrshire) written by Himself*, Glasgow, 1759, p. 85; a rare tract of 111 pages :—

The next business (as I spake of before) was the Lord's goodness and providence towards me, in that particular, with Mr. Alexander Dunlop, our minister, when he fell first into his reveries and distractions of groundless jealousy of his wife with sundry gentlemen, and of me in special. First, I have to bless God on my part he had not so much as a presumption (save his own fancies) of my misbehaviour in any sort; for as I shall be accountable to that great God, before whose tribunal I must stand and give an account at that great day, I was not only free of all actual villany with that gentlewoman his wife, but also of all scandalous misbehaviour either in private or public: yea, further, as I shall be saved at that great day, I did not so much as kiss her mouth in courtesy (so far as my knowledge and memory serves me) seven years before his jealousy brake forth: this was the ground of no small peace to my mind * * * and last of all, the Lord brought me cleanly off the pursuit, and since he and I has keeped general fashions of common civility to this day, 12 *December*, 1637. I pray God may open his eyes and give him a sight of his weakness and insufficiency both one way and other. Now praise, honour, glory, and dominion be to God only wise (for this and all other his providences and favours unto me) now and ever—Amen. I subscribe with my hand the truth of this. JAMES MITCHELL.

In a curious work containing much information on the fashions of the time, entitled "*The Ladies' Dictionary; being a*

General Entertainment for the Fair Sex. London, printed for John Dunton, at the Raven in the Poultry, 1694," the "Author N. H.," article "Kissing," thus remarks :—

But kissing and drinking both are now grown (it seems) to be a greater custom amongst us than in those dayes with the *Romans*. Nor am I so austere to forbid the use of either, both which, though the one in surfeits, the other in adulteries may be abused by the vicious; yet contrarily at customary meetings and laudable banquets, they by the nobly disposed, and such whose hearts are fixt upon honour, may be used with much modesty and continence.

This extract would prove that the custom continued down to some years in the reign of William and Mary. The following is told in the *Retrospective Review*, 2d Series, vol. ii. p. 240 :—

The proud and pompous Constable of Castile, on his visit to the English Court soon after the accession of James I., was right well pleased to bestow a kiss on Anne of Denmark's lovely maids of honour, "according to the custom of the country, and any neglect of which is taken as an affront."

In Hone's *Year Book*, col. 1087, this custom is also noticed by a correspondent as follows :—

Another specimen of our ancient manners is seen in the French embrace. The gentleman, and others of the male sex, lay hands on the shoulders, and touch the side of each other's cheek; but on being introduced to a lady, they say to her father, brother, or friend, *Permettez-moi*, and salute each of her cheeks . . . And was not this custom in England in Elizabeth's reign? Let us read one of the epistles of the learned Erasmus, which being translated, is in part as follows :—

Although, Faustus, if you knew the advantages of Britain, truly you would hasten thither with wings to your feet; and, if your gout would not permit, you would wish you possessed the *heart* [sic] of Dædalus. For, just to touch on one thing out of many here, there are lasses with heavenly faces; kind, obliging, and you would far prefer them to all your Muses. There is, besides, a practice never to be sufficiently commended. If you go to any place, you are received with a *kiss* by all; if you depart on a journey, you are dismissed with a *kiss;* you return, *kisses* are exchanged. They come to visit you, a *kiss* the first thing; they leave you, you *kiss* them all round. Do they meet you any where, *kisses* in abundance. Lastly, wherever you move, there is nothing but *kisses*. And if you, Faustus, had but *once* tasted them! how soft they are—how *fragrant!* on my honour you would wish not to reside here for ten years only, but for life.

"HELL IS PAVED WITH GOOD INTENTIONS."

Coleridge, in quoting this saying, attributes it to Baxter. Boswell, in his *Life of Johnson* (*sub* 15th April, 1775), says that Johnson, in allusion to the unhappy failure of pious resolves, said to an acquaintance, "Sir, hell is paved with good intentions." Upon which Malone adds a note :—

This is a proverbial saying. "Hell," says Herbert, "is full of good meanings and wishings."—*Jacula Prudentum*, p. 11, ed. 1631."

But he does not say where else the proverbial saying is to be found. The last editor, Croker, adds :—

Johnson's phrase has become so proverbial, that it may seem rather late to ask what it means—why "*paved?*" perhaps as making the *road* easy, *facilis descensus Averni.*

Sir Walter Scott, in a letter to Miss Joanna Baillie, dated October 12, 1825 (Lockhart's *Life of Sir W. S.*, vol. vi. p. 82), says :—

I well intended to have written from Ireland, but alas! as some stern old divine says, "Hell is paved with good intentions." There was such a whirl of laking, and boating, and wondering, and shouting, and laughing, and carousing— [He alludes to his visiting among the Westmoreland and Cumberland lakes on his way home, especially] so much to be seen, and so little time to see it; so much to be heard, and only two ears to listen to twenty voices, that upon the whole I grew desperate, and gave up all thoughts of doing what was right and proper on post-days, and so all my epistolary good intentions are gone to Macadamise, I suppose, "the burning marle" of the infernal regions.

How easily a showy absurdity is substituted for a serious truth, and taken for granted to be the right sense. Without having been there, we may venture to affirm that "Hell is *not* paved with good intentions," such things being *all lost or dropt on the way* by travellers who reach "that bourne;" for, where "hope never comes," "good intentions" cannot exist any more than they can be formed, since to fulfil them were impossible. The authentic and emphatical figure in the saying is, "The *road* to hell is paved with good intentions;" and it was uttered by the "stern old divine," whoever he might be, as a warning *not* to let "good intentions" miscarry for want of being realized at the time and upon the spot. The moral, moreover, is manifestly this, that people may be going to hell with "the best intentions in the world," substituting all the while *well-meaning* for *well-doing*.

THE NAME OF BACON.

It has been suggested that the word *bacon* had the obsolete signification of "*dried wood.*" Old Richard Verstegan, famous for Saxon lore and archæological research, explains it thus:—

> Bacon, *of the Beechen tree*, anciently called Bucon; and, whereas swines-flesh is now called by the name of Bacon, it grew only at the first unto such as were fatted with Bucon or *beechmast.*—Chap. ix. p. 299.

There is one agreeable feature in this explanation, viz., that it professes somewhat naturally to account for the mysterious relation between the flesh of the unclean animal, and the name of a very ancient and honorable family. But its chief value is to be found in the singular *authentication* of it in Collins's *Baronetage.* In the very ample and particular account there given of the pedigree of the Premier Baronet, it will be seen that the *first* man who assumed the surname of Bacon, was one William (temp. Rich. I.), a great grandson of the Grimbaldus, who came over with the Conqueror and settled in Norfolk. Of course there was *some* reason for his taking that name; and though Collins makes no comment on it, he does in fact unconsciously supply that reason (elucidated by Verstegan), by happily noting of this *sole* individual, that he *bore for his arms*, "argent, *a beech-tree* proper!" The family name, Bacon, then, undoubtedly signifies "of the beechen tree," and is therefore of the same class with many others such as ash, beech, &c., latinized in ancient records by De Fraxino, De Fago, &c.

A modern motto of the Somersetshire Bacons has an ingenious rebus—

ProBa-conScientia;

the capitals, thus placed, giving it the double reading, Proba conscientia, and Pro Bacon Scientia.

ON A LADY WHO WAS PAINTED.

(*From the Latin.*)

It sounds like paradox—and yet 'tis true,
You're like your picture though it's not like you.

GOSSIPING HISTORY.

This is the Jew
That Shakspeare drew.

I do not know by whom or when the above couplet was first imputed to Pope. The following extracts will show how a story grows, and the parasites which, under unwholesome cultivation, adhere to it. The restoration of Shakspeare's text, and the performance of Shylock as a serious part, are told as usual.

In the dumb action of the trial scene he was amazingly descriptive, and through the whole displayed such unequalled merit, as justly entitled him to that very comprehensive, though concise, compliment paid to him by Mr. Pope, who sat in the stage-box on the third night of the reproduction, and who emphatically exclaimed :—

"This is the Jew
That Shakspeare drew."

Life of Macklin, by J. T. Kirkman, vol i. p. 264 : London, 1799, 2 vols. 8vo.

The book is ill-written, and no authorities are cited.

A few days after, Macklin received an invitation to dine with Lord Bolingbroke at Battersea. He attended the rendezvous, and there found Pope and a select party, who complimented him very much on the part of Shylock, and questioned him about many little particulars, relative to his getting up the play, &c. Pope particularly asked him why he wore a *red hat*, and he answered, because he had read that Jews in Italy, particularly in Venice, wore hats of that color.

"And pray, Mr. Macklin," said Pope, "do players in general take such pains?" "I do not know, sir, that they do; but as I had staked my reputation on the character, I was determined to spare no trouble in getting at the best information." Pope nodded, and said, "It was very laudable."—*Memoirs of Macklin*, p. 94, Lond. 1804.

The above work has not the author's name, and is as defective in references as Mr. Kirkman's. It is, however, not quite so trashy. Being published five years later, the author must have seen the preceding *Life*, and his not repeating the story about the couplet is strong presumption that it was not then believed. It appears again in the *Biographia Dramatica*, vol. i. p. 469, London, 1812.

Macklin's performance of this character (Shylock) so forcibly struck a gentleman in the pit, that he, as it were, involuntarily exclaimed, "This is," &c. It has been said that this gentleman was Mr. Pope.

I am not aware of its alteration during the next forty years, but this was the state of the anecdote in 1853:—

Macklin was a tragedian, and the personal friend of Alexander Pope. He had a daughter, a beautiful and accomplished girl, who was likewise on the stage. On one occasion Macklin's daughter was about to take a benefit at Drury Lane Theatre, and on the morning of that evening, whilst the father and daughter were at breakfast, a young nobleman entered the apartment, and, with the most undisguised ruffianism, made overtures of a dishonorable character to Macklin for his daughter. The exasperated father, seizing a knife from the table, rushed at the fellow, who on the instant fled, on which Macklin pursued him along the street with the knife in his hand. The cause of the tragedian's wild appearance in the street soon got vent in the city. Evening came, and Old Drury seldom saw so crowded a house. The play was the *Merchant of Venice*, Macklin sustaining the part of Shylock, and his interesting daughter that of Jessica. Their reception was most enthusiastic; but in that scene where the Jew is informed of his daughter being carried off, the whole audience seemed to be quite carried away by Macklin's acting. The applause was immense, and Pope, who was standing in the pit, exclaimed:—

"That's the Jew that Shakspeare drew."

Macklin was much respected in London. He was a native of Monaghan, and a Protestant. His father was a Catholic, and died when he was a child; and his mother being a Protestant, he was educated as such.—*Dublin Weekly Telegraph*, Feb. 9, 1853.

One more version is given in the *Irish Quarterly Review*, and quoted approvingly in *The Leader*, Dec. 17, 1853.

The house was crowded from the opening of the doors, and the curtain rose amidst the most dreadful of all awful silence, the stillness of a multitude. The Jew enters in the third scene, and from that point to the famous scene of Tubal, all passed off with considerable applause. Here, however, and in the trial scene, the actor was triumphant, and in the applause of a thousand voices the curtain dropped. The play was repeated for nineteen successive nights, with increased success. On the third night of representation all eyes were directed to the stage-box, where sat a little deformed man; and whilst others watched *his* gestures, as if to learn his opinion of the performers, he was gazing intently upon Shylock, and as the actor panted, in broken accents of rage, and sorrow, and avarice—"Go, Tubal, fee me an officer, bespeak him a fortnight before: I will have the heart of him, if he forfeit; for were he out of Venice, I can make what merchandise I will: go, Tubal, and meet me at our synagogue; go, good Tubal; at our synagogue, Tubal," the little man was seen to rise, and, leaning from the box as Macklin passed it, he whispered:—

"This is the Jew
That Shakspeare drew."

The speaker was Alexander Pope, and, in that age, from his judgment in criticism there was no appeal.

No reference to contemporary testimony is given by these historians.

Galt, in his *Lives of the Players*, Lond. 1831, does not notice the story.

Pope was at Bath on the 4th of February, 1741, as appears

from his letter to Warburton of that date; but as he mentions his intention to return to London, he may have been there on the 14th. That he was not in the pit we may be confident; that he was in the boxes is unlikely. His health was declining in 1739. In his letter to Swift, quoted in Croly's edition, vol. i. p. lxxx, he says:—

Having nothing to tell you of my poetry, I come to what is now my chief care, my health and amusement; the first is better as to headaches, worse as to weakness and nerves. The changes of weather affect me much; the mornings are my life, *in the evenings I am not dead indeed, but sleepy and stupid enough.* I love reading still better than conversation, but my eyes fail, and the hours when most people indulge in company, I am tired, and find the labor of the past day sufficient to weigh me down; *so I hide myself in bed, as a bird in the nest, much about the same time,* and rise and chirp in the morning.

I hope I have said enough to stop the farther growth of this story; but before laying down my pen, I wish to call attention to the practice of giving anecdotes without authorities. This is encouraged by the newspapers devoting a column to "varieties," which are often amusing, but oftener stale. A paragraph is now commencing the round, telling how a lady took a linendraper to a barber's, and on pretence of his being a mad relative, had his head shaved, while she absconded with his goods. It is a bad version of an excellent scene in Foote's *Cozeners.*

TALFOURD.

The noble sentiments uttered by Justice Talfourd in his last moments gave a charm to his sudden death, and shed a hallowed beauty about the painfully closing scenes of this great man. They may be placed with a passage from his beautiful tragedy of *Ion*, which may be considered as a transcript of those thoughts which filled his mind on the very eve of quitting the high and honorable duties of his earthly course. It forcibly illustrates the loving soul, the kind heart, and the amiable character of this deeply lamented judge.

After speaking of the peculiar aspect of crime in that part of the country where he delivered his last charge, he goes on to say:—

> I cannot help myself thinking it may be in no small degree attributable to that separation between class and class, which is the great curse of British society, and for which we are all, more or less, in our respective spheres, in some degree responsible, and which is more complete in these districts than in agricultural districts, where the resident gentry are enabled to shed around them the blessings resulting from the exercise of benevolence, and the influence and example of active kindness. I am afraid we all of us keep too much aloof from those beneath us, and whom we thus encourage to look upon us with suspicion and dislike. Even to our servants we think, perhaps, we fulfil our duty when we perform our contract with them—when we pay them their wages, and treat them with the civility consistent with our habits and feelings—when we curb our temper, and use no violent expressions towards them. But how painful is the thought, that there are men and women growing up around us, ministering to our comforts and necessities, continually inmates of our dwellings, with whose affections and nature we are as much unacquainted as if they were the inhabitants of some other sphere. This feeling, arising from that kind of reserve peculiar to the English character, does, I think, greatly tend to prevent that mingling of class with class, that reciprocation of kind words and gentle affections, gracious admonitions and kind inquiries, which often, more than any book-education, tend to the culture of the affections of the heart, refinement and elevation of the character of those to whom they are addressed. And if I were to be asked what is the great want of English society—to mingle class with class—I would say, in one word, the want is the want of sympathy.

Act I. Sc. 2. After Clemanthe has told Ion that, forsaking all within his house, and risking his life with strangers, he can do but little for their aid, Ion replies:—

> It is little:
> But in these sharp extremities of fortune,
> The blessings which the weak and poor can scatter
> Have their own season. 'Tis a little thing

To give a cup of water; yet its draught
Of cool refreshment, drain'd by fever'd lips,
May give a shock of pleasure to the frame
More exquisite than when nectarean juice
Renews the life of joy in happiest hours.
It is a little thing to speak a phrase
Of common comfort, which, by daily use,
Has almost lost its sense; yet, on the ear
Of him who thought to die unmourn'd, 'twill fall
Like choicest music; fill the glazing eye
With gentle tears; relax the knotted hand
To know the bonds of fellowship again;
And shed on the departing soul a sense,
More precious than the benison of friends
About the honour'd death-bed of the rich,
To him, who else were lonely, that another
Of the great family is near and feels.

REVERSIBLE EPIGRAMS.

In a small work, entitled *Specimens of Macaronic Poetry*, 8vo. 1831, the following verses are stated to have been written by some poet (not named) in praise of Pope Clement VI. or Pius II., but of which learned authorities do not agree, though it is stated in the book called *Les Bigarrures du Seigneur des Accords*, p. 173, of the edit. 1662, that the lines were written by Philelphus on Pope Pius II. It seems the poet was afraid he might not receive such a reward as, according to his own estimate, he deserved, and therefore retained the power of converting his flattery into abuse, by simply giving his friends the cue to commence from the last word, and begin backwards.

Laus tua, non tua fraus; virtus non copia rerum,
  Scandere te fecit hoc decus eximium,
Pauperibus tua das; nunquam stat janua clausa;
  Fundere res quæris, nec tua multiplicas.
Conditio tua sit stabilis! non tempore parvo
  Vivere te faciat hic Deus omnipotens.

When reversed, it reads thus :—

Omnipotens Deus hic faciat te vivere parvo
  Tempore! Non stabilis sit tua conditio.
Multiplicas tua, nec quæris res fundere; clausa
  Janua stat, nunquam das tua pauperibus.
Eximium decus hoc fecit te scandere rerum
  Copia, non virtus; fraus tua, non tua laus.

The following are other verses of the same sort :—

AD JULIUM III. PONTIFICEM MAXIMUM.

Pontifici sua sint Divino Numine tuto
Culmina, nec montes hos petat omnipotens.

AD CAROLUM V. CÆSAREM.

Cæsareum tibi sit felici sidere nomen,
Carole, nec fatum sit tibi Cæsareum.

Patrum dicta probo, nec sacris belligerabo
Belligerabo sacris, nec probo dicta patrum.

The first verse is from a Catholic, the second from a Huguenot.

Again, a third :—

Retro mente labo, non metro continuabo;
Continuabo metro; non labo mente retro.

A tutor, explaining one of the odes of Horace to his scholars, after the explanation of each ode dictated in hexameter verses the ode he had explained. He did this, he said, as an exercise. It cost him some trouble; he hesitated sometimes in his dictation, and substituted other words occasionally. His pupils thought the composition had been prepared. Some thought he would not succeed in his effort, and others maintained that, having begun, it was a point of honor to complete his task. The context gave rise to the distich.

There is another clever line :—

Sacrum pingue dabo non macrum sacrificabo.

Thus written it is an hexameter, and refers to Abel's sacrifice. But read backwards, thus:—

Sacrificabo macrum non dabo pingue sacrum,

it is a pentameter, and refers to that of Cain.

IDEES NAPOLEONIENNES.

We hear a vast deal in these ages of what are called Idées Napoléoniennes," the wisdom of Napoleon, and so forth. Some of this is invented by the writers, and ascribed to Napoleon; some of it is no wisdom at all; and some is what may be called second-hand wisdom, an old familiar face with a new dress. Of the latter sort is the famous saying:—

From the sublime to the ridiculous there is but a step.

For this remark Napoleon has obtained considerable notice; but the truth is, he borrowed it from Tom Paine; Tom Paine borrowed it from Hugh Blair, and Hugh Blair from Longinus. Napoleon's words are:—

Du sublime au ridicule il n'y a qu'un pas.

The passage in Tom Paine, whose writings were translated into French as early as 1791, stands thus:—

The sublime and the ridiculous are often so nearly related, that it is difficult to class them separately; one step above the sublime makes the ridiculous, and one step above the ridiculous makes the sublime again.

Blair has a remark akin to this:—

It is indeed extremely difficult to hit the precise point where true wit ends and buffoonery begins.

But the passage in Blair, from which Tom Paine adopted his notion of the sublime and the ridiculous, is that in which Blair, commenting on Lucan's style, remarks:—

It frequently happens that where the second line is sublime, the third, in which he meant to rise still higher, is perfectly bombast.

Lastly, this saying was borrowed by Blair from his brother rhetorician, Longinus, who, in his *Treatise on the Sublime*, has the following sentence at the beginning of Section III :—

Τεθόλωται γὰρ τῇ φράσει, καὶ τεθορύβηται ταῖς φαντασίας μᾶλλον, ἢ δεδείνωται, κᾂν ἕκαστον αὐτῶν πρὸς αὐγὰς ἀνασκοπῇς, ἐκ τοῦ φοβεροῦ κατ' ὀλίγον ὑπονοστει πρὸς τὸ εὐκαταφρόνητον.

It will be seen that the original saying, in its various peregrinations, has undergone a slight modification, Longinus making the transition a gradual one, " κατ' ὀλίγον," while Blair, Paine, and Napoleon make it but "a step." Yet, notwithstanding this disguise, the marks of its paternity are sufficiently traceable.

So much for this celebrated "mot." And, after all, there is very little wit or wisdom in it that is not expressed or suggested by Rousseau's remark :—

Tout état qui brille est sur son déclin;

or by Beaumarchais' exclamation :—

Que les gens d'esprit sont bêtes!

or by the old French proverb :—

Les extrêmes se touchent;

or by the English adage :—

The darkest hour is nearest the dawn;

or, lastly, by any of the following passages in our own poets :—

Wit, like tierce claret, when't begins to pall,
Neglected lies, and's of no use at all;
But in its full perfection of decay
Turns vinegar, and comes again in play.—*Rochester.*

There's but the twinkling of a star
Between a man of peace and war.—*Butler.*

Th' extremes of glory and of shame,
Like east and west become the same:
No Indian prince has to his palace
More followers, than a thief to the gallows.—*Butler.*

For as extremes are short of ill or good,
And tides at highest mark regorge the flood;
So fate, that could no more improve their joy,
Took a malicious pleasure to destroy.—*Dryden.*

Extremes in nature equal ends produce,
And oft so mix, the difference is too nice
Where ends the virtue or begins the vice.—*Pope.*

Other instances might be adduced, but these are sufficient to show that the sentiment owes nothing to Napoleon but the sanction of his great name and the pithy sentence in which he has embodied it.

THUNDER.

The following singular definition of *thunder* occurs in Bailey's *Dictionary*, vol. i. 17th edit., 1759:—

Thunder [Dunder, Sax. &c.], a noise known by persons not deaf.

In Bailey's 2d vol. 2d edition, 1731, the word is much more scientifically treated.

"MY MIND TO ME A KINGDOM IS."

"My mind to me a kingdom is," will be found to be of much earlier date than Nicholas Breton. Percy *partly* printed it from William Byrd's *Psalmes, Sonets, and Songs of Sadnes* (no date, but 1588 according to Ames), with some additions and *improvements* (?) from a B. L. copy in the Pepysian collection.

The following copy is from a contemporary MS. containing many of the poems of Sir Edward Dyer, Edward Earl of Oxford, and their contemporaries, several of which have never been published. The collection appears to have been made by Robert Mills, of Cambridge. It is, at least, much more genuine than the *composite* one given by Bishop Percy.

My mynde to me a kyngdome is,
  Such preasente joyes therein I fynde,
That it excells all other blisse,
  That earth affordes or growes by kynde;
Thoughe muche I wante which moste would have,
Yet still my mynde forbiddes to crave.

No princely pompe, no wealthy store,
  No force to winne the victorye,
No wilye witt to salve a sore,
  No shape to feade a loving eye;
To none of these I yielde as thrall,
For why? my mynde dothe serve for all.

I see howe plenty suffers ofte,
  And hasty clymers sone do fall,
I see that those which are alofte
  Mishapp dothe threaten moste of all;
They get with toyle, they keepe with feare,
Suche cares my mynde could never beare.

Content to live, this is my staye,
  I seeke no more than maye suffyse,
I presse to bear no haughty swaye;
  Look what I lack, my mynde supplies:
Lo, thus I triumph like a kynge,
Content with that my mynde doth brynge.

Some have too muche, yet still do crave,
  I little have and seek no more,
They are but poore, though muche they have,
  And I am ryche with lyttle store;
They poore, I ryche, they begge, I gyve,
They lacke, I leave, they pyne, I lyve.

I laughe not at another's losse,
  I grudge not at another's payne;
No worldly wants my mynde can toss,
  My state at one dothe still remayne:
I feare no foe, I fawn no friende,
I lothe not lyfe nor dreade my ende.

Some weighe their pleasure by theyre luste,
Theyre wisdom by theyre rage of wyll,
Theyre treasure is theyre onlye truste,
A cloked crafte theyre store of skylle;
But all the pleasure that I fynde
Is to mayntayne a quiet mynde.

My wealthe is healthe and perfect ease,
My conscience cleere my chiefe defence,
I neither seek by brybes to please,
Nor by deceyte to breed offence;
Thus do I lyve, thus will I dye,
Would all did so as well as I.

FINIS. E. DIER.

STONE-PILLAR WORSHIP IN IRELAND.

In a work recently published by the Earl of Roden, entitled *Progress of the Reformation in Ireland*, there occurs a curious account of a remnant of this ancient form of fetichism still existing in Inniskea, an island off the coast of Mayo, with about three hundred and eighty inhabitants, amongst whom, he says,—

A stone carefully wrapped up in flannel is brought out at certain periods to be adored; and when a storm arises, this god is supplicated to send a wreck on their coast.—P. 51.

A correspondent in the same volume writes to Lord Roden that—

They all speak the Irish language, and among them is a trace of that government by chiefs, which in former times prevailed in Ireland: the present chief or king of Inniskea is an intelligent peasant called CAIN, whose authority is acknowledged, and the settlement of all disputes is referred to his decision. Though nominally Roman Catholics, these islanders have no priest resident among them; they know nothing of the tenets of that church, and their worship consists in occasional meetings at their chief's house, with visits to a holy well called *Derivla*. The absence of religion is supplied by the open practice of pagan idolatry. In the south island a stone idol, called in the Irish *Neevougi*, has been from time immemorial religiously preserved and worshipped.

This god resembles in appearance a thick roll of homespun flannel, which arises from the custom of dedicating to it a dress of that material whenever its aid is sought; this is sewed on by an old woman, its priestess. Of the early history of this idol no authentic information can be procured, but its power is believed to be immense; they pray to it in time of sickness, it is invoked when a storm is desired to dash some hapless ship upon their coast, and again it is solicited to calm the waves to admit of the islanders fishing or visiting the main land.—*Ib.* pp. 53, 54.

This statement, irrespective of graver reflections, is suggestive of a curious inquiry, whether this point of Ireland, on the utmost western verge of Europe, be not the last spot in Christendom in which a trace can now be found of stone-pillar worship?—the most ancient of all forms of idolatry known to the records of the human race; and the most widely extended, since at one time or another it has prevailed in every nation of the old world, from the shores of Lapland to the confines of India; and, I apprehend, vestiges of its former existence are to be traced on the continent of America.

In all parts of Ireland these stone pillars are to be found in comparative frequency. Accounts of them will be found in *The Ancient and Present State of the County Down*, A. D. 1744; in Wakeman's *Handbook of Irish Antiquities*, and in various similar authorities. A writer in the *Archæologia* for A. D. 1800, says that many of the stone crosses which form so interesting and beautiful a feature in Irish antiquities were originally pagan pillar-stones, on which the cross was sculptured subsequent to the introduction of Christianity, in order that—

The common people, who were not easily to be diverted from their superstitious reverence for these stones, might pay a kind of justifiable adoration to them when thus appropriated to the use of Christian memorials by the sign of the cross.—*Archæol.* vol. xiii. p. 208.

The tenacity of the Irish people to this ancient superstition is established by the fact of its continuance to the present day in the sequestered island of Inniskea. It would be an object of curious inquiry to ascertain whether this be the last remnant of pillar-worship now remaining in Europe; and especially whether any further trace of it is to be found in any other portion of the British dominions.

GALLOSHES.

In the *Promptorium Parvulorum* we find—

GALACHE or GALOCHE, undersolynge of manny's fote.

Mr. Way says in his note:—

The galache was a sort of patten, fastened to the foot by cross latchets, and worn by men as early as the time of Edward III. Allusion is made to it by Chaucer:—

Ne were worthy to unbocle his galoche.
Squires Tale, 10,869.

Among other quotations, Mr. Way gives the following:—

To geten hym gilte spores,
Or galoches y-couped.
Piers Ploughman, 12,099.

And in the *Wardrobe Book of Prince Henry*, A. D. 1607, are mentioned—

1 pair of golossians, 6*s.*: 16 gold buckles with pendants and toungs to buckle a pair of golosses.—*Archæol.* xi. 93.

Cole, in his English dictionary, 1724, has—

Geleges, galages, galloches, galloshoes, Fr., wooden shoes all of a piece. With us outward shoes or cases for dirty weather, &c.

The word itself most likely comes to us from the French. The dictionaries refer to Spenser as using it under the form *galage;* and it occurs written *galege*, *galosh*, *calosh*, &c.

Boyer's *Dictionnaire Royal*, edit. 1753, has the following definition:—

Galoche (espèce de mule que l'on porte par dessus les souliers), galoshoe.

The French borrowed the term from the Latin *Gallicæ;* but

the Romans first derived the idea and the thing itself from Gaul, *Gallicæ* denoting Gallic or Gaulish shoes. Cicero speaks of the *Gallicæ* with contempt: " Cum calceis et toga, nullis nec *gallicis* nec lacerna; " and again, " Cum *gallicis* et lacerna cucurristi " (*Philip*. ii. 30). Blount, in his *Law Dictionary* (1670), gives the following, which refers to one very early use of the term in this country:—

> GALEGE (*galiciæ*), from the French *galloches*, which signified of old a certain shoe worn by the Gauls in foul weather, *as at present the signification with us does not much differ*. It is mentioned 4 Edw. IV. cap. 7, and 14 & 15 Hen. VIII. cap. 9.

Therefore the thing itself and the word were known among us before America was discovered. As it regards the Latin word *Gallicæ*, it is used by Cicero, Tertullian, and A. Gellius. The last named, in the *Noctes Atticæ*, gives the following anecdote and observations relating to this word: T. Castricius, a teacher of rhetoric at Rome, observing that some of his pupils were, on a holiday, as he deemed, unsuitably attired, and shod (*soleati*) with *gallicæ* (*galloches*, *sabots*, wooden shoes or clogs), he expressed in strong terms his disapprobation. He stated it to be unworthy of their rank, and referred to the above-cited passage from Cicero. Some of his hearers inquired why he called those *soleati* who wore goloshes (*gallicæ*) and not shoes (*soleæ*). The expression is justified by a statement which sufficiently describes the goloshes, viz., that they call *soleæ* (shoes) all those which cover only the lower portions of the foot, and are fastened with straps. The author adds:—

> I think that *gallicæ* is a new word, which was begun to be used not long before Cicero's time, therefore used by him in the Second of the *Antonians*. " Cum gallicis," says he, " et lacerna cucurrusti." Nor do I read it in any other writer of authority, but other words are employed.

The Romans named shoes after persons and places as we do:

for examples, see Dr. W. Smith's *Dictionary of Greek and Roman Antiquities*, sub voc. "Calceus."

WHIG AND TORY.

The derivation of these terms, as applied to the two extreme parties in politics, is a much vexed question, which will probably never be satisfactorily settled. That stanch tory, Roger North, in his *Examen*, has referred the origin of the name of his party to their connection with the Duke of York and his popish allies.

> It is easy (says North) to imagine how rampant these procurators of power, the Exclusioners, were under such circumstances of advantage as at that time prevailed; everywhere insulting and menacing the royalists, as was done in all the terms of common conversation, and the latter had the wind in their faces, the votes of the house and the rabble into the bargain. This trade, then not much opposed, naturally led to a common use of slighting and opprobrious names, such as Yorkist. That served for mere distinction, but did not scandalize or reflect enough. Then they came to Tantivy, which implied riding post to Rome. Observe, all the while the royal church party were passive; the outrage lay wholly on the other side. These observing that the Duke favored Irishmen, all his friends, or those accounted such by appearing against the Exclusion, were straight become Irish; thence bog-trotters, and in the copia of the factious language, the word *Tory* was entertained, which signified the most despicable savages among the wild Irish; and being a vocal and clear-sounding word, readily pronounced, it kept its hold, and took possession of the foul mouths of the faction.

Burton, in vol. ii. of his *Parliamentary Diary* on the state of Ireland, under date of June 10, 1657, has the following passage:—

> Tory is said to be the Irish word *Toree*, that is, *Give me*, which was the summons of surrender used by the banditti, to whom the name was originally applied.

In support of this assertion it may be as well to state that Tory or Terry Island, on the coast of Donegal, is said to have taken its name from the robbers by whom it was formerly infested. Dr. Johnson also supports Burton's derivation of the word; he calls it a cant term, signifying a savage. Mr. G. O. Borrow (alias Lavengro), who has devoted much attention to the Celtic dialect, in a paper which he contributed some years back to the *Norfolk Chronicle*, suggested that the etymology of the word Tory might be traced to the Irish adherents of Charles II. during the Cromwellian era; the words *Tar-a-Ri* (pronounced Tory, and meaning *Come, O King*), having been so constantly in the mouths of the Royalists as to have become a by-word to designate them. Lingard says that

> The name *Tory* is derived from *toringhim*, to pursue for the sake of plunder. The name was given to certain parties in Ireland, who, refusing to submit to Cromwell, retired into bogs and fastnesses, formed bodies of armed men, supporting themselves and their followers by the depredations which they committed on the occupiers of their estates. They were called *Raperees* and *Tories*.

Concerning the word Whig, Burnet says:—

> The south-west counties of Scotland have seldom corn enough to serve them round the year; and the northern parts producing more than they need, those in the west come in the summer to buy at Leith the stores that came from the north; and from a word, Whiggam, used in driving their horses, all that drove were called Whiggamors, and shorter, the Whiggs. Now, in that year (*i. e.* 1648), after the news came down of Duke Hamilton's defeat, the ministers animated their people to rise and march to Edinburgh; and they came up marching on the head of their parishes with an unheard-of fury, praying and preaching all the way as they came. The Marquis of Argyle and his party came and bearded them, they being about 6,000. This was called the Whiggamors' inroad, and ever after that, all that opposed the court came in contempt to be called Whiggs; and from Scotland the word was brought into England, where it is now one of our unhappy terms of disunion.—Burnet's *History of his own Times*, vol. i. p. 43.

Such is Burnet's account of the derivation of this word, in which he is followed by Samuel Johnson, who has transcribed the above passage in his *Dictionary*. Kirkton, also, in his *History of the Church of Scotland*, edited by C. K. Sharpe, Esq., in 1817, adheres to the same opinion. Under the year 1667, he says :—

That the term Whig was originally derived from Scotland, is a well-ascertained fact; but while some of our etymologists follow the opinion of Burnet, others with greater show of reason, adhere to the opinion of Roger North, and the historians Laing and Lingard, all of whom were of opinion that the original Scotch Whigs were called so, not, as Burnet supposes, from the word used by them in driving their horses, but from the word Whig being vernacular in Scotland from sour whey, which was a common drink with the people.

It is also suggested that the name "Whig" is derived from the Celtic *ugham*, a sort of large saddle, with bags attached to it, in use among the freebooters of the borders of Scotland: hence those robbers were known to the Highlanders by the name of *Whiggam-more*, or "big-saddle thieves;" and when the civil war broke out, the Highlanders and Irish, who supported the king, called themselves *a taobh Righ*, *i. e.* "the king's party," and gave the name of *Whiggamore thieves* to their opponents.

LINE ON FRANKLIN.

The line on Franklin—

Eripuit cœlo fulmen, sceptrumque tyrannis,

was written by Turgot, Louis XVI.'s minister and controller-general of finance. This verse, however, so happily applied to the American philosopher and statesman's double title to renown, is merely the modification of one in the *Anti-Lucretius* of Cardinal Polignac, the 37th of the first book, "Eripuitque Jovi fulmen, Phœboque sagittas," which again had for its model that of Marcus Manilius, a poet of the Augustan age. It is the 104th of his *Astronomicon*, where he says of Epicurus (lib. v.), "Eripuitque Jovi fulmen, viresque Tonanti." This appears to be the original source of the phrase, so far as I could trace it. Turgot, though highly appreciated by his sovereign, and promoted to the prime ministry in consequence, was only suffered to hold the responsible situation for a short time, from August, 1774, to May, 1776, when he fell a sacrifice to court intrigues, which the weak king had not the energy to resist, while emphatically saying, "Il n'y a que Turgot et moi qui aimions le peuple." This eminent statesman's advocacy of the freedom of commerce, state economy, and general liberty of the subject, exposed him not only to courtly, but to popular hostility. The French were certainly ill prepared for such innovations on their policy or habits, nor, even now, notwithstanding the constantly alternating schemes of government, from despotic to constitutional, in the long-interposed period, do they appear fully to appreciate, or anxious to introduce these desirable improvements.

ANAGRAMS.

The following anagram was found on the fly-leaf of a book in manuscript, date 1653, in the neat Italian hand of the period. The book had probably belonged to one of the English exiles who accompanied Charles II. in his banishment. I have never met with it in any collection of anagrams hitherto published.

Carolus Stuartus, Angliæ, Scotiæ, et Hiberniæ Rex,
Aulâ, statû, regno exueris, ac hostili arte necaberis.

Polemics apart, the following will strike most persons as most remarkably happy :—

But, holie father, I am certifyed
That they youre power and policye deride ;
And how of you they make an anagram,
The best and bitterest that the wits could frame.
As thus :
Supremus Pontifex Romanus.
Annagramma :
O non sum super petram fixus.

It occurs in Taylor's *Suddaine Turne of Fortune's Wheele*, lately printed for private circulation, under the care of Mr. Halliwell.

The anagram by George Herbert on *Roma*, is a good specimen of what may be called "learned trifling."

Roma dabit oram, Maro,
Ramo, armo, mora, et amor.

Henriot, an ingenious anagrammatist, discovered the following anagram for the occasion of the 15th :—

Napoleon Bonaparte sera-t-il consu à vie,
La [le] peuple bon reconnoissant votera Oui.

There is only a trifling change of *a* to *e*.—*Gent. Mag.*, Aug. 1802, p. 771.

The following is singular :—

Quid est veritas ?=Vir qui adest.

NOTES AND QUERIES.

The history of books and periodicals of a similar character ought to be an object of interest to the readers of this work. The number of works in which answers have been given to proposed questions is not small. Not to mention the *Spectator* and its imitators, nor the class of almanacs which give riddles and problems, nor mathematical periodicals of a more extensive character—though all these ought to be discussed in course of time—there yet remains a class of books in which general questions proposed by the public are answered periodically, either by the public or by the editors.

In 1736 and 1737, appeared the *Weekly Oracle; or, Universal Library. Published by a Society of Gentlemen.* One folio sheet was published weekly, usually ending in the middle of a sentence. (Query. What is the technical name for this mode of publication? If none, what ought to be?) I have one folio volume of seventy numbers, at the end of which notice of suspension is given, with prospect of revival in another form: probably no more was published. The introduction is an account of the editorial staff: to wit, a learned divine who "hath entered with so much discernment into the true spirit of the schoolmen, especially Thomas Aquinas and Duns Scotus, that he is qualified to resolve, to a hair's breadth, the nicest cases of conscience." A physician who "knows, to a mathematical point, the just tone and harmony of the rising pulses. . . ." A lawyer who, "what he this day has proved to be a contingent remainder, to-morrow he will, with equal learning, show must operate as an executory devise or as a springing use." A philosopher "able to give the true reason of all things, from the composition of watches to the raising of minced pies . . . and who, if he is closely questioned about the manner of squaring the circle, or by what means the perpetual motion, or longitude, may be discovered, we believe has honesty, and we are sure that he has skill enough to say that he knows—nothing of the matter." A moral philosopher who has "discovered a *perpetuum mobile* of government." An eminent virtuoso who understands "what is the best pickle to preserve a rattlesnake or an Egyptian mummy, better than the nature of the government he lives under, or the economy and welfare of himself and family." Lastly, a *man of mode.* "Him the beaus and the ladies may consult in the affairs of love, dress, and equipage."

There is a great deal of good answering to tolerably rational questions, mixed with some attempts at humor and other eccentricities, and occasionally a freedom, both of question and answer, by which we might, were it advisable, confirm the fact, that the decorums of 1736 and of 1850 are two different things.

There are many other works of a similar character. Thus, we have *Memoirs for the Ingenious*, 1693, 4to., edited by I. de la Crose; *Memoirs for the Curious*, 1701, 4to.; *The Athenian Oracle*, 1704, 8vo.; *The Delphick Oracle*, 1720, 8vo.; *The British Apollo*, 1708 to 1711, 12mo.; with several others of less note. The three last quoted answer many singular questions in theology, law, medicine, physics, natural history, popular superstitions, &c., not always very satisfactorily or very intelligently, but still, often amusingly and ingeniously.

The first number of *The British Apollo* was issued on February 13, 1708, and it was published twice a week. It completed its career in March, 1711, having attained the bulk of three volumes folio. An abridgment of this curious periodical, "containing 2,000 Answers to Questions in most Arts and Sciences," was published in 1726 and 1740, 3 vols. 12mo. The principal part is occupied by questions and replies, to which is added a page of very indifferent poetry; a short letter concerning foreign news (in one number, commencing: "Feb. 22, 1710. Sir, yesterday we received a *male* from Holland, by which we have confirmation from Warsaw," &c.); and a few advertisements of "good Bohee at 24*s.* per lb.;" quack doctors; a reward for a runaway negro in a suit of grey livery, &c., &c. The questions and answers are somewhat of a miscellaneous character, some on deep religious subjects; as on free will, election, &c.: one begins, "Resplendent sages, pray oblige your adorer with an exposition of Matt. xxiii. 35." Some on medical topics, and apparently from those who have a personal interest in the reply, as, "Whether thin people are most liable to consumption?" "whether three half-pints of good punch per diem is good for that complaint?" "on the wholesomeness of cyder;" "on the properties of crabs' eyes;" "respecting the virtues of raisons of the sun." One is: "Gentlemen, I being very willing to keep my carcass in health as much as I can, I would fain know which is the best for me to drink in the morning, tea or chocolate?" Another, "Gentlemen, pray give your opinion of mushrooms." Of the miscellaneous ones, the following may serve as specimens: What sort of a person was Xenophon? What were the Carpocratians? Whether music has any virtue to drive away devils? Is a person who has just eaten his breakfast heavier than before? How ancient is the use of rattles for children? Answer, attributing the invention to Archytas of Tarentum, the tutor of Plato. "How old was Adam when Eve was created?—Is it lawful to eat black pudding?—Whether the moon in Ireland is like the moon in England?—Where is hell situated?—Do cocks lay eggs?" &c. In answer to the question, "Why is gaping catching?" the querists are gravely told—

Gaping or yawning is infectious, because the steams of the blood being ejected out of the mouth, doth infect the ambient air, which being received by the nostrils into another man's mouth, doth irritate the fibres of the hypogastric muscle to open the mouth to discharge by expiration the unfortunate gust of air infected with the streams of blood, as aforesaid.

The feminine gender, we are further told, is attributed to a ship, "because a ship carries burdens, and therefore resembles a pregnant woman." What dependence are we to place in the origin it attributes to two very common words, a *bull*, and a *dun?*—

Why, when people speak improperly, is it termed a bull? It became a proverb from the repeated blunders of one *Obadiah Bull*, a lawyer of London, who lived in the reign of King Henry VII.

Now for the second:—

Pray tell me whence you can derive the original of the word *dun?* Some falsely think it comes from the French, where *donnez* signifies *give me*, implying a demand of something due; but the true original of this expression owes its birth to one *Joe Dun*, a famous bailiff of the town of Lincoln, so extremely active, and so dexterous at the management of his rough business, that it became a proverb, when a man refused to pay his debts, "Why don't you *Dun* him?" that is, why don't you send Dun to arrest him? Hence it grew a custom, and is now as old as since the days of Henry VII.

Were these twin worthies, Obadiah Bull the lawyer, and Joe

Dun the bailiff, men of straw for the nonce, or veritable flesh and blood? They both flourished, it appears, in the reign of Henry VII.; and to me it is doubtful whether one reign could have produced two worthies capable of cutting so deep a notch in the English tongue.

It gives this account of the origin of "Nine Tailors make a Man."

It happen'd ('tis no great matter in what year), that eight taylors, having finish'd considerable pieces of work at a certain person of quality's house (whose name authors have thought fit to conceal), and receiving all the money due for the same, a virago servant-maid of the house observing them to be but slender-built animals, and in their mathematical postures on their shop-board appearing but so many pieces of men, resolv'd to encounter and pillage them on the road. The better to compass her design, she procured a very terrible great black-pudding, which (having waylaid them) she presented at the breast of the foremost: they, mistaking this prop of life for an instrument of death, at least a blunder-buss, readily yielded up their money; but she, not contented with that, severely disciplin'd them with a cudgel she carry'd in the other hand, all of which they bore with a philosophical resignation. Thus, eight not being able to deal with one woman, by consequence could not make a man, on which account a ninth is added. 'Tis the opinion of our curious virtuosos, that this want of courage ariseth from their immoderate eating of cucumbers, which too much refrigerates their blood. However, to their eternal honour be it spoke, they have been often known to encounter a sort of cannibals, to whose assaults they are often subject, not fictitious, but real man-eaters, and that with a lance but two inches long; nay, and although they go arm'd no further than their middle finger.

"To dine with Duke Humphrey," we are told, arose from the practice of those who had shared his dainties when alive being in the habit of perambulating St. Paul's, where he was buried, at the dining time of day; what dinner they then had, they had with Duke Humphrey, the defunct.

The following are some questions discussed in the *Athenian Oracle*:—

Adam and Eve, whether they had navels?
Angels, why painted in petticoats?
Babel tower, what was the height of it?
Brethren, two born in one, had they two souls?

This must have referred to a case similar to the Siamese twins, now living in North Carolina, married to two sisters, and having families.

Females, if they went a-courting, would there be more marriages than now?
Hairs, an equal number in any two men's heads?

Answered in the affirmative, the number of persons living at any one time greatly exceeding the number of hairs in any man's head.

Negroes, shall they rise so at the last day?

Answered in the negative, as all men will then be as near perfection as possible.

Peter and Paul, did they use notes?
Queen of Sheba, had she a child by Solomon?
Wife, whether she may beat her husband?
Women, whether they have souls?
Women, whether not bantered into a belief of being angels?

A readable volume might be compiled from these "Notes and Queries," which amused our grandfathers.

QUEEN ELIZABETH.

In the *Travels* of Hentzner, who resided some time in England in the reign of Elizabeth, as tutor to a young German nobleman, there is given a very interesting account of the "Maiden Queen," and the court which she then maintained at "the Royal Palace of Greenwich." After noticing the appearance of the presence-chamber—"the floor, after the English fashion, strewed with hay,"—the writer gives a descriptive portrait of Her Majesty. He states:—

Next came the Queen, in her sixty-fifth year, as we were told, very majestic; her face oblong, fair, but wrinkled; her eyes small, but black and pleasant; her nose a little hooked; her lips narrow, and her teeth black (a defect the English seem subject to, from their too great use of sugar.) She had in her ears two *pearls*, with very rich drops. She wore false hair, and that red.

NURSERY TALE.

I saddled my sow with a sieve full of buttermilk, put my foot into the stirrup, and leaped nine miles beyond the moon into the land of temperance, where there was nothing but hammers, and hatchets, and candlesticks, and there lay bleeding Old Noles. I let him lie, and sent for Old Hippernoles, and asked him if he could grind green steel nine times finer than wheat flour? He said he could not. Gregory's wife was up in the pear-tree gathering nine corns of buttered peas to pay Saint James' rent. Saint James was in the meadow mowing oat cakes; he heard a noise, hung his scythe at his heels, stumbled at the battledore, tumbled over the barn-door ridge,. and broke his shins against a bag of moonshine that stood behind the stairsfoot door, and if that isn't true, you know as well as I.

MILTON'S BORROWINGS.

There is perhaps nothing in "Lycidas" which has so commended itself to the memory and lips of men, as that exquisite strain of tender regret and pathetic despondency in which occur the lines—

> Fame is the spur which the clear spirit doth raise
> (That last infirmity of noble minds),
> To scorn delights, and live laborious days.

May not that graceful glorifying of Fame as "the last infirmity of noble minds" have been suggested by the profound remark of Tacitus, in his character of the stoical republican, Helvidius Priscus (*Hist.*, l. iv. c. 6) :—

> Erant, quibus appetentior famæ videretur, quando etiam sapientibus cupido gloriæ novissima exuitur.

The great Englishman has condensed and intensified the expression of the concise and earnest Roman. This is one of those delightful obligations which repay themselves: Milton has more than returned the favor of the borrowed thought by lending it a heightened expression.

Warton's edition of the *Minor Poems of Milton*, with its formidable array of parallel passages from other and elder poets, furnishes an abounding example of a prevailing characteristic of Milton's mind, that of reflecting (perhaps unconsciously) the axioms and bright sayings of all ages of literature, stored in his capacious brain-treasury.

No writer of the same rank in genius has, perhaps, to a greater extent re-fused the sentences of other authors which were worth preserving. Warton, it is said, produced his edition in no friendly spirit towards the old republican, whom he hated for his politics, but to manifest the abundance of the poet's obligations to his predecessors. There is no question that Milton "borrowed," and unscrupulously; but it was not an Israelitish "borrowing" of the Egyptians; he returned the thoughts he had appropriated with added lustre, or, to preserve the image in its integrity, with compound interest.

Leigh Hunt, speaking on this very subject, acknowledged in his fanciful and humorous vein of language:—"Oh, yes! Milton 'borrowed' other poets' thoughts, but he did not 'borrow' as gipsies borrow children, spoiling their features that they may not be recognized. No, he returned them improved. Had he 'borrowed' your coat, he would have restored it, *with a new nap upon it!*"

ERASMUS.

The following epigram is written in a fly-leaf of a copy of the *Epistolæ Obscurorum Virorum*, published at Frankfort, 1624:—

Ut Rhadamantheum stetit ante tribunal Erasmus,
Ante jocos scribens serio damnor, ait
Cui Judex, libri dant seria damna jocosi,
Si tibi culpa jocus, sit tibi pœna jocus.

Anglicè. T. CORBETT.

Erasmus standeinge fore hell's tribune said,
For writeinge iest I am in earnest paid.
The iudge replied, Iests will in earnest hurt,
Sport was thy fault, then let thy paine be sport.

HERMITS, ORNAMENTAL AND EXPERIMENTAL.

Keeping a poet is a luxury enjoyed by many, from the Queen down to Messrs. Moses, Hyam & Co.; but the refinement of keeping a hermit would appear to be a more *recherché* and less ordinary appendage of wealth and taste.

Here is an advertisement *for*, and two actual instances of *going a hermiting*:—

A young man, who wishes to retire from the world and live as an hermit in some convenient spot in England, is willing to engage with any nobleman or gentleman who may be desirous of having one. Any letter directed to S. Lawrence (post-paid) to be left at Mr. Otton's, No. 6. Colman's Lane, Plymouth, mentioning what gratuity will be given, and all other particulars, will be duly attended to.—*Courier*, Jan. 11th, 1810.

It is not probable that this retiring young man was engaged in the above capacity, for soon after an advertisement appeared in the papers which there are reasons for thinking was by the same hand.

Wants a situation in a pious regular family, in a place where the Gospel is preached, a young man of serious mind, who can wait at table and milk a cow.

The immortal Dr. Busby asks—

When energising objects men pursue,
What are the prodigies they cannot do

Whether it is because *going a hermiting* does not come under the Doctor's "energising objects" is uncertain; but this is clear, that the two following instances proved unsuccessful:—

M. Hamilton, once the proprietor of Payne's Hill, near Cobham, Surrey, advertised for a person who was willing to become a hermit in that beautiful retreat of his. The conditions were, that he was to continue in the hermitage seven years, where he should be provided with a Bible, optical glasses, a mat for his bed, a hassock for his pillow, an hour-glass for his timepiece, water for his beverage, food from the house, but never to exchange a syllable with the servant. He was to wear a camlet robe, never to cut his beard or nails, nor ever to stray beyond the limits of the grounds. If he lived there, under all these restrictions, till the end of the term, he was to receive seven hundred guineas. But on breach of any of them, or if he quitted the place any time previous to that term, the whole was to be forfeited. One person attempted it, but a three weeks' trial cured him.

Mr. Powyss, of Marcham, near Preston, Lancashire, was more successful in this singularity: he advertised a reward of 50*l.* a-year for life, to any man who would undertake to live seven years under ground, without seeing any thing human: and to let his toe and finger nails grow, with his hair and beard, during the whole time. Apartments were prepared under ground, very commodious, with a cold bath, a chamber organ, as many books as the occupier pleased, and provisions served from his own table. Whenever the recluse wanted any convenience, he was to ring a bell, and it was provided for him. Singular as this residence may appear, an occupier offered himself, and actually stayed in it, observing the required conditions for four years.

CIRCULATION OF THE BLOOD.

There is a passage in Longinus (ch. xxii.) which indicates that the fact of the circulation of the blood was well established in the days of Plato. The father of critics, to exemplify, and illustrate the use and value of *trope* in writing, has garbled from the Timæus a number of sentences descriptive of the anatomy of the human body, where the circulation of the blood is pointed at in terms singularly graphic. The exact extent of professional knowledge arrived at in the time of the great philosopher is by no means clearly defined. He speaks of the fact, however, not with a view to prove what was contested or chimerical, but avails himself of it to figure out the surpassing wisdom of the gods in constructing the human frame. The venerable Bede, in a tract *De Minutione Sanguinis sive de Phlebotomia* (which occurs in the folio editions, Basle, vol. i. p. 472; Colon., vol. i. p. 898), in the enumeration of the veins from which blood may be taken, says:—

> De brachio tres, *qui per totùm corpus reddunt sanguinem*, capitanea linea, matricia, capsale.

The subject of bleeding is again referred to in *Eccl. Hist.*, vol. iii., but not to the purpose.

PRÆ-RAFFAELISM.

If at a distance you would paint a pig,
 Make out each single bristle of his back;
Or, if your meaner subject be a wig,
 Let not the caxon a *distinctness* lack;
Else all the lady critics will so stare,
And angry vow, "'Tis not a bit like hair!"

. . . .

Claude's distances are too confused—
 One floating scene—nothing made out—
For which he ought to be abused,
 Whose works have been so cried about.

Give me the pencil whose amazing style
Makes a bird's beak appear at twenty mile;
And to my view, eyes, legs, and claws will bring,
With every feather of his tail and wing.

Peter Pindar, *Lyric Odes for* 1783, Ode VIII.

NEGUS.

Wine and water, it is said, first received the name of Negus from Colonel Francis Negus, who was commissioner for executing the office of Master of the Horse during the reign of George I. Among other anecdotes related of him, one is, that party spirit running high at that period between Whigs and Tories, wine-bibbing was resorted to as an excitement. On one occasion some leading Whigs and Tories having, *par accident*, got over their cups together, and Mr. Negus being present, and high words ensuing, he recommended them in future to dilute their wine, as he did, which suggestion fortunately directed their attention from an argument which probably would have ended seriously, to one on the merits of wine and water, which concluded by their nick-naming it *Negus*. A correspondent in the *Gentleman's Mag.* for Feb. 1799, p. 119, farther states, "that Negus is a family name, and that the said liquor took its name from an individual of that family, the following relation (on the veracity of which you may depend) will, I think, ascertain: "It is now nearly thirty years ago, that being on a visit to a friend at Frome, in Somersetshire, I accompanied my friend to the house of a clergyman of the name of Potter. The house was decorated with many paintings, chiefly family portraits, amongst which I was particularly pleased with that of a gentleman in a military dress, which appeared, by the style, to have been taken in or about the reign of Queen Anne. In answer to my inquiries concerning the original of the portrait, Mrs. Potter informed me it was a Colonel Negus, an uncle of her husband's; that from this gentleman the liquor usually so called had its name, it being his usual beverage. When in company with his junior officers, he used to invite them to join him by saying, 'Come, boys, join with me; taste my liquor!' Hence it soon became fashionable in the regiment, and the officers, in compliment to their colonel, called it *Negus*."

ERRONEOUS BIBLE QUOTATIONS.

The *apple* is a fruit never connected in Scripture with the fall of man; Eve was not Adam's *helpmate*, but merely a help *meet* for him; Absalom's long hair, of which he was so proud, and which has consequently so often served "to point a moral and adorn a tale," had nothing to do with his death, his head itself, and not the hair upon it, having been caught in the boughs of the tree.

LORD BROOK.

The following fine lines form the "Chorus Sacerdotum," at the end of Lord Brook's *Mustapha.* (See his Works, fol. 1633, p. 159.)

O wearisome condition of humanity!
Borne under one Law, to another bound:
Vainely begot, and yet forbidden vanity;
Created sick, commanded to be sound:
What meaneth Nature by these diverse Lawes?
Passion and reason self division cause.
Is it the mark or majesty of power
To make offences that it may forgive?
Nature herself doth her own self defloure
To hate those Errors she herself doth give.
For how should Man think that he may not do
If Nature did not fail and punish too?
Tyrant to others, to herself unjust,
Only commands things difficult and hard,
Forbids us all things, which it knows is lust,
Makes easy pains, impossible reward.
If Nature did not take delight in blood,
She would have made more easy ways to good.
We that are bound by vows and by promotion,
With pomp of holy sacrifice and rites,
To teach belief in good and still devotion,
To preach of Heaven's wonders and delights;
Yet when each of us in his own heart looks,
He finds the God there far unlike his Books.

There should be a collected edition of the works of the two noble Grevilles, Fulke and Robert, Lords Brook; the first the friend of Sir Philip Sidney, the second the honored of Milton. The little treatise on *Truth* of the latter, which Wallis answered in his *Truth Tried,* is amply sufficient to prove that he possessed powers of no common order.

SWEARING OF THE ENGLISH.

The revolting habit of swearing, which of late years has happily diminished, has been a marked characteristic of the English for *many centuries;* and the national adjuration which has given us a *nick-name* on the continent, appears to have prevailed at an earlier period than is generally supposed.

"The English," observes Henry, "were remarkable in this period (between 1399 and 1485) among the nations of Europe, for the absurd and impious practice of profane swearing in conversation." Of this the trial of Joan of Arc (ann. 1429) affords us a distinct proof. One of the witnesses, Colette, being asked who "Godon" was, made answer that the term was a nickname generally applied to the English on account of their continual use of the exclamation, "G—d d—n it," and not the designation of any particular individual. This fact from Sharon Turner's *Hist. Middle Ages,* 8vo. edit. vol. ii. p. 555.

The Count of Luxemburg, accompanied by the Earls of Warwick and Stafford, visited the Maid of Orleans in her prison at Rouen, where she was chained to the floor and loaded with irons. The Count, who had sold her to the English, pretended that he had come to treat with her about her ransom. After addressing him with contempt and disdain, she turned her eyes towards the two Earls, and said, "I know that you English are determined to put me to death, and imagine that, after I am dead, you will conquer France: but though there were a hundred thousand

G——dammees more in France than there are, they will never conquer that kingdom." So early had the English got this odious nickname by their frequent and common use of that horrid and disgusting imprecation.

Swearing is, however, no longer considered essential to good breeding, but is now quite discountenanced in good society. Yet the army and navy continue to keep up its respectability, and prevent it becoming utterly vulgar." They have made it professional and official; in fact, part of their uniform. A sentence in conversation not rounded by *an oath* is unworthy the dignity of either Mars or Neptune, and an order not endorsed with a *curse* or shotted with a *damn* is scarcely valid, and certainly not so efficacious.

The severe epigram of Sir John Harrington is but too just:—

In older times, an ancient custom was,
To swear in mighty matters by the *mass;*
But when the mass went down, as old men note,
They swore then by the *Cross* of this same groat:
And when the *Cross* was likewise held in scorn,
Then by their *faith*, the common oath was sworn;
Last, having sworn away all faith and truth,
Only *G—d d——n them*, is the common oath:
Thus custom kept decorum by gradation,
That losing *mass*, *Cross*, *faith*, they find *damnation*.

The only work expressly on the subject that I have heard of is, *Remarks on the Profane and Absurd Use of the Monosyllable Damn, by the Rev. Matthew Towgood*, 1746, 8vo.

Byron notices it in the 11th Canto of *Don Juan*:—

Juan, who did not understand a word
  Of English, save their shibboleth, "God damn!"
And even *that*, he had so rarely heard,
  He sometimes thought 'twas only their "Salām,"

> Or "God be with you!" and 'tis not absurd
> To think so: for half English as I am,
> (To my misfortune) never can I say,
> I heard them wish "God with you" save that way.—Stanza XII.

See also Stanza XLIII. of the same Canto.

Our sovereigns had each their favorite oath; thus, William the Conqueror swore by the *splendor of God;* William Rufus, by *St. Luke's face;* John, by *God's tooth.* Elizabeth's ordinary oath was peculiarly impious and irreverent. Lord Herbert of Cherbury gives the following extraordinary excuse for James I.'s habit of cursing:—

> It fell out one day that the Prince of Condé coming to my house, some speech happ'ned concerning the King my master, in whom, tho' he acknowledged much learning, knowledge, clemency, and divers other virtues, yet he said he had heard that the king *was much given to cursing;* I answered that it was out of his *gentleness:* but the Prince demanding how cursing could be gentleness? I replied yes; for tho' he could punish men himself, yet he left them to God to punish: which defence of the King my master was afterwards much celebrated in the French Court.

PROSPERO'S ISLAND.

We cannot assert that Shakspeare, in the *Tempest,* had any particular island in view as the scene of his immortal drama, though by some this has been stoutly maintained. Chalmers prefers one of the Bermudas. The Rev. J. Hunter, in his *Disquisition on the Scene, &c., of the Tempest,* endeavors to confer the honor on the Island of Lampedosa. In reference to this question, a statement of the pseudo-Aristotle is remarkable. In his work "περὶ θαυμασίων ἀκουσμάτων,," he mentions Lipara, one of the Æolian Islands, lying to the north of Sicily, and nearly in the course of Shakspeare's Neapolitan fleet from Tunis to Naples. Among the πολλὰ τερατώδη found there, he tells us:—

> Ἐξακούεσθαι γὰρ τυμπάνων καὶ κυμβάλων ἦχον γέλωτά τε μετὰ θορύβου

καὶ κροτάλων ἐναργῶς. λέγουσι δέ τι τερατωδέστερον γεγονέναι περὶ τὸ σπήλαιον.

If we compare this with the aerial music heard by Ferdinand (*Tempest* I. 2), especially as the orchestra is represented by the genial burin of M. Retsch in the fifth plate of his well-known sketches (*Umrisze*), it will appear probable that Shakspeare was acquainted with the Greek writer either in the original or through a translation.

EARLY DELIGHTS OF PHILADELPHIA.

In Gabriel Thomas's *Description of the Settlement of Philadelphia* occurs the following passage :—

> In the said city are several good schools of learning for youth, for the attainment of arts and sciences, also reading and writing. Here is to be had, on any day in the week, cakes, tarts, and pies ; we have also several cook-shops, both roasting and boiling, as in the city of London : happy blessings, for which we owe the highest gratitude to our plentiful Provider, the great Creator of heaven and earth.

AMERICANISMS.

Most of these are either English words that have become obsolete in the mother-country, or words and phrases used in a way that is now out of use there. The words *guess* and *reckon*, used to signify *suppose* or *think*, are instances.

Locke, in his *Essay on Education,* in sect. 28, says, " Once in four-and-twenty hours is enough, and nobody, *I guess*, will think it too much."

In sect. 167 : " But yet, *I guess*, this is not to be done with children whilst very young." And in sect. 174 : " And he whose design it is to excel in English poetry would not, *I guess*, think the way to it was to make his first essay in Latin verses."

Where the New Englander, or resident of the Middle States, says *I guess*, the Virginian says *I reckon*, and in this he has the sanction of the translators of the Bible in the days of James I., who rendered Romans viii. 18, thus: "For I *reckon* that the sufferings of this present time are not worthy to be compared with the glory which shall be revealed in us."

To progress.—Americans have been ridiculed by some English writers for using this verb. It was in use in England in the time of Queen Elizabeth.

PRINT FROM AN ENGRAVING BY HOGARTH.

Some time since a gentleman sent his box to a working jeweller for repair; the embossed frame which surrounded the lid had become loose. The box was of silver, plain in its shape, but ornamented on the top with a group of figures, somewhat after the manner of Watteau, engraved upon the plate.

Upon removing the border, it was found necessary to take the upper part of the box entirely to pieces. While minutely inspecting the landscape and figures, the jeweller perceived, at the edge of the plate, which had been concealed by its frame, the name of William Hogarth. This naturally excited his attention, and he mentioned the circumstance to a neighbor, whom he knew to be thoroughly conversant with all matters of art. It was suggested by this gentleman that a few impressions of the subject should be taken off, as he knew a great Hogarthian collector, and he might probably obtain something for the ingenious workman, who had a large family to support by one pair of hands. Some twenty copies were printed on India paper, the plate restored to its original destination, but so soldered and riveted to the exterior embossing as to prevent the possibility of its ever again being subjected to the process of the printing press.

The circumstances of the case were communicated, the twenty copies shown to the collector, Mr. W——, and their price demanded. Five pounds were named, and immediately paid. Mr.

W—— then carefully examined his purchase, selected the best impression, and threw the remaining nineteen into the fire, exclaiming, "Now I have in my possession a unique work of my idol's [Query, why not idol?]. No man can boast that he has a copy of this *fête champêtre* but myself, and I would not part with it for fifty pounds."

His feelings were less enviable than those of the person who had enabled him to possess this treasure. With what delight did he hand over the smaller sum to the honest workman, whose gratitude was equal to his surprise at such an unexpected Godsend.

The passion for destroying what is valuable in order to monopolize, instead of diffusing pleasure and information, is the vice of a virtuoso, and a proof of imperfect knowledge in a connoisseur.—From *A Pinch—of Snuff*, by Pollexenes Digit Snift, Dean of Brazen-Nose. London, Robert Tyas, 1840, p. 79.

THE SOUND OF "OUGH."

TWO ATTEMPTS TO SHOW THE SOUND OF "OUGH" FINAL.

1.

Though from rough cough, or hiccough free,
  That man has pain enough
Whose wounds through plough, sunk in a slough,
  Or lough begins to slough.

2.

'Tis not an easy task to show
How *o*, *u*, *g*, *h* sound; since *though*
An Irish *lough* and English *slough*,
And *cough*, and hic*cough*, all allow
Differ as much as *tough* and *through*,
There seems no reason why they do.

SHENSTONE'S LINES ON AN INN.

The circumstances which gave occasion to the composition of Shenstone's well-known lines on an inn, are thus narrated in a pleasing little volume* by his friend, the Rev. Richard Graves of Mickleton :—

About the year 1750 (notwithstanding his reluctance to leave home), Mr. Shenstone had resolution enough to take a journey of near seventy miles across the country to visit his friend, Mr. Whistler, in the southernmost part of Oxfordshire. Mr. Whistler, with manly sense and a fine genius, had a delicacy of taste and a softness of manners bordering on effeminacy. He laid a stress on trivial circumstances in his domestic economy, which Mr. Shenstone affected to despise. As people in small families find it difficult to retain a valuable servant, Mr. Whistler made it a rule to prevent, as much as possible, any intercourse with strange servants, and, without making any apology for it, had sent Mr. Shenstone's servant to a little inn in the village. This was a little disgusting, but unfortunately, while Mr. Shenstone was there, Mr. Whistler thought proper to give a ball and supper to two or three of the most respectable families in the neighborhood.

Mr. Shenstone (as he says in a letter on that occasion)—

never liked that place. There was too much trivial elegance, punctilio, and speculation in that polite neighborhood. They do nothing but play at cards, and on account of my ignorance of any creditable game, I was forced to lose my money, and two evenings out of seven, at Pope Joan with Mr. P.'s children.

This disposed him to ridicule Mr. Whistler's great solicitude in preparing for his entertainment; instead, therefore, of paying any regard to the hints given him, that it was time to dress for their company, Shenstone continued lolling at his ease, taking snuff, and disputing rather perversely on the folly and absurdity of laying a stress upon such trifles; and, in short, the dispute ran

* *Recollections of some Particulars in the Life of the late William Shenstone, Esq.*: London (Dodsley), 1788, 12mo.

so high, that although Shenstone suppressed his choler that evening, yet he curtailed his visit two or three days, took a cool leave the next morning, and decamped. Traversing the whole county, he reached Edge Hill that night, where, in a summer-house, he wrote the lines in question.

Both Shenstone and Whistler seemed afterwards conscious of their childish conduct on this occasion; each seemed solicitous to know how his account stood with the other. Whistler still expressed the highest regard for Shenstone, and Shenstone retained the same warmth of affection for his old friend until his death.

Mr. Graves remarks "that there were more stanzas added to to this effusion afterward, which diminished the force of the principal thought." The additions are thus given in Dodsley's edition of Shenstone's *Works*, vol. i. p. 218, where the whole is inscribed:—

WRITTEN AT AN INN AT HENLEY.

To thee, fair Freedom! I retire
From flattery, cards, and dice, and din;
Nor art thou found in mansions higher
Than the low cot or humble inn.

'Tis here with boundless pow'r I reign;
And every health which I begin
Converts dull port to bright champagne;
Such freedom crowns it, at an inn.

I fly from pomp, I fly from plate!
I fly from falsehood's specious grin;
Freedom I love, and form I hate,
And chuse my lodgings at an inn.

Here waiter! take my sordid ore,
Which lacqueys else might hope to win;
It buys, what courts have not in store,
It buys me freedom at an inn.

Whoe'er has travell'd life's dull round,
Where'er his stages may have been,
May sigh to think he still has found
The warmest welcome at an inn.

The statement of Mr. Graves, that the lines were written in a summer-house at Edge Hill (Mr. Jago's), is inconsistent with the title prefixed to these stanzas. Perhaps the lines so often quoted were all that were produced at Edge Hill; and the other stanzas may have been written afterwards at the inn at Henley.

"LONG SIR T. RCBINSON."

"Till how he did a dukedom gain,
And Robinson was Aquitain?"

At the last coronation the Duke of Normandy, not Aquitain, was represented by Sir Thomas Robinson, a Yorkshire baronet, more generally known as "Long Sir Thomas," on account of his uncommon height of stature; in allusion to which the following happy epigram was written:—

Unlike to Robinson shall be my song,
It shall be witty, and it shan't be long.

A ludicrous anecdote is related of the introduction of Sir Thomas to a Russian nobleman, who persuaded himself that he was addressing no less a character than Robinson Crusoe. Sir Thomas was a specious empty man, and a great pest to persons of high rank or in office. He was very troublesome to the *Earl of Burlington*, and when in his visits to him he was told that his lordship was gone out, would desire to be admitted to look at the clock, or to play with a monkey that was kept in the hall, in hopes of being sent for in to the earl. This he had so frequently done that all in the house were tired of him. At length it was concerted among the servants that he should receive a summary answer to his usual questions, and accordingly, at his next coming, the porter, as soon as he had opened the gate, and without waiting for what he had to say, dismissed him with these words: "Sir, his lordship is gone out, the clock stands, and the monkey is dead."—Churchill's *Poetical Works*, 1804, vol. ii. p. 183.

MIND YOUR P'S AND Q'S.

There are several explanaticns given as to the origin of this term. Some have thought it to be derived from the ancient custom of hanging a slate behind the alehouse door, on which was written *P.* or *Q.* (i. e. *pint* or *quart*) against the name of each customer, according to the quantity which he had drunk, and which was not expected to be paid for till the Saturday evening, when the wages were settled.

The expression so familiar to schoolboys of "*going tick*," may perhaps be traced to this, a *tick* or mark being put for every glass of ale.

Others have thought that this phrase was, originally, "Mind your *toupées* and your *queues*,"—the *toupée* being the artificial locks of hair on the head, and the *queue* the pigtail of olden time.

There used to be an old riddle as follows:—Who is the best person to keep the alphabet in order? Answer: A barber, because he ties up the *queue*, and puts *toupées* in irons.

But the most plausible explanation as to origin, seems to be the following, by Charles Knight, who says:—

I have always thought that the phrase, "Mind your P's and Q's," was derived from the school-room or the printing-office. The forms of the small "p" and "q," in the Roman type, have always been puzzling to the child and the printer's apprentice. In the one, the downward stroke is on the left of the oval; in the other, on the right. Now, when the types are reversed, as they are when in the process of distribution they are returned by the compositor to his case, the mind of the young printer is puzzled to distinguish the "p" from the "q." In sorting *pie*, or a mixed heap of letters, where the "p" and the "q" are not in connection with any other letters forming a word, I think it would be almost impossible for an inexperienced person to say which is which upon the instant. "Mind your *p*'s and *q*'s"—I write it thus, and not "Mind your P's and Q's" has a higher philosophy than mind your *toupées* and your *queues*, which are things essentially different, and impossible to be mistaken. It means, have regard to small differences; do not be deceived by apparent resemblances; learn to discriminate between things essentially distinct, but which look the same; be observant; be cautious.

DE GUSTIBUS, &c.

A clergyman in the south-west of England, calling lately on one of his parishioners, who kept a public house, remarked to her how sorry he was, when passing along the road, to hear such noises proceeding from her house. "I wonder," said he, "that any woman can keep a public house, especially one where there is so much drunkenness and depravity as in yours." "Oh, sir," she replied, "that is the very reason why I like to keep such a house, because I see every day so much of the *worst part of human nature*."

THE ROSE.

Lines supposed to have been addressed, with the present of a white rose, by a Yorkist, to a lady of the Lancastrian faction.

If this fair rose offend thy sight,
It on thy bosom wear,
'Twill blush to find itself less white,
And turn Lancastrian there.

But if thy ruby lip it spy,
As kiss it thou may'st deign,
With envy pale 'twill lose its dye,
And Yorkist turn again.

The origin of the blush imparted to the rose is most beautifully described by Carey:—

As erst in Eden's blissful bowers
Young Eve surveyed her countless flowers,

An opening rose of purest white
She marked with eye that beamed delight;
Its leaves she kissed, and straight it drew
From Beauty's lip the vermeil hue.

A CHAPTER ON PLANTS AND FLOWERS.

Christians in times past loved to think that as all created nature shared in man's fall, so did she sympathize in his Redemption; that she hailed with glad welcome the nativity of the Saviour; and that, after the Incarnate Deity had risen and ascended on high, inspired with a mysterious joy, she looked up once more, and

The lonely world seem'd lifted nearer heaven.

As Adam of St. Victor sings :—

Mundi renovatio
Nova parit gaudia
Resurgenti Domino
Consurgunt omnia.

Then the flowers "gladlier grew," shed a grateful fragrance to their risen King, and with silent aspirations whispered of love, and peace, and hope.

There is the beautiful *Legend of the Tree of Life.* In the words of Evelyn :—

Trees and woods have twice saved the whole world; first by the *Ark*, then by the *Cross;* making full amends for the evil fruit of the tree in Paradise by *that* which was borne on the Tree in Golgotha.—*Silva*, p. 604: York, 1776, 4to.

And of Calderon :

Arbol donde el cielo quiso
Dar el fruto verdadero
Contra el bocado primero,
Flor del nuevo Paraiso.

The ancient botanists have handed down to us many an allusive name and legend, and even yet

> Many a sign
> Of the great Sacrifice which won us heaven,
> The woodman and the mountaineer can trace
> On rock, on herb, and flower.
>
> *Wood Walk and Hymn*, by Mrs. Hemans.

Thus we have *Holy Rood Flower*, *Passion Flower*, *St. Andrew's Cross*, *St. James's Cross*, *Cross of Jerusalem*, *Cross of Malta*, *Cross Flower*, *Cross Wort*, *Cross Mint*, *Crossed Heath.*

The legend of the Aspen-tree (*Populus tremula*) is thus beautifully told by Mrs. Hemans :—

> *Father.* Hast thou heard, my boy
> The peasant's legend of that quivering tree ?
> *Child.* No, father : doth he say the fairies dance
> Amidst the branches ?
> *Father.* Oh ! a cause more deep,
> More solemn far the rustic doth assign
> To the strange restlessness of those wan leaves.
> The Cross, he deems, the blessed Cross, whereon
> The meek Redeemer bow'd His head to death,
> Was form'd of aspen wood : and since that hour
> Through all its race the pale tree hath sent down
> A thrilling consciousness, a secret awe
> Making them tremulous, when not a breeze
> Disturbs the airy thistle-down, or shakes
> The light lines of the shining gossamer.
>
> *Wood Walk and Hymn.*

Lightfoot ascribes this legend to the Highlanders of Scotland. Another legend runs thus :—

At that awful hour of the Passion, when the Saviour of the world felt deserted in His agony, when—

> The sympathising sun his light withdrew,
> And wonder'd how the stars their dying Lord could view,—

when earth, shaken with horror, rung the passing bell for Deity, and universal nature groaned; then from the loftiest tree to the lowliest flower all felt a sudden thrill, and trembling, bowed their heads, all save the proud and obdurate *aspen*, which said, "Why should *we* weep and tremble? we trees, and plants, and flowers are pure and never sinned!" Ere it ceased to speak, an involuntary trembling seized its every leaf, and the word went forth that it should never rest, but tremble on until the day of judgment.

With regard to the Passion Flower, it is only necessary to refer to Mrs. Hemans' lines in the poem above quoted. The legend of the *Arum maculatum* is similar to that of the Robin Redbreast:—

These deep inwrought marks
The villager will tell thee (and with voice
Lower'd in his true heart's reverent earnestness)
Are the flower's portion from the atoning blood,
On Calvary shed. Beneath the Cross it grew,
And in the vase-like hollow of the leaf,
A few mysterious drops transmitted thus
Unto the groves and hills their sealing stains—
A heritage for storm or vernal wind
Never to waft away.—*Wood Walk and Hymn.*

The beautiful shrub, *Cereis silignastrum*, or *Arbor Judæ*,

Is thought to be that whereon Judas hanged himselfe, and not upon the elder-tree as it is vulgarly said.—Gerarde's *Herbal* (by Johnson): Lond. 1633, folio.

Of Adam's Apple-tree, or West Indian plantain (*Musa serapionis*), the same writer says:—

If it (the fruit) be cut according to the length, oblique, transverse, or any other way whatsoever, may be seen *the shape and forme of a Crosse, with a man fastened thereto.* Myselfe have seene the fruit and cut it in pieces, which was brought me from Aleppo in pickle. *The Crosse I might perceive as the forme of a Spred Egle in the root of Ferne;* but the man I leave to be sought by those who have better eies and judgment than myselfe. . . . The Grecians and Christians w[h] inhabit Syria, and the Jews also, suppose it to be that tree of whose fruit Adam did taste.

In a work by a bright star of the dreary eighteenth century, Jones of Nayland, entitled *Reflections on the Growth of Heathenism among Modern Christians*, the following passage occurs :—

Botany, which in ancient times was full of the blessed Virgin Mary, and had many religious memorials affixed to it, is now as full of the heathen Venus, the Mary of our modern virtuosi. Amongst the ancient names of plants, we found the *Calceolus Mariæ*, *Carduus Mariæ*, *Carduus benedictus*, Our Lady's Thistle, Our Lady's Mantle, the Alchymilla, &c.; but modern improvements have introduced the Speculum Veneris, Labrum Veneris, Venus's Looking-glass, Venus's Basin, Venus's Navelwort, Venus's Flytrap, and such like; and whereas the ancient botanists took a pleasure in honouring the memory of the Christian saints with the St. John's Wort, St. Peter's Wort, Herb Gerard, Herb Christopher, and many others, the modern ones, more affected to their own honour, have dedicated several newly-discovered genera of plants to one another, of which the Hottonia, the Sibthorpia, are instances, with others, so numerous and familiar to men of science, that they need not be specified.

Sir Thomas Browne, in one of his *Dialogues*, makes the Puritan Prynne say—

In our zeal we visited the gardens and apothecaries' shops. So *Ungentium Apostolicum* was commanded to take a new name, and besides, to find security for its good behaviour for the future. *Carduus benedictus*, Angelica, St. John's Wort, and Our Lady's Thistle, were summoned before a class and forthwith ordered to distinguish themselves by more sanctified appellations.—Quoted in Southey's *Colloquies*, i. p. 373, and in Teale's *Life of William Jones*, p. 367.

Ah! what ravages Botany has made in the poetry of flowers! Truly there was exquisite beauty in many of our old-fashioned country appellations. How many a tale of rustic love yet lives in some of their names! Who can doubt whence arose such as *Mary-gold*, *None-so-pretty*, *Goldilock*? And by the very name were village maidens warned against *Love-in-idleness* and *London Pride*; and long delicious walks in the deep summer twilights, and lingerings before the old grey cottage, and partings at the wicket—they all live in one little plant, *Kiss-me-at-the-garden-gate!* The *Forget-me-not* is so called in every Christian tongue. In village botany, too, lingers many a quaint and lovely superstition; look, for example, at the *Fox-glove*, that is, *Folks'-glove* or *Faries'-glove*. What needed the villager to lament his poverty, when his meadows gave him *Money-wort*, and *Shepherd's-purse* flowered in the waysides? Why needed he to envy the skill of the physician, when for his sight he had *Eye-bright*, for his hurts he had *Wound-wort*, for ointment *Ploughman's-spikenard*, for sprains *Chafe-weed*, against infection *Pestilent-wort*, in the burning summer, *Fever-few;* in the unhealthy autumn, *Spleen-wort;* if hurt by poison, *Adder-wort;* for condiments, *Poor-man's-pepper;* finally, against all possible accidents, *All-heal?* Merrily might the traveller wend on his way when there was the little *Speedwell* to cheer him, *Waybread* to support him, *Gold-of-pleasure* to enrich him, *Travellers'-joy* to welcome him; when, though *Dent-de-lion* and *Wolf's-claw* might meet his eye, he would find no further trace of those evil beasts. Animals, too, have left their names; so we have *Snake-weed*, and from its sweetness *Ox-lips* or *Cows'-lips;* and how pretty are the names *Day's-eye* and *Night-shade!* Sage men, too, have given such titles as *Honesty*, and *Thrift*, and *Heart's-ease*, and *Loose-strife;* and even in this cold age we have *St. John's Wort*, *St. Peter's Wort*, *St. Barnaby's Thistle*, ay, and best of all, *Everlasting!*

Palæophilus.—Yes, our boasted wisdom has fallen very short here in the unpronounceable and hideous names which we fasten on our delicate plants.—*Hierologus*, p. 171: Lond. 1846.

PURITAN SIMILES.

1. Indeed there is an ignorance that is no better than a dancing-roome for the satyre.—Sydenham's *Serm.*, 1637, p. 198.

2. Our Church is full crammed with Pastours, our Pastours with the Worde, and our Congregations with both, *and our Parloures sometimes with all three.—Ibid*, p. 223.

3. That hande is vnshapen and little better than monstrous, where all the fingers are the same length.—*Ibid*, p. 295. (*Touching the Degrees of Church Ministry.*)

4. Between a toad under a sill, and the sunne in the firmament.—Baxter's *Saints' Rest*, 1649, p. 270.

5. When God will, he takes up whom He will amongst the wicked and trusseth him up so or so, quarters him, and hangs up his quarters; setts him up as a mark, and shoots him clean thorow.—Lockyer's *England Watched*, 1646, p. 308.

6. Malice should be looked on as an implacable thing, and

the men in whose breasts it is, as fire shovels fetched from Hell. —*Ibid*, p. 402.

7. Vindication of conscience! ah, what a thing 'tis! 'tis a granado shot into the house in the night, when all are abed and asleep: which awakens, breaks open, teares open windows, doores, eyes, and bowels, and fetches the sleeper outc piecemeal.—*Ibid*, p. 499.

8. As all the beastes tremble when the lion roreth, soe let all men harken when God teacheth.—Smith's *Serm.*, 1622, p. 311.

9. But if they bee vsed as beautifull baites to couer a barbed hooke, I will there *lay a strawe*, and reject them.—Frewen's *Serm.*, 1612, c. 4.

10. They returned home with the same sinnes they carried away; like new moones, they had a new face and appearance, but the same spots remained still.—Stillingfleet's *Serm.*, 1666, p. 9.

11. Hell paved with skulls of children.—Watson's *Art of Contentment*, 1653, p. 27.

12. His house made an habitation for *Zim* and *Jim*, and every unclean thing.—*Godly Man's Portion*, 1663, p. 129.*

13. A covenant with them is like a *loose collar aboute an ape's neck*, which they can put off and on at pleasure.—Calamy's *Serm.*, p. 27; Gibson's *Serm.*, 1645, p. 22.

Pray'r is Faith's pump, where't works till the water come;
If't comes not free at first, Faith puts in some.
Pray'r is the sacred bellows; when these blow,
How doth that live-coal from God's altar glow.

Faithful Teate's Ter Tria, 1658.

Walking in the streets, I met a cart that came near the wall; so I stept aside, to avoid it, into a place where I was secure enough. *Reflection*. Lord, sin is that great evill of which Thou

* See the margin of the authorized version of Isaiah xiii. 21, 22, where these words occur: Gesenius makes *Zim* to be animals, *i. e.* jackals, ostriches, wild beasts. The *Jim*, he says, were jackals.

complainest that Thou art pressed as a cart is pressed; how can it then but bruise me to powder?—Caleb Trenchfield's *Christian Chymestree.*

ANTIQUITY OF THE "BONES."

And with his right drew forth a truncheon of a white ox rib, and two pieces of wood of a like form; one of black Eben, and the other of incarnation Brazile; and put them betwixt the fingers of that hand, in good symmetry. Then knocking them together, made such a noise as the lepers of Britany used to do with their clappering clickets; yet better resounding, and far more harmonious.—*Rabelais*, book ii. c. 19.

COLLEGE SALTING.

There formerly prevailed an odd custom at Oxford and Cambridge, entitled *Salting*, which was the ceremony of initiating a freshman into the company of senior students. There is an account of it given in the *Life of Anthony Wood*, who was admitted a student at Oxford, 1647. At various periods, from All Saints till Candlemas, "there were Fires of Charcole made in the Common hall."

At all these Fires every Night, which began to be made a little after five of the clock, the Senior Under-Graduats would bring into the hall the Juniors or Freshmen between that time and six of the clock, and there make them sit down on a Forme in the middle of the Hall, joyning to the Declaiming Desk: which done, every one in Order was to speake some pretty Apothegme, or make a Jest or Bull, or speake some eloquent Nonsense, to make the Company laugh: But if any of the Freshmen came off dull or not cleverly, some of the forward or pragmatical Seniors would *Tuck* them, that is, set the nail of their Thumb to their chin, just under the Lipp, and by the help of their other Fingers under the Chin, they would give him a chuck, which sometimes would produce Blood. On Candlemas day, or before (according as Shrove Tuesday fell out), every Freshman had warning given him to provide his Speech, to be spoken in the public Hall before the Under-Graduats and Servants on Shrove-

Tuesday night that followed, being alwaies the time for the observation of that Ceremony. According to the said Summons A. Wood provided a Speech as the other Freshmen did.

Shrove Tuesday Feb. 15, the Fire being made in the Common hall before 5 of the Clock at night, the Fellowes would go to Supper before six, and making an end sooner than at other times, they left the Hall to the Libertie of the Undergraduats, but with an Admonition from one of the Fellowes (who was the Principall of the Undergraduats and Postmasters) that all things should be carried in good Order. While they were at Supper in the Hall, the Cook (Will. Noble) was making the lesser of the brass Pots full of Cawdle at the Freshmans Charge; which, after the Hall was free from the Fellows, was brought up and set before the Fire in the said Hall. Afterwards every Freshman, according to seniority, was to pluck off his Gowne and Band, and if possibly to make himself look like a Scoundrell. This done, they were conducted each after the other to the high Table, and there made to stand on a Forme placed thereon; from whence they were to speak their Speech with an audible voice to the Company: which, if well done, the person that spoke it was to have a Cup of Cawdle and no *salted Drinke;* if indifferently, some Cawdle and some *salted Drinke;* but if dull, nothing was given to him but *salted Drinke*, or *salt* put in College Bere, with Tucks to boot. Afterwards when they were to be admitted into the Fraternity, the Senior Cook was to administer to them an Oath over an old Shoe, part of which runs thus: *Item tu jurabis, quod penniless bench non visitabis, &c.*: the rest is forgotten, and none there are that now remembers it. After which spoken with gravity, the Freshman kist the Shoe, put on his Gowne and Band, and took his place among the Seniors.

Mr. Wood gives part of his speech, which is ridiculous enough. It appears that it was so satisfactory that he had cawdle and sack without any salted drink. He concludes thus:—

This was the way and custome that had been used in the College, time out of mind, to initiate the Freshmen; but between that time and the restoration of K. Ch. 2. it was disused, and now such a thing is absolutely forgotten.

LIFE.

It has been ingeniously said that "Life is an epigram, of which death is the point." Alas for human nature! good points are rare, and no wonder, according to this wicked but witty

EPIGRAM BY LA MONNOYE.

The world of fools has such a store,
That he who would not see an ass,
Must bide at home, and bolt his door,
And break his looking glass.

CHILDREN CRYING AT THEIR BIRTH.

When I was born, I drew in the common air, and fell upon the earth, which is of like nature, *and the first voice which I uttered was crying, as all others do.*—*Wisd.* vii. 3.

Tum porro Puer, ut sævis projectus ab undis
Navita, *nudus humi jacet,* Infans, indigus omni
Vitali auxilio; cum primum in luminis oras
Nixibus ex alvo matris natura profudit:
Vagituque locum lugubri complet, ut æquum est,
Cui tantum in vita restet transire malorum.

Lucret. De Rer. Nat., v. 223.

For the benefit of the lady readers of "N. & Q." I subjoin a translation of these beautiful lines of Lucretius:—

The infant, as soon as Nature with great pangs of travail hath sent it forth from the womb of its mother into the regions of light, lies, like a sailor cast out from the waves, *naked upon the earth* in utter want and helplessness; *and fills every place around with mournful wailings* and piteous lamentation, as is natural for one who has so many ills of life in store for him, so many evils which he must pass through and suffer.

Thou must be patient: we came crying hither;
Thou know'st, the first time that we smell the air,
We wawle and cry—
When we are born, we cry that we are come
To this great stage of fools.—Shakspeare's *Lear.*

Who remindeth me of the sins of my infancy? "For in Thy sight none is pure from sin, not even the infant whose life is but a day upon the earth." (Job xxv. 4.) Who remindeth me? Doth not each little infant, in whom I see what of myself I remember not? What then was my sin? Was it that I *hung upon the breast and cried?*—St. Austin, *Confess.*, lib. i. 7.

For man's sake it should seeme that Nature made and produced all other creatures besides; though this great favour of hers, so bountifull and beneficiall in that respect, hath cost them full deere. Insomuch as it is hard to judge, whether in so doing she hath done the part of a kind mother, or a hard and cruell stepdame. For first and foremost, of all other living creatures, man she hath brought forth all naked, and cloathed him with the good and riches of others. To all the rest she hath given sufficient to clad them everie one according to their kind: as namely shells, cods, hard hides, prickes, shagge, bristles, haire, downe, feathers, quils, skailes, and fleeces of wool. The verie trunkes and stemmes of trees and plants, shee hath defended with bark and rind, yea, and the same sometime double against the injuries both of heat and cold: man alone, poore wretch, she hath laid *all naked upon the bare earth, even on his birth-day, to cry and wraule presently from the very first houre that he is borne into this world:* in suche sort as, *among so many living creatures, there is none subject to shed teares and weepe like him. And verily to no babe or infant is it given once to laugh before he be fortie daies old*, and that is counted verie early and with the soonest. . . . The child of man thus untowardly borne, and who another day is to rule and command all other, loe how he lyeth bound hand and foot, weeping and crying, and beginning his life with miserie, as if he were to make amends and satisfaction by his punishment unto Nature, for this onely fault and tresspass, that he is borne alive.—Plinie's *Naturall Historie*, by Phil. Holland, Lond. 1601, fol., intr. to b. vii.

The following queries are extracted from Sir Thomas Browne's "Common-place Books," *Aristotle, Lib. Animal.*:—

Whether till after forty days children, though they cry, weep not; or, as Scaliger expresseth it, "Vagiunt sed oculis siccis."

Whether they laugh not upon tickling?

Why, though some children have been heard to cry in the womb, yet *so few cry at their birth*, though their heads be out of the womb?—Bohn's ed. iii. 358.

Thomson follows Pliny, and says that man is "taught *alone* to weep" ("Spring," 350); but—not to speak of the

> Cruel, crafty crocodile,
> Which, in false grief hiding his harmful guile,
> Doth weep full sore and sheddeth tender tears,

as Spenser sings—the camel weeps when overloaded, and the deer when chased sobs piteously. Thomson himself, in a passage he has stolen from Shakspeare, makes the stag weep :—

——he stands at bay;
The big round tears run down his dappled face;
He groans in anguish.—Autumn, 452.

Steller relates this of the *Phoca Ursina*, Pallas of the camel, and Humboldt of a small American monkey.—Laurence *On Man*, Lond. 1844, p. 161.

Risibility, and a sense of the ridiculous, is generally considered to be the property of man, though *Le Cat* states that he has seen a chimpanzee laugh.

Grose (quoted in Brand) tells us there is a superstition that a child who does not cry when sprinkled in baptism will not live; and the same is recorded in Hone's *Year-Book*.

EPIGRAMS IN THE BRITISH MUSEUM.

The following epigrams are transferred from the letters of Mr. Martyn, a *littérateur* of temporary fame in the first half of the eighteenth century, addressed to Dr. Birch, which are among the Birch MSS. in the British Museum. Mr. Martyn, if I remember right, gives them as not his own.

EPITAPH ON ARCHBISHOP POTTER.

Alack and well-a-day,
Potter himself is turned to clay.

Two epigrams on the coffins of Dr. Sacheverel and Sally Salisbury, being found together in the vault of St. Andrew's :—

Lo! to one grave consigned, of rival fame,
A reverend Doctor and a wanton dame.
Well for the world both did to rest retire,
For each, while living, set mankind on fire.

———

A fit companion for a high-church priest;
He non-resistance taught, and she profest.

CINDERELLA.

Two centuries ago furs were so rare, and therefore so highly valued, that the wearing of them was restricted by several sumptuary laws to kings and princes. Sable, in those laws called *vair*, was the subject of countless regulations: the exact quality permitted to be worn by persons of different grades, and the articles of dress to which it might be applied, were defined most strictly. Perrault's tale of *Cinderella* originally marked the dignity conferred on her by the fairy, by her wearing a slipper of *vair*, a privilege then confined to the highest rank of princesses. An error of the press, now become inveterate, changed *vair* into *verre*, and the slipper of *sable* was suddenly converted into a *glass* slipper.

A story somewhat similar to that of Cinderella has been handed down from the Greek. It is reported of Rhodopis, "that one day when she was in the bath, an eagle snatched one of her slippers from an attendant, and carried it to Memphis. The King was then sitting on his tribunal; the eagle, settling above his head, let fall the slipper into his bosom; the prince, astonished at this singular event, and at the smallness of the slipper, ordered search to be made through the country for the woman to whom it belonged. Having found her at Naucratis, she was presented to the King, who made her his wife."

CORNELIS DREBBEL.

In a very curious little book, entitled *Kronycke van Alcmaer*, and published in that town anno 1645, are the following particulars about Cornelis Drebbel, a native of the same city.

Being justly renowned as a natural philosopher, and having made great progress in mechanics, our Drebbel was named tutor of the young Prince of Austria, by the Emperor Ferdinandus II., an office which he fulfilled so well, that he was afterwards chosen councillor to His Majesty, and honored with a rich pension for past services. But, alas! in the year 1620, Prague, the place he dwelt in, was taken by Frederick, then King of Bohemia, several members of the imperial council were imprisoned, and some of them even put to death.

Bereft of every thing he possessed, a prisoner as well as the others, poor Drebbel would perhaps have undergone the same lot if the High Mighty States of the United Provinces had not sent a message to the King of England, asking him to interfere in their countryman's favor. They succeeded in their benevolent request; for his English Majesty obtained at last from his son-in-law, the Dutch philosopher's liberation, who (I don't exaggerate) was *made a present of* to the British King; maybe a sort of *lion*, which the King of Morocco had never yet thought of bestowing upon the monarch as a regal offering.

Drebbel, however, did not forget how much he owed to the intercession of King James, and, to show his gratitude, presented him with an object of very peculiar make. I will try to give you an exact version of its not very clear description in the Dutch book.

> A glass or crystal globe, wherein he blew or made a perpetual motion by the power of the four elements. For every thing which (by the force of the elements) passes, in a year, on the surface of the earth (sic!) could be seen to pass in this cylindrical wonder in the shorter lapse of twenty-four hours. Thus were marked by it, all years, months, days, hours; the course of the sun, moon, planets, and stars, &c. It made you understand what cold is, what the cause of the *primum mobile*, what the first principle of the sun, how it moves; the firmament, all stars, the moon, the sea, the surface of the earth, what occasions the ebb, flood, thunder, lightning, rain, wind, and how all things wax and multiply, &c.—as every one can be informed of by Drebbel's own works; we refer the curious to his book, entitled *Eeuwige Beweginghe* (Perpetual Motion).

Can this instrument have been a kind of Orrery?

He built a ship, in which one could row and navigate *under water*, from Westminster to Greenwich, the distance of two Dutch miles; even five or six miles, as far as one pleased. In this boat, a person could see under the surface of the water, and without candlelight, as much as he needed to read in the Bible or any other book. Not long ago, this remarkable ship was yet to be seen lying on the Thames or London river.

Aided by some instruments of his own manufacture, Drebbel could make it rain, lighten, and thunder at every time of the year, so that you would have sworn it came in a natural way from heaven.

By means of other instruments, he could, in the midst of summer, so much refrigerate the atmosphere of certain places, that you would have thought yourself in the very midst of winter. This experiment he did once on His Majesty's request, in the great Hall of Westminster; and although a hot summer day had been chosen by the King, it became so cold in the Hall, that James and his followers took to their heels in hasty flight.

With a certain instrument, he could draw an incredible quantity of water out of a well or river.

By his peculiar ingenuity, he could, at all times of the year, even in the midst of winter, hatch chickens and ducklings without using hens or ducks.

He made instruments, by means of which were seen pictures and portraits; for instance, he could show you kings, princes, nobles, although residing at that moment in foreign countries. And there was no paint nor painter's work to be seen, so that you saw a picture in appearance, but not in reality.

Perhaps a magic lantern?

He could make a glass, that placed in the dark near him or another, drew the light of a candle, standing at the other end of a long room, with such force, that the glass near him reflected so much light as to enable him to see to read perfectly.

Was this done by parallel parabolical mirrors?

He could make a plane glass, without grinding it on either side, in which people saw themselves reflected seven times.

He invented all these and many other curiosities, too long to relate, without the aid of the black art; but by natural philosophy alone, if we may believe the *tongues*, whose *eyes* saw it. By these experiments, he so gained the King's favor, His Majesty granted him a pension of 2,000 guilders. He died in London, anno 1634, the sixtieth year of his age.

HORNS.

When I was at Rome, among many other visits to the tomb of Julius II., I went thither once with a Prussian artist, a man of great genius and vivacity of feeling. As we were gazing on Michael Angelo's Moses, our conversation turned on the horns and beard of that stupendous statue; of the necessity of each to support the other; of the superhuman effect of the former, and the necessity of the existence of both to give a harmony and *integrity* both to the image and the feeling excited by it. Conceive them removed, and the statue would become *un*natural, without being *super*natural. We called to mind the horns of the rising sun, and I repeated the noble passage from Taylor's *Holy Dying*. That horns were the emblem of power and sovereignty among the Eastern nations; and are still retained as such in Abyssinia; the Achelous of the ancient Greeks; and the probable ideas and feelings that originally suggested the mixture of the human and the brute form in the figure, by which they realized the idea of their mysterious Pan, as representing intelligence blended with a darker power, deeper, mightier, and more universal than the conscious intellect of man; than intelligence—all these thoughts passed in procession before our minds.—Coleridge's *Biographia Literaria*, vol. ii. p. 127, edit. 1817.

The passage from Taylor's *Holy Dying*, which Coleridge repeated, is subjoined.

As when the sun approaches towards the gates of the morning, he first opens a little eye of heaven, and sends away the spirits of darkness, and gives light to a cock, and calls up the lark to matins, and by and bye gilds the fringes of a cloud, and peeps over the eastern hills, thrusting out his golden horns like those which decked the brows of Moses, when he was forced to wear a veil, because himself had seen the face of God; and still, while a man tells the story, the sun gets up higher, till he shows a fair face and a full light, and then he shines one whole day, under a cloud often, and sometimes weeping great and little showers, and sets quickly; so is man's reason and his life.—*Holy Dying*.

OUR WORLD.

Who is the author of the following lines ?—

'Tis an excellent world that we live in,
To lend, to spend, or to give in;
But to borrow or beg, or get a man's own,
'Tis just the worst world that ever was known.

PHILOLOGICAL NOTES.

The following is from that storehouse of choice things, *Howell's Letters*, part 4, letter xix. :—

I find that there are some single words antiquated in the French which seem to be more significant than those that come in their places, as *Maratre, paratre, filatre, serourge*, a step-mother, a step-father, a son or daughter-in-law, a sister-in-law, which they now express in two words, *belle mère, belle père, belle sœur.* Moreover I find there are some words now in French which are turned to a counter-sense, as we use the Dutch word *crank* in English, to be well disposed, which in the original signifieth to be sick. The word *pleiger* is also to drink after one is drunken unto, whereas the first true sense of the word was, that if the party drunk unto was not disposed to drink himself, he would put another for a pledge to do it for him, else the party who began would take it ill. Besides this word, *Abry* derived from the Latin *Apricus* is taken in French for a close place or shelter, whereas in the original it signifieth an open free sunshine. They now term in French a free boon companion *Roger bon temps*, whereas the original is *rouge bon temps*, reddish and good weather. They also use in France, when one hath a good bargain, to say *Il a joué à boule veue*, whereas the original is *bonne veue.* A beacon or watch-tower is called *Beffroy*, whereas the true word is *L'Effroy.* A travelling warrant is called *passeport*, whereas the original is *passe partout.* . . . . . I will add hereunto another proverb which had been quite lost, had not our order of the Garter preserved it, which is, *Honi soit qui mal y pense:* this we English, Ill to him who ill thinks, though the true sense be, Let him be bewrayed that thinks any ill.

Furthermore, I find in the French language, that the same fate hath attended some French words as usually attend men; among whom some rise to preferment, others fall to decay, and an under value: I will instance in a few.

The word *Maistre* was a word of high esteem in former times among the French, and applied to noblemen and others in high office only, but now 'tis fallen from the baron to the boor, from the count to the cobbler, or any other mean artisan; as, *Maistre Jean le Suavetier*, Mr. John the cobbler; *Maistre Jacquet le Cubaretier*, Mr. Jammy the tapster. *Sire* was also appropriated only to the king, but now, adding a name after it, 'tis applicable to any mean man, upon the endorsement of a letter, or otherwise. *Mareshal* was at first the name of a smith, farrier, or one that dressed horses, but it is climbed by degrees to that height that the chiefest commanders of the gendarmery and militia of France are come to be called *marshals.*

The letter contains also several other curious bits of philological information. In the piece quoted is an example of the use of the word *party* as it is employed in our time.

CALIFORNIA AND ITS GOLD.

In the *Voyage round the World*, by Captain George Shelvocke, begun Feb. 1719, he says of California (*Harris's Collection*, vol. i. p. 233):

The soil about Puerto, Seguro, and very likely in most of the valleys, is a rich black mould, which, as you turn it fresh up to the sun, appears as if intermingled with gold dust; some of which we endeavoured to purify and wash from the dirt; but though we were a little prejudiced against the thoughts that it could be possible that this metal should be so promiscuously and universally mingled with common earth, yet we endeavoured to cleanse and wash the earth from some of it; and the more we did the more it appeared like gold. In order to be further satisfied I brought away some of it, which we lost in our confusion in China.

In Hakluyt's *Voyages*, printed in 1599–1600, will be found much earlier notices on this subject. California was first discovered in the time of the Great Marquis, as Cortes was usually called. There are accounts of these early expeditions by Francisco Vasquez Coronada, Ferdinando Alarchon, Father Marco de Niça, and Francisco de Ulloa, who visited the country in 1539 and 1540. It is stated by Hakluyt that they were as far to the north as the 37th degree of latitude, which would be about one degree south of St. Francisco. I am inclined, however, to believe from the narrations themselves that the Spanish early discoveries did not extend much beyond the 34th degree of latitude, being little higher than the Peninsular or Lower California. In all these accounts, however, distinct mention is made of abundance of gold. In one of them it is stated that the natives used plates of gold to scrape the perspiration off their bodies!

The most curious and distinct account, however, is that given in "The famous voyage of Sir Francis Drake into the South Sea, &c. in 1577," which will be found in the third volume of Hakluyt, page 730. At page 737 is this passage:—

> The 5th day of June (1579) being in 43 degrees wards the pole Arctike, we found the ayre so colde, that our men being grievously pinched with the same, complained of the extremitie thereof, and the further we went, the more the colde increased upon us. Whereupon we thought it best for that time to seeke the land, and did so, finding it not mountainous, but low plaine land, till we came within thirty degrees toward the line. In which height it pleased God to send us into a faire and good baye, with a good winde to enter the same. In this baye wee anchored."

A glance at the map will show that "in this baye" is now situated the famous city of San Francisco.

Their doings in the bay are then narrated, and from page 738 the following is extracted:—

> When they [the natives with their king] had satisfied themselves [with dancing, &c.] they made signes to our General [Drake] to sit downe, to whom the king and divers others made several orations, or rather supplications, that hee would take their province or kingdom into his hand, and become their king, making signes that they would resigne unto him their right and title of the whole land, and become his subjects. In which, to persuade us the better, the king and the rest with our consent, and with great reverence, joyfully singing a song, did set the crowne upon his head, inriched his necke with all their chaines, and offred unto him many other things, honouring him by the name of Hioh, adding thereunto, as it seemed, a sign of triumph; which thing

our Generall thought not meet to reject, because he knew not what honour and profit it might be to our countrey. Whereupon, in the name and to the use of Her Majestie, he took the scepter, crowne, and dignitie of the said country into his hands, wishing that the riches and treasure thereof might so conveniently be transported to the enriching of her kingdom at home, as it aboundeth in y[e] same.

Our Generall called this countrey Nova Albion, and that for two causes; the one in respect of the white bankes and cliffes, which lie towards the sea, and the other, because it might have some affinities with our countrey in name, which sometime was so called.

Then comes the curious statement—

There is no part of earth heere to be taken up, wherein there is not some probable show of gold or silver.

The narrative then goes on to state that formal possession was taken of the country by putting up a "monument" with "a piece of sixpence of current English money under the plate," &c.

Drake and the bold cavaliers of that day probably found that it paid better to rob the Spaniard of the gold and silver ready made in the shape of "the Acapulco galleon," or such like, than to sift the soil of the Sacramento for its precious grains. At all events, the wonderful richness of the "earth" seems to have been completely overlooked or forgotten. So little was it suspected, until the Americans acquired the country at the peace with Mexico, that in the fourth volume of Knight's *National Cyclopædia*, published early in 1848, in speaking of Upper California, it is said, "very little mineral wealth has been met with!" A few months after, intelligence reached Europe how much the reverse was the case.

THE UNIVERSITIES.

The following epigrams are from Hartshorne's *Book-rarities in the University of Cambridge.* After mentioning the donation to that University by George I. of the valuable library of Dr.

Moore, Bishop of Ely, which his Majesty had purchased for six thousand guineas, the author adds:—

When George I. sent these books to the University, he sent at the same time a troop of horse to Oxford, which gave occasion to the following well-known epigram from Dr. Trapp, smart in its way, but not so clever as the answer from Sir William Browne:

The King, observing, with judicious eyes,
The state of both his Universities,
To one he sent a regiment; for why?
That learned body wanted loyalty:
To th' other he sent books, as well discerning
How much that loyal body wanted learning.

THE ANSWER.

The King to Oxford sent his troop of horse,
For Tories hold no argument but force:
With equal care, to Cambridge books he sent,
For Whigs allow no force but argument.

The books were received Nov. 19, 20, &c., 1715.

INDIA RUBBER.

India Rubber is now so cheap and common, that it seems worth while to make a note of the following passage in the *Monthly Review* for Feb. 1772. It occurs at p. 71, in an article on "A familiar Introduction to the Theory and Practice of Perspective, by Joseph Priestly, LL.D. F.R.S., 8vo. 5*s*., boards. Johnson."

Our readers, perhaps, who employ themselves in the art of drawing, will be pleased with a transcript of the following advertisement:—"I have seen," says Dr. Priestly, "a substance, excellently adapted to the purpose of wiping from paper the marks of a black lead pencil. It must, therefore, be of singular use to those who practise drawing. It is sold by Mr. Nairne, mathematical instrument-maker, opposite the Royal Exchange. He sells a cubical piece, of about half an inch, for three shillings; and, he says, it will last several years."

JUVENAL'S TENTH SATIRE.

Amongst the poems of the Rev. Thos. Warton, vicar of Basingstoke, who is best remembered as the father of two celebrated sons, is one entitled *The Universal Love of Pleasure*, commencing :—

> All human race, from China to Peru,
> Pleasure, howe'er disguised by art, pursue.
> &c., &c.

Warton died in 1745, and his Poems were published in 1748.

Johnson's *Vanity of Human Wishes* appeared in 1749; but Boswell believes that it was composed in the preceding year. That Poem, as we well remember, commences thus tamely :—

> Let observation with extensive view,
> Survey mankind from China to Peru.

Though so immeasurably inferior to his own, Johnson may have noticed these verses of Warton's with some little attention, and unfortunately borrowed the only prosaic lines in his poem. Besides the imitation before quoted, both writers allude to Charles of Sweden. Thus Warton says :—

> 'Twas hence rough Charles rush'd forth to ruthless war.

Johnson, in his highly-finished picture of the same monarch, says :—

> War sounds the trump, he rushes to the field.

This reminds me of a conversation, many years since, with the late William Wordsworth, in which some mention had been made of the opening lines of the tenth satire of Juvenal :—

> Omnibus in terris, quæ sunt a Gadibus usque
> Auroram, et Gangem, pauci dignoscere possunt
> Vera bona, atque illis multum diversa, remotâ
> Erroris nebulâ.

"Johnson's translation of this," said Wordsworth, "is extremely bad :—

'Let observation, with extensive view,
Survey mankind from China to Peru.'

"And I do not know that Gifford's is at all better :—

'In every clime, from Ganges' distant stream,
To Gades, gilded by the western beam,
Few, from the clouds of mental error free,
In its true light, or good or evil see.'

"But," he added, musing, "what is Dryden's? Ha! I have it :—

'*Look round the habitable world*, how few
Know their own good, or, knowing, it pursue.'

"This is indeed the language of a poet; it is better than the original."

"SIR GAMMAR VANS."

AN IRISH NURSERY STORY.

Last Sunday morning at six o'clock in the evening, as I was sailing over the tops of the mountains in my little boat, I met two men on horseback riding on one mare: so I asked them, "Could they tell me whether the little old woman was dead yet, who was hanged last Saturday week for drowning herself in a shower of feathers?" They said they could not positively inform me, but if I went to Sir Gammar Vans he could tell me all about it. "But how am I to know the house?" said I. "Ho, 'tis easy enough," said they, "for it's a brick house, built entirely of flints, standing alone by itself in the middle of sixty or seventy others just like it." "Oh, nothing in the world is easier," said I. "Nothing *can* be easier," said they; so I went on my way. Now this Sir G. Vans was a giant, and bottlemaker. And as all giants, who *are* bottlemakers, usually pop out of a little thumb bottle from behind the door, so did Sir G. Vans. "How d'ye do?" says he. "Very well, I thank you," says I. "Have some breakfast with me?" "With all my heart," says I. So he gave me a slice of beer, and a cup of cold veal; and there was a little dog under the table that picked up all the crumbs. "Hang him," says I. "No, don't hang him," says he; "for he killed a hare yesterday; and if you don't believe me, I'll show you the hare alive in a basket." So he took me into his garden to show me the curiosities. In one corner there was a fox hatching eagle's eggs; in another there was an iron apple-tree, entirely covered with pears and lead; in the third there was the hare which the dog killed yesterday alive in the basket; in the fourth there were twenty-four *hipper** *switches* threshing tobacco, and at the sight of me they threshed so hard that they drove the plug through the wall, and through a little dog that was passing by on the other side. I, hearing the dog howl, jumped over the wall; and turned it as neatly inside out as possible, when it ran away as if it had not an hour to live. Then he took me into his park to show me his deer: and I remembered that I had a warrant in my pocket to shoot venison for His Majesty's dinner. So I set fire to my bow, poised my arrow, and shot amongst them. I broke seventeen ribs on one side, and twenty-one and a half on the other; but my arrow passed clean through without ever touching it, and the worst was I lost my arrow: however, I found it again in the hollow of a tree. I felt it; it felt clammy. I smelt it; it smelt honey. "Oh, ho!" said I, "here's a bee's nest," when out sprung a covey of partridges. I shot at them; some say I killed eighteen; but I am sure I killed thirty-six, besides a dead salmon which was flying over the bridge, of which I made the best apple pie I ever tasted.

This worthy is mentioned in that curious little chap-book, *A Strange and Wonderful Relation of the Old Woman that was drowned at Ratcliff Highway*, in two parts. I now quote the passage from a copy of the genuine Aldermary churchyard edition:—

At last I arrived at Sir John Vang's house. 'Tis a little house entirely alone, encompassed about with forty or fifty houses, having a brick wall made of flint stone round about it. So, knocking at the door, "Gammer Vangs," said I, "is Sir John Vangs within?" "Walk in," said she, "and you shall see him in the little, great, round, three-square parlour." This Gammer Vangs had a little old woman her son. Her mother was a churchwarden of a large troop of horse, and her grandmother was a Justice of the Peace; but when I came into the said great, little, square, round, three-corner'd parlour, I could not see Sir John Vangs, for he was a giant. But I espied abundance of nice wicker bottles. And just as I was going out, he called to me and asked me

*A description of osiers used in coarse basket-making.

what I would have? So looking back I espied him just creeping out of a wicker bottle. It seems by his profession he was a wicker bottle maker. And after he had made them, he crept out at the stopper holes.

It is said that the Rev. Thomas Kerrich, the well-known librarian of the University of Cambridge, could repeat by heart the whole of the eight and forty pages of this strange gallimawfrey.

SATIRICAL POEMS ON WILLIAM III.

Some years since I copied from a MS. vol., compiled before 1708, the following effusions of a Jacobite poet, who seems to have been "a good hater" of King William. I have made ineffectual efforts to discover the witty author, or to ascertain if these compositions have ever been printed. My friend, in whose waste-book I found them—a beneficed clergyman in Worcestershire, who has been several years dead—obtained them from a college friend during the last century.

UPON KING WILLIAM'S TWO FIRST CAMPAGNES.

'Twill puzzle much the author's brains,
  That is to write your story,
To know in which of these campagnes
  You have acquired most glory;
For when you march'd the foe to fight,
  Like Heroe, nothing fearing,
Namur was taken in your sight,
  And Mons within your hearing.

ON THE OBSERVING THE 30TH OF JANUARY, 1691.

Cease, Hippocrites, to trouble heaven,
How can ye think to be forgiven
  The dismal deed you've done?
When to the martyr's sacred blood,
This very moment, if you could,
  You'd sacrifice his son.

ON KING WILLIAM'S RETURN OUT OF FLANDERS.

Rejoice, yee fops, yor idoll's come agen
To pick yor pocketts, and to slay yor men;
Give him yor millions, and his Dutch yor lands;
Don't ring yor bells, yee fools, but wring yor hands.

GRENDON.

EXECUTION OF CHARLES I.

In Lilly's *History of his Life and Times*, is the following interesting account in regard to the vizored execution of Charles I., being part of the evidence he gave when examined before the first parliament of King Charles II. respecting the matter :—

Liberty being given me to speak, I related what follows, viz.: That the next Sunday but one after Charles I. was beheaded, Robert Spavin, Secretary to Lieutenant-general Cromwell at that time, invited himself to dine with me, and brought Anthony Pearson and several others along with him to dinner. That their principal discourse all dinner time was only who it was that beheaded the King. One said it was the common hangman; another, Hugh Peters; others were also nominated, but none concluded. Robert Spavin, as soon as dinner was done, took me by the hand, and carried me to the south window. Saith he, " They are all mistaken; they have not named the man that did the fact: it was Lieutenant-colonel Joice. I was in the room when he fitted himself for the work; stood behind him when he did it; when done, went in with him again: there is no man knows this but my master, viz., Cromwell, Commissary Ireton, and myself." "Doth Mr. Rushworth know it?" saith I. "No, he doth not know it," saith Spavin. The same thing Spavin since has often related to me, when we were alone.

A NOTE ON "SMALL WORDS."

"And ten low words creep on in one dull line."

Most ingenious! most felicitous! but let no man despise little words, despite of the little man of Twickenham. He himself knew better, but there was no resisting the temptation of such a line as that. Small words, he says, in plain prosaic criticism, are generally "stiff and languishing, but they may be beautiful to express melancholy."

The English language is a language of small words. It is, says Swift, "overstocked with monosyllables." It cuts down all its words to the shortest possible dimensions: a sort of half-Procrustes, which lops but never stretches. In one of the most magnificent passages in Holy Writ, that, namely, which describes the death of Sisera:—

> At her feet he bowed, he fell: at her feet he bowed, he fell, he lay down; where he bowed, there he fell down dead.

There are twenty-two monosyllables to three of greater length, or rather to the same dissyllable thrice repeated; and that, too, in common parlance pronounced as a monosyllable. The passage in the Book of Ezekiel, which Coleridge is said to have considered the most sublime in the whole Bible,—

> And He said unto me, son of man, can these bones live? And I answered, O Lord God, thou knowest,—

contains seventeen monosyllables to three others. And in that most grand passage which commences the Gospel of St. John, from the first to the fourteenth verses, inclusive, there are polysyllables twenty-eight, monosyllables two hundred and one. This, it may be said, is poetry, but not verse, and therefore makes but little against the critic. Well, then, out of his own mouth shall he be confuted. In the fourth epistle of his *Essay on Man*, a specimen selected purely at Random from his works, and extending altogether to three hundred and ninety-eight lines, there are no less than twenty-seven (that is, a trifle more than one out of every fifteen) made up *entirely* of monosyllables: and over and above these, there are one hundred and fifteen which have in them only one word of greater length; and yet there are few dull creepers among the lines of Pope.

The early writers, the "pure wells of English undefiled," are full of "small words."

Hall, in one of the most exquisite of his satires, speaking of the vanity of "adding house to house, and field to field," has these most beautiful lines :—

Fond fool! six feet shall serve for all thy store,
And he that cares for most shall find no more!

"What harmonious monosyllables!" says Mr. Gifford; and what critic will refuse to echo his exclamation? The same writer is full of monosyllabic lines, and he is among the most energetic of satirists. By the way, it is not a little curious that in George Webster's *White Devil, or Vittoria Corombona,* almost the same thought is also clothed in two monosyllabic lines :—

His wealth is summ'd, and this is all his store :
This poor men get, and great men get no more.

Was Young dull? Listen, for it is indeed a "solemn sound:"—

The bell strikes one. We take no note of time
Save by its loss; to give it then a tongue
Was wise in man.

Was Milton tame? Hear the "lost archangel" calling upon Hell to receive its new possessor :—

One who brings
A mind not to be chang'd by place or time,
The mind is in its own place, and in *itself*
Can make a heav'n of hell,—a hell of heav'n.
What *matter* where, if I be still the same,
And what I should be; all but less than he
Whom *thunder* hath made *greater?* Here at least
We shall be free; the *Almighty* hath not built
Here for his *envy;* will not drive us hence:
Here we may reign *secure;* and in my choice
To reign is worth *ambition,* though in hell:
Better to reign in hell, than serve in heav'n!

A great conjunction of little words! Are monosyllables passionless? Listen to the widowed Constance:—

> Thou may'st, thou shalt! I will not go with thee!
> I will *instruct* my *sorrows* to be proud;
> For grief is proud, and makes his *owner* stout;
> To me, and to the state of my great grief,
> Let kings *assemble;* for my grief's so great,
> That no *supporter* but the huge firm earth
> Can hold it up; here I and *sorrow* sit;
> Here is my throne: bid kings come bow to it.

Six polysyllables only in eight lines!

Hear Lear:—

> *Lear.* Thou know'st the first time that we smell the air,
> We wawl, and cry:—I will preach to thee; mark me.
> [*Gloster.* Alack! alack the day!]
> *Lear.* When we are born, we cry, that we are come
> To this great stage of fools.—This a good block?—*King Lear*, Act IV. Sc. 6.

In this passage [I bracket Gloster] we find no fewer than *forty-two monosyllables* following each other consecutively. In *King John*, Act III. Sc. 3, where the king is *pausing* in his wish to incense Hubert to Arthur's murder, he says:—

> Good friend, thou hast no cause to say so yet:
> But thou shalt have; and creep time ne'er so slow,
> Yet it shall come, for me to do thee good.
> I had a thing to say,—But let it go:—

forty monosyllables.

Again:—

> ——————— but through his lips do throng
> Weak words, so thick come, in his poor heart's aid,
> That no man could *distinguish* what he said.
> *Rape af Lucreece*, Stanza 255.

In Beaumont and Fletcher's *Boadicea*, Act III. Sc. 1 (Edinburgh, 1812), are the following lines in Caratach's Apostrophe to

"Divine Andate," and which seem to corroborate the theory on the employment of monosyllables by Shakspeare, when he wished to express violent and overwhelming emotion; at least they appear to be used much in the same way by these celebrated dramatists:—

Give us this day good hearts, good enemies,
Good blows on both sides, wounds that fear or flight
Can claim no share in; steel us both with anger,
And warlike executions fit thy viewing.
Let Rome put on her best strength, and thy Britain,
Thy little Britain, but as great in fortune,
Meet her as strong as she, as proud, as daring!
And then look on, thou red-eyed God; who does best,
Reward with honour; who despair makes fly,
Unarm for ever, and brand with infamy!

This passage contains one hundred and twenty-six words, one hundred and ten of which are monosyllables, and the remainder words of only two syllables.

New light new love, new love new life hath bred;
A life that lives by love, and loves by light;
A love to Him to whom all loves are wed;
A light to whom the sun is darkest night:
Eye's light, heart's love, soul's only life He is;
Life, soul, love, heart, light, eye, and all are His;
He eye, light, heart, love, soul; He all my joy and bliss.
Phineas Fletcher's *Purple Island*, Canto I. Stanza 7.

In seventy words only *one* of more than a syllable; the alliteration in the second line is likewise noticeable.

In the following passage in Churchill, the structure of the second couplet must surely have been suggested by Pope's line:—

Conjunction, adverb, preposition, join
To add new vigour to the nervous line:—
In monosyllables his thunders roll,
He, she, it, and, we, ye, they, fright the soul.
Censure on Mossop.

Moore, in his Journals, notes, on the other side of the question, a conversation between Rogers, Crowe, and himself, "on the beauty of monosyllabic verses. 'He jests at scars,' &c.; the couplet, 'Sigh on my lip,' &c.; 'Give all thou canst,' &c. &c., and many others, the most vigorous and musical, perhaps, of any." (Lord John Russell's *Moore*, vol. ii. p. 200.)

The frequency of monosyllabic lines in English poetry will hardly be wondered at, however it may be open to such criticisms as Pope's and Churchill's, when it is noted that our language contains, of monosyllables formed by the vowel *a* alone, considerably more than five hundred; by the vowel *e*, about four hundred and fifty; by the vowel *i*, nearly four hnndred; by the vowel *o*, rather more than four hundred; and by the vowel *u*, upwards of two hundred and sixty; a calculation entirely exclusive of the large number of monosyllables formed by diphthongs.

The ingenuity of Pope's line is great, but the criticism false. We applaud it only because we have never taken the trouble to think about the matter, and take it for granted that all monosyllabic lines must "creep" like that which he puts forward as a specimen. The very frequency of monosyllables in the compositions of our language is one grand cause of that frequency passing uncommented upon by the general reader. The investigation prompted by the criticism will serve only to show its unsoundness.

HE THAT FIGHTS AND RUNS AWAY.

The often-quoted lines—

> For he that fights and runs away
> May live to fight another day,

generally supposed to form a part of *Hudibras*, are to be found (as Mr. Cunningham points out at p. 602 of his *Handbook for London*), in the *Musarum Deliciæ*, 12mo. 1656; a clever collection of "witty trifles," by Sir John Mennis and Dr. James Smith.

The passage, as it really stands in *Hudibras* (book iii. canto iii. verse 243), is as follows:—

For those that fly may fight again,
Which he can never do that's slain.

But there is a much earlier authority for these lines than the *Musarum Deliciæ;* a fact which I learn from a volume now open before me, the great rarity of which will excuse my transcribing the title-page in full:—

Apophthegmes, that is to saie, prompte, quicke, wittie, and sentencious saiynges, of certain Emperours, Kynges, Capitaines, Philosophiers, and Oratours, as well Grekes as Romaines, bothe veraye pleasaunt and profitable to reade, partely for all maner of persones, and especially Gentlemen. First gathered and compiled in Latine by the right famous clerke, Maister Erasmus, of Roteradame. And now translated into Englyshe by Nicolas Udall. *Excu sam typis Ricardi Grafton*, 1542. 8vo.

The work consists of only two books of the original, comprising the apophthegms of Socrates, Aristippus, Diogenes, Philippus, Alexander, Antigonus, Augustus Cæsar, Julius Cæsar, Pompey, Phocion, Cicero, and Demosthenes.

On folio 239, occurs the following apophthegm, which is the one relating to the subject before us:—

That same man, that renneth awaie,
Maie again fight, an other daie.

¶ Judgeyng that it is more for the benefite of one's countree to renne awaie in battaile, then to lese his life. For a ded man can fight no more; but who hath saved hymself alive, by rennyng awaie, may, in many battailles mo, doe good service to his countree.

§ At lest wise, if it be a poinct of good service, to renne awaie at all times, when the countree hath most neede of his helpe to sticke to it.

Menage observes, in speaking of Monsieur Perier's abuse of Horace for running away from the battle of Philippi, "Relictâ non bene parmulâ," "Mais je le pardonne, parce qu'il ne sait peut-être pas que les Grecs ont dit en faveur des *Fuiars.*"

'Ανὴρ ὁ φεύγων καὶ πάλιν μαχήσεται.
Menagiana, vol. i. p. 248. Amst. 1713.

Perhaps Erasmus translated this "*apophthegme.*"

The following extract from Collet's *The Relics of Literature*, published in 1820, may prove interesting, as further illustrating the disputed passage:—

Few popular quotations have more engaged the pens of critics than the following:—

For he that fights and runs away
Will live to fight another day.

These lines are almost universally supposed to form a part of *Hudibras;* and, so confident have even scholars been on the subject, that in 1784 a wager was made at Bootle's, of twenty to one, that they were to be found in that inimitable poem. Dodsley was referred to as the arbitrator, when he ridiculed the idea of consulting him on the subject, saying, "Every fool knows they are in *Hudibras.*" George Selwyn, who was present, said to Dodsley, "Pray, sir, will you be good enough, then, to inform an old fool, who is at the same time your wise worship's very humble servant, in what canto they are to be found?" Dodsley took down the volume, but he could not find the passage; the next day came, with no better success; and the sage bibliopole was obliged to confess, "that a man might be ignorant of the author of this well-known couplet without being absolutely a fool."

JOHNSON AS A DEDICATOR.

As a writer of dedications Samuel Johnson was the giant of his time. He once said to Boswell, the subject arising at a dinner-party, "Why, I have dedicated to the royal family all round,"—and the *honest chronicler* proves that he spoke advisedly.

BOOKS BY THE YARD.

Many readers have heard of books bought and sold by weight—in fact it is questionable whether the *number* of books sold in that way is not greater than those sold "over the counter"—but few have probably heard of books sold "by the yard." Having purchased at St. Petersburg, the library left by an old Russian nobleman of high rank, I was quite astonished to find a copy of *Œuvres de Frederick II.*, originally published in 15 vols., divided into 60, to each of which a new title had been printed; and several hundred volumes lettered outside *Œuvres de Miss Burney*, *Œuvres de Swift*, &c., but containing, in fact, all sorts of French waste paper books. These, as well as three editions of *Œuvres de Voltaire*, were all very neatly bound in calf, gilt, and with red morocco backs. My curiosity being aroused, I inquired into the origin of these circumstances, and learnt that during the reign of Catharine, every courtier who had hopes of being honored by a visit from the Empress, was expected to have a library, the greater or smaller extent of which was to be regulated by the fortune of its possessor, and that, after Voltaire had won the favor of the Autocrat by his servile flattery, one or two copies of his works were considered indispensable. Every courtier was thus forced to have a room fitted up with mahogany shelves, and filled with books, by far the greater number of which he never read or even opened. A bookseller of the name of Klostermann, who, being of an athletic stature, was one of the innumerable favorites of the lady, "who loved all things save her lord," was usually employed, not to select a library, but to fill a certain given space of so many yards, with books, at so much per volume, and Mr. Klostermann, the "Libraire de la Cour Imperiale," died worth a plum, having sold many thousand yards of books (among which I understood there were several hundred copies of Voltaire), at from 50 to 100 roubles a yard, "according to the binding."

PUZZLING EPITAPH.

The following epitaph is stated to be in a churchyard in Germany. The first two lines, and many similar specimens of learned trifling, will be found in *Les Bigarrures et Touches du Seigneur des Accords*, cap. iii., *autre Façon de Rebus*, p. 35, ed. 1662.

O quid tua te
be bis bia abit
ra ra ra
es
et in
ram ram ram
i i
Mox eris quod ego nunc.

The reading is—

O superbe quid superbis? tua superbia te superabit. Terra es et in terram ibis. Mox eris quod ego nunc.

BILL OF FARE OF 1626.

The following *actual* bill of fare in a gentleman's house, anno 1626, is from the account book of Sir Edward Dering, Knt. and Bart.:—

A dinner att London, made when my Lady Richardson, my sister E Ashbornham, and Kate Ashb,—my brother John Ashb, my cosen Walldron and her sister, and S[r] John Skeffington, were with me att Aldersgate streete, December 23, 1626. My sister Fr Ashb and cosen Mary Hill did fayle of coming

Wine - - - - - - - -	3*s.* 10*d.*
Stourgeon - - - - - - -	7*s.*
a joll of brawne - - - - - -	5*s.*
pickled oystres a barrell - - - - -	1*s.* 6*d.*
viniger - - - - - - - -	3*d.*
Rabetts a couple—larkes a dozen—plovers 3 and snikes 4 -	7*s.*
Carrowaye and comfites - - - - - -	6*d.*
a Banquet* and 2 dozen and a half of glasse plates to set itt out in	1*l.* 3*s.*
Half a doe—which in y[e] fee and charge of bringing itt out of Northhampton - - - - - - -	8*s.*
a warden† py that the cooke made—we finding y[e] wardens -	2*s.* 4*d.*
ffor a venison pasty, we finding y[e] venison - - -	4*s*

* Banquet was a name given to a dessert, and it was usually set out in another room.
† Warden is a large baking pear.

ffor 2 minct pyes - - - - - -	2s. 6d.
a breast of veale - - - - - -	2s. 4d.
a legg of mutton - - - - - -	2s.
Sum totall expended - - - -	3l. 10s. 3d.

The dinner was att ye first course—

a peece of Brawne.
a boiled ducke in white broathe.
a boiled haunch of powdered venison.
2 minct pyes.
a boyled legge of mutton.
a venison pasty.
a roast ducke.
a powdered goose roasted.
a breast of veale.
a cold Capon py.

Second course—

a couple of rabitts.
3 plovers.
12 larks.
4 snikes.
pickled oysters—two dishes.
a cold warden py.
a joull of Sturgeon.

Complement—

Apples and Carrawayes.
wardens bakt and cold.
a Cake and
Cheese.

A banquett ready in ye next room.

Memd—we had out of ye country ye goose, ye duckes, ye capon py, ye Cake and wardens, and ye venison; but that is allways pd for, though given.

The above seems to have been a family dinner.

THE POETS.

This sonnet, by Leigh Hunt, appeared many years ago in the *Examiner* :—

Were I to name, out of the times gone by,
The poets dearest to me, I should say,
Pulci for spirits, and a fine, free way,
Chaucer for manners, and a close, silent eye;
Spenser for luxury and sweet sylvan play,
Horace for chatting with from day to day;
Milton for classic taste and harp strung high,
Shakspeare for all—but most, society.
But which take with me could I take but one?
Shakspeare, as long as I was unoppress'd
With the world's weight, making sad thoughts intenser;
But did I wish out of the common sun
To lay a wounded heart in leafy rest,
And dream of things far off and healing—Spenser.

NOTES ON COFFEE.

The earliest account we have of coffee is said to be taken from an Arabian MS. in the Bibliothèque du Roi in Paris.

Schehabeddin Ben, an Arabian author of the ninth century of the Hegira, or fifteenth of the Christians, attributes to Gemaleddin, Mufti of Aden, a city of Arabia Felix, who was nearly his contemporary, the first introduction into that country of drinking coffee. He tells us that Gemaleddin, having occasion to travel into Persia, during his abode there saw some of his countrymen drinking coffee, which at that time he did not much attend to; but, on his return to Aden, finding himself indisposed, and remembering that he had seen his countrymen drinking coffee in Persia, in hopes of receiving some benefit from it, he determined to try it on himself; and, after making the experiment, not only recovered his health, but perceived other useful qualities in that liquor; such as relieving the headache, enlivening the spirits, and, without prejudice to the constitution, preventing drowsiness. This last quality he resolved to turn to the advantage of his profession; he took it himself, and recommended it to the Dervises, or religious Mahometans, to enable them to pass the night in prayer, and other exercises of their religion, with greater zeal and attention. The example and authority of the mufti gave reputation to coffee. Soon men of letters, and persons belonging to the law, adopted the use of it. These were followed by the tradesmen and artisans that were under the necessity of working in the night, and such as were obliged to travel late after sunset. At length the custom became general in Aden; and it was not only drunk in the night by those who were desirous of being kept awake, but in the day for the sake of its other agreeable qualities.

Before this time coffee was scarce known in Persia, and very little used in Arabia, where the tree grew. But, according to Schehabeddin, it had been drunk in Æthiopia from time immemorial.

Coffee being thus received at Aden, where it has continued in use ever since without interruption, passed by degrees to many neighboring towns; and not long after reached Mecca, where it was introduced as at Aden, by the Dervises, and for the same purposes of religion.

The inhabitants of Mecca were at last so fond of this liquor, that, without regarding the intention of the religious and other studious persons, they at length drank it publicly in coffee-houses, where they assembled in crowds to pass the time agreeably, making that the pretence. From hence the custom extended itself to many other towns of Arabia, particularly to Medina, and then to Grand Cairo in Egypt, where the Dervises of Yemen, who lived in a district by themselves, drank coffee on the nights they intended to spend in devotion.

Coffee continued its progress through Syria, and was received at Damascus and Aleppo without opposition; and in the year 1554, under the reign of Solyman, one hundred years after its introduction by the Mufti of Aden, became known to the inhabitants of Constantinople, when two private persons of the names of Schems and Hekin, the one coming from Damascus, and the other from Aleppo, opened coffee-houses.

"It is not easy," says Ellis, "to determine at what time, or upon what occasion, the use of coffee passed from Constantinople to the western parts of Europe. It is, however, likely that the Venetians, upon account of the proximity of their dominions, and their great trade to the Levant, were the first acquainted with it; which appears from part of a letter wrote by Peter della Valle, a Venetian, in 1615, from Constantinople; in which he tells his friend, that, upon his return, he should bring with him some coffee, which he believed was a thing unknown in his country."

Mr. Garland tells us he was informed by M. de la Croix, the King's interpreter, that M. Thevenot, who had travelled through the East, at his return in 1657, brought with him to Paris some coffee for his own use, and often treated his friends with it.

It was known some years sooner at Marseilles; for, in 1644, some gentlemen who accompanied M. de la Haye to Constantinople, brought back with them, on their return, not only some coffee, but the proper vessels and apparatus for making it. However, until 1660, coffee was drunk only by such as had been accustomed to it in the Levant, and their friends; but that year some bales were imported from Egypt, which gave a great number of persons an opportunity of trying it, and contributed very much to bringing it into general use; and in 1661, a coffee-house was opened at Marseilles, in the neighborhood of the Exchange.

Before 1669, coffee had not been seen at Paris, except at M. Thevenot's, and some of his friends; nor scarce heard of but from the account of travellers. In that year, Soliman Aga, ambassador from the Sultan Mahomet the Fourth, arrived, who, with his retinue, brought a considerable quantity of coffee with them, and made presents of it to persons both of the court and city, and is supposed to have established the custom of drinking it.

Two years afterwards, an Armenian of the name of Pascal, set up a coffee-house, but meeting with little encouragement, left Paris and came to London.

From Anderson's *Chronological History of Commerce*, it appears that the use of coffee was introduced into London some years earlier than in Paris. For in 1652, one Mr. Edwards, a Turkey merchant, brought home with him a Greek servant, whose name was Pasqua, who understood the roasting and making of coffee, till then unknown in England. This servant was the first who sold coffee, and kept a house for that purpose in George Yard, Lombard Street.

The first mention of coffee in our statute books is anno 1660 (12 Car. II. c. 24), when a duty of 4*d.* was laid upon every gallon of coffee, made and sold, to be paid by the maker.

The statute 15 Car. II. c. 11, § 15, an. 1663, directs that all coffee-houses should be licensed at the general quarter sessions of the peace for the county within which they are to be kept.

In 1675 King Charles II. issued a proclamation to shut up the coffee-houses, but in a few days suspended the proclamation by a second. They were charged with being seminaries of sedition.

The first European author who has made any mention of coffee is Rauwolfus, who was in the Levant in 1573.

Anthony Wood, in his *Diary*, records, under the year 1654, that—

> Coffey, which had been drank by some persons in Oxon. 1650, was this yeare publickly sold at or neare the Angel, within the Easte Gate of Oxon., as also chocolate, by an outlander or Jew.

And in another place he says :—

This yeere Jacob a Jew opened a Coffey-house at the Angel, in the parish of St. Peter in the East, Oxon., and there it was by some, who delighted in noveltie, drank. When he left Oxon. he sold it in Old Southampton Buildings in Holborne, near London, and was living there in 1671.

Aubrey, in his account of Sir Henry Blount (MS. in the Bodleian Library), says of this worthy knight :—

When coffee first came in he was a great upholder of it, and hath ever since been a constant frequenter of coffee-houses, especially Mr. Farres at the Rainbowe, by Inner Temple Gate, and lately John's Coffee-house, in Fuller's Rents. The first coffee-house in London was in St. Michael's Alley, in Cornhill, opposite to the church, which was set up by one —— Bowman (coachman to Mr. Hodges, a Turkey merchant, who putt him upon it), in or about the yeare 1652. 'Twas about 4 yeares before any other was sett up, and that was by Mr. Farr. Jonathan Paynter, over against to St. Michael's Church, was the first apprentice to the trade, viz. to Bowman.—Mem. The Bagneo, in Newgate Street, was built and first opened in Decemb. 1679: built by . . . . . Turkish merchants.

Of this James Farr, Edward Hatton, in his *New View of London*, 1708, (vol. i. p. 30,) says :—

I find it recorded that one James Farr, a barber, who kept the coffee-house which is now the Rainbow, by the Inner Temple Gate (one of the first in England), was in the year 1657 prosecuted by the inquest of St. Dunstan's in the West, for making and selling a sort of liquor called coffee, as a great nuisance and prejudice to the neighborhood, &c., and who would then have thought London would ever have had near three thousand such nuisances, and that coffee world have been, as now, so much drank by the best of quality and physicians.

1637. There came in my tyme to the College, Oxford, one Nathaniel Conopios, out of Greece. He was the first I ever saw drink coffee, which custom came not into England till thirty years after.—*Evelyn's Diary.*

George Sandys, the translator of Ovid's *Metamorphoses*, travelled in the Turkish empire in 1610. He first published his

Notes in 1615. The following is from the 6th edit. 1652, p. 52:—

Although they be destitute of taverns, yet have they their coffa-houses, which something resemble them. There sit they, chatting most of the day, and sip of a drink called coffa (of the berry that it is made of), in little *China* dishes, as hot as they can suffer it; black as soot, and tasting not much unlike it (why not that black broth which was in use among the Lacedæmonians?) which helpeth, as they say, digestion, and procureth alacrity, &c.

Burton also (*Anatomy of Melancholy*) describes it as "like that black drink which was in use among the Lacedæmonians, and perhaps the same."

James Howell, in a letter addressed "to his highly esteemed friend and compatriot, Judge Rumsey, upon his *Provang*, or rare pectorale Instrument, and his rare experiments of Cophie and Tobacco"—and prefixed to the latter's *Organon Salutis: an Instrument to cleanse the stomach, as also divers new experiments of the virtue of Tobacco and Coffee*, London, 1657, 8vo.—says:—

Touching coffee, I concurre with them in opinion, who hold it to be that black-broth which was us'd of old in Lacedemon, whereof the Poets sing; Surely it must needs be salutiferous, because so many sagacious and the wittiest sort of Nations use it so much; as they who have conversed with Shashes and Turbants doe well know. But, besides the exsiccant quality it hath to dry up the crudities of the Stomach, as also to comfort the Brain, to fortifie the sight with its steem, and prevent Dropsies, Gouts, the Scurvie, together with the Spleen and Hypocondriacall windes (all which it doth without any violence or distemper at all), I say, besides all these qualities, 'tis found already, that this Coffee-drink hath caused a greater sobriety among the nations: For whereas formerly Apprentices and Clerks with others, used to take their mornings' draught in Ale, Beer, or Wine, which by the dizziness they cause in the Brain, make many unfit for businesse, they use now to play the Good-fellows in this wakefull and civill drink: Therefore that worthy Gentleman, Mr. Mudiford, who introduced the practice hereof first to London, deserves much respect of the whole Nation.

Of Judge Rumsey and his *Provang* (which was a flexible

whalebone from two to three feet long, with a small linen or silk button at the end, which was to be introduced into the stomach to produce the effect of an emetic), the reader may find some account in Wood's *Athen.* (Bliss's edit., vol. iii. p. 509), and this is not the place to speak of them, except as they had to do with coffee; on that point a few more words may be allowed.

Besides the letter of Howell already quoted, two others are prefixed to the book; one from the author to Sir Henry Blount, the other Sir Henry's reply. In the former the Judge says:—

I lately understood that your discovery, in your excellent book of travels, hath brought the use of the Turkes Physick, of Cophie, in great request in England, whereof I have made use, in another form than is used by boyling of it in Turkie, and being less loathsome and troublesome, &c.

And Sir Henry, after a fervent panegyric on coffee, replies:—

As for your way of taking both Cophie and Tobacco, the rarity of the invention consists in leaving the old way: For the water of the one and the smoke of the other may be of inconvenience to many: but your way in both takes in the virtue of the Simples without any additional mischief.

As this may excite the reader's curiosity to know what was the Judge's new and superior "way" of using coffee, I will add his prescription for making "electuary of cophy," which is, I believe, the only preparation of it which he used or recommended:—

Take equall quantity of Butter and Sallet-oyle, melt them well together, but not boyle them: Then stirre them well that they may incorporate together: Then melt therewith three times as much Honey, and stirre it well together: Then add thereunto Powder of Turkish Cophie, to make it a thick Electuary.—p. 5.

A very little consideration may convince one that this electuary was likely to effect the purpose for which it was recommended.

Whether (says the Judge) it be in time of health or sickness, whensoever you find any evill disposition in the stomach, eat a convenient meal of what meat and drink you please, then walk a little while after it: Then set down your body bending, and thrust the said Whalebone Instrument into your stomach, stirring it very gently, which will make you vomit; then drink a good draught of drink, and so use the Instrument as oft as you please, but never doe this upon an empty stomach. To make the stomach more apt to vomit, and to prepare the humours thereunto before you eat and drink, Take the bigness of a Nutmeg, or more of the said Electuary of Cophie, &c., into your mouth; then take drink to drive it down; then eat and drink, and walk, and use the instrument as before."—p. 19.

CUPID CRYING.

Who was the author of the original of the following translation?

CUPID CRYING.

Why is Cupid crying so?—
  Because his jealous mother beat him.—
What for?—For giving up his bow
  To Cœlia, who contrived to cheat him.

The child! I could not have believed
  He'd give his weapons to another.—
He would not; but he was deceived:
  She smiled; he thought it was his mother.

"UNDER THE ROSE."

I. "The expression, 'under the rose,' took its origin," says Jenoway, "from the wars between the Houses of York and Lancaster. The parties respectively swore by the red or the white rose, and these opposite emblems were displayed as the *signs of two taverns;* one of which was by the side of, and the other opposite to, the Parliament House in Old Palace Yard, Westminster. Here the retainers and servants of the noblemen attached to the Duke of York and Henry VI. used to meet. Here also, as disturbances were frequent, measures either of defence or annoyance were taken, and every transaction was said to be done 'under the rose;' by which expression the most profound secrecy was implied."

II. According to others, this term originated in the fable of Cupid giving the rose to Harpocrates, the god of silence, as a bribe to prevent him betraying the amours of Venus, and was hence adopted as the emblem of silence. The rose was for this reason frequently sculptured on the ceilings of drinking and feasting rooms, as a warning to the guests that what was said in moments of conviviality should not be repeated; from which, what was intended to be kept secret was said to be held "under the rose." To this derivation the following verses refer:—

Est Rosa flos Veneris, quem, quo sua furta laterent,
Harpocrati, Matris dona, dicavit Amor.
Inde rosam mensis hospes suspendit amicis,
Convivæ ut sub eâ dicta tacenda sciant.

III. Roses were consecrated as presents from the Pope. In 1526 they were placed over the goals of confessionals as the symbols of secrecy. Hence the origin of the phrase, "Under the Rose."

THE PURSUITS OF LITERATURE.

Many years ago, the satirical poem, entitled *The Pursuits of Literature*, engaged public attention for a very considerable time; the author concealed his name; and from 1796 at least to 1800, the world continued guessing at who could be the author. Amongst the names to which the poem was ascribed were those of Anstey, Colman, Jun., Coombe, Cumberland, Harry Dampier, Goodall, Hudderford, Knapp, MATHIAS, Mansell, Wrangham, Stephen Weston, and many others, chiefly Etonians. George Steevens, it is believed, fixed upon the real author at an early period: at least in the *St. James's Chronicle*, from Tuesday, May 1, to Thursday, May 3, 1798, we find—

THE PURSUER OF LITERATURE PURSUED.

Hic niger est.

With learned jargon and conceit,
With tongue as prompt to lie as
The veriest mountebank and cheat,
Steps forth the black * * * * * * *.

At first the world was all astounded,
Some said it was *Elias:*
But when the riddle was expounded,
'Twas little black * * * * * * *.

This labored work would seem the job
Of hundred-handed *Gyas;*
But proves to issue from the nob
Of little black * * * * * * *.

Through learned shoals of garbled Greek
We trace his favorite bias,
But when the malice comes to speak,
We recognize * * * * * * *.

What strutting *Bantam,* weak but proud,
E'er held his head so high as
This pigmy idol of the crowd,
The prancing pert * * * * * *.

Τουτο το βιβλιον, he'll swear,
Is *πληρον τῆς σοφιας*,
But men of sense and taste declare
'Tis little black * * * * * * *.

Oh! were this scribbler, for a time,
Struck dumb like *Zacharias,*
Who could regret the spiteful rhyme
Of little black * * * * * * *.

Small was his stature who in fight
O'erthrew the great *Darius,*
But small in genius as in height
Is little black * * * * * * *.

Say, couldst thou gain the butt of sack
And salary that *Pye* has,
Would it not cheer thy visage black,
Thou envious rogue * * * * * * *.

When next accus'd deny it not!
Do think of *Ananias!*
Remember how *he* went to pot,
As thou may'st, friend * * * * * * *.

REVIVALS.

Every man ought to read the jest-books, that he may not make himself disagreeable by repeating "old Joes" as the very last good things. One book of this class is little more than the copy of another as to the points, with a change of the persons; and the same joke, slightly varied, appears in as many different countries as the same fairy-tale. Seven years ago I found at Prague the "Joe" of the Irishman saying that there were a hundred judges on the bench, because there was one with two cyphers. The valet-de-place told me that when the Emperor and Metternich were together they were called "the council of ten," because they were *eins und zero*.

It is interesting to trace a joke back, of which process here is an example. In the very clever version of the Chancellor of Oxford's speech on introducing the new doctors (*Punch*, No. 622) are these lines :—

En Henleium! en Stanleium! Hic eminens prosator:
Ille, filius pulchro patre, hercle pulchrior orator;
Demosthenes in herbâ, *sed in ore retinens illos*
Quos, antequam peroravit, Græcus respuit lapillos.

Ebenezer Grubb, in his description of the opposition in 1814, thus notices Mr. F. Douglas :—

He is a forward and frequent speaker; remarkable for a graceful inclination of the upper part of his body in advance of the lower, and speaketh, I suspect (*after the manner of an ancient*), *with pebbles in his mouth*.—*New Whig Guide*, 1819, p. 47.

In Foote's *Patron*, Sir Roger Dowlas, an East India proprietor, who has sought instruction in oratory from Sir Thomas Lofty, is introduced to the *conversazione*:—

Sir Thomas. Sir Roger, be seated. This gentleman has, in common with the greatest orator the world ever saw, a small natural infirmity; he stutters a little; but I have prescribed the same remedy that Demosthenes used, and don't despair of a radical cure. Well, sir, have you digested those general rules?

Sir Roger. Pr-ett-y well, I am obli-g'd to you, Sir Th-omas.

Sir Thomas. Did you open at the last general court?

Sir Roger. I att-empt-ed fo-ur or five times.

Sir Thomas. What hindered your progress?

Sir Roger. *The pe-b-bles.*

Sir Thomas. *Oh, the pebbles in his mouth;* but they are only put in to practise in private: *you should take them out when you are addressing the public.*

I cannot trace the joke farther, but as Foote, though so rich in wit, was a great borrower, it might not be new in 1764.

If we believe any thing to have happened in our own day, that is, in Liverpool or Castlereagh time, it is the anecdote of the boroughmonger who would answer nothing to the excuses of the minister, except "There are five of us." This story was told as an old one in the *Telegraph* in 1798, and a long dialogue was given between Lord Falmouth, who wanted the Captaincy of the Yeomen of the Guard, and Henry Pelham, who had promised it elsewhere. To all the poor minister could say, the peer could only answer, "There are *seven* of us." I hope that, in an age when coincidences are sought for, Wordsworth will not be suspected of plagiarism.

Again, what reader of gossip does not know that when George III. went to Weymouth, the Mayor, in making his address, mistook the private directions of his prompter for parts of his address, and gave it the King as follows: "Hold up your head, and look like a man—what the —— do you mean? . . . By ——, Sir, you'll ruin us all." This story was told in a newspaper in 1797, as having happened between James II. and the Mayor of Winchester.

In the *Monthly Magazine* in 1798, is a paper on peculiarities of expression, among which are several which we flatter ourselves belong to our own time. For instance, "to *cut* a person," which was then current: some tried to change it into *spear*, but failed. Also, to *vote*, as in "he voted it a bad lounge;" and the words *bore*, *done up*, *dished*, &c.; not forgetting *spilt* for "upset" in a carriage.

The parliamentary phrases of "catching the speaker's eye," "being upon his legs," "meeting the ideas of the house," "committing himself," "taking shame to himself," "being free to confess," "putting a question roundly," "answering it fairly," "pushing an investigation," are all noted as then worthy of remark. And, if we are to trust the article cited, the word *truism* was born and bred in the House of Commons, in the sense of a forcible and undeniable truth. And the same origin is given to the idiom "in my own mind" as in "I feel no doubt, in my own mind."

RIGHTS OF WOMEN.

Single women, who were freeholders, voted in the State of New Jersey as late as the year 1800. In a newspaper of that date is a complimentary editorial to the female voters for having unanimously supported Mr. John Adams (the defeated candidate) for President of the United States, in opposition to Mr. Jefferson, who was denounced as wanting in religion.

CHARLES LAMB'S EPITAPH.

The following lines are copied from the gravestone of Charles Lamb, who lies in the churchyard at Edmonton :—

Farewell, dear friend; that smile, that harmless mirth,
No more shall gladden our domestic hearth ;
That rising tear, with pain forbid to flow,
Better than words, no more assuage our woe,
That hand outstretch'd from small but well-earned store,
Yield succor to the destitute no more.

Yet art thou not all lost: thro' many an age
With sterling sense and humor shall thy page
Win many an English bosom, pleased to see
That old and happier vein revived in thee.
This for our earth, and if with friends we share
Our joys in heav'n, we hope to meet thee there.

According to Mr. Thorne (*Rambles by Rivers*, 1st series, p. 190), the inscription in the churchyard at Edmonton, to the memory of Charles Lamb, was written "by his friend, Dr. Cary, the translator of Dante." Mr. Thorne gives an anecdote concerning this inscription :—

We heard a piece of criticism on this inscription that Lamb would have enjoyed. As we were copying it, a couple of canal excavators came across the churchyard, and read it over with great deliberation; when they had finished, one of them said, "A very fair bit of poetry that." "Yes," replied his companion, "I'm blest if it isn't as good a bit as any in the churchyard; rather too long, though."

HOAX ON SIR WALTER SCOTT.

The following passage occurs in one of Sir Walter Scott's letters to Southey, written in September, 1810 :—

A witty rogue, the other day, who sent me a letter subscribed "Detector," proved me guilty of stealing a passage from one of Vida's Latin poems, which

I had never seen or heard of; yet there was so strong a general resemblance as fairly to authorize "Detector's" suspicion.

Lockhart remarks thereupon :—

The lines of Vida which "Detector" had enclosed to Scott, as the obvious original of the address to "Woman" in *Marmion*, closing with—

"When pain and anguish wring the brow,
A ministering angel thou!"

end as follows: and it must be owned that if Vida had really written them, a more extraordinary example of casual coincidence could never have been pointed out.

"Cum dolor atque supercilio gravis imminet angor,
Fungeris angelico sola ministerio."

"Detector's" reference is Vida *ad Eranen*, El. ii. v. 21; but it is almost needless to add there are no such lines, and no piece bearing such a title in Vida's works. "Detector" was, no doubt, some young college wag; for his letter has a Cambridge post-mark.

It may interest to know that the author of this clever hoax was Henry I. T. Drury, then of King's College, Cambridge, and afterwards one of the Masters at Harrow. The lines will be found in the *Arundines Cami.*

SHAKSPEARE'S PLAYS.

MEMORIA TECHNICA

For the Plays of Shakspeare, omitting the Historical English Dramas,
"quos versu dicere non est."

Cymbeline, Tempest, Much Ado, Verona,
Merry Wives, Twelfth Night, As You Like it, Errors,
Shrew Taming, Night's Dream, Measure, Andronicus,
Timon of Athens.

Wintry Tale, Merchant, Troilus, Lear, Hamlet,
Love's Labour, All's Well, Pericles, Othello,
Romeo, Macbeth, Cleopatra, Cæsar,
Coriolanus.

PICNIC.

The word is in Ménage (*Dictionnaire étymologique*, folio, 1694) :—

Piquenique.—Nous disons *faire un repas à piquenique*, pour dire faire un repas où chacun paye son écot : ce que les Flamans disent, *parte bétal, chacun sa part.* Ce mot n'est pas ancien dans notre langue ; et il est inconnu dans la plupari de nos provinces.

Picnics were known and practised in the reign of James I. An amusing description of one is given in a letter from Sir Philip Mainwaring, dated Nov. 22, 1618. The knight is writing to Lord Arundel from Newmarket :—

The Prince his birth-day hathe beene solemnised heare by those few Marquises and Lords which found themselves heare, and to supplie the want of the Lords, Knights and Squires were admitted to a consultation, wherein it was resolved that such a number should meete at Gamiges, and bring every man his dish of meate. It was left to their own choyces what to bring : some strove to be substantiall, some curios, and some extravagant. Sir George Goring's invention bore away the bell ; and that was foure huge brawny piggs, pipeing hott, bitted and harnised with ropes of sarsiges, all tyde to a monstrous bag-pudding.

And on the 28th of the same month, Mr. Chamberlain wrote to Sir Dudley Carleton :—

We hear nothing from Newmarket, but that they devise all the means they can to make themselves merry ; as of late there was a feast appointed at a farmhouse not far off, whither every man should bring his dish. The King brought a great chine of beef, the Marquis of Hamilton four pigs incircled with sausages, the Earl of Southampton two turkies, another six partridges, and one a whole tray full of buttered eggs ; and so all passed off very pleasantly.—Nichol's *Progresses of James I.*, vol. iii. pp. 495, 496.

Picnic Supper.—This season (1802), says the *Annual Register*, has been marked by a new species of entertainment, common to the fashionable world, called a Picnic supper. It consists of a variety of dishes. The subscribers to the entertainment have a bill of fare presented to them, with a number against each dish. The lot which he draws obliges him to furnish the dish marked against it; which he either takes with him in a carriage, or sends by a servant. The proper variety is preserved by the taste of the maître-d'hotel who forms the bill of fare.

MY LOVE AND I FOR KISSES PLAY'D.

In the *Common-place Book* of Justinian Paget, a lawyer of James the First's time, preserved among the Harleian MSS. in the British Museum, is the following sonnet:—

My love and I for kisses play'd;
 Shee would keepe stakes, I was content;
But when I wonn she would be pay'd,
 This made me ask her what she ment;
Nay, since I see (quoth she), you wrangle in vaine,
 Take your owne kisses, give me mine againe.

The initials at the end, "W. S." probably stand for William Stroud or Strode, whose name is given at length to some other rhymes in the same MS.

They likewise occur in the MS. volume from which James Boswell extracted "Shakspeare's Verses on the King," but with a much better reading of the last couplet:—

Nay, then, quoth shee, is this your wrangling vaine?
Give me my stakes, take your own stakes againe.

They are entitled, "Upon a Lover and his Mistris playing for Kisses," and are there without any name or signature. They remind us of Lilly's very elegant "Cupid and Campaspe."

THE MOSQUITO COUNTRY.

A quarto volume published by Cadell in 1789, entitled *The Case of His Majesty's Subjects having Property in and lately established upon the Mosquito Shore*, gives the fullest account of the early connection between the Mosquito Indians and the English. The writer says that Jeremy, King of the Mosquitos, in Charles II.'s reign, after formally ceding his country to officers sent to him by the Governor of Jamaica to receive the cession, went to Jamaica, and thence to England, where he was generously received by Charles II., " who had him often with him in his private parties of pleasure, admired his activity, strength, and manly accomplishments; and not only defrayed every expense, but loaded him with presents." Is there any notice of this visit in any of our numerous memoirs and diaries of Charles II.'s reign?

A curious tract, printed in the sixth volume of Churchill's *Voyages*, " The Mosquito Indian and his Golden River, being a familiar Description of the Mosquito Kingdom, &c., written in or about the Year 1699, by M. W.," from which Southey drew some touches of Indian manners for his " Madoc," speaks of another King Jeremy, son of the previous one; who, it is said, esteemed himself a subject of the King of England, and had visited the Duke of Albemarle in Jamaica. His father had been carried to England, and received from the King of England a crown and commission. The writer of this account says that the Mosquito Indians generally esteem themselves English :—

> And, indeed, they are extremely courteous to all Englishmen, esteeming themselves to be such, although some Jamaica men have very much abused them.

There is the following amusing passage in a speech of Governor Johnstone, in a debate in the House of Commons on the Mosquito country in 1777 :—

> I see the noble lord [Lord North] now collects his knowledge by piecemeal from those about him. While my hon. friend [some one was whispering Lord North] now whispers the noble lord, will he also tell him, and the more aged gentlemen of the House, before we yield up our right to the Mosquito shore, that it is from thence we receive the greatest part of our delicious turtle? May I tell the younger part, before they give their consent, that it is from thence comes the sarsaparilla to purify our blood?—*Parl. Hist.*, vol. xix. p. 54.

UMBRELLAS.

Thomas Coryat, in his *Crudities*, vol. i. p. 134, gives us a curious notice of the early use of the umbrella in Italy. Speaking of fans, he says :—

> These fans are of a mean price, for a man may buy one of the fairest of them for so much money as countervaileth one English groat. Also many of them (the Italians) do carry other fine things of a far greater price, that will cost at the least a ducat, which they commonly call in the Italian tongue *umbrellaes*, that is, things that minister shadow unto them for shelter against the scorching heat of the sun. These are made of leather, something answerable to the form of a little canopy, and hooped in the inside with diverse little wooden hoops that extend the *umbrella* in a pretty large compass. They are used especially by horsemen, who carry them in their hands when they ride, fastening the end of the handle upon one of their thighs : and they impart so long a shadow unto them, that it keepeth the heat of the sun from the upper parts of their bodies.

In Fynes Moryson's *Itinerary*, "printed by John Beale, 1617, part iii. booke i. chap. ii. p. 21," is the following passage :—

> In hot regions, to auoide the beames of the sunne, in some places (as in Italy), they carry Vmbrels, or things like a little canopy, over their heads; but a learned Physician told me, that the use of them was dangerous, because they gather the heate into a pyramidall point, and thence cast it down perpendicularly vpon the head, except they know how to carry them for auoyding that danger.

The following passage is from the fourth edition of Blount's *Glossographia*, published as far back as 1674 :—

> *Umbrello* (Ital. *Ombrella*), a fashion of round and broad Fans, wherewith the *Indians* (and from them our great ones), preserve themselves from the heat of the sun or fire; and hence any little shadow, Fan, or other thing, wherewith the women guard their faces from the sun.

And in Phillips's *New World of Words*, 7th ed., 1720 :—

> *Umbrella* or *Umbrello*, a kind of broad Fan or Skreen, which in hot countries People hold over their heads to keep off the Heat of the Sun ; or such as

are here commonly us'd by women to shelter them from Rain: Also, a wooden Frame cover'd with cloth or stuff, to keep off the sun from a window.

Parasol (*Fr.*), a small sort of canopy or umbrello, which women carry over their Heads, to shelter themselves from Rain, &c.

Gay mentions umbrellas in his *Trivia, or Art of Walking the Streets of London*, published 1712:—

Good housewives all the winter's rage despise,
Defended by the ridinghood's disguise;
Or, underneath th' *umbrella's* oily shade,
Safe through the wet on clinking pattens tread.
Let Persian dames the *umbrella's* ribs display,
To guard their beauties from the sunny ray;
Or sweating slaves support the shady load,
When Eastern monarchs show their state abroad;
Britain in winter only knows its aid,
To guard from chilling showers the walking maid.
Book i. lines 209–218.

That it was, perhaps, an article of curiosity rather than use in the middle of the seventeenth century, is evident in the fact of its being mentioned in the "*Musæum Tradescantianum, or Collection of Rarities*, preserved at South Lambeth near London, by John Tradescant." 12mo. 1656. It occurs under the head of "Utensils," and is simply mentioned as "*An Umbrella.*"

Lt.-Col. (afterwards Gen.) Wolfe, writing from Paris, in the year 1752, says:—

The people here use umbrellas in hot weather to defend them from the sun, and something of the same kind to secure them from snow and rain. I wonder a practice so useful is not introduced in England (where there are such frequent showers), and especially in the country, where they can be expanded without any inconveniency.

The introduction of this article of general convenience is attributed to Jonas Hanway, the Eastern traveller, who on his return to his native land rendered himself justly celebrated by his practical benevolence. In a little book with a long title, published in 1787, written by "*John Pugh*," are to be found many curious anecdotes related of Hanway, and apropos of umbrellas, in describing his dress Mr. Pugh says,—"When it rained, a small parapluie defended his face and wig; thus he was always prepared to enter into any company without impropriety, or the appearance of negligence. And he (Hanway) was the first man who ventured to walk the streets of London with an umbrella over his head: after carrying one near thirty years, he saw them come into general use." Hanway died 1786.

PHONETIC PECULIARITY.

It is a very curious phonetic peculiarity, that we have in the English language a large number of monosyllabic words ending in *sh*, all of which are expressive of some violent action or emotion. The following are a few which have occurred without search, in alphabetical order: "Brush, brash, crash, crush, dash, gash, gush, hash, gnash, lash, mash, pash, push, quash, rush, slash, mash, squash, splash, thrash.

HIGH CHURCH AND LOW CHURCH.

A Universal History of Party; with the Origin of Party Names, would form an acceptable addition to literary history. Such names as *Puritan*, *Malignant*, *Evangelical*, can be traced up to their first commencement, but some obscurity hangs on the mintage-date of the names we are about to consider.

As a matter of fact, the distinction of *High Church* and *Low Church* always existed in the Reformed English Church, and the history of these parties would be her history. But the *names* were not coined till the close of the seventeenth century, and were not stamped in full relief as party names till the first year of Queen Anne's reign.

In October, 1702, Anne's first Parliament and Convocation assembled :—

From the disputes in Convocation at this period, the appellations *High Church* and *Low Church* originated, and they were afterwards used to distinguish the clergy. It is singular that the bishops were ranked among the Low Churchmen (see Burnet, v. 138 ; Calamy, i. 643 ; Tindal's *Cont.*, iv. 591).—Lathbury's *Hist. of the Convocation*, Lond. 1842, p. 319.

Mr. Lathbury is a very respectable authority in matters of this kind, but if he use "originated" in its strict sense, he is probably mistaken, as I am tolerably certain that I have met with the words several years before 1702. At the moment, however, I cannot lay my hands on a passage to support this assertion.

The disputes in Convocation gave rise to a number of pamphlets, such as *A Caveat against High Church*, Lon. 1702, and *The Low Churchmen vindicated from the unjust Imputation of being No Churchmen, in Answer to a Pamphlet called "The Distinction of High and Low Church considered:"* Lond. 1706, 8vo. Dr. Sacheverell's trial gave additional zest to the *dudgeon ecclesiastick*, and produced a shower of pamphlets. This is the title of one of them: *Pulpit War, or Dr. S—l, the High Church Trumpet, and Mr. H—ly, the Low Church Drum, engaged by way of Dialogue*, Lond. 1710, 8vo.

To understand the cause of the exceeding bitterness and virulence which animated the parties denominated *High Church* and *Low Church*, we must remember that until the time of William of Orange, the Church of England, *as a body*—her sovereigns and bishops, her clergy and laity—comes under the *former* designation; while those who sympathized with the Dissenters were comparatively few and weak. As soon as William was head of the Church, he opened the floodgates of Puritanism, and admitted into the Church what previously had been more or less external to it. This element, thus made part and parcel of the Anglican Church, was denominated *Low Church*. William supplanted the bishops and clergy who refused to take oaths of allegiance to him as king *de jure;* and by putting Puritans in their place, made the latter the dominant party. Add to this the feelings of exasperation produced by the murder of Charles I., and the expulsion of the Stuarts, and we have sufficient grounds, political and religious, for an irreconcilable feud. Add, again, the reaction resulting from the overthrow of the tyrannous hot-bed and forcing system, where a sham conformity was maintained by coercion; and the *Church-Papist*, as well as the *Church-Puritans*, with ill-concealed hankering after the mass and the preaching-house, by penal statutes were forced to do what their souls abhorred, and play the painful farce of attending the services of "The Establishment."

A writer in a *High Church* periodical of 1717 (prefacing his article with the passage from Proverbs vi. 27) proceeds:—

> The old way of attacking the Church of England was by mobs and bullies, and hard sounds; by calling *Whore*, and *Babylon*, upon our worship and liturgy, and kicking out our clergy as *dumb dogs:* but now they have other irons in the fire; a new engine is set up under the cloak and disguise of *temper, unity, comprehension, and the Protestant religion.* Their business now is not to storm the Church, but to *lull it to sleep:* to make us relax our care, quit our defences, and neglect our safety . . . . These are the politics of their Popish fathers: when *they* had tried all other artifices, they at last resolved to sow schism and division in the Church: and from thence sprang up *this* very generation, who by a fine stratagem endeavoured to set us one against the other, and they gather up the stakes. *Hence the distinction of High and Low Church.—The Scourge*, p. 251.

In another periodical of the same date, in the Dedication "To the most famous University of Oxford," the writer says:—

> These enemies of our religious and civil establishment have represented you as instillers of *slavish doctrines and principles* . . . if to give to God and Cæsar his due be such tow'ring, and *High Church* principles, I am sure St. Peter and St. Paul will scarce escape being censured for *Tories* and *Highflyers.— The Entertainer*, Lond. 1717.

If those who have kept their first love, and whose robes have not been defiled, endeavour to stop these innovations and corruptions that their enemies would introduce, they are blackened for *High Church Papists*, favourers of I know not who, and fall under the public resentment.—*Ib.* p. 301.

The following are a few extracts from *Low Church* writers (quoted in *The Scourge*), who thus designate their opponents :—

A pack or party of scandalous, wicked, and profane men, who appropriate to themselves the name of *High Church* (but may more properly be said to be Jesuits or Papists in masquerade), do take liberty to teach, preach, and print, publickly and privately, sedition, contentions, and divisions among the Protestants of this kingdom.—*Motives to Union*, p. 1.

These men glory in their being members of the *High Church* (Popish appellation, and therefore they are the more fond of that); but these pretended sons are become her persecutors, and they exercise their spite and lies both on the living and the dead.—*The Snake in the Grass brought to Light*, p. 8.

Our common people of the *High Church* are as ignorant in matters of religion as the bigotted Papists, which gives great advantage to our Jacobite and Tory priests to lead them where they please, or to mould them into what shapes they please.—*Reasons for an Union*, p. 39.

The minds of the populace are too much debauched already from their loyalty by seditious arts of the *High Church faction*.—*Convocation Craft*, p. 34.

We may see how closely our present *Highflyers* pursue the steps of their Popish predecessors, in reckoning those who dispute the usurped power of the Church to be hereticks, schismaticks, or what else they please.—*Ib.* p. 30.

All the blood that has been spilt in the late unnatural rebellion, may be very justly laid at the doors of the *High Church* clergy.—*Christianity no Creature of the State*, p. 16.

We see what the *Tory Priesthood* were made of in Queen Elizabeth's time, that they were ignorant, lewd, and seditious: and it must be said of 'em that they are true to the stuff still.—*Toryism the Worst of the Two*, p. 21.

The *Tories* and *High Church*, notwithstanding their pretences to loyalty, will be found by their actions to be the greatest rebels in nature.—*Reasons for an Union*, p. 20.

Sir W. Scott, in his *Life of Dryden*, Lond. 1808, observes that—

Towards the end of Charles the Second's reign, the *High-Church-men* and the Catholics regarded themselves as on the same side in political questions, and not greatly divided in their temporal interests. Both were sufferers in the plot, both were enemies of the sectaries, both were adherents of the Stuarts. Alternate conversion had been common between them, so early as since Milton made a reproach to the English Universities of the converts to the Roman faith daily made within their colleges: of those sheep—

> Whom the *grim wolf* with privy paw
> Daily devours apace, and nothing said.

Life, 3d edit. 1834, p. 272.

This passage is quoted as a preface to the remark that in James II.'s reign, and at the time these party names originated, the Roman Catholics were in league with the Puritans or *Low Church* party against the High Churchmen, which increased the acrimony of both parties.

In those days religion was politics, and politics religion, with most of the belligerents. Swift, however, as if he wished to be thought an exception to the general rule, chose one party for its politics and the other for its religion.

Swift carried into the ranks of the Whigs the opinions and scruples of a *High Church* clergyman . . . Such a distinction between opinions in Church and State has not frequently existed: the *High Churchmen* being usually *Tories*, and the *Low Church* divines universally *Whigs*.—Scott's *Life*, 2d edit. Edin. 1824, p. 76.

See Swift's *Discourse of the Contests and Dissensions between the Nobles and Commons of Athens and Rome:* Lond. 1701.

In his quaint *Argument against abolishing Christianity*, Lond. 1708, the following passage occurs:—

There is one advantage, greater than any of the foregoing, proposed by the abolishing of Christianity: that it will utterly extinguish parties among us by removing those factious distinctions of *High* and *Low Church*, of *Whig* and *Tory*, Presbyterian and Church of England.

Scott says of the *Tale of a Tub*:—

The main purpose is to trace the gradual corruptions of the Church of Rome, and to exalt the English Reformed Church at the expense both of the

Roman Catholic and Presbyterian establishments. It was written with a view to the interests of the *High Church* party.—*Life*, p. 84.

Most men will concur with Jeffrey, who observes:—

It is plain, indeed, that Swift's *High Church* principles were all along but a part of his selfishness and ambition; and meant nothing else, than a desire to raise the consequence of the order to which he happened to belong. If he had been a layman, we have no doubt he would have treated the pretensions of the priesthood as he treated the persons of all priests who were opposed to him, with the most bitter and irreverent disdain.—*Ed. Rev.*, Sept. 1816.

The following lines are from a squib of eight stanzas which occurs in the works of Jonathan Smedley, and are said to have been fixed on the door of St. Patrick's Cathedral on the day of Swift's instalment (see Scott, p. 174):—

For *High Churchmen* and policy,
He swears he prays most hearty;
But would pray back again to be
A Dean of any party.

This reminds us of the Vicar of Bray, of famous memory, who, if I recollect aright, commenced his career thus:—

In good King Charles's golden days,
When loyalty no harm meant,
A zealous *High Churchman* I was,
And so I got preferment.

How widely different are the men we see classed under the title *High Churchmen!* Evelyn and Walton,* the gentle, the Christian; the arrogant Swift, and the restless Atterbury.

The great principle of religious toleration is a discovery of very recent date. Butler's exquisitely witty lines on "The True Church *Militant*," apply as well to Papists as Puritans, to High Church as well as Low Church.

Wordsworth, and most Anglican writers down, are ever ex-

* Of Izaak Walton, his biographer, Sir John Hawkins, writing in 1760, says, "He was a friend to a hierarchy, or, as we should now call such a one, a *High Churchman*."

tolling the Golden Mean and the moderation of the Church of England. Wordsworth says:—

High and *Low*,
Watchwords of party, on all tongues are rife;
As if a Church, though sprung from heaven, must owe
To opposites and fierce extremes her life;—
Not to the golden mean and quiet flow
Of truths, that soften hatred, temper strife.

A fine old writer of the same Church (Dr. Joseph Beaumont) seems to think that this love of the Mean can be carried too far:—

And witty too in self-delusion, we
Against highstreined piety can plead,
Gravely pretending that extremity
Is Vice's clime; that by the Catholick creed
Of all the world it is acknowledged that
The temperate *mean* is always Virtue's seat.
Hence comes the race of mongrel goodness; hence
Faint tepidness usurpeth fervour's name;
Hence will the earth-born meteor needs commence,
In his gay glaring robes, sydereal flame;
Hence foolish man, if moderately evil,
Dreams he's a saint because he's not a devil.

Psyche, cant. xxi. 4, 5.

The High Churchmen, unfortunately, had recourse to an argument which cuts both ways; they taught their opponents "the holy text of pike and gun," and to

Decide all controversies by
Infallible artillery;
And prove their doctrine orthodox
By apostolic blows and knocks.

By penal laws and acts of uniformity they erected an "Establishment" at the loss of a Church; and by abject servility to the State they gained their temporalities at the loss of spiritual power. They were all this time tying a halter round their own necks; and, by a curious moral retribution, they eventually found themselves, *in one half* of Great Britain, hunted, persecuted "Dissenters," utterly crippled *in the other*, and barely tolerated as a *party* in a Church they once called their own.

The principle of private judgment, and the precedent of separation, being introduced by the Reformers, intolerance and a forced conformity came awkwardly from their followers, though this inconsistency had the authority of Luther and Calvin, &c.; and the experiment was especially hazardous with a nation allowed to be about as "stiff-necked" as the Israelites of old, and thus described by one of their own countrymen:—

> In their religion they are so uneven,
> That each man goes his own by-way to heaven:
> Tenacious of mistakes to that degree
> That every man pursues it separately:
> And fancies none can find the way but he.
> So shy of one another are they grown,
> As if they strove to get to heav'n alone.
> Rigid and zealous, positive and grave,
> And every grace but charity they have.
> This makes them so ill-natured and uncivil,
> That all men think an Englishman the devil.*

All the Dissenters wanted at first was toleration, and a free exercise of their religion according to their conscience; and most of them would have been content to leave the wealth and power of the Establishment to the Churchmen; but no, the latter would not let them alone, they *must conform.* As external conformity was all they could control, they thus filled the Church with secret enemies, the mildest of whom mocked at Church principles as at best a conventional farce, a mere system of unreality. These turned the tables on their masters when they got the opportunity; and determined not to give up the temporalities of the Church they were forced into, nor their own principles neither.

* The True-Born Englishman. A Satyr. Printed in the year MDCCI.—P. 16.

When it was too late, the Churchmen began to wish they had let the Dissenters alone, and allowed them to stay where they were. But now the latter not only would not go out themselves, but threatened to oust the Churchmen, who soon had cause to rue the violent hurry they had been in to make the Dissenters conform, and bitterly regretted that they had compelled them to enter the Anglican Church. They who introduced the principle that *might makes right*—who mutilated the consciences, and forced the minds and bodies of others to fit in the procrustean bed of the Establishment—have no cause to complain if they be served according to the same measure.

The question of conformity, especially *occasional* conformity, was the great bone of contention between the parties of Queen Anne's reign.

Dissenters they were to be pressed
To go to common-prayer,
And turn their faces to the East,
As God were only there:

Or else no place of price or trust
They ever could obtain;
Which shows that saying very just,
That "Godliness is gain." *

James Owen, a dissenting minister, published a pamphlet with a very lengthy title, commencing :—

* From "The History and Fall of the Conformity Bill," London, 1705. "Being an excellent new Song, chanted to the tune of *Chevy Chace.*" On the celebrated bill for preventing occasional conformity (which passed the House of Commons, December 7, 1703, but was rejected by the Lords), Swift remarks, in a letter to Stella, dated December 16, 1703, "I wish you had been here for ten days, during the highest and warmest reign of party and faction that I ever knew or read of, upon the bill against occasional conformity, which two days ago was rejected by the Lords. It was so universal that I observed the *dogs* in the streets much more contumelious and quarrelsome than usual; and the very night before the bill went up, a committee of Whig and Tory *cats* had a very warm and loud debate upon the roof of our house. But why should we wonder at that, when the very *ladies* are split asunder into *High Church* and *Low*, and out of zeal for *religion* have hardly time to say their prayers?"

Moderation, a Virtue; or, the Occasional Conformist justified from the Imputation of Hypocrisy. Wherein is shown the Antiquity, Catholic Principles, and Advantage of Occasional Conformity to the Church of England, &c. London, 1703, 4to.

Defoe replied in—

The Sincerity of the Dissenters vindicated from the Scandal of Occasional Conformity. London, 1703, 4to.

Leslie attacked both in another long-named pamphlet—

The Wolf stript of his Shepherd's Clothing. . . . . By one called a High Churchman. . . . . . London, 1704, 4to., pp. 108.

To which Defoe replied in—

The Dissenters' Answer to the High-Church Challenge. London, 1704, 4to., pp. 55.

The numerous works published by Defoe and other writers on this subject, for obvious reasons, must be passed over in these pages. It is impossible to give here even a summary of what Defoe has written on party; the most we can do with a man who has published not less than *two hundred and ten works* is to make a selection.

In the following passage Defoe shows how the spirit of party had diffused itself every where, and leavened all ranks in his time:—

The strife is gotten into your kitchens, your parlours, your counting-houses, nay, into your very beds. The poor despicable scullions learn to cry *High Church! No Dutch kings! No Hanover!* that they may do it dexterously when they come into the next mob. Here their antagonists of the dripping-pan practise the other-side clamour, *No French Peace! No Pretender! No Popery!* Up stairs the 'prentices, standing some on one side of the shop and some on the other, throw *High Church* and *Low Church* at each other's heads, like battledore and shuttlecock; and, instead of posting their books, are fighting and railing at the Pretender and the House of Hanover. If we go one story higher, the ladies, instead of their innocent sports and diversions, are falling out amongst each other; the mothers and the daughters, the children and the servants, nay, even the little sisters. If the chambermaid is a slattern, and does not please, I warrant she is a High-Flyer or a Whig: I never knew one of that sort good for any thing in my life. Nay, go up to your very bed-chambers, and even in bed the man and wife shall quarrel about it. People! people! what will become of you at this rate? *

The periodical literature of Queen Anne's reign is very remarkable, and deserves the careful attention of all inquirers into the history of English party.

In the early part of this reign the most remarkable periodicals are, *The Observator*, of which the first number was published April 1, 1702, conducted by John Tutchin, a Whig and Low Churchman. *The Review*, which commenced February 19, 1704, conducted by Defoe, who comes under the same classification, but, like Henry of the Wynd, generally fought for his own band, and occupied that anomalous position ascribed by tradition to Mahomet's tomb, and assumed in our own times by Dr. Arnold. This periodical was continued until May, 1713, when it was finally relinquished, after a steady publication of more than nine years. A copy of the last volume of this work is not known to be in existence. (See Wilson, vol. iii. p. 295.) The remaining periodical of this period of any note is *The Rehearsal*, conducted by the High-Church champion, Charles Leslie. It commenced August 2, 1704, and was discontinued at the end of March, 1709. Another writer revived it shortly after, but it soon fell to the ground. *The Rehearsal* was published in folio, and was reprinted in 6 vols. 12mo. in 1750.

In the succeeding reign, also, the most remarkable party periodicals are three in number, *The Scourge*, *The Entertainer*, and *The Independent Whig*.

The Scourge, in vindication of the Church of England, was edited by Thomas Lewis, and contains forty-three numbers, 8vo.,

* From Defoe's ironical *Reasons against the Succession of the House of Hanover.* . . . . "Si Populus vult decipi decipiatur:" London, 1713, pp. 45.

commencing with February 4, 1717, and ending November 25, 1717. It was reprinted in a handsome 8vo. vol. in 1720, with a rubricated title-page and a frontispiece, containing in five medallion portraits the royal family of the Stuarts. The title runs thus :—

The Scourge : in Vindication of the Church of England. To which are added, 1. The Danger of the Church Establishment of England, from the Insolence of Protestant Dissenters, occasioned by a Presentment of the Forty-second Paper of the Scourge at the King's Bench Bar, by the Grand Jury of the Hundred of Ossulston. 2. The Anatomy of the Heretical Synod of Dissenters at Salters' Hall. By T. L. : London, printed in the year M.DCCXX. Price six shillings, pp. 384.

The latter tract has a curious frontispiece prefixed, representing the Synod.

The next on our list is—

The Entertainer : containing Remarks upon Men, Manners, Religion, and Policy ; to which is prefixt a Dedication to the most famous University of Oxford. . . . . London, printed by N. Mist.

It contains forty-three numbers, from November 6, 1717, to August 27, 1718; pp. 307, 12mo.

The Independent Whig contains fifty-four numbers, from January 20, 1720, to January 18, 1721. In the preface to the last edition the editor says :—

To gratify the usual curiosity of readers, I have, at the end of each paper, put the initial letter of the name of the gentleman who wrote it. As there were only *three* gentlemen concerned in the undertaking, and as their names are well known, it will be easy to distinguish them by this mark.

The initials appended are G., T., and C. The first stands for Thomas Gordon; the second for John Trenchard; (?) the third initial.

The last edition (the eighth) was issued in 4 vols. 12mo. in 1752; but the original periodical ends at p. 173 of the 2d vol.

The editor, Thomas Gordon, has added the remaining pages himself. The title of the 1st vol. is—

The Independent Whig; or, a Defence of Primitive Christianity, and of our Ecclesiastical Establishment, against the exorbitant Claims and Encroachments of Fanatical and Disaffected Clergymen. By Thomas Gordon, Esq. The eighth edition, with additions and amendments, in 4 vols.: London, 1753.

The 2d vol. has the same title: the 3d the same, except that it is "the third edition." The 4th is entitled—

The Independent Whig: being a Collection of Papers, all written, some of them published, during the late Rebellion. The second edition.

After a scurrilous dedication follows "A Letter to the Publisher," full of rancour against the famous Bishop of Sodor and Man, Dr. Wilson, with that prelate's "Bull against *The Independent Whig*," and extolling that "honest and brave magistrate, the Governor of Man, Capt. Horne," for his conduct in the affair.

The titles of some of the papers may serve to give some idea of this work:—

7. Of Uninterrupted Succession. 12. The Enmity of the High Clergy to the Reformation, and their Arts to defeat the end of it. 13, 14. The Church proved a Creature of the Civil Power by Acts of Parliament and the Oaths of the Clergy, by the Canons, and their own public Acts. 15. The Absurdity and Impossibility of Church Power, as independent of the State. 16. The Inconsistency of the Principles and Practice of the High Church. 17. Reasons why the High Church are the most wicked of all Men. 19. Ecclesiastical Authority, as claimed by the High Clergy, an Enemy to Religion. 21. A Comparison between the High Church and the Quakers. 33. The Ignorance of the High Church vulgar, and its Causes. 37. The Enmity of the High Clergy to the Bible. 42–46. Of High-Church Atheism. 51. Of the three High Churches in England.

In the index to the 1st. vol. we have—

High-Church priests . . . . . subscribe the Articles without believing them, and abuse those that do. Mislead those that follow them, and curse those that leave them. Allow us to read the Bible, but not to make use of it. . . . . Damn all the world, without taking one step to convert it. Low Churchmen the best and only friends of the Church: High Churchmen its bitterest enemies.

No. 51 is a curious paper on "The Three High Churches in England:"—

The High-Churches, which differ from this Establishment, are three in number: 1. *Dr. Bungey's** High Church; 2. *Mr. Lesley's* High Church; and 3. *Dr. Brett's* High Church.

Here is a curious quotation from this virulent publication:—

A *High Churchman* may be denominated from divers marks and exclamations. He must be devout in damning of Dissenters; he must roar furiously for the Church and its great modern apostle, the late Duke of Ormond, with some other pious and forsworn gentlemen, who are well affected to the Pretender and the Convocation; he must rebel for *passive obedience;* he must uphold *divine right* by diabolical means; and he must be loud and zealous for *hereditary, indefeasible*, and the like *orthodox nonsense.* But there is one sign more of a *true Churchman*, which is more lasting and universal than all the rest, and that is a firm and senseless persuasion that *the Church is in danger.*† If a man believe this it is enough, his reputation is raised; and though his life show more of the demon than the Christian, he shall be deemed an *excellent Churchman.* This is so true, that if an honest atheistical Churchman will but curse and roar against a toleration of Dissenters, he shall be sure to find a toleration himself for the blackest iniquities, be rewarded with reputation, and, if possible, with power. . . . . Now for the *Low Church* clergy.—Vol. iii. pp. 157–163.

In Sir Walter Scott's edition of the *Somers Tracts*, vol. xii. p. 320, occurs a doggrel of six-and-twenty lines, entitled "High-Church Miracles, or Modern Inconsistencies, printed in the year 1710." It commences thus:—

The High Church have a right divine from Jove,
By signs and wonders they pretend to prove
They can a mortal soul immortal make;
They can by prayers our constitution shake.

* A name for Dr. Sacheverell.

† Defoe calls this "the motto" of the Church party. (See a curious passage in *The Review*, ii. 230.)

And ends with the lines—

But I defy themselves and all their devils
To wash the Ethiop white, and purge High Church from evils.

Any Notes on the present subject would be imperfect without a reference to some of the voluminous writings of the author of *Robinson Crusoe*, the indomitable Daniel Defoe. It is necessary to notice, also, some of the writings of Charles Leslie the Nonjuror, who is styled by Puritan writers the great champion of High Churchmen—the Coryphæus of his party.

Defoe's most celebrated pamphlet is thus entitled :—

The Shortest Way with the Dissenters; or, Proposals for the Establishment of the Church. London: printed in the year 1702. 4to., pp. 29.

The irony of this satire was so exquisite, that it deceived both *High* and *Low;* and many of the more violent of the former party welcomed it as an admirable production. When the writer was found out, and his scope perceived, the fury and indignation of High Churchmen knew no bounds. Defoe was prosecuted for libel, and condemned to pay a fine of two hundred marks to the queen,* to stand three times in the pillory, to be imprisoned during the queen's pleasure, and to find sureties for his good behaviour for seven years. A High-Church writer thus speaks of the pamphlet :—

It passed currently as the work of one of those they called *High Churchmen:* and though the pretended zeal and earnestness of the author, to have the Dissenters treated according to their deserts, was universally condemned by Churchmen in general, yet it served the purpose well enough *to brand that whole body with bloodthirstiness and a persecuting spirit*, till, by the diligence of the government, it appeared that no Churchman had been so little a Christian; but that it was done by one of the chief scribes of the other party with a mere design *to halloo the mob to make the world believe that the Dissenters' throats were to be cut the shortest way, and to provoke these to begin first for their own preservation:*

* By Defoe's long imprisonment on this occasion, he lost upwards of 3,500*l.*, and was reduced to ruin.

for which wicked attempt the author had his just reward. But the party were so little ashamed of it, that whenever it was objected against them, it was only grinned off as a piece of wit and management.*

To complete the punishment, the book was burnt by the hands of the common hangman by order of Parliament. However, the man who wrote a "Hymn to the Pillory" was not likely to mind the latter indignity; accordingly, Defoe remarks in one of his works:—

I have heard a bookseller in King James's time say, "That if he would have a book sell, he would have it burnt by the hands of the common hangman."—*Essay on Projects*, p. 173.

Shortly after he wrote—

A Brief Explanation of a late Pamphlet, entitled "The Shortest Way with the Dissenters." London, 1703, 4to.†

And next year our "unabashed Defoe" publishes—

"More Short Ways with the Dissenters." London, 1704, 4to., pp. 24.

The keen satire entitled *The Shortest Way with the Dissenters*, drew forth a vast number of replies and animadversions. One is mentioned for the sake of the title:—

The Fox with his Firebrand unkennelled and ensnared; or, a Short Answer to Mr. Daniel Defoe's "Shortest way with the Dissenters." As also to his "Brief Explication" of the same. Together with some Animadversions upon the Sham Reflections made upon his "Shortest Way," and printed with the same. London: printed in the year 1703, 4to.

Defoe's satire was not altogether uncalled for, and is justified by many writings of the *High Church* party. It seems to have

* "A Caveat against the Whigs, in a Short Historical View of their Transactions. Wherein are discovered their many Attempts and Contrivances against the established Government, both in Church and State, since the Restoration of King Charles II. London: 1711, 8vo." The third and fourth parts of this work were published in 1712. The passage above cited is from Part IV., pp. 88, 89.

† Defoe gives an "explanation" of this satire in another work also: see *The Present State of Parties in Great Britain*, London, 1712, 8vo., pp. 18, 21.

especial reference to a sermon of Dr. Sacheverell's, preached before the University of Oxford, and printed with the *imprimatur* of the Vice-Chancellor, dated June 2, 1702. It is entitled—

The Political Union: A Discourse, showing the Dependence of Government on Religion in General; and of the English Monarchy on the Church of England in particular.

In it occurs the following passage:—

Men must be strange infatuated sots and bigots to be so much in love with their ruin, as to seek and court it: and it is as unaccountable and amazing a contradiction to our reason, as the greatest reproach and scandal upon our Church, however others may be seduced or misled, that any pretending to that sacred and inviolable character of being her true sons, pillars, and defenders, should turn such apostates and renegadoes to their oaths and professions, such false traitors to their trusts and offices, as to strike sail with a party that is such an open and avowed enemy to our Communion; and against whom every man that wishes its welfare *ought to hang out the Bloody Flag and Banner of Defiance*. But in this, as well as most other circumstances, both our Church and State share the same common fate, that they can be ruined by none but themselves; and that, if ever they receive a mortal stab or wound, it must be in the house of their friends.

Dennis replied to this sermon in a pamphlet entitled—

The Danger of Priestcraft to Religion and Government; with some Politick Reasons for a Toleration, &c. London, 1702.

Which was answered by Charles Leslie in—

The New Association of those called *Moderate* Churchmen, with the Modern Whigs and Fanaticks, to undermine and blow up the present Church and Government. Occasioned by a late Pamphlet, entitled "The Danger of Priestcraft," &c. With a Supplement on occasion of the New Scotch Presbyterian Covenant. By a True Churchman. London, 1702, 4to.

Upon Nov. 5, 1709, Dr. Sacheverell preached his famous sermon at St. Paul's, *The Perils among False Brethren;* which, after his being impeached before the House of Commons, and condemned by the Lords, was burned by the hangman.

Dr. Sacheverell's trial, and the agitation of the Tory mob,

produced many publications. Ned Ward, one of the inferior grade of High Church partisans, published some effusions in separate cantos, and afterwards collected them into a volume with the following title :—

Vulgus Britannicus; or, The British Hudibras, in Fifteen Cantos. The Five Parts complete in One Volume. Containing the Secret History of the late London Mob; their Rise, Progress, and Suppression by the Guards; intermixed with the Civil Wars betwixt *High Church* and *Low Church*, down to this Time. Being a Continuation of the late ingenious Mr. Butler's "Hudibras." Written by the Author of "The London Spy." The Second Edition, adorned with Cuts of Battles, Emblems, and Effigies, engraven on Copper Plates. London: printed for Sam. Briscoe, &c., 1710, 8vo, pp. 180.

At this period Defoe published his—

Instructions from Rome in favour of the Pretender. Inscribed to the most elevated Don Sacheverellio, and his Brother Don Higginisco. And which all Perkinites, Non-Jurors, High-Flyers, Popish-Desirers, *Wooden-shoe Admirers*,* and Absolute Non-resistance Drivers, are obliged to pursue and maintain, under pain of his Unholinesses Damnation, in order to carry on their intended Subversion of a Government fixed upon Revolution Principles. London: J. Baker, 1710, 8vo.

And also—

The High Church Address to Dr. Henry Sacheverell, for the great Service he has done the Established Church and Nation: wherein is shown the Justice of the Proceedings of those Gentlemen who have encouraged the pulling down and destroying those Nurseries of Schism, the Presbyterian Meeting-houses. Submitted to the Consideration of all Good Churchmen and Conscientious Dissenters. London: J. Baker, 1710. Price One Penny.

---

* Wooden shoes rank among the chief evils from which we were delivered in "that never-to-be-forgotten year of grace, 1688." They are gratefully enumerated in the famous Orange toast: "To the Glorious, Pious, and Immortal Memory of the Great Deliverer, &c., who rescued us from Popery, Prelacy, Brass Money, and *Wooden Shoes*." They may be said to form part of the *Greater Litany* of the Puritans. The Lesser Litany runs simply:—

From Plague, Pestilence, and Famine;
From Bishops, Priests, and Deacons;
Good Lord, deliver us!

In 1704 Defoe published a pamphlet, entitled *The Christianity of the High Church considered*, London, 1704, 4to., pp. 20.

In 1705 a violent party work appeared, entitled—

The Memorial of the Church of England, humbly offered to the Consideration of all the True Lovers of our Church and Constitution. London, 1705, 4to., pp. 56.

Defoe replied to it in—

The High Church Legion; or, The Memorial examined. Being a New Test of Moderation; as 'tis recommended to all that love the Church of England and the Constitution. London, 1705, 4to., pp. 21.

The *Memorial* itself was subjected to the fashionable process of the time, for it was presented at the Old Bailey, and ordered by the Court to be burnt by the common hangman.

In *The Review* for October 30, 1705, Defoe inserted the following advertisement, which was probably a *jeu d'esprit*, as the work never appeared:—

Preparing for the press, and to be published in a few days, the first volume of twenty-six centuries of *Highflying Churchmen* in England, who have sworn allegiance to the Government, and get their bread under the protection of it; basely and villainously betray the nation and the Church, by openly and maliciously aiding, siding with, and abetting the Popish and non-juring party in England; abusing the queen, the bishops, and the best Churchmen in the kingdom; fomenting divisions amongst Protestants, and diligently widening the unhappy breaches of the nation. To which are added large collections of their wise sayings and common maxims in favour of Popery, and an abhorrence of moderation: together with the characters and abridgments of their respective histories; and a large examination of two new *High-Church* maxims: 1. I had rather be a Papist than a Presbyterian; 2. I had rather go to hell than to a meeting-house; both learnedly asserted by two vigorous defenders of *High Church* principles; one a man of the gown, and the other of the sword.

In the same year he wrote—

The Experiment; or, the Shortest Way with the Dissenters exemplified. Being the case of Mr. Abraham Gill, a Dissenting Minister in the Isle of Ely, and a full account of his being sent for a soldier, by Mr. Fern (an Ecclesiastical Justice of Peace) and other conspirators, to the eternal honour of the temper and moderation of *High-Church* principles. London, 1705, 4to., pp. 58.

As this book did not sell well, it was issued with a new title-page as a second edition. It was then called—

The Modesty and Sincerity of those Worthy Gentlemen, commonly called High Churchmen, exemplified in a modern Instance. London, 1707.

ANTIQUITY OF THE POLKA.

The description of the *lavolta*, in Sir John Davies's poem on dancing, *The Orchestra* (1596), shows that it must have closely resembled the dance which we fondly boast of as one of the great inventions of the nineteenth century. It runs as follows :—

Yet is there one, the most delightful kind,
A lofty jumping, or a leaping round,
Where arm in arm two dancers are entwined,
And whirl themselves with strict embracements bound;
And still their feet an anapæst do sound;
An anapæst is all their music's song,
Whose first two feet are short, and third is long.

The "anapæst" is conclusive; it points exactly to the peculiar nature of the polka, the pause on the *third* step. Moreover, it appears, that as there is no especial figure for the polka, so there was none for the lavolta; for it is classed among those dances

Wherein that dancer greatest praise has won,
Which, with best order, can all orders shun;
For every where he wantonly must range,
And turn and wind with unexpected change.

Who can doubt after that? The polka was certainly danced before Queen Elizabeth!

To this valuable historical parallel, it may be added that the galliard and coranto also were apparently danced *ad libitum* (observing only a particular measure), just as our waltz and gallop also are :—

For more diverse and more pleasing show,
A swift, a *wandering* dance, he [Love] did invent,
With *passages uncertain* to and fro,
Yet with a certain answer and consent,
To the quick music of the instrument.

A CUSTOM OF "YE ENGLYSHE."

When a more than ordinarily doubtful matter is offered us for credence, we are apt to inquire of the teller if he "sees any green" in our optics, accompanying the query by an elevation of the right eyelid with the forefinger. Now, regarding this merely as a "fast" custom, I marvelled greatly at finding a similar action noted by worthy Master Blunt, as conveying to his mind an analogous meaning. I can scarcely credit its antiquity; but what other meaning can I understand from the episode he relates? He had been trying to pass himself off as a native, but—

The third day, in the morning, I, prying up and down alone, met a Turke, who, in Italian, told me, Ah! are you an Englishman? and with a *kind of malicious posture laying his forefinger under his eye*, methought he had the lookes of a designe.—*Voyage in the Levant, performed by Mr. Henry Blunt*, p. 60: Lond. 1650.

—a silent, but expressive, "posture," tending to eradicate any previously-formed opinion of the verdantness of Mussulmans!

THE FALLACY OF TRADITIONS.

Several communications have already proved how little reliance is to be placed upon the traditions repeated by vergers and guides to wondering lionizers. A collection of other instances, where the test of science and archæological investigation have exposed their falsity, would be interesting and instructive. In spite of Sir Samuel Meyrick's judicious arrangement of the armor in the tower, the beef-eaters still persist in relating the old stories handed down. At Warwick Castle the rib of the dun cow is ascertained to be a bone of a fossil elephant, and Guy's porridge-pot a military cooking utensil of the time of Charles I. St. Crispin's chair, carefully preserved in Linlithgow Cathedral by insertion in the wall, is of mahogany—an American wood! The chair of Charles I. at Leicester bears a crown, which, having been the fashionable ornament after the Restoration, together with the form, betrays the date. Queen Eleanor's crosses, it now appears, were not built by her affectionate husband, but by her own direction and her own money. The fire-place and other objects in belted Will's bedroom, at Naworth Castle, are manifestly of later date. The curious bed treasured up near Leicester as that occupied by Richard III., immediately before the battle of Bosworth, is in the style commonly called Elizabethan. Queen Mary's bed at Holyrood is of the last century; and her room at Hardwicke is in a house which was not erected till after her death; the tapestry and furniture, however, may have been removed from the old hall where she was imprisoned. The tower of Caernarvon Castle, in which the first Prince of Wales is supposed to have been born, is not of so early a period. In short, archæologists seem to show that there is not only nothing *new* under the sun, but that there is also nothing *true* under the sun.

DESCENDANTS OF DEFOE.

A son of Daniel shines in Pope's *Dunciad.* Does the following notice refer to a son of that son? It is extracted from an old Wiltshire paper :—

On the 2 Jan. 1771, two young men, John Clark and John Joseph Defoe, said to be a grandson * to the celebrated author of the *True Born Englishman*,

* It appears from Wilson's Life that he was a great-grandson.

&c., were executed at Tyburn for robbing Mr. F——, the banker, of a watch and a trifling sum of money on the highway,—

and the writer then proceeds to moralize on the inequality of that code of laws, which could visit with death the author of a burglary committed on another man, who, by the failure of his bank, had recently produced an unexampled scene of distress, in the ruin of many families, and was yet suffered to go scatheless.

Another notice, which is also extracted from a Wiltshire paper, is dated 1836.

In a street adjoining Hungerford Market, there is now living, "to fortune and to fame unknown," the great-grandson of the author of *Robinson Crusoe.* His trade is that of a carpenter, and he is much respected in the neighborhood. His father, a namesake of this great progenitor, was for many years a creditable tradesman in the old Hungerford Market.

It is doubtless of the latter that the *Edinburgh Review* (Oct. 1815, p. 487) speaks. It is there stated that he was then living in London, "a creditable tradesman in Hungerford Market. His manners give a favorable impression of his sense and morals. He is neither unconscious of his ancestor's fame, nor ostentatious of it." He is there stated to be a great-grandson of Defoe, and not a grandson, as is implied in the preceding notice.

ZACHARY BOYD.

The well known *couplet* about Pharaoh—

And was not Pharaoh a saucy rascal?
That would not let the children of Israel, their wives
And their little ones, their flocks and their herds, go
Out into the wilderness forty days
To eat the Pascal.

is from a certain *History of the Bible* or *Bible History*, by the Rev. Dr. Zachary Boyd, of Todrig, who was either Principal or Professor of Divinity at Glasgow in the seventeenth century.

He left considerable property to the College there, on condition that his bust should be placed in the quadrangle, and his great work printed under the care of the Academical Senatus. The bust was placed accordingly, and is, or lately was, to be seen in a niche over the inner doorway. The *History* was also printed, it is said, but never published. However, curious visitors have always been allowed a peep into it, and a few choice morsels are current. This is one stave of the lamentation of Jonah :—

Lord! what a doleful place is this!
There's neither coal nor candle;
And nothing I but fishes' tripes
And greasy guts do handle.

Speaking of Zackariah Boyd, Granger says (vol. ii. p. 379) :—

His translation of the Scripture, in such uncouth verse as to amount to burlesque, has been often quoted, and the just fame of a benefactor to learning has been obscured by that cloud of miserable rhymes. Candor will smile at the foible, but applaud the man.

Macure, in his account of Glasgow, p. 223, informs us he lived in the reign of Charles I.

ODD TITLES.

In 1686 a pamphlet was published in London, entitled *A most Delectable Sweet Perfumed Nosegay for God's Saints to Smell at.* About the year 1649, there was published a work entitled *A Pair of Bellows to blow off the Dust cast upon John Fry;* and another, called *The Snuffers of Divine Love.* Cromwell's time was particularly famous for title-pages. The author of a work on charity entitled his book, *Hooks and Eyes for Believers' Breeches.* Another, who professed a wish to exalt poor human nature, calls his labors *High-heeled Shoes for Dwarfs in Holiness.* And another, *Crumbs of Comfort for the Chickens of the Covenant.* A Quaker, whose outward man the powers that were thought proper to imprison, published *A Sigh of Sorrow for the Sinners of Zion, breathed out of a Hole in the Wall of an Earthly Vessel, known among Men by the Name of Samuel Fish.* About the same time there was also published, *The Spiritual Mustard Pot, to make the Soul Sneeze with Devotion; Salvation's Vantage-ground, or a Louping Sand for Heavy Believers.* Another, *A Shot aimed at the Devil's Head-quarters, through the Tube of the Cannon of the Covenant.* This is an author who speaks plain language, which the most illiterate reprobate cannot fail to understand. Another, *A Reaping-hook, well tempered, for the Stubborn Ears of the coming Crop; or, Biscuit Baked in the Oven of Charity, carefully conserved for the Chickens of the Church, the Sparrows of the Spirit, and the sweet Swallows of Salvation.* To another we have the following copious description of its contents :—

> *Seven Sobs of a Sorrowful Soul for Sin, or the Seven Penitential Psalms of the Princely Prophet David; whereunto are also added, William Humius's Handful of Honeysuckles, and divers Godly and Pithy Ditties now newly augmented.*

Another work has the following quaint title :—

> *The Christian Sodality: or, Catholic Hive of Bees, sucking the Honey of the Churches' Prayer from the Blossomes of the Word of God, blowne out of the Epistles and Gospels of the Divine Service throughout the yeare. Collected by the Puny Bee of all the Hive, not worthy to be named otherwise than by these Elements of his Name, F. P. Printed in the Yeare of our Lord,* 1652.

OMISSION OF "DEI GRATIA."

Ruding, in his *Annals of the Coinage*, iv. 9, furnishes a precedent for the omission of the words Dei Gratia from the coinage, in the case of the Irish half-pence and farthings coined at the Tower in 1736–7. And he supplies, also, a precedent for the dissatisfaction with which their omission from the new florin has been received, in the shape of two epigrams written at that time, for which he is indebted (as what writer upon any point of English literature and history is not) to Sylvanus Urban. The first (from the *Gentleman's Magazine* for June, 1837) is as follows:—

No Christian kings that I can find,
However match'd or odd,
Excepting ours, have ever coin'd
Without the *grace of God.*

By this acknowledgment they show
The mighty King of Kings,
As him from whom their riches flow,
From whom their grandeur springs.

Come, then, Urania, aid my pen,
The latent cause assign,—
All other kings are mortal men,
But GEORGE, 'tis plain, 's divine.

SHAKSPEARIAN NAMES.

The following Shakspearian note is from a periodical now defunct:—

It appears from an old MS. in the British Museum, that amongst canoniers serving in Normandy in 1436, were "Wm. Pistail—R. Bardolf."

Query: Were these common English names, or did these identical canoniers transmit a traditional fame, good or bad, to the time of Shakspeare, in song or story?

Mr. Collier (Life prefixed to the edit. of *Shakspeare*, p. 139) was the first to notice that Bardolph, Fluellen, and Awdrey, were names of persons living at Stratford in the lifetime of the poet; and Mr. Halliwell (*Life of Shakspeare*, pp. 126–7) has carried the subject still further, and shown that the names of ten characters in the plays are also found in the early records of that town. Poins was, I believe, a common Welsh name.

FIELD OF FORTY FOOTSTEPS.

Mr. Cunningham, in his *Handbook of London*, has given no account of a piece of ground of which a strange story is recorded by Southey, in his *Common-Place Book* (Second Series, p. 21). After quoting a letter received from a friend, recommending him to "take a view of those wonderful marks of the Lord's hatred to *duelling*, called the '*Brother's Steps*,'" and giving him the description of the locality, Mr. Southey gives an account of his own visit to the spot (a field supposed to bear ineffaceable marks of the footsteps of two brothers, who fought a fatal duel about a love affair) in these words:—

> We sought for nearly half an hour in vain. We could find no steps at all, within a quarter of a mile, no nor half a mile, of Montague House. We were almost out of hope, when an honest man who was at work directed us to the next ground adjoining to a pond. There we found what we sought, about three quarters of a mile north of Montague House, and about five hundred yards east of Tottenham Court Road. The steps answer Mr. Walsh's description. They are of the size of a large human foot, about three inches deep, and lie nearly from northeast to southwest. We counted only seventy-six, but we were not exact in counting. The place where one or both brothers are supposed to have fallen, is still bare of grass. The labourer also showed us the bank where (the tradition is) the wretched woman sat to see the combat.

Mr. Southey then goes on to speak of his full confidence in the tradition of their indestructibility, even after ploughing up, and of the conclusions to be drawn from the circumstance.

The fields behind Montague House were, from about the year 1680, until towards the end of the last century, the scenes of robbery, murder, and every species of depravity and wickedness of which the heart can think. They appear to have been originally called the Long Fields, and afterwards (about Strype's time) the Southampton Fields. These fields remained waste and useless, with the exception of some nursery grounds near the New Road to the north, and a piece of ground enclosed for the Toxopholite Society, towards the northwest, near the back of Gower Street. The remainder was the resort of depraved wretches, whose amusements consisted chiefly in fighting pitched battles, and other disorderly sports, especially on the Sabbath day. Such was their state in 1800.

Tradition had given to the superstitious at that period a legendary story of the period of the Duke of Monmouth's Rebellion, of two brothers who fought in this field so ferociously as to destroy each other; since which, their footsteps, formed from the vengeful struggle, were said to remain, with the indentations produced by their advancing and receding; nor could any grass or vegetable ever be produced where these *forty footsteps* were thus displayed. This extraordinary arena was said to be at the extreme termination of the northeast end of Upper Montague Street; and, profiting by the fiction, Miss Porter and her sister produced an ingenious romance thereon, entitled, *Coming Out, or the Forty Footsteps.* The Messrs. Mayhew also, some twenty years back, brought out, at the Tottenham Street Theatre, an excellent melo-drama piece, founded upon the same story, entitled *The Field of Forty Footsteps.*

The latest account of these *footsteps*, previous to their being built over, with which I am acquainted, is the following, extracted from one of Joseph Moser's *Common-place Books*:—

June 16, 1800.—Went into the fields at the back of Montague House, and there saw, for the last time, the *forty footsteps*; the building materials are there ready to cover them from the sight of man. I counted more than *forty*, but they might be the footprints of the workmen.

This extract is valuable, as it establishes the period of the final demolition of the footsteps, and also confirms the legend that *forty* was the original number.

CHARADES.

Can any one tell who is the author of the following charade? It has been said that Dr. Robinson, a physician, wrote it:—

Me, the contented man desires,
The poor man has, the rich requires;
The miser gives, the spendthrift saves,
And all must carry to their graves.

It can scarcely be necessary to add that the answer is, *nothing.*

BOOKSELLING IN CALCUTTA.

Any one who may have visited the capital of British India will recollect the native *kitaub-wallahs* or booksellers, who drive a good trade in the streets of Calcutta, by thrusting their second-hand literature into the *palanquins* of the passers, and their pertinacity and success in fixing *master* with a bargain. These *flying bibliopoles* draw their supplies from the daily auctions arising out of the migratory habits of the mortality to which the residents in that city are subject; and it would somewhat astonish our *Sothebys* and *Putticks* to see the extent of these sales of literary property, and derange their *tympanums* to hear the clamorous competition among the aforesaid half-naked dealers for lots not catalogued with their bibliographical precision. The books thus purchased are subject to the overhaul of the better-informed of the tribe before they make their appearance in the streets; when deficiencies are made good, bindings vamped, and lettering attempted: finally, they are placed in the hands of the hawkers, when the following peculiarities are detectable:—Where a title or last leaf may have been wanting, these *Calcutta editions* occasionally display a *prophane* book with a *sacred* title; or a *pious treatise*, for the sake of the word "Finis," made complete by affixing the last leaf of *Tristram Shandy* or the *Devil on Two*

Sticks! Less intelligent jobbers will open their book, and, finding the first word "Preface," clap it incontinently in gilt letters on the back! The imagination of the reader can fill up the *cross-readings* which would likely result from such practices.

Some twenty years ago, then, the dingy tribes were startled, and the auctioneer gratified by the appearance of a new face in the *bidders' box*—a brisk little European, who contested every lot, aiming, apparently, at a monopoly in the second-hand book trade. Shortly thereafter, this individual, having located himself in a commanding position, came forth in the daily papers as a candidate for public favor; and, in allusion to the reformation he contemplated, and his sovereign contempt for his black brethren, headed his address, to the no small amusement of the lieges, in the *Falstaffian* vein:—

> . . No eyes hath seen such *scarecrows.*
> I'll not march thro' Coventry with them, that's flat!

This joke was no doubt thrown away upon his Hindoo and Mussulman rivals, but alas for the reformer! he little knew the cold indifference of the Anglo-Indian about such matters, and, as might have been expected, he failed in establishing himself in business, and ultimately fell a victim to the climate. He was a son of Thomas Holcroft, a dramatist of repute in his day.

THE MAIDS AND WIDOWS.

The following petition, signed by sixteen maids of Charleston, South Carolina, was presented to the Governor of that province on March 1, 1733–4, "the day of the feast:"

To His Excellency Governor Johnson.

The humble Petition of all the Maids whose names are underwritten:

Whereas we the humble petitioners are at present in a very melancholy disposition of mind, considering how all the bachelors are blindly captivated by widows, and our more youthful charms thereby neglected: the consequence of this our request is, that your Excellency will for the future order that no widow shall presume to marry any young man till the maids are provided for; or else to pay each of them a fine for satisfaction, for invading our liberties; and likewise a fine to be laid on all such bachelors as shall be married to widows. The great disadvantage it is to us maids, is, that the widows, by their forward carriages, do snap up the young men; and have the vanity to think their merits beyond ours, which is a great imposition upon us who ought to have the preference.

This is humbly recommended to your Excellency's consideration, and hope you will prevent any farther insults.

And we poor Maids as in duty bound will ever pray.

P. S.—I, being the oldest Maid, and therefore most concerned, do think it proper to be the messenger to your Excellency in behalf of my fellow subscribers.

BLACKGUARD.

The following from Butler and Fuller, refer obviously to a popular superstition, during an age when the belief in witchcraft and hobgoblins was universal; and when such creatures of fancy were assigned as *Black Guards* to his Satanic majesty. "Who can conceive," says Fuller, "but that such a Prince-principal of Darkness must be proportionally attended by a Black Guard of monstrous opinions?" (*Church History*, b. ix. c. xvi.) Hudibras, when deceived by Ralpho counterfeiting a ghost in the dark—

> Believed it was some drolling sprite
> That *staid upon the guard* at night:

and thereupon in his trepidation discourses with the Squire as follows:—

> Thought he, How does the *Devil* know
> What 'twas that I design'd to do?
> His office of intelligence,
> His oracles, are ceas'd long since;
> And he knows nothing of the Saints,
> But what some treach'rous spy acquaints.

This is some petty-fogging *fiend*,
Some under door-keeper's friend's friend,
That undertakes to understand,
And juggles at the second-hand:
And now would pass for spirit Po,
And all men's dark concerns foreknow.
I think I need not fear him for't;
These rallying *devils* do not hurt.
With that he roused his drooping heart,
And hastily cry'd out, What art?—
A wretch, quoth he, whom want of grace
Has brought to this unhappy place.
  I do believe thee, quoth the knight;
Thus far I'm sure thou'rt in the right,
And know what 'tis that troubles thee,
Better than thou hast guess'd of me.
Thou art some paltry, *blackguard sprite*,
Condemn'd to drudg'ry in the night;
Thou hast no work to do in th' house,
Nor half-penny to drop in shoes;
Without the raising of which sum
You dare not be so troublesome;
To pinch the slatterns black and blue,
For leaving you their work to do.
This is your business, good Pug Robin,
And your diversion, dull dry bobbing.

Hudibras, Part III. Canto 1, line 1385, &c.

It will be seen that Butler, like Fuller, uses the term in the simple sense as a *guard* of the Prince of Darkness. But the concluding lines of Hudibras's address to Ralpho explain the process by which, at a late period, this term of the *Black Guard* came to be applied to the lowest class of domestics in great establishments.

The Black Guard of Satan was supposed to perform the domestic drudgery of the kitchen and servants' hall, in the infernal household. This extract from Hobbes refers to this:—

Since my Lady's decay, I am degraded from a cook; and I fear the Devil himself will entertain me but for one of his *black guard*, and he shall be sure to have his roast burnt.

Hence came the popular superstition that these goblin scullions, on their visits to the upper world, confined themselves to the servants' apartments of the houses which they favored with their presence, and which at night they swept and garnished; pinching those of the maids in their sleep who, by their laziness, had imposed such toil on their elfin assistants; but *slipping money into the shoes* of the more tidy and industrious servants, whose attention to their own duties before going to rest had spared the goblins the task of performing their share of the drudgery. Hudibras apostrophises the ghost as—

. . . some paltry *blackguard* sprite
Condemn'd to drudgery in the night;
Thou hast no work to do in th' house
Nor half-penny to drop in shoes;

and therefore, as the knight concluded—"this devil full of malice" had found sufficient leisure to taunt and rally him in the dark upon his recent disasters.

This belief in the visits of domestic spirits, who busy themselves at night in sweeping and arranging the lower apartments, has prevailed in the North of Ireland and in Scotland from time immemorial: and it is explained in Sir Walter Scott's notes to the *Lay of the Last Minstrel*, as his justification for introducing the goblin page Gilpin Horner amongst the domestics of Branksome Hall. Perhaps, from the association of these elves with the lower household duties, but more probably from a more obvious cause, came at a later period the practice described by Gifford in his note on Ben Jonson, by which—

In all great houses, but particularly in the Royal Residences, there were a number of mean, dirty dependents, whose office it was to attend the wool-yard, sculleries, &c. Of these, the most forlorn wretches seem to have been selected to carry coals to the kitchens, halls, &c. To this smutty regiment, who attended the progresses, and rode in the carts with the pots and kettles, the people, in derision, gave the name of the *black guards.*

This is no doubt correct: and hence the expression of Beaumont and Fletcher, in the *Elder Brother*, that—

> . . . . . from the *black guard*
> To the grim Sir in office, there are few
> Hold other tenets:

meaning from the lowest domestic to the highest functionary of a household. This, too, explains the force of the allusion, in Jardine's *Criminal Trials*, to the apartments of Euston House being "far unmeet for her Highness, but fitter for the Black Guard"—that is, for the scullions and lowest servants of an establishment. Swift employs the word in this sense when he says, in the extract quoted by Dr. Johnson in his *Dictionary* in illustration of the meaning of *blackguard*—

Let a black-guard boy be always about the house to send on your errands, and go to market for you on rainy days.

Burton likewise affords an instance of a similar use of the word:—

The same author, Cardan, in his *Hyperchen*, out of the doctrine of the Stoicks, will have some of these genii (for so he calls them), to be desirous of men's company, very affable and familiar with them, as dogs are; others again, to abhor as serpents, and care not for them. The same, belike, Trithemius calls *igneos et sublunares, qui nunquam demergunt ad inferiora, aut vix ullum habent in terris commercium: generally they far excel men in worth, as a man the meanest worm;* though some there are *inferiour to those of their own rank in worth, as the black guard in a princes court, and to men again, as some degenerate, base, rational creatures are excelled of brute beasts.—Anat. of Mel.*, Part I. sec. 2, Mem. 1, Subs. 2.

It will thus be seen, that of the authors quoted, no one makes use of the term *black guard* in an opprobrious sense, such as attaches to the more modern word "blackguard;" and that they all wrote within the first fifty years of the seventeenth century. It must therefore be subsequent not only to that date, but to the reign of Queen Anne, that we are to look for its general acceptance in its present contumelious sense.

Within the last two centuries, a number of words of honest origin have passed into an opprobrious sense; for example, the oppressed tenants of Ireland are spoken of by Spenser and Sir John Davies as "*villains.*" In our version of the Scriptures, "*cunning*" implies merely skill in music and in art. Shakspeare employs the word "*vagabond*" as often to express pity as reproach; and it will be found, that as a *knave*, prior to the reign of Elizabeth, meant merely a serving man, so a *blackguard* was the name for a pot-boy or scullion in the reign of Queen Anne. The transition into its more modern meaning took place at a later period, on the importation of a foreign word, to which, being already interchangeable in sound, it speedily became assimilated in sense.

The following document is in the Lord Steward's offices. The name blackguard in it is applied to the number of masterless boys hanging about the verge of the Court and other public places, palaces, coal-cellars, and palace stables; ready with links to light coaches and chairs, and conduct, and rob people on foot, through the dark streets of London; nay, to follow the Court in its progresses to Windsor and Newmarket. Pope's "link-boys vile" are the black-guard boys of the following Proclamation.

At the Board of Green Cloth,
in Windsor Castle,
this 7th day of May, 1683.

WHEREAS of late a sort of vicious, idle, and masterless boyes and rogues, commonly called the Black-guard, with divers other lewd and loose fellowes, vagabonds, vagrants, and wandering men and women, do usually haunt and follow the Court, to the great dishonour of the same, and as Wee are informed have been the occasion of the late dismall fires that happened in the towns of Windsor and Newmarket, and have, and frequently do commit divers other misdemeanonrs and disorders in such places where they resort, to the prejudice of His Majesty's subjects, for the prevention of which evills and misdemeanours hereafter, Wee do hereby strictly charge and command all those so called the Black-guard as aforesaid, with all other loose, idle, masterless men, boyes, rogues, and wanderers, who have intruded themselves into His Majesty's Court or stables, that within the space of twenty-four houres next after the publishing of this order, they depart, upon pain of imprisonment, and such other punishments as by law are to be inflicted on them.

(Signed) ORMOND.
H. BULKELEY.
H. BROUNCKER.
RICH. MASON.
STE. FOX.

The following lines by Charles, Earl of Dorset and Middlesex (the writer of the famous old song, "To all you ladies now at land"), are an instance of the application of this term to the turbulent link-boys, against whom the proclamation was directed. Their date is probably a short time before that of the proclamation:—

Belinda's sparkling wit and eyes,
United cast so fierce a light,
As quickly flashes, quickly dies;
Wounds not the heart, but burns the sight.
Love is all gentleness, Love is all joy:
Sweet are his looks, and soft his pace:
Her Cupid is a *black-guard boy,*
That runs his link full in your face.

In a curious old pamphlet of twenty-three pages, entitled *Everybody's Business is Nobody's Business answer'd Paragraph by Paragraph,* by a Committee of Women-Servants and Footmen, London, printed by T. Read for the author, and sold by the booksellers of London, and . . . price one penny (without date), the following passage occurs:—

The next great Abuse among us is, that under the Notion of cleaning our Shoes, above ten Thousand Wicked, Idle, Pilfering Vagrants are permitted to stroll about our City and Suburbs. These are called the *Black-Guard,* who Black your Honour's Shoes, and incorporate themselves under the Title of the *Worshipful Company of Japanners.* But the Subject is so low that it becomes disagreeable even to myself; give me leave therefore to propose a Way to clear the streets of those Vermin, and to substitute as many honest and industrious persons in their stead, who are now starving for want of bread, while those execrable villains live (though in Rags and Nastiness) yet in Plenty and Luxury.

A(nswer). *The next Abuse you see is,* Black your shoes, your Honour, *and the* Japanners *stick in his Stomach. We shall not take upon us to answer for these pitiful Scrubs, but in his own words;* the Subject is so low, that it becomes disagreeable even to us, *as it does* even to himself, *and he may* clear the Streets of these Vermin *in what Manner he pleases if the Law will give him leave, for we are in no want of them; we are better provided for already in that respect by our Masters and their Sons.*

SONNET (QUERY, BY MILTON).

In a *Collection of Recente and Witty Pieces by several eminente hands*, London, printed by W. S. for Simon Waterfou, 1628, p. 109, is the following sonnet, far the best thing in the book:—

ON THE LIBRARIE AT CAMBRIDGE.

In that great maze of books I sighed and said,—
It is a grave-yard, and each tome a tombe;
Shrouded in hempen rags, behold the dead,
Coffined and ranged in crypts of dismal gloom,
Food for the worm and redolent of mold,
Traced with brief epitaph in tarnished gold—
Ah, golden lettered hope!—ah, dolorous doom!
Yet mid the common death, where all is cold,
And mildewed pride in desolation dwells,
A few great immortalities of old
Stand brightly forth—not tombes but living shrines,
Where from high sainte or martyr virtue wells,
Which on the living yet work miracles,
Spreading a relic wealth richer than golden mines.

J. M. 1627.

Attached to it, it will be seen, are the initials J. M. and the date 1627. Is it possible that this may be an early and neglected sonnet of Milton?

"THE PORRIDGE" CONTROVERSY.

An analysis of the "divers pamphlets published against the Book of Common Prayer" would make a very curious volume. Take a passage from the *Anatomy of the Service Book*, for instance:—

The cruellest of the American Savages, called the Mohaukes, though they fattened their captive Christians to the slaughters, yet they eat them up at once; but the Service-book and savages eat up the servants of God by piecemeal: keeping them alive (if it may be called a life) *ut sentiant se mori*, that they may be the more sensible of their dying.—p. 56.

Sir Walter Scott quotes a curious tract in *Woodstock*, entitled *Vindication of the Book of Common Prayer against the contumelious slanders of the Fanatic Party terming it "Porridge."* The author of this singular and rare tract (says Sir W.) indulges in the allegorical style, till he fairly hunts down the allegory. The learned divine chases his metaphor at a very cold scent, through a pamphlet of six mortal quarto pages.

The following are some titles of books written on the Porridge controversy:—

Messe of Pottage, very well seasoned and crumbed with Bread of Life, and easie to be digested, against the contumelious Slanderers of the Divine Service. A Pottage, set forth by Gyles Calfine. London, 1642, 4to.

Answer to lame Giles Calfine's *Messe of Pottage*, proving that the Service Booke is no better than Pottage, in comparison of divers Weeds which are chopt into it to poyson the taste of the Children of Grace, by the Advice of the Whore of Babylon's Instruments and Cooks. London, 1642, 4to.

Answer, in Defence of a *Messe of Pottage well seasoned and crumb'd*, against the last, which falsely says the Common Prayers are unlawfull, and no better than the Pope's Porrage. London, 1642, 4to.

Fresh Bit of Mutton for those fleshly-minded Cannibals that cannot endure Pottage; or, a Defence of Giles Calfine's *Messe of Pottage*, against the idle yet insolent exceptions of his monstrous Adversary. London, 1642, 4to.

Another curious-titled book is George Lightbodie's:—

Against the Apple of the Left Eye of Antichrist; or The Masse-Booke of

Lurking Darknesse (*The Liturgy*), making Way for the Apple of the Right Eye of Antichrist, the Compleate Masse-Booke of Palpable Darknesse. London. 1638. 8vo.

GROG.

Jack loves to give a pet nickname to his favorite officers. The gallant Edward Vernon (a Westminster man by birth) was not exempted from the general rule. His gallantry and ardent devotion to his profession endeared him to the service. In bad weather he was in the habit of walking the deck in a rough *grogram* cloak, and thence had obtained the nickname of *Old Grog*. Whilst in command of the West India station, and at the height of his popularity on account of his reduction of Porto Bello with six men-of-war only, he introduced the use of rum and water by the ship's company. When served out, the new beverage proved most palatable, and speedily grew into such favor that it became as popular as the brave admiral himself, and in honor of him was surnamed by acclamation "Grog."

THE ORIGIN OF GROG.

Written on board the Berwick, a few days before Admiral Parker's engagement with the Dutch fleet, on the 5th of August, 1781. By Dr. TROTTER.

'Tis sung on proud Olympus' hill
The Muses bear record,
Ere half the gods had drank their fill
The sacred nectar sour'd.

At Neptune's toast the bumper stood,
Britannia crown'd the cup;
A thousand Nereids from the flood
Attend to serve it up.

"This nauseous juice," the monarch cries,
"Thou darling child of fame,
Tho' it each earthly clime denies,
Shall never bathe thy name.

"Ye azure tribes that rule the sea,
And rise at my command,
Bid *Vernon* mix a draught for me
To toast his native land."

Swift o'er the waves the Nereids flew,
Where *Vernon's* flag appear'd;
Around the shores they sung "True Blue,"
And Britain's hero cheer'd.

A mighty bowl on deck he drew,
And filled it to the brink;
Such drank the Burford's* gallant crew,
And such the gods shall drink.

The sacred robe which Vernon wore
Was drenched within the same;
And hence his virtues guard our shore,
And *Grog* derives its name.

THE FORLORN HOPE.

In John Dymmoks' *Treatise of Ireland*, written about the year 1600, and published among the *Tracts relating to Ireland, printed for the Irish Archæological Society*, vol. ii., is the following paragraph.—

Before the vant-guard marched the *forelorn hope*, consisting of forty shott and twenty shorte weapons, with order that they should not discharge untill they presented theire pieces to the rebells' breasts in their trenches, and that soodenly the short weapons should enter the trenches pell-mell: vpon eyther syde of the vant-guarde (which was observed in the batle and reare-guarde) marched wings of shott enterlyned with pikes, to which were sent secondes with as much care and diligence as occasion required. The baggage, and a parte of the horse, marched before the battell; the rest of the horse troopes fell in before the *rearewarde* except thirty, which, in the head of the *rearelorne hope*, conducted by Sir Hen. Danvers, made the retreit of the whole army.—P. 32.

* Flag-ship at the taking of Porto-Bello.

The terms *rearelorne hope* and *forlorne hope* occur constantly in the same work, and bear the same signification as in the foregoing.

The late Dr. Graves wrote the following notice of the word in the *Dublin Quarterly Journal of Medical Science*, in Feb. 1849 :—

Military and civil writers of the present day seem quite ignorant of the true meaning of the words *forlorn hope*. The adjective has nothing to do with despair, nor the substantive with the "charmer which lingers still behind;" there was no such poetical depth in the words as originally used. Every corps marching in any enemy's country had a small body of men at the head (*haupt* or *hope*) of the advanced guard; and which was termed the *forlorne hope* (*lorn* being here but a termination similar to *ward* in *forward*), while another small body at the head of the rere guard was called the *rear-lorn hope* (xx). A reference to Johnson's *Dictionary* proves that civilians were misled as early as the time of Dryden by the mere sound of a technical military phrase; and, in process of time, even military men forgot the true meaning of the words. It grieves me to sap the foundations of an error to which we are indebted for Byron's beautiful line—

The full of hope, misnamed *forlorn*.

THE WANDERING BEE.

High mountains closed the vale,
Bare, rocky mountains, to all living things
Inhospitable; on whose sides no herb
Rooted, no insect fed, no bird awoke
Their echoes, save the eagle, strong of wing;
A lonely plunderer, that afar
Sought in the vales his prey.

Thither towards those mountains Thalaba
Advanced, for well he ween'd that there had Fate
Destined the adventure's end.
Up a wide vale, winding amid their depths,
A stony vale between receding heights
Of stone, he wound his way.

A cheerless place! *The solitary Bee,*
Whose buzzing was the only sound of life,
Flew there on restless wing,
Seeking in vain one blossom, where to fix.
Thalaba, book VI. 12, 13.

This incident of the wandering bee, highly poetical, seems at first sight very improbable, and passes for one of the many strange creations of this wild poem. But yet it is quite true to nature, and was probably suggested to Southey, an omnivorous reader, by some out-of-the-way book of travels.

In Hurton's *Voyage to Lapland*, vol. ii. p. 251, published a few years since, he says that as he stood on the verge of the North Cape—

The only living creature that came near me was a *bee*, which hummed merrily by. What did the busy insect seek there? Not a blade of grass grew, and the only vegetable matter on this point was a cluster of withered moss at the very edge of the awful precipice, and it I gathered at considerable risk, as a memorial of my visit.

So in Frémont's *Exploring Expedition to the Rocky Mountains*, 1842, p. 69, he speaks of standing on the crest of the snow-peak, 13,570 feet above the Gulf of Mexico, and adds :—

During our morning's ascent, we had met no sign of animal life, except the small sparrow-like bird already mentioned. A stillness the most profound, and a terrible solitude, forced themselves constantly on the mind as the great features of the place. Here on the summit, where the stillness was absolute, unbroken by any sound, and the solitude complete, we thought ourselves beyond the region of animated life; but while we were sitting on the rock, a *solitary bee* (*Bromus*, the humble bee), came winging his flight from the eastern valley, and lit on the knee of one of the men.

It was a strange place, the icy rock and the highest peak of the Rocky Mountains, for a lover of warm sunshine and flowers; and we pleased ourselves with the idea that he was the first of his species to cross the mountain barrier, a solitary pioneer to foretell the advance of civilization. I believe that a moment's thought would have made us let him continue his way unharmed, but we carried out the law of this country, where all animated nature seems at war; and seizing him immediately, put him in at least a fit place, in the leaves of a large book, among the flowers we had collected on our way.

WEATHER RULES.

Thomas Passenger, who dwelt at the Three Bibles and Star, on London Bridge, was very celebrated during the latter part of the seventeenth century for publishing popular histories and chap-books. His shop seems to have been the principal place of resort for the hawkers who then supplied the provinces with literature. Many of the works which issued from his press are now very rare: one of the most curious, and, at the same time, the rarest, is *The Shepherd's Kalendar; or, the Citizen's and Country Man's Daily Companion*, &c. The contents of this book are of a very singular nature, it being a kind of epitome of the facts it was then thought necessary for a countryman to be acquainted with. A considerable portion of the work is occupied by remarks on the weather, and on lucky and unlucky days.

We are informed, under the head "Observations on Remarkable Days, to know how the whole Year will succeed in Weather, Plenty," &c., that—

If the sun shine clear and bright on Christmas-day, it promiseth a peaceable year from clamours and strife, and foretells much plenty to ensue; but if the wind blow stormy towards sunset, it betokeneth sickness in the spring and autumn quarters.

If January 25 (being St. Paul's day), be fair, it promises a happy year; but if cloudy, windy, or rainy, otherwise: hear in this case what an ancient judicious astrologer writes:—

If St. Paul be fair and clear,
It promises then a happy year;
But if it chance to snow or rain,
Then will be dear all sorts of grain:
Or if the wind do blow aloft,
Great stirs will vex the world full oft;
And if dark clouds do muff the sky,
Then foul and cattle oft will die.

Mists or hoar frosts on tde tenth of March betokens (*sic*) a plentiful year, but not without some diseases.

If, in the fall of the leaf in October, many of them wither on the bows, and hang there, it betokens a frosty winter and much snow.

Under "The Signs of Rain in Creatures" we have the following:—

When the hern or bitron flies low, the air is gross, and thickening into showers.

The froggs much croaking in ditches and pools, &c., in the evening, foretells rain in little time to follow: also, the sweating of stone pillars or tombs denotes rain.

The often doping or diving of water-fowl foreshows rain is at hand.

The peacock's much crying denotes rain.

TELEGRAPHING THROUGH WATER.

Dr. Franklin, in 1748, thus wrote to his friend Peter Collinson of London:—

Chagrined a little that we have hitherto been able to produce nothing in this way of use to mankind, and the hot weather coming on when electrical experiments are not so agreeable, it is proposed to put an end to them for the season, somewhat humorously, in a party of pleasure on the banks of the Schuylkill. Spirits at the same time are to be fired by *a spark sent from side to side through the river without any other conductor than the water; an experiment which we some time since performed to the amazement of many.* A turkey is to be killed for our dinner by the electric shock, and roasted by the electric jack, before a fire kindled by the electrified bottle; when the health of all the famous electricians of England, Holland, France, and Germany, are to be drunk in electrified bumpers, under a discharge of guns from the electrical battery.

LIFE AND DEATH.

1. *To die is better than to live.*

I praised the dead which are already dead more than the living which are yet alive. Yea, better is he than both they, which hath not yet been, who hath not seen the evil work that is done under the sun —*Eccles.* iv. 2, 3.

Great travail is created for every man, and a heavy yoke upon the sons of

Adam, from the day that they go out of their *mother's womb*, till the day that they return to the *mother of all things*.—*Ecclus.* xl. 1 : cf. 2 *Esdr.* vii. 12, 13.

Never to have been born, the wise man first
Would wish; and, next, as soon as born to die.
Anth. Græc. (Posidippus).

In the affecting story of Cleobis and Biton, as related by Herodotus, we read :—

The *best end of life* happened to them, and the Deity showed in their case that *it is better for a man to die than to live.*

Διέδεξέ τε ἐν τούτοισι ὁ Θεὸς ὡς ἄμεινον εἴη ἀνθρώπῳ τεθάναι μᾶλλον ἢ ζώειν. —Herod., ΚΛΕΙΩ. i. 32.

As for all other living creatures, there is not one but, by a secret instinct of nature, knoweth his owne good and whereto he is made able. . . . . Man onely knoweth nothing unlesse hee be taught. He can neither speake nor goe, nor eat, otherwise than he is trained to it: and, to be short, apt and good at nothing he is naturally, but to pule and crie. And hereupon it is that some have been of this opinion, *that better it had been, and simply best, for a man never to have been born, or else speedily to die.*—Pliny's *Nat. Hist.* by Holland, Intr. to b. vii

Happy the mortal man, who now at last
Has through this doleful vale of misery passed;
Who to his destined stage has carry'd on
The tedious load, and laid his burden down;
Whom the cut brass or wounded marble shows
Victor o'er Life, and all her train of woes.
He, happier yet, who, privileged by Fate
To shorter labour and a lighter weight,
Received but yesterday the gift of breath,
Order'd to-morrow to return to death.
But O! beyond description, *happiest he*
Who ne'er must roll on life's tumultuous sea;
Who with bless'd freedom, from the general doom
Exempt, must never face the teeming womb,
Nor see the sun, nor sink into the tomb!
Who breathes must suffer; and who thinks must mourn;
And he alone is blessed who ne'er was born.
Prior's *Solomon*, b. iii.

"I have learned from religion, that an early death has often been the reward of piety," said the Emperor Julian on his death-bed. (See Gibbon, ch. xxiv.)

2. *Judge none blessed before his death.*

"Ante mortem ne laudes hominem," saith the son of Sirach, xi. 28.

Of this sentiment St. Chrysostom expresses his admiration, Hom. li. in. S. Eustath.; and heathen writers afford very close parallels:—

"Πρὶν δ' ἂν τελευτήσῃ ἐπισχέειν μηδὲ καλέειν κω ὄλβιον ἀλλ' εὐτυχέα," says Solon to Crœsus (Herod., ΚΛΕΙΩ. i. 32): cf. Aristot., *Eth. Nic.* ch. x., for a comment on this passage.

Sophocles, in the last few lines of the *Œdipus Tyrannus*, thus draws the moral of his fearful tragedy:—

Ὥστε θνητὸν ὄντ', ἐκείνην τὴν τελευταίαν ἰδεῖν
Ἡμέραν ἐπισκοποῦντα, μηδέν' ὀλβίζειν, πρὶν ἂν
Τέρμα τοῦ βίου περάσῃ, μηδὲν ἀλγεινὸν παθών.

Elmsley, on this passage, gives the following references:— Trach. I. Soph. Tereo, fr. 10; ibid. Tyndar. fr. 1; Agam., 937; Androm., 100; Troad., 509; Heracl., 865; Dionys., ap. Stob., ciii. p. 560; Gesn., cv. p. 431; Grot. To which may be added the oft-quoted lines:—

Ultima semper
Expectanda dies, homini dicique beatus
Ante obitum nemo supremaque funera debet.

In farther illustration of this passage from Ecclus., let us consider the *Death of the Righteous.*

"Let me die *the death* of the righteous, and let my *last end* be like his!" exclaims the truth-compelled and reluctant prophet, Numb. xxiii. 10.

The Royal Psalmist, after reflecting on the prosperity of the wicked in this world, adds:—

Then thought I to understand this,
But it was too hard for me,
Until I went into the sanctuary of God:
Then understood I the end of these men.—*Ps.*

And again:—

I have seen the wicked in great power,
And spreading himself like a green bay-tree;
Yet he passed away, and, lo! he was not;
Yea, I sought him, but he could not be found.
  Mark the perfect man,
And behold the upright,
For *the end* of that man is *peace*.
Ps. xxxvii. 35–37: cf. the Prayer-book version.

The prophet Isaiah declares:—

The righteous man is taken away because of the evil;
He shall go in peace, he shall rest in his bed;
Even the perfect man, he that walketh in the straight
path.—Ch. lvii., Bp. Lowth's Trans.

Sure *the last end*
Of the good man is peace! How calm his exit!
Night-dews fall not more gently to the ground,
Nor weary worn-out winds expire so soft.
Behold him! in the evening tide of life,
A life well spent, whose early care it was
His riper years should not upbraid his green:
By unperceived degrees he wears away;
Yet, like the sun, seems larger at his setting!
High in his faith and hopes, look how he reaches
After the prize in view! and, like a bird
That's hamper'd, struggles hard to get away!
Whilst the glad gates of sight are wide expanded
To let new glories in, the first fair fruits
Of the fast-coming harvest.—Blair's *Grave*.

How blest the righteous when he dies!
  When sinks the weary soul to rest!
How mildly beam the closing eyes!
  How gently heaves the expiring breast!

So fades the summer cloud away;
So sinks the gale when storms are o'er;
So gently shuts the eye of day;
So dies a wave upon the shore.

Life's duty done, as sinks the clay,
Light from its load the spirit flies;
While heaven and earth combine to say,
How blest the righteous when he dies!

Mrs. Barbauld.

An eve
Beautiful as the good man's quiet *end*,
When all of earthly now is passed away,
And heaven is in his face.—*Love's Trial.*

He sets
As sets the Morning Star, which goes not down
Behind the darken'd West, nor hides obscured
Among the tempests of the sky, but melts away
Into the light of heaven.
As sweetly as a child,
Whom neither thought disturbs nor care encumbers,
Tired with long play, at close of summer's day
Lies down and slumbers.

A holy life is the only preparation to a happy death, says Bishop Taylor. And we have seen how much importance even heathen minds attached to *peace at the last.* Truly, as Kettlewell said while expiring, "There is no *life* life a happy *death.*"

"Consider," says that excellent writer, Norris of Bemerton, "that *this* life is wholly in order to *another*, and the *time* is that sole opportunity that God has given us for transacting the great business of *eternity:* that our work is great, and our day of working short; much of which also is lost and rendered useless through the cloudiness and darkness of the morning, and the thick vapours and unwholesome fogs of the evening; the ignorance and inadvertency of youth, and the disease and infirmities of old age; that our portion of time is not only *short* as to its duration, but also *uncertain* in the possession: that the loss of it is irreparable to the loser, and profitable to nobody else:. that it shall be severely accounted for at the great judgment, and lamented in a sad eternity."—"Of the Care and Improvement of time," *Miscel.*, 6th edit., p. 118.

A NOTE ON GULLIVER'S TRAVELS.

If one may argue from the silence of the edition of *Gulliver's Travels, with Notes*, by W. C. Taylor, LL.D., Trinity College, Dublin, the preface to which is dated May 1st, 1840, one may say that all the commentators on Swift—all, at least, down to that late date—have omitted to refer to a work containing incidents closely resembling some of those recorded in the "Voyage to Lilliput."

The work alluded to is a little dramatical composition, the Bambocciata, or puppet-show, by Martelli, entitled *The Sneezing of Hercules.* Goldoni, in his *Memoirs*, has given us the following account of the manner in which he brought it out on the stage :—

Count Lantieri was very well satisfied with my father, for he was greatly recovered, and almost completely cured: his kindness was also extended to me, and to procure amusement for me he caused a puppet-show, which was almost abandoned, and which was very rich in figures and decorations, to be refitted.

I profited by this, and amused the company by giving them a piece of a great man, expressly composed for wooden comedians. This was the *Sneezing of Hercules*, by Peter James Martelli, a Bolognese.

. . . .

The imagination of the author sent Hercules into the country of the pigmies. Those poor little creatures, frightened at the aspect of an animated mountain with legs and arms, ran and concealed themselves in holes. One day, as Hercules had stretched himself out in the open fields and was sleeping tranquilly, the timid inhabitants issued out of their retreats, and armed with prickles and rushes, mounted on the monstrous man, and covered him from head to foot, like flies when they fall on a piece of rotten meat. Hercules waked, and felt something in his nose, which made him sneeze; on which, his enemies tumbled down in all directions. This ends the piece.

There is a plan, a progression, an intrigue, a catastrophe, and winding up; the style is good and well supported; the thoughts and sentiments are all well proportionate to the size of the personages. The verses even are short, and every thing indicates pigmies.

A gigantic puppet was requisite for Hercules: every thing was well executed. The entertainment was productive of much pleasure; and I could lay a bet, that I am the only person who ever thought of executing the Bambocciata of Martelli.—*Memoirs of Goldoni* translated by John Black; vol. i. ch. 6.

EPITAPHIANA.

The following epitaph is copied from Lavenham Church, Norfolk:—

John Weles, Ob. 1694.
Quod fuit esse, quod est
Quod non fuit esse, quod esse,
Esse quod non esse,
Quod est, non est, erit, esse.

The word *est* has evidently been omitted in the third line; with this restored, the lines will read as a couple of hexameters:—

Quod fuet esse, quod est; quod non fuit esse, quod esse;
Esse quod (est), non esse; quod est, non est, erit, esse.

And the literal meaning will be, "What was existence, is that which lies here; that which was not existence, is that which is existence; to be what is now, is not to be; that which is now, is not existence, but will be hereafter."

This, perhaps, is as enigmatical as the original; but the following lines will render the meaning plainer, though it is difficult to preserve the brevity of the Latin in an English version:—

All that I really was lies here in dust;
That which was death before is life, I trust.
To be what *is*, is not, I ween, to *be*;
Is not, but *will be* in eternity.

The Latin inscription has been thus paraphrased:—

What we have been, and what we are,
The present and the time that's past,
We cannot properly compare
With what we are to be at last.

Tho' we ourselves have fancied Forms,
And Beings that have never been;
We into something shall be turn'd,
Which we have not conceived or seen.

There is a similar epitaph in another churchyard, which may serve to elucidate its meaning:—

That which a Being was, what is it? show:
That being which it was, it is not now.
To be what 'tis is not to be, you see;
That which now is not shall a Being be.

In one of Dr. Byrom's Common-place Books now in the possession of his respected descendant, Miss Atherton, of Kersal Cell, is the following arrangement and translation of this enigmatical inscription, probably made by the Doctor himself:—

Quod fuit esse quod est quod non fuit esse quod esse
Esse quod est non esse quod est non est erit esse.

Quod fuit esse quod,
Est quod non fuit esse quod,
Esse esse quod est,
Non esse quod est non est
Erit esse.

What was John Wiles is what John Wiles was not,
The mortal Being has immortal got.
The Wiles that was but a non Ens is gone,
And now remains the true eternal John.

THE REMAINS OF JAMES THE SECOND.

The following curious account was given to the writer in 1840 by Mr. Fitzsimmons, an Irish gentleman upwards of eighty years, who taught French and English at Toulouse. He stated that he had been a runaway monk:—

I was a prisoner in Paris, in the convent of the English Benedictines in the Rue St. Jaques, during part of the revolution. In the year 1793 or 1794, the body of King James II. of England was in one of the chapels there, where it had been deposited some time, under the expectation that it would one day be sent to England for interment in Westminster Abbey. It had never been buried. The body was in a wooden coffin, inclosed in a leaden one; and that again inclosed in a second wooden one, covered with black velvet. That while I was so a prisoner, the sans-culottes broke open the coffins to get at the lead to cast into bullets. The body lay exposed nearly a whole day. It was swaddled like a mummy, bound tight with garters. The sans-culottes took out the body, which had been embalmed. There was a strong smell of vinegar and camphor. The corpse was beautiful and perfect. The hands and nails were very fine. I moved and bent every finger. I never saw so fine a set of teeth in my life. A young lady, a fellow prisoner, wished much to have a tooth; I tried to get one out for her, but could not, they were so firmly fixed. The feet also were very beautiful. The face and cheeks were just as if he were alive. I rolled his eyes: the eye-balls were perfectly firm under my finger. The French and English prisoners gave money to the sans-culottes for showing the body. They said he was a good sans-culotte, and they were going to put him into a hole in the public churchyard like other sans-culottes; and he was carried away, but where the body was thrown I never heard. King George IV. tried all in his power to get tidings of the body, but could not. Around the chapel were several wax moulds of the face hung up, made probably at the time of the king's death, and the corpse was very like them. The body had been originally kept at the palace of St. Germain, from whence it was brought to the convent of the Benedictines. Mr. Porter, the prior, was a prisoner at the time in his own convent.

BURKE AND WARREN HASTINGS.

The following epigram was thrown to Burke while he was making his celebrated speech against Warren Hastings:—

Oft have we wondered that on Irish ground
No poisonous reptile has e'er yet been found;
Reveal'd the secret stands of nature's work,
She saved her venom to create a Burke.

These lines have been always erroneously attributed to Mr. Law (Lord Ellenborough), but the real author was Hastings himself; his private secretary (Mr. Evans) sat by his side during the trial, and saw him write the above. Our authority is a niece of Mr. Evans, who formed one of her uncle's family at the period of the trial.

A WHALE IN THE THAMES.

In the British Museum library is a tract of four leaves only, with the following title:—

London's Wonder. Being a most true and positive relation of the taking and killing of a great Whale neer to Greenwich; the said Whale being fifty-eight foot in length, twelve foot high, fourteen foot broad, and two foot between the eyes. At whose death was used Harping-irons, Spits, Swords, Guns, Bills, Axes, and Hatchets, and all kind of sharp Instruments to kill her: and at last two Anchors being struck fast into her body, she could not remoove them, but the blood gush'd out of her body, as the water does out of a pump. The report of which Whale hath caused many hundred of people both by land and water to go and see her: the said Whale being slaine hard by *Greenwich* upon the third day of June this present yere 1658, which is largely exprest in this following discourse.—*London, printed for Francis Grove, neere the Sarazen's head on Snowhill*, 1658.

Evelyn, who lived near Greenwich, and was most probably one of the wonder-struck spectators of the huge monster of the deep which had been so rash as to visit our shores, notes in his *Diary* under the above-mentioned date—

A large whale was taken betwixt my land butting on the Thames and Greenwich, which drew an infinite concourse to see it by water, horse, coach, and on foote, from London and all parts. It appear'd first below Greenwich at low water, for at high water it would have destroyed all ye boates; but lying now in shallow water encompass'd with boates, after a long conflict it was kill'd with a harping yron, struck in ye head, out of which spouted blood and water by two tunnells, and after an horrid grone it ran quite on shore and died. Its length was 58 foote, height 16; black-skin'd like coach leather, very small eyes, greate tail, only 2 small finns, a picked snout, and a mouth so wide that divers men might haue stood upright in it: no teeth, but suck'd the slime onely as thro' a grate of that bone which we call whale-bone; the throate yet so narrow as would not have admitted the least of fishes. The extreames of the cetaceous bones hang downewards from the upper jaw, and was hairy towards the ends and bottom within side: all of it prodigious, but in nothing more wonderfull then that an animal of so greate a bulk should be nourished onely by slime thro' those grates.

WATER CURE.

A noble lord distinguished for a total neglect of religion, and who, boasting the superior excellence of some water-works which he had invented and constructed, added, that after having been so useful to mankind, he expected to be very *comfortable* in the next world, notwithstanding his ridicule and disbelief of religion. "Ah," replied the clergyman, "if you mean to be *comfortable* there, you must take your *water-works* along with you."—Daniel's *Sports*, Supplement, p. 305.

THE BIRDS' CARE FOR THE DEAD.

It is not uncommon to find in poets of all ages some allusion to the pious care of particular birds for the bodies of the dead. Is there any truth in the idea? for certainly the old ballad of "The Children in the Wood" has made many a kind friend for the Robin Redbreast by the affecting lines:—

No burial this pretty pair
Of any man receives,
Till Robin Redbreast piously
Did cover them with leaves.

Herrick also alludes to the same tradition in his verses "upon Mrs. Elizabeth Wheeler, under the name of Amarillis:"—

Sweet Amarillis, by a spring's
Soft and soule-melting murmurings,
Slept; and thus sleeping, thither flew
A Robin Redbreast; who, at view,
Not seeing her at all to stir,
Brought leaves and moss to cover her;

But while he, perking, there did prie
About the arch of either eye,
The lid began to let out day,
At which poor Robin flew away;
And seeing her not dead, but all disleav'd,
He chirpt for joy, to see himself disceav'd.

In the earlier editions of Gray's Elegy, before the Epitaph, the following exquisite lines were inserted:—

There scatter'd oft, the earliest of the year,
By hands unseen, are showers of violets found;
The Redbreast loves to build and warble there,
And little footsteps lightly print the ground.

About the same time Collins' "Dirge in Cymbeline" had adorned the "fair Fidele's grassy tomb" with the same honor:—

The Redbreast oft, at evening hours,
  Shall kindly lend his little aid,
With hoary moss, and gather'd flowers,
  To deck the ground where thou art laid.

Horace, too, affords an example in a passage in one of his odes (III. iv. 9) thus translated by Milman:—

The vagrant infant, on Mount Vultur's side,
Beyond my childhood's nurse, Apulia's bounds
  By play-fatigued and sleep,
    Did the poetic *doves*
With young leaves cover.

The following beautiful legend occurs in a book entitled *Communications with the Unseen World*, p. 26:—

Eusebia.—Like that sweet superstition current in Brittany, which would explain the cause why the robin redbreast has always been a favourite and *protégé* of man. While our Saviour was bearing His cross, one of these birds, they say, took one thorn from His crown, which dyed its breast; and ever since that time robin redbreasts have been the friends of man.

CURT CRITICISM.

In a copy of Herbert's *Travels in Africa, Asia, &c.*, folio, 1634, there is a very characteristic note in the autograph of Dean Swift, to whom the book formerly belonged :—

> If this book were stript of its impertinence, conceitedness, and tedious digressions, it would be almost worth reading, and would then be two thirds smaller than it is. 1720. J. Swift.

The author published a new edition in his older days, with many additions, upon the whole more insufferable than this. He lived several years after the Restoration, and some friends of mine knew him in Ireland. He seems to have been a coxcomb both ævi vitio et sui.

BONAPARTE AND LORD WHITWORTH.

I send you an account of the very memorable scene which occurred at Madame Bonaparte's drawing-room on the 13th of March, 1803. I believe I am the only living witness, as those who were near the person of Lord Whitworth were members of the corps diplomatique, Cobenzel, Marcoff, Lucchesini, all dead. Many years after I became intimately acquainted with the Marchese Lucchesini at Florence, when I had an opportunity of referring to that remarkable conversation.

It was announced that Madame Bonaparte was to receive on the following Sunday, and it was reported that she was to have maids of honor for the first time; a little curiosity was excited on this score. The apartment of Madame B. was on the opposite side of the Tuilleries in which Bonaparte held his levees. I was acquainted with Lord Whitworth, who told me to place myself near to him, in order to afford facility for presentation, as Madame B. would occupy an arm-chair to which he pointed, and on each side of which were two tabourets. As all foreigners had been presented to General B. at his levee, his presence was not expected. The rooms, two in number, were not very large; the ladies were seated round the rooms in arm-chairs: a passage was left, I suppose, for Madame B. to pass without obstacle. When the door of the adjoining room was opened, instead of Madame B. the First Consul entered; and as Lord Whitworth was the first ambassador he encountered, he addressed him by inquiring about the Duchess of Dorset's health, she being absent from a cold. He then observed that we had had fifteen years' war; Lord W. smiled very courteously, and said it was fifteen years too much. We shall probably, replied General B., have fifteen years more: and if so, England will have to answer for it to all Europe, and to God and man. He then inquired where the armaments in Holland were going on, for he knew of none. Then for a moment he quitted Lord W. and passed all the ladies, addressing Mrs. Greathead only, though the Duchess of Gordon and her daughter, Lady Georgiana, were present. After speaking to several officers in the centre of the room, which was crowded, he returned to Lord W. and asked why Malta was not given up. Lord W. then looked more serious, and said he had no doubt that Malta would be given up when the other articles of the treaty were complied with. General B. then left the room, and Madame B. immediately entered. As soon as the drawing-room was over, I observed to Lord W. that it was the first cabinet council I had ever witnessed; he laughingly answered, by far the most numerously attended. Lord W. then addressed the American Minister, who was very deaf, and repeated what had passed, and I perceived that he was very much offended at what had occurred. In justice to the First Consul, I must say that the impropriety consisted in the unfitness of the place for such a subject; the tone of his voice was not raised, as was said at the time. He spoke in the same tone as when he inquired for the Duchess of Dorset.

J. Sandford.

EPIGRAMS ON BURNET AND FRANKLIN.

Does any one know where the following epigram in MS. in an old folio copy of Burnet's *History*, comes from?—

> If Heaven is pleas'd when sinners cease to sin,
> If Hell is pleas'd when sinners enter in,
> If men are pleas'd at parting with a knave,
> Then all are pleas'd—for Burnet's in his grave.

Who was the author of the following lines, written shortly after Dr. Franklin's attendance at the Privy Council in January, 1774, in allusion to Wedderburn's severe remarks upon him?—

> Sarcastic Sawney, full of spite and hate,
> On modest Franklin poured his venal prate;
> The calm philosopher without reply
> Withdrew—and gave his country liberty

BOWYER AND HIS BIBLE.

Bowyer being a poor youth in search of employment, and withal moody enough at his prospects, he was one day walking down Newgate Street, and pausing to look at a print or two in a shop window, it struck him he could take a likeness; so he went home to his indifferent lodging, having procured implements suitable, seated himself before a glass, and took his own portrait, which he considered was as successful as a first effort could be. Encouraged thereby, he was soon employed to paint others, and such note did he acquire that his miniatures were carried into court-circles, so that he became a sort of celebrity in that line, and Queen Charlotte appointed him her official miniature-painter —if such be the proper term.

He soon struck out much more important occupation, planning various publications, the most promising of which was his large edition of Hume's *History of England;* and this was so ponderous an undertaking that it was only at last disposed of by a lottery. His fondness for taking portraits never left him. He was much pleased with one of his successes. Just before George III. was secluded finally from public view, he and another artist, an old acquaintance, went one Sunday together to the Chapel Royal at Windsor, and during the service each sketched the King on *one of his nails:* they adjourned to an inn, and while the impression was yet fresh, transferred to a sheet of paper the likeness of the venerable monarch. On returning with it to London, Bowyer sent it for the inspection of the Prince Regent, who was so pleased with this rough pencil-drawing, that he sent word back he would never part with it, and begged to know Bowyer's price. The latter said one hundred and five pounds, which the Prince Regent immediately forwarded.

I once found Bowyer drawing at a table, a wig placed on a stick before him, and he was taking the likeness of a very old friend, who was dead and gone, from memory. In this attempt he entirely succeeded, even to the surprise of all who knew the deceased.

About ten years ago a little book, called *Henry VIII. and His Contemporaries*, by B. Bensley, contained, concerning the earlier impressions of the Bible, the following note:—

I trust to be pardoned for introducing a little anecdote relative to the Bible, exactly three hundred years after the period about which I am writing, that is not the less appropriate for being likewise illustrative of *episcopal shrewdness.* [The text is recording an instance of the then Bishop of London being bitten in an arrangement with a bookseller.] The most splendid Bible ever issued was that published by Macklin, printed by my late father, and the execution of which, even his son may say, would alone hand down his name to posterity. *Bowyer*, publisher of another great national work—the folio edition of Hume's *History of England,* also a splendid specimen of my father's typography —had a copy of Macklin's Bible, which he employed his leisure during many years to illustrate, having the best opportunities, from his pursuits as an artist, publisher of prints, &c. On the completion of his labours, he valued the massy product, consisting of an immense number of prints, at 2500*l.*; and, after unsuccessful efforts to procure a purchaser, he put it up to be raffled for, issuing proposals to the nobility and gentry, &c. Among others, an aged *bishop* sent his name as a subscriber to this kind of lottery, and shortly after called at the rooms in Pall Mall to pay the two guineas; but, before he did so, he drew Mr. Bowyer apart, and gravely told him he could not quite make out how, by paying that sum, he could *insure* possession of the great work. Upon its being explained to his lordship, that he could only take a chance with 1249 others, he expressed surprise and vexation, and declined to pay two guineas for the chance, which he *then*, probably, saw was objectionable in a moral point of view, as a species of gambling! The parties are all long since dead.

BOTANICAL NOTES FROM THEOPHRASTUS.

Difficult as it often is to identify plants described therein, Theophrastus's *History of Plants* is full of interest, as showing the state of the science 2,100 years since, as also from its incidental illustrations of ancient manners. It may be worth mentioning, that the vegetable kingdom was subdivided by Theophrastus into trees, bushes, plants, and herbs. That he observed the sexual differences of certain flowers; the ascent of sap; the diseases of plants, such as smut and rust; and the growth of madrepores, corallines, and sponges. Wild trees and plants, however, were mostly unnamed in his time. He speaks of grafting and budding as practised by gardeners; and informs us that the roots of plants were extensively used in pharmacy, numerous receipts being given in the latter part of the work.

The following will interest the general reader:—Marsh-mallow, birch, and willow stems were used for light walking-sticks, of which the best and most fashionable were made at Sparta; and the laurel for those of old persons. Painters' tablets were manufactured from heart of pine. Drinking-cups, in Arcadia, from the tuberous nodules in the stems of trees; and in Syria, from the black terebinth, equal to the best Thericlean pottery. Elm was the most prized for the doors of houses; and the large doors of the Temple of Diana, at Ephesus, were made of cypress, the only wood then known to take a polish. A kind of holm oak was principally used in the manufacture of wheels, especially the single wheels of wheelbarrows. The bark of the alder was used in tanning skins generally, and the sumach in staining them white. The Persian apple and citron were used to flavor the breath, and put with clothes to keep away the moth. Double flutes were manufactured from a jointed reed, the best kinds of which grew near Orchomenos; shields, from the willow and vine; elastic couches, from the ash or beech; coblers' sharpening-strops, from the gritty wild pear; cat-traps, from elm; hinges, from elm; seals, from worm satin-wood; images (εἴδωλα), from palm-wood; statues (ἀγαλματα), some of which were noted for sweating, from cedar, cypress, lotus, and box; bread, from dates as well as wheat; ships, from the pines which grew in great abundance at Sinope, but not from oak, of which five species were known.

Corinth and Bœotia were famous for radishes; Philippi for double roses; Macedonia and Bœotia for heavy, Attica and Laconia for light crops, Attica being especially a barley-growing country. The caper plant, the artichoke, spring asparagus, and lettuces, were ancient as well as modern luxuries; and Theophrastus mentions a kind of *omelet soufflet* (ἐκπνευματουμενος), made of cheese, honey, and garlick, which however was so strong as to set people sneezing. It is amusing to find that walnut-trees were beaten in order to increase their bearing, in those days as well as in ours; though it may well be doubted whether the custom is much more conducive to any good end than another. Our author mentions of sowing cummin with oaths and curses in order to insure a good crop. Mushrooms, we are told, as every rustic now knows, grow in thunder; and Egyptian beer (βρυτον) was made from barley.

The attention of the curious in ancient herbal lore, will be well directed to the store of anecdotes and observations in the too neglected writings of the pupil and heir of Aristotle, whose popularity was such, that his disciples are said to have numbered two thousand.

FIRST ENGLISH ENVOY TO RUSSIA.

In the review of the late embassy to China, *Quarterly Review*, for 1817, p. 476, is given this notice of the spirited conduct of Sir Jerom Bowes, who was sent as ambassador from Queen Elizabeth to Jan Vasilovitch :—

On entering the presence chamber [at Moscow], the ambassador was desired by the Emperor to take his seat at ten paces distance, and to send to him her Majesty's letter and present. Sir Jerom thinking this not reasonable, stept forwards towards the Emperor, but was intercepted by the chancellor, who would have taken his letters; to whom the ambassador said, "that her Majesty had directed no letters to him," and so went forward and delivered them himself to the Emperor's own hands. In the course of his mission, however, he offended the Emperor, "because he would not yield to every thing he thought fit," who, with a stern and angry countenance, told him "that he did not reckon the Queen of England to be his fellow." Upon which Sir Jerom "disliked these speeches," and unwilling to suffer this autocrat to derogate from the honour and greatness of her Majesty, boldly told him to his face, "that the Queen his mistress was as great a prince as any was in Christendom, equal to him that thought himself the greatest, and well able to defend herself against the malice of any whomsoever." The Emperor on this was so enraged that he declared "if he were not an ambassador, he would throw him out of doors." Sir Jerom replied coolly, "that he was in his power, but that he had a mistress who would revenge any injury done unto him." The Emperor unable to bear it longer, bade him "get home," when Sir Jerom, with no more reverence than such usage required, saluted the Emperor and departed.

This Juan Vasilowidg nailed a French ambassador's hat to his head. Sir Jerom Boze, a while after, came as ambassador, and put on his hat and cocked it before him; at which, he sternly demanded how he durst do so, having heard how he chastised the French ambassador. Sir Jerom answered, he represented a cowardly King of France, but I am the ambassador of the invincible Queen of England, who does not vail her bonnet, nor bare her head, to any prince living; and if any of her ministers shall receive any affront abroad, she is able to revenge her own quarrel. Look you there (quoth Juan Vasilowidg to his boyars), there is a brave fellow, indeed, that dares do and say thus much for his mistress; which whoreson of you all dare do so much for me, your master? This made them envy Sir Jerom, and persuade the Emperor to give him a wild horse to tame; which he did, managing him with such rigour, that the horse grew so tired and tamed, that he fell down dead under him. This being done, he asked His Majesty if he had any more wild horses to tame? The Emperor afterwards much honoured him, for he loved such a daring fellow as he was, and a mad blade to boot.—Dr. Collins' *Present State of Russia*, 120, 1671; quoted in *Retrospective Review*, xiv. 40.

Pepys, under the date September 5, 1662, has the following entry:—

To Mr. Bland's, the merchant, by invitation: where I found all the officers of the customs, very grave, fine gentlemen, and I am glad to know them: viz., Sir Job Harvy, &c., very good company. And among other discourse, some was of Sir Jerom Bowes, ambassador from Queen Elizabeth to the Emperor of Russia; who, because some of the noblemen there would go up stairs to the Emperor before him, he would not go up till the Emperor had ordered those two men to be dragged down stairs, with their heads knocking upon every stair, till they were killed. And when he was come up, they demanded his sword of him before he entered the room. He told them if they would have his sword, they should have his boots too; and so he caused his boots to be pulled off, and his nightgown, and nightcap, and slippers, to be sent for; and made the Emperor stay till he could go in his nightdress, since he might not go as a soldier. And lastly, when the Emperor, in contempt, to show his command of his subjects, did command one to leap from the window down, and broke his neck in the sight of our ambassador, he replied, that his mistress did set more by, and make better use of, the necks of her subjects; but said, that to show what her subjects would do for her, he would and did fling down his gauntlet before the Emperor; and challenged all the nobility there to take it up in defence of the Emperor against his Queen; for which, at this very day, the name of Sir Jerom Bowes is famous and honoured there.

SALLY LUNN.

The bun so fashionable, called the *Sally Lunn*, originated with a young woman of that name at Bath, about thirty years ago. [This was written in 1826.] She first cried them in a basket, with a white cloth over it, morning and evening. Dalmer, a respectable baker and musician, noticed her, bought her business, and made a song and set it to music in behalf of Sally Lunn. This composition became the street favorite, barrows were made to distribute the nice cakes, Dalmer profited thereby and retired, and to this day the *Sally Lunn Cake* claims pre-eminence in all the cities of England.—Hone's *Everyday Book*, ii. 1561.

ALLITERATION.

One of the best specimens of alliteration in the English language, will be found in Quarles' *Divine Emblems*, book ii. emblem ii. Beyond all question, Quarles was a poet that needed not "apt alliteration's artful aid" to add to the vigor of his verse, or lend liquidity to his lines. Quarles is often queer, quaint, and querulous, but never prolix, prosy, or puling.

We sack, we ransack, to the utmost sands
Of native kingdoms, and of foreign lands:
We travel sea and soil; we pry, we prowl,
We progress, and we prog from pole to pole.

THE SEVENTH SON OF A SEVENTH SON.

Apropos of the peculiar powers and qualities superstitiously attributed by the common sort of people to the seventh son of a seventh son, there is a rare old printed copy of "The Quack Doctor's Speech," which was spoken by the witty Lord Rochester, in character, and mounted on a stage; it is altogether a very humorous and lengthy address, partaking of the licence of language not uncommon to the courtiers of that period, abounding in much technical phraseology, and therefore unsuited for an introduction *in extenso*. The titles assumed, however, are in character with the pretensions claimed by virtue of being the seventh begotten son of a seventh begotten father :—

Gentlemen,

I, Waltho Van Clauterbauck, High German Doctor, Chymist and Dentrificator—Native of Arabia Deserta, Citizen and Burgomaster of the City of Brandipolis—Seventh son of a Seventh son, unborn Doctor of above sixty years' experience, having studied over Galen, Hypocrates, Albumazur, and Paracelsus, am now become the Æsculapius of this age. Having been educated at twelve Universities, and travelled through fifty-two Kingdoms, and been Counsellor to the Counsellors of several grand Monarchs, natural son of the wonder-working chymical Doctor Signior Hanesio, lately arrived from the farthest parts of Utopia, famous throughout all Asia, Europe, Africa, and America, from the Sun's oriental exaltation to his occidental declination, out of mere pity to my own dear self and languishing mortals, have by the earnest prayers and entreaties of several Lords, Dukes, and honorable Personages been at last prevailed upon to oblige the World with this notice, &c., &c.

Veniente occurrite morbo—Down with your dust.
Principiis obsta—No cure no money.
Querenda Pecunia Premium—Be not sick too late.

You that are willing to render yourselves immortal, Buy this pacquet, or else repair to the sign of the Pranceis, in Vico vulgo dicto Ratcliffero, something south-east of Templum Dancicum, in the Square of Profound Close, not far from Titter Tatter Fair; and you may hear, see, and return Re-infecta.

THE GROANING-BOARD.

The English public has ever been distinguished by an enormous amount of gullibility.

Ha ha, ha ha! this world doth pass
Most merrily I'll be sworn;
For many an honest Indian ass
Goes for an unicorn.

So sung old Thomas Weelkes in the year 1608.

In a volume in the British Museum, marked MS. Sloane 958, is the following hand-bill pasted on the first page :—

At the sign of the Wool-sack, in Newgate Market, is to be seen a strange and wonderful thing, which is an *elm board*, being touched with a hot iron, doth express itself as if it were a man dying *with groans*, and trembling, to the great admiration of all the hearers. It hath been presented before the king and his nobles, and hath given great satisfaction. *Vivat Rex.*

At the top of the bill is the king's arms, and the letters C. R., and in an old hand is written the date 1682. On the same page is an autograph of the original possessor of the volume, "Ex libris Jo. Coniers, Londini, pharmacopol, 1673."

In turning to Malcolm (*Anecdotes of the Manners and Customs of London*, 4to. 1811, p. 427), we find the following elucidation of this mysterious exhibition :—

One of the most curious and ingenious amusements ever offered to the publick ear was contrived in the year 1682, when an elm plank was exhibited to the king and the credulous of London, which being touched by a hot iron, invariably produced a sound resembling deep groans. This sensible, and very irritable board, received numbers of noble visitors; and other boards, sympathizing with their afflicted brother, demonstrated how much affected they might be by similar means. The publicans in different parts of the city immediately applied ignited metal to all the woodwork of their houses, in hopes of finding sensitive timber; but I do not perceive any were so successful as the landlord of the Bowman Tavern in Drury Lane, who had a mantle tree so extremely prompt and loud in its responses, that the sagacious observers were nearly unanimous in pronouncing it part of the same trunk which had afforded the original plank.

The following paragraph is also given by Malcolm, from the *Loyal London Mercury*, Oct. 4, 1682 :—

Some persons being this week drinking at the Queen's Arms Tavern, in St. Martin's-le-Grand, in the kitchen, and having laid the fire-fork in the fire to light their pipes, accidentally fell a discoursing of the *groaning-board*, and what might be the cause of it. One in the company, having the fork in his hand to light his pipe, would needs make trial of a long dresser that stood there, which, upon the first touch, made a great noise and groaning, more than ever the board that was showed did; and then they touched it three or four times, and found it far beyond the other. They all having seen it, the house is almost filled with spectators day and night, and any company calling for a glass of wine may see it; which, in the judgment of all, is far louder, and makes a longer groan than the other; which to report, unless seen, would seem incredible.

Among the *Bagford Ballads* in the Museum (three vols., under the press-mark 643, m.), is preserved the following singular broadside upon the subject, which is now reprinted for the first time :—

A NEW SONG, ON THE STRANGE AND WONDERFUL GROANING-BOARD.

What fate inspir'd thee with groans,
To fill phanatick brains?
What is't thou sadly thus bemoans,
In thy prophetick strains?

Art thou the ghost of *William Pryn*,
Or some old politician?
Who, long tormented for his sin,
Laments his sad condition?

Or must we now believe in thee,
The old cheat transmigration?
And that thou now art come to be
A call to reformation?

The giddy vulgar to thee run,
Amaz'd with fear and wonder;
Some dare affirm, that hear thee groan,
Thy noise is petty thunder.

One says and swears, you do foretell
A change in Church and State;
Another says, you like not well
Your master *Stephen's* fate.*

* This was *Stephen* College, a joiner by trade, but a man of an active and violent spirit, who, making himself conspicuous by his opposition to the Court, obtained the name of the Protestant joiner. His fate is well known.

Some say you groan much like a *whigg*,
Or rather like a *ranter;*
Some say as loud, and full as big,
As *Conventicle Canter*.

Some say you do petition,
And think you represent
The woe and sad condition
Of Old *Rump Parliament*.

The wisest say you are a cheat;
Another politician
Says, 'tis a mistery as great
And true as *Hatfield's vision*.*

Some say, 'tis a *new evidence*,
Or witness of the *plot;*
And can discover many things,
Which are the Lord knows what.

And lest you should the *plot* disgrace,
For wanting of a name,
Narrative Board henceforth we'll place
In registers of fame.

London: Printed for T. P., in the year 1682.

The extraordinary and long-lived popularity of the "groaning-board" is fully evinced by the number of contemporary allusions: a few will suffice.

Mrs. Mary Astell, in her *Essay in Defence of the Female Sex*, 1696, speaking of the character of a "coffee-house politician," observes:—

He is a mighty listener after prodigies: and never hears of a whale or a comet, but he apprehends some sudden revolution in the State, and looks upon a *groaning-board*, or a speaking-head, as forerunners of the day of judgment.

* Martha Hatfield, a child twelve years old in Sept. 1652, who pretended to have visions "concerning Christ, faith, and other subjects." She was a second edition of the "holy maid of Kent."

Swift, in his *Tale of a Tub*, written in the following year (1697), says of Jack :—

He wore a large plaister of artificiall causticks on his stomach, with the fervor of which he would set himself a *groaning* like the famous *board* upon application of a red-hot iron.

Steele, in the 44th number of the *Tatler*, speaking of Powell, the "puppet showman," says :—

He has not brains enough to make even wood speak as it ought to do: and I, that have heard the *groaning-board*, can despise all that his puppets shall be able to speak as long as they live.

So much for the "story" of the *groaning-board*. As to "how it was done," we leave the matter open to the reader's sagacity.

The following notice of the "Groaning-Board" is given in a Memoir of Sir Thomas Molyneux, Bart. M. D., in the Dublin University Magazine, Sept. 1841, written by W. R. Wilde :—

In one of William Molyneux's communications, he mentions the exhibition of "the groaning elm-plank" in Dublin, a curiosity that attracted much attention and many learned speculations about the years 1682 and 1683. He was, however, too much of a philosopher to be gulled with the rest of the people who witnessed this so-called "sensible elm-plank," which is said to have groaned and trembled on the application of a hot iron to one end of it. After explaining the probable cause of the noise and tremulousness by its form and condition, and by the sap being made to pass up through the pores or tubuli of the plank which was in some particular condition, he says: "But, Tom, the generality of mankind is lazy and unthoughtful, and will not trouble themselves to think of the reason of a thing: when they have a brief way of explaining any thing that is strange by saying 'The devil's in it,' what need they trouble their heads about pores, and matters, and motion, figure, and disposition, when the devil and a witch shall solve all the phenomena of nature."

EARTH TO EARTH.

Earth walks on Earth,
    Glittering in gold:
Earth goes to Earth,
    Sooner than it wold:
Earth builds on Earth,
    Palaces and towers:
Earth says to Earth,
    Soon, all shall be ours.

In the church of Stratford upon Avon, was painted an angel holding a scroll, upon which were seven stanzas in old English, being an allegory of mortality. The two following stanzas stand third and fourth in the inscription :—

Erth apon erth wynnys castellys and towrys,
Then seth erth unto erth thys ys all owrys.
When erth apon erth hath bylde hys bowrys,
Then schall erth for erth suffur many hard schowrys.

Erth goth apon erth as man apon mowld,
Lyke as erth apon erth never goo schold,
Erth goth apon erth as gelsteryng gold,
And yet schall erth unto erth rather than he wold.

The following epitaph is from an old brass in the church of St. Helen's, London :—

Here lyeth ye bodyes of
James Pomley, ye sonne of ould
Dominick Pomley and Jane his
Wyfe: ye said James deceased ye 7th
day of Januarie, Anno Domini, 1592
he beyng of ye age of 88 years, and
ye sayd Jane deceased y^e^ — day
of —— D——.

Earth goeth upō earth as moulde upō moulde;
Earth goeth upō earth all glittering as golde,
As though earth to ye earth never turne shoulde;
And yet shall earth to ye earth sooner than he woulde

The following two epitaphs are from monuments in the church-yard of Llangerrig, Montgomeryshire :—

O earth, O earth! observe this well—
That earth to earth shall come to dwell:
Then earth in earth shall close remain,
Till earth from earth shall rise again.

From earth my body first arose;
But here to earth again it goes.
I never desire to have it more,
To plague me as it did before.

YANKEE DOODLE.

The origin of *Yankee Doodle* is by no means as clear as American antiquaries desire. The statement that the air was composed by Dr. Shuckburg, in 1755, when the Colonial troops united with the British regulars near Albany for the conquest of Canada, and that it was produced in derision of the old-fashioned manners of the provincial soldiers, when contrasted with the neat and dandified appearance of the regulars, was published some years ago in a musical magazine printed in Boston. The account there given as to the origin of the song is this :—During the attacks upon the French outposts in 1755, in America, Governor Shirley and General Jackson led the force directed against the enemy lying at Niagara and Frontenac. In the early part of June, whilst these troops were stationed on the banks of the Hudson, near Albany, the descendants of the " Pilgrim fathers " flocked in from the eastern provinces; never was seen such a motley regiment as took up its position on the left wing of the British army. The band played music some two centuries of age, officers and privates had adopted regimentals each man after his own fashion; one wore a flowing wig, while his neighbor rejoiced in hair cropped closely to the head; this one had a coat with wonderful long skirts, his fellow marched without his upper garment; various as the colors of the rainbow were the clothes worn by the gallant band. It so happened that there was a certain Dr. Shuckburgh, wit, musician, and surgeon, and one evening after mess he produced a tune, which he earnestly commended as a well-known piece of military music, to the officers of the militia. The joke succeeded, and Yankee Doodle was hailed by acclamation "their own march."

This account is somewhat apocryphal, as there is no song: the tune in the United States is a march; there are no words to it of a national character. The only words ever affixed to the air in this country is the following doggerel quatrain:—

Yankee Doodle came to town
Upon a little pony,
He stuck a feather in his hat
And called it macaroni.

It has been asserted by writers in this country, that the air and words of these lines are as old as Cromwell's time. The only alteration is in making *Yankee Doodle* of what was *Nankee Doodle.* It is asserted that the tune will be found in the *Musical Antiquities of England*, and that *Nankee Doodle* was intended to apply to Cromwell, and the other lines were designed to "allude to his going into Oxford with a single plume, fastened in a knot called a macaroni." The tune was known in New England before the Revolution as *Lydia Fisher's Jig*, and there were verses to it commencing:—

Lucy Locket lost her pocket,
Lydia Fisher found it,
Not a bit of money in it,
Only binding round it.

The regulars in Boston in 1775 and 1776 are said to have sung verses to the same air:—

Yankee Doodle came to town,
For to buy a firelock;
We will tar and feather him,
And so we will John Hancock, &c.

The manner in which the tune came to be adopted by the Americans, is shown in the following letter of the Rev. W. Gordon. Describing the battles of Lexington and Concord, before alluded to, he says:—

The brigade under Lord Percy marched out [of Boston] playing, by way of contempt, *Yankee Doodle:* they were afterwards told they had been made to dance it.

NOTES ON MANNERS, COSTUME, ETC.

Billiards.—Evelyn (*Mem.*, vol. i. p. 516) describes a *new* sort of billiards, "with more hazards than ours commonly have." The game was therefore already known. The new game was with *posts* and *pins.* The balls were struck with "the small end of the billiard stick, which is shod with brass or silver."

Buckles.—Charles II. attempted in 1666 to introduce what was called a Persian dress (Evelyn's *Mem.*, vol. i. p. 398) into national use. One point of this alteration was to change "shoe-strings and garters into buckles, of which some were set with precious stones." The attempt wholly failed, and soon went out of fashion, except the buckles, which appear never to have been wholly lost. The shoe-buckles were pushed to a great size by the fops about 1775: the largest were called Artois-buckles, after the Comte d'Artois, the French king's brother. But on the Revolution they became unpopular, and at one time it would have been dangerous to wear them. The republican Roland was the first person who ventured to Court without buckles. This matter made a sensation so great as to deserve the ridicule of the *Antijacobin:* "Roland the Just with ribands in his shoes!" The opportunity which buckles afford of ornament and expense has preserved them as a part of the court dress; and of late years they have appeared a little in private society. They are generally, though not always, worn when a prince of the royal family is of the party; and at the king's private parties, although the rest of the dress be that usually worn, buckles are almost indispensable. Knee-strings came in with shoe-strings, and have had about the same vogue. We see in the great roses worn by peers and knights of the orders with their robes, the fashion of shoe and garter knots, which were common in the reigns of Charles II. and Louis XIV.

Baits.—Bull and bear baiting are well-known amusements; but in Evelyn's *Memoirs*, vol. i. p. 408, he tells us that—

> A very gallant horse was baited to death by dogs; but he fought them all, so as the fiercest of them could not fasten on him till they (the assistants) ran him through with their swords. This wicked and barbarous sport should have been punished on the contrivers of it, to get money under pretence that the horse had killed a man; which was false.

Cloaks.—After being out of fashion for near a century, cloaks are come a little into fashion again (1822). For officers in the army they are better than great coats, as the latter spoil the epaulets and lace; but for common life they are cumbrous and more expensive. I do not think the fashion will last. It is said that when the common Irish wish to excite a quarrel in a fair, one of them drags a cloak or coat along the ground as a signal of defiance—(*Edgeworth*). This practice is of older date and higher origin than may be supposed. Sandras de Courtiez, in his *Mémoires du Compte de Rochefort*, states that one of the unbecoming follies of the Duke of Orleans was that he took pleasure "*à tirex les manteaux sur le Pont Neuf.*" This probably means that his royal highness amused himself in stealing cloaks, but the practices were probably originally the same.

Visiting Cards.—About six or eight years ago a house in Dean Street, Soho, was repaired (I think No. 79), and, on removing a marble chimney-piece in the front drawing-room, four or five visiting cards were found, one with the name of Isaac Newton on it. The names were all written on the back of common playing cards. Hogarth's "Marriage à-la-Mode," plate iv., supplies an additional proof of playing cards having done duty as visiting cards and cards of invitation during the middle of the last century. There are several lying on the floor, in the right-hand corner of the picture. One is inscribed—"Count Basset begs to no how Lade Squander sleapt last nite."

Vails to Servants.—The old and expensive custom of "vails-giving" received its death-blow at Newcastle House. Sir Timothy Waldo, on his way from the Duke's dinner table to his carriage, put a crown into the hand of the cook, who returned it, saying, "Sir, I do not take silver." "Don't you, indeed?" said Sir Timothy, putting it in his pocket; "then I do not give gold." Hanway's "Eight Letters to the Duke of ——," had their origin in Sir Timothy's complaint.—*Cunningham's London.*

Coats.—Full dress coats have no capes nor cuffs, morning or riding coats had; whence are derived the ordinary coat now worn all through Europe called *frocks*, and all uniforms. The full dress was made to fit, but the riding dress was loose, and long in the collar and arms to protect the neck and wrists. When the weather was fine, or that the wearer came into a house, he doubled down his cape and doubled up his cuffs; and as in those days the coats were lined with different colored stuffs, the color of the lining became the color of the cape and cuffs. Uniforms had the same origin, the facings, as they are called, being only the old linings. This is still preserved in the French word *revers*, which is more correct than our word *facing;* though that also, if well considered, has the same meaning; for it was the custom to face the breasts of coats with a slip of lining, which, when buckled back, became what is now called a facing, as in hats and boots, in which a corresponding alteration has taken place. The frocks being cut down straight to cover the thighs (as grooms' frocks still are), were inconvenient to walk in; the opposite corners of each skirt were therefore furnished with a hook and eye, by which the skirt was fastened back, and hence the form of the flaps of military coats, of a different color from the coats, with an ornament in the place of a hook and eye. When I was a child (1790), I had a kind of military uniform which was made in this fashion, and I have seen uniforms of the Irish Volunteers in this style. This is the reason why a standing collar is essential to a full-dress coat; and that the Windsor uniform, rich, handsome, and laced as it was, and worn with a sword, cocked hat, and buckles, was not full dress, because it was a frock; because the cape and collars were red, while the coat was blue; and because the cape was a double one. Of this Windsor uniform there were three classes in the last thirty years of George III.: the common blue frock with red cape and cuffs, worn in the morning; the *laced* blue frock, with gold-laced button-holes on the breasts, pocket-flaps, capes, and cuffs; with this coat, white breeches, and a cocked hat and sword, were worn. It was the dress of those who attended the king when not actually at court. The third was a blue full-dress coat with standing collar, embroidered, with red silk breeches; this was a complete *court* dress, but worn only by cabinet ministers and the great officers of the crown. The Princes of the Blood, and the Lord Lieutenant of Ireland, have a kind of frock uniform; blue for the former, &c.; the latter the color he may choose, lined with silk, and with a button bearing the initial and coronet of the Prince or Lord Lieutenant; but not otherwise differing from the usual frock coat. The uniform of George IV., when Prince of Wales, was blue lined with buff, and buff waistcoat and breeches. When he became Prince Regent, the buttons bore G. P. R., and also the members of his government wore it. There was also established a kind of full dress of blue, with black cape and cuffs, and gold frogs, and Brandenberg embroidery; but it did not take.

The origin of these uniforms was a coat which the court of Louis XIV. wore in that monarch's visits to Marley, which was a kind of retirement, and to which it was therefore a great honor to be invited. The *habit de Marly* was therefore, at one time a great distinction. But every thing changes: when the Marquis of Vardes, a former favorite, returned to court, after a long exile, he thought it clever to appear in the old *habit de Marly*, with which he had been formerly honored, but it was so old-fashioned that he was laughed at; on which he said to the king, " Sire, loin de V. M. on n'est pas seulement malheureux, on devient encore ridicule." A few of us who had the Windsor uniform under the old king, continue still to wear it on some half-dress occasions, such as the Speaker's dinners, Lord Mayor's Day, &c.; but, much as it was once admired, it begins to grow strange. William IV. has established some official uniforms with graduated degrees of splendor: red velvet facings for his household, black velvet for diplomatists, and white for the Admiralty; with deep embroideries and white-feather hat trimmings for the greater officers, and lighter embroideries and black hat trimmings for the subordinates. This kind of livery (if I may use the expression), though in some respects convenient, and though it gives variety to a court which much wanted it, is not quite in accordance with our customs and manners; nor is, I think, the arrangement consistent with the principles on which our court dresses have been regulated; for a century and a half it has been too servilely borrowed from the foreign courts, where, as every thing is military, these civil dresses partook of the nature of a military uniform; hence the capes and cuffs of a different material and color from the coat itself. It is observable that the second Windsor uniform was copied by the Emperor of Russia for his civil service. We have since returned the compliment.

Old Costume.—Dress is mutable, who denies it? but still old fashions are retained to a far greater extent than one would at first imagine. The Thames watermen rejoice in the dress of Elizabeth; while the royal beefeaters (buffetiers) wear that of private soldiers of the time of Henry VII.; the blue-coat boy, the costume of a London citizen of the reign of Edward VI.; the London charity-school girls, the plain mob cap and long gloves of the time of Queen Anne. In the brass badge of the cabmen, we see a retention of the dress of Elizabethan retainers; while the shoulder-knots that once decked an officer now adorn a footman. The attire of the sailor of William III.'s era is now seen amongst our fishermen. The university dress is as old as the age of the Smithfield martyrs. The linen bands of the pulpit and the bar are abridgments of the falling collar.

Other costumes are found lurking in provinces, and amongst some trades. The butchers' blue is the uniform of a guild. The quaint little head-dress of the market women of Kingswood, Gloucestershire, is in fact the gipsy hat of George II. Scarlet has been the color of soldiers' uniforms from the time of the Lacedemonians. The blue of the army we derived from the Puritans; of the navy from the colors of a mistress of George I.

Dishes.—Part of the payment of the king's servants used to consist of a certain number of dishes of meat. The lord president of the council was formerly allowed ten dishes of meat per diem; these ten dishes were eventually compounded for at £1000 per annum, while his salary was only £500. The lord steward had, I think, sixteen dishes. At the installations of knights of the garter, the knights were liberally provided. "On St. George's Day, 1667, each knight," says Evelyn, "had forty dishes to his mess, piled up five or six high." N. B.—This festival seems to have been kept in the banqueting-house.

Pantaloons, a kind of tight trowsers fitting the knee and leg, came into fashion about 1790, and were so called: the name, however, existed long before, but meant loose trowsers, such, perhaps, as were worn by the "lean and slippered *pantaloon*" of Shakspeare, and probably by the pantaloons of the stage. "The pantaloon," says Evelyn (*Tyrannus, or the Mode*), "are too exorbitant, and of neither sex." They were "set in plaits," not, it seems, unlike the fashion of Cossack trowsers, which came into fashion in Europe after the French campaigns to Russia, and still more after the Russian campaigns into France.

Mourning.—Mr. Bray (in his note on a passage in Evelyn's *Memoirs*, vol. ii. p. 80), stating that he had *received* gratis a complete mourning to attend Mr. Pepys's funeral) observes that "this is a curious circumstance." Mr. Bray seems strangely misinformed on this point; mourning is always given gratis. The custom is lost amongst the higher orders, except in scarves, gloves, and hat-bands, which are still given; but our servants still understand that mourning is to be a gratuitous gift, and female servants, who are seldom allowed clothes at their master's cost, always have their mourning. The clergy have always, I believe, received and used for private purposes the mourning decorations of churches. The kings of France mourn in violet; our kings, as kings of France, used to do the same. Dangeau tells us that on some public occasion at the court of France, after his exile, James II. wore violet. "It surprised us," says Dangeau, "to see two kings of France." The anecdote is creditable to both the monarchs.

Wig.—At Paris the Prince (Charles I. on his expedition to Spain) spent one day to view the city and court, shadowing himself the most he could under a bushy peruque, which none in former days but bald people used, but now generally intruded into a fashion; and the Prince's was so big that it was hair enough for his whole face.—Arthur Wilson, *Hist. Eng.*, 1653, p. 226.

Swords worn in public.—Sir Lucius O'Trigger talks of Bath in 1774, near twenty years after Nash's reign, and, even at that time, only says that swords were "not worn *there*"—implying that they were worn elsewhere; and we know that Sheridan's own duel at Bath was a rencontre, he and his adversary, Mathews, both wearing swords. In a set of characteristic sketches of eminent persons about the year 1782, several wear swords; and one or two members of the House of Commons, evidently represented in the attitude of speaking, have swords. In a picture of the Mall in St. James's Park, of about that date, the men have swords. They probably began to go out of common use about 1770, and were nearly left off in ordinary life in 1780; but were still occasionally worn, both in public and private, till the French Revolution, when they totally went out, except in court dress.

Muffs worn by Gentlemen.—In Lamber's *Travels in Canada and the United States* (1815), vol. i. p. 307, is the following passage:—

> I should not be surprised if those *delicate young soldiers* were to introduce muffs; they were in general use among the men under the French government, and are still worn by two or three old gentlemen.

In the year 1592 the Duke of Nevers was despatched by Henry IV. with all speed to a place called Bully, in order to cut off the retreat of the Duke of Guise, lately defeated near Bures. Sully speaks of him thus:—

> The Duke of Nevers, the slowest of men, began by sending to make choice of the most favourable roads, and marched with a slow pace towards Bully, with his hands and his nose in his muff, and his whole person well packed up in his coach.—*Memoirs of Sully*, vol. i. p. 235, English edit., Edinburgh, 1773.

The writer of a series of papers in the *New Monthly Magazine*, entitled "Parr in his later years," thus (vol. xvi. p. 482) describes the appearance of that learned Theban:—

> He had on his dressing-gown, which, I think, was flannel or cotton, and the skirts dangled around his ankles; over this he had drawn his great coat, buttoned close; and his hands, for he had been attacked with erysipelas not

long before, were kept warm in a silk muff, not much larger than the poll of a common hat.

In an anonymous poetical pamphlet (*Thoughts concerning Feasting and Dancing*, 12mo., London, 1800) is a little poem entitled "The Muff," in the course of which the following lines occur:—

A time there was (that time is now no more,
At least in England 'tis not now observ'd!)
When muffs were worn by *beaux* as well as belles.
Scarce has a century of time elaps'd,
Since such an article was much in vogue;
Which, when it was not on the arm sustain'd,
Hung, pendant by a silken ribbon loop
From button of the coat of well-dress'd beau.
'Tis well for manhood that the use has ceased!
For what to *woman* might be well allow'd,
As suited to the softness of her sex,
Would seem effeminate and wrong in *man*.

In a portrait of Erasmus, prefixed to a translation of his Colloquies, London, 1671, he is represented with his hands in a muff.

CHATTERTON.

The following account of the whole of the proceedings at the inquest which was held at the Three Crows, Brook Street, Holborn, on Friday, Aug. 27, 1770, before Swinson Carter, Esq., and ten jurymen, whose names are mentioned, is from a MS. copy.

I am not acquainted with any printed work which contains a report of the inquest. It is not in the large collection of Chatterton's *Works* and *Lives*, and the innumerable newspaper and magazine cuttings, which fill several volumes, and which belonged to Mr. Haslewood; nor is it in Barrett's *Bristol*, or Herbert Croft's *Love and Madness*.

Account of the Inquest held on the body of THOMAS CHATTERTON, deceased, at the Three Crows, Brook Street, Holborn, on Friday, the 27th August, 1770, before Swinson Carter, Esq., and the following jury:—Charles Skinner, —— Meres, John Hollier, John Park, S. G. Doran, Henry Dugdale, G. J. Hillsley, C. Sheen, E. Manley, C. Moore, —— Nevett.

MARY ANGELL, sack-maker, of No. 17 Brook Street, Holborn, deposed, that the deceased came to lodge at her house about nine or ten weeks ago; he took the room below the garret; he always slept in the same room; he was always very exact in his payments to her; and at one time, when she knew that he had paid her all the money he had in the world, she offered him sixpence back, which he refused to take, saying, "I have that here (pointing to his forehead) which will get me more." He used to sit up nearly all night, and she frequently found his bed untouched in the morning, when she went to make it; she knew that he always bought his loaves—one of which lasted him for a week—as stale as possible, that they might last the longer: and, two days before his death, he came home in a great passion with the baker's wife, who had refused to let him have another loaf until he paid her 3*s.* 6*d.* which he owed her previously. He, the deceased, appeared unusually grave on the 28th August; and, on her asking him what ailed him, he answered, pettishly, "Nothing, nothing—why do you ask?" On the morning of the 24th August, he lay in bed longer than usual; got up about ten o'clock, and went out with a bundle of paper under his arm, which he said "was a treasure to any one, but there were so many fools in the world that he would put them in a place of safety, lest they should meet with accident." He returned about seven in the evening, looking very pale and dejected; and would not eat any thing, but sat moping by the fire with his chin on his knees, and muttering rhymes in some old language to her. Witness saw him for the last time when he got up to go to bed; he then kissed her (a thing he had never done in his life before), and then went up stairs, stamping on every stair as he went slowly up, as if he would break it. Witness stated that he did not come down next morning, but she was not alarmed, as he had lain longer than usual on the day before; but at eleven o'clock, Mrs. Wolfe, a neighbour's wife, coming in, they went and listened at the door, and tried to open it, but it was locked. At last, they got a man who was near to break it open; and they found him lying on the bed with his legs hanging over, quite dead: the bed had not been lain on. The floor was covered all over with little bits of paper; and on one piece the man read, in deceased's handwriting, "I leave my soul to its Maker, my body to my mother and sister, and my curse to Bristol. If Mr. Ca . . ."

The rest was torn off. The man then said he must have killed himself, which we did not think till then, not having seen the poison till an hour after. Deceased was very proud, but never unkind to any one. I do not think he was quite right in his mind lately. The man took away the paper, and I have not been able to find him out.

Frederick Angell deposed to the fact of deceased lodging at their house; was from home when deceased was found. Always considered him something wonderful, and was sometimes afraid he would go out of his mind. Deceased often came home very melancholy: and, on his once asking him the reason, he said, "Hamilton has deceived me;" but could get no more from him. Deceased was always writing to his mother or sister, of whom he appeared to be very fond. I never knew him in liquor, and never saw him drink any thing but water.

Edwin Cross, apothecary, Brook Street, Holborn. Knew the deceased well from the time he came to live with Mrs. Angell in the same street. Deceased used generally to call on him every time he went by his door, which was usually two or three times in a day. Deceased used to talk a great deal about physic, and was very inquisitive about the nature of different poisons. I often asked him to take a meal with us, but he was so proud that I could never but once prevail on him, though I knew he was half-starving. One evening he did stay, when I unusually pressed him. He talked a great deal, but all at once became silent, and looked quite vacant. He used to go very often to Falcon Court, Fleet Street, to a Mr. Hamilton, who printed a magazine; but who, he said, was using him very badly. I once recommended him to return to Bristol, but he only heaved a deep sigh; and begged me, with tears in his eyes, never to mention the hated name again. He called on me on the 24th August, about half past eleven in the morning, and bought some arsenic, which he said was for an experiment. About the same time next day, Mrs. Wolfe ran in for me, saying deceased had killed himself. I went to his room, and found him quite dead. On his window was a bottle containing arsenic and water; some of the little bits of arsenic were between his teeth. I believe if he had not killed himself, he would soon have died of starvation; for he was too proud to ask of any one. Witness always considered deceased as an astonishing genius.

Anne Wolfe, of Brook Street. Witness lived three doors from Mrs. Angell's; knew the deceased well; always thought him very proud and haughty. She sometimes thought him crazed. She saw him one night walking up and down the street at twelve o'clock, talking loud, and occasionally stopping, as if to think on something. One day he came in to buy some curls, which he said he wanted to send to his sister; but he could not pay the price, and went away seemingly much mortified. On the 25th August, Mrs. Angell asked her to go up stairs with her to Thomas's room: they could make no one hear. And, at last, being frightened, they got a man who was going by to break open the door, when they found him dead on the bed. The floor was covered with little bits of paper, and the man who was with them picked up several and took away with him.

Verdict.—Felo de se.

EPIGRAMS.

The following are from a MS. commonplace book of the date of January 11th, 1697–8, in a very good handwriting of that time:—

ON THE COVETOUS.

He, Hercules' *nil ultra* does pass by,
And Carolus' *plus ultra* doth apply.

LAW AND PHYSIC.

If mortals would, as Nature dictates, live,
They need not fees to the physician give.
If men were wise they need not have their cause
Pleaded, prolong'd by the ambiguous laws.
So Bartolus might (feeless) go to bed,
And mice corrode Hippocrates unread.

OF TIME.

Age all things brings—all things bears hence with it.
All things have time, and time all things fit.

A HARD FATHER.

A sparing father is most liberall
To his son, for, dying, he doth leave him all.

VIRTUE'S COMPLAINT.

Rare's love of Love, love of Virtue's rare:
Price is now priz'd, and honours honor'd are:
Riches are prostitute; coyn money byes [*sic*];
And Virtue's vile, she must her own worth prize.

VIRESCIT VULNERE VIRTUS.

For injur'd Virtue, trampled on, revives;
More beauteous seems, and by oppression thrives!
Custom it is, that all the world to slavery brings,
And the dull excuse for doing silly things.
Custom, which sometimes Wisdom overrules,
And serves instead of Reason to the ffools.

WEIGHT OF REVOLUTIONARY OFFICERS.

On the 10th of August, 1778, the American officers at West Point were weighed, with the following result:—

	Lbs.		Lbs.
Gen. Washington	209	Col. Michael Jackson	252
Gen. Lincoln	224	Col. Henry Jackson	238
Gen. Knox	280	Lt. Col. Huntingdon	212
Gen. Huntingdon	182	Lieut. Col. Cobb	182
Gen. Greaton	166	Lt. Col. Humphreys	221
Col. Swift	319		

Only three of the eleven weighed less than two hundred pounds—a result which does not confirm the Abbé Raynal's theory of the deterioration of mankind in America.

THE "PERCY ANECDOTES."

The *Percy Anecdotes*, published in forty-four parts, in as many months, commencing in 1820, were compiled by "Sholto and Reuben Percy, Brothers of the Benedictine Monastery of Mont Benger." So said the title-pages, but the names and the locality were *supposé*. Reuben Percy was Mr. Thomas Byerley, who died in 1824: he was the brother of Sir John Byerley, and the first editor of the *Mirror*, commenced by John Limbird in 1822. Sholto Percy was Mr. Joseph Clinton Robertson, who died in 1852: he was the projector of the *Mechanics' Magazine*, which he edited from its commencement to his death. The name of the collection of Anecdotes was not taken from the popularity of the *Percy Reliques*, but from the Percy Coffee-house in Rathbone Place, where Byerley and Robertson were accustomed to meet to talk over their joint work. The idea was, however, claimed by my clever master and friend, Sir Richard Phillips, who stoutly maintained that it originated in a suggestion made by him to Dr. Tilloch and Mr. Mayne, to cut the anecdotes from the many years' files of the *Star* newspaper, of which Dr. Tilloch was then editor, and Mr. Byerley assistant editor; and to the latter overhearing the suggestion, Sir Richard contested, might the *Percy Anecdotes* be traced. I have not the means of ascertaining whether Sir Richard's claim is correct; and I should be equally sorry to reflect upon his statement as upon that of Mr. Byerley, my predecessor in the editorship of the *Mirror*. The *Percy Anecdotes* were among the best compilations of their day: their publisher, Mr. Thomas Boys, of Ludgate Hill, realized a large sum by the work; and no inconsiderable portion of their success must be referred to Mr. Boys's excellent taste in their production: the portrait illustrations, mostly engraved by Fry, were admirable.

JOHN TIMBS.

MONKISH VERSE.

The merit of this fine specimen will be seen to be in its being at once acrostic, mesostic, and telestic.

Inter cuncta micans **I**gniti sidera cœl**I**
Expellit tenebras **E** toto Phœbus ut orb**E**;
Sic cæcas removet J E **S** U S caliginis umbra**S**,
Vivificansque simul **V**ero præcordia mot**V**,
Solem justitiæ **S**ese probat esse beati**S**.

The following translation preserves the acrostic and mesostic, though not the telestic form of the original:—

In glory rising see the sun, Illustrious orb of day,
Enlightening heaven's wide expanse, Expel night's gloom away.
So light into the darkest soul, JESUS, thou dost impart,
Uplifting Thy life-giving smiles Upon the deaden'd heart:
Sun Thou of Righteousness Divine, Sole King of Saints thou art.

SWIFT AND ADDISON.

The biographer and the critic, down to the pamphleteer and the lecturer, have united in painting St. Patrick's immortal Dean in the blackest colors. To their (for the most part) unmerited scandal and reproach thus heaped upon his memory (as little in accordance with truth as with Christian charity) we oppose the following brief but emphatic testimony on the bright side of the question, of the virtuous, the accomplished Addison :—

To Dr. Jonathan Swift, The Most Agreeable Companion, The Truest Friend, and the Greatest Genius of his Age, This Book is presented by his most Humble Servant the Authour.

The above inscription, in the autograph of Addison, is on the fly-leaf of his *Remarks on several Parts of Italy, &c.*, 8vo. 1705.

"SPEECH GIVEN TO MAN TO CONCEAL HIS THOUGHTS."

This remarkable saying, like most good things of that kind, has been repeated by so many distinguished writers, that it is impossible to trace it to any one in particular, in the precise form in which it is now popularly received. I shall quote, in succession, all those who appear to have expressed it in words of the same or a nearly similar import.

I cannot help thinking that the first place should be assigned to Jeremy Taylor, as he must have had the sentiment clearly in view in the following sentence :—

There is in mankind an universal contract implied in all their intercourses; and *words being instituted* to *declare the mind, and for no other end,* he that hears me speak hath a right in justice to be done him, that, as far as I can, what I speak be true; for else he by words does not know your mind, and then as good and better not speak at all.

Next we have David Lloyd, who in his *State Worthies*, thus remarks of Sir Roger Ascham :—

None is more able for, yet none is more averse to, that circumlocution and contrivance wherewith some men shadow their main drift and purpose. *Speech was made to open man to man, and not to hide him;* to promote commerce, and not betray it.

Dr. South, Lloyd's contemporary, but who survived him more than twenty years, expresses the sentiment in nearly the same words:—

In short, this seems to be the true inward judgment of all our politick sages, that *speech was givin to the ordinary sort of men, whereby to communicate their mind, but to wise men whereby to conceal it.*

The next writer in whom this thought occurs is Butler, the author of *Hudibras.* In one of his prose essays on the "Modern Politician," he says:—

He (the modern politician) believes a man's words and his meanings should never agree together: for he that says what he thinks lays himself open to be expounded by the most ignorant; and *he who does not make his words rather serve to conceal than discover the sense of his heart,* deserves to have it pulled out, like a traitor's, and shown publicly to the rabble.

In *Gulliver's Travels* (1727), Voyage to the Houyhnhnms, the minister, Gulliver says, "applies his words to all uses except to the indication of his mind."

Young has the thought in the following couplet on the duplicity of courts:—

When Nature's end of language is declin'd,
And men talk only to *conceal their mind.*

From Young it passed to Voltaire, who, in the dialogue entitled "Le Chapon et la Poularde," makes the former say of the treachery of men:—

Ils n'emploient les paroles que pour *déguiser leurs pensées.*

Goldsmith about the same time, in his paper in *The Bee,* produces it in the well known words:—

Men who know the world, hold that the true use of speech is not so much to *express* our wants, as to *conceal* them.

Then comes Talleyrand, who is reported to have said:—

La parole n'a été donnée à l'homme que pour *déguiser sa pensée.*

The latest writer who adopts this remark without acknowledgment is, I believe, Lord Holland. In his *Life of Lope de Vega* he says of certain Spanish writers, promoters of the *cultismo* style:—

Those authors do not avail themselves of the invention of letters for the purpose of *conveying, but of concealing, their ideas.*

From these passages it will be seen that the germ of the thought occurs in Jeremy Taylor; that Lloyd and South improved upon it; that Butler, Young, and Goldsmith repeated it; that Voltaire translated it into French; that Talleyrand echoed Voltaire's words; and that it has now become so familiar an expression that any one may quote it, as Lord Holland has done, without being at the trouble of giving his authority.

PLUM-PUDDING.

Southey, in his *Omniana*, vol. i. p. 7, quotes the following receipt for English plum-pudding, as given by the Chevalier d'Arvieux, who in 1658 made a voyage in an English forty-gun ship:—

Leur pudding était détestable. C'est un composé de biscuit pilé, ou de farine, de lard, de raisins de Corinthe, de sel, et de poivre, dont on fait une pâte, qu'on enveloppe dans une serviette, et que l'on fait cuire dans le pot avec du bouillon de la viande; on la tire de la serviette, et on la met dans un plat, et on rappe dessus du vieux fromage, qui lui donne une odeur insupportable. Sans ce fromage la chose en elle-même n'est pas absolument mauvaise.

WILLIAM COWPER.

In the midsummer holidays of 1799, being on a visit to an old and opulent family of the name of Deverell, in Dereham, Norfolk, I was taken to the house of an ancient lady (a member of the aforesaid family), to pay my respects to her, and to drink tea. Two visitors were *particularly* expected. They soon arrived. The first, if I remember rightly (for my whole attention was singularly riveted to the *second*), was a pleasant-looking, lively young man, very talkative and entertaining; his companion was above the middle height, broadly made, but not stout, and advanced in years. His countenance had a peculiar charm that I could not resist. It alternately exhibited a deep sadness, a thoughtful repose, a fearful and an intellectual fire, that surprised and held me captive. His manner was embarrassed and reserved. He spoke but little. Yet *once* he was roused to animation; then his voice was full and clear. I have a faint recollection that I saw his face lighted up with a momentary smile. His hostess kindly welcomed him as "Mr. Cooper." After tea, we walked for a while in the garden. I kept close to his side, and once he addressed me as "My little master." I returned to school; but that variable, expressive, and interesting countenance I did not forget. In after years, standing, as was my wont, before the shop windows of the London booksellers (I have not *quite* left off this old habit!), reading the title-pages of tomes that I intensely longed, but had not then the money to purchase, I recognised at a shop in St. Paul's Churchyard that well-remembered face, prefixed to a volume of poems, "written by William Cowper, of the Inner Temple, Esq." The *cap* (for when I saw "Mr. Cooper" he wore a wig, or his hair, for his age, was unusually luxuriant) was the only thing that puzzled me. To make "assurance doubly sure," I hastened to the house of a near relation hard by, and I soon learnt that "Mr. Cooper" was William Cowper. The welcome present of a few shillings put me in *immediate* possession of the coveted volumes. I will only just add, that I read and re-read them; that the man whom, in my early boyhood, I had so mysteriously reverenced, in my youth I deeply and devotedly admired and loved! Many, many years have since passed away; but that reverence, that admiration, and that love have experienced neither diminution nor change.

It was something, said Washington Irving, to have seen even the *dust* of Shakspeare. It is something, too, to have beheld the face and to have heard the voice of Cowper. GEORGE DANIEL.

SHAKSPEARE'S BEDSIDE.

The accompanying BALLAD originally appeared in the *Gentleman's Magazine* for 1797, page 912. The author, fancifully enough, imagines the various editions of Shakspeare brought in succession to the sick-bed of the immortal bard, and has curiously detailed the result of their several prescriptions:—

Old Shakspeare was sick—for a doctor he sent—
But 'twas long before any one came;
Yet at length his assistance Nic Row did present;
Sure all men have heard of his name.

As he found that the poet had tumbled his bed;
He smooth'd it as well as he could;
He gave him an anodyne, comb'd out his head,
But did his complaint little good.

Doctor Pope to incision at once did proceed,
And the Bard for the simples he cut;
For his regular practice was always to bleed,
Ere the fees in his pocket he put.

Next Theobald advanced, who at best was a quack,
And dealt but in old women's stuff;
Yet he caused the physician of Twick'nam to pack,
And the patient grew cheerful enough.

Next Hanmer, who fees ne'er descended to crave,
In gloves lily-white did advance;
To the Poet the gentlest of purges he gave,
And, for exercise, taught him to dance.

One Warburton, then, tho' allied to the Church,
Produced his alterative stores;
But his med'cines the case so oft left in the lurch
That Edwards* kick'd him out of doors.

Next Johnson arrived to the patient's relief,
And ten years he had him in hand;
But, tired of his task, 'tis the gen'ral belief,
He left him before he could stand.

Now Capel drew near, not a Quaker more prim,
And number'd each hair in his pate;
By styptics, call'd stops, he contracted each limb,
And crippled for ever his gait.

From Gopsal then strutted a formal old goose,
And he'd cure him by inches, he swore;
But when the poor Poet had taken one dose,
He vow'd he would swallow no more.

But Johnson, determined to save him or kill,
A second prescription display'd;
And that none might find fault with his drop or his pill,
Fresh doctors he called to his aid.

First, Steevens came loaded with black-letter books,
Of fame more desirous than pelf;
Such reading, observers might read in his looks,
As no one e'er read but himself.

Then Warner, by Plautus and Glossary known,
And Hawkins, historian of sound;†
Then Warton and Collins together came on,
For Greek and potatoes renown'd.

* One Edwards, an apothecary, who seems to have known [more] of the poet's case than some of the regular physicians who undertook to cure him.

† From the abilities and application of Sir J. Hawkins, the publick is now furnished with a compleat history of the science of musick.

With songs on his pontificalibus pinn'd,
Next, Percy the Great did appear;
And Farmer, who twice in a pamphlet had sinn'd,
Brought up the empirical rear.

"The cooks the more num'rous the worse is the broth,"
Says a proverb I well can believe;
And yet to condemn them untried I am loth,
So at present shall laugh in my sleeve.

RIGDUM FUNNIDOS.

[At page 1108 of the same volume will be found the following reply :—

ANSWER TO SHAKSPEARE'S BEDSIDE; OR THE DOCTORS ENUMERATED.

How could you assert, when the Poet was sick,
None hit off a method of cure;
When Montagu's pen, like a magical stick,
His health did for ever ensure?]

NAPOLEON.

The Bonapartes are said to have adopted the name of *Napoleon* from Napoleon des Ursins, a distinguished character in Italian story, with one of whose descendants they became connected by marriage; and the first of the family to whom it was given was a brother of Joseph Bonaparte, the grandfather of Napoleon I. Many are the *jeux de mots* that have been made on this name; but the following, in *Littérature Française Contemporaine*, vol. ii. p. 266, is perhaps the most remarkable.

The word *Napoleon*, being written in Greek characters, will form seven different words, by dropping the first letter of each in succession; namely, Ναπολεων, Απολεων, Πολεων, Ολεων, Λεων,

Εων, Ων. These words make a complete sentence, and are thus translated into French: "Napoléon étant le lion des peuples, al lait détruisant les cités."

PRICES OF TEA.

From Read's *Weekly Journal or British Gazetteer*, Saturday, April 27, 1734:—

Green Tea - - - - -	9*s.* to 12*s.* per lb.
Congou - - - - -	10*s.* to 12*s.* "
Bohea - - - - - -	10*s.* to 12*s.* "
Pekoe - - - - - -	14*s.* to 16*s.* "
Imperial - - - - -	9*s.* to 12*s.* "
Hyson - - - - - -	20*s.* to 25*s.* "

PUNNING MOTTOES.

The following are some specimens of this curious class of motto:—

Deo paget.—PAGET.
Του αριστευειν ἑνεκα.—HENNIKER.
Forte scutum salus ducum.—FORTESCUE.
Hoc in loco dens.—HOCKIN.
Fides montium Deo.—HILL.
Et juste et vrai.—WRAY.
Fari fac.—FAIRFAX.
Recipiunt fœmina sustentacula a nobis.—PATTENMAKERS' COMPANY.
God the only Founder.—FOUNDERS' COMPANY.
Omnia subjecisti sub pedibus, oves et boves.—BUTCHERS'.

GUANO.

It may not be altogether uninteresting to ascertain the date when the knowledge of *Guano* and its fertilising properties was first introduced to the English public. There is a mention of this substance in 1670, in a little work then printed, called the *Art of Metalls*, translated from the Spanish. Although the title-page of that edition does not mention the name of the translator, he is known to have been Edward Montagu, Earl of Sandwich. The title was thus :—

The First Book of the Art of Metalls; written in Spanish by Albano Alonzo Barba, Master of Art, born in the Town of Lepe in Andalusia, Curate of St. Bernard's Parish in the Imperial City of Potosi, in the Kingdom of Peru in the W. I., in the Year 1640. Translated into English in the Year 1669: Lond., sm. 8vo., 1670.

At p. 16 is the passage alluded to, viz. :—

Cardanus, amongst his curiosities, makes mention of another kinde of earth, anciently called *Britannica* (from the country where it is found); they were fain to dig very deep mines to come at it. It was white; and after they had separated the plate it contained, they manured their tilth-fields with the earth, which were put in heart thereby for 100 years after. Out of islands in the South Sea, not far from the city of Arica, they fetch earth that doth the same effect as the last afore-mentioned. It is called *Guano* (i. e. dung); not because it is the dung of sea-fowls (as many would have it), but because of its admirable virtue in making ploughed ground fertile. And that which is brought from the island of *Iqueyque* is of a dark gray colour, like unto tobacco ground small. Although from other islands near Arica they get a white earth, inclining to sallow, of the same virtue. It instantly colours water whereinto it is put, as if it was the best ley, and smells very strong. The qualities and virtues of this, and of many other simples of the new world, are a large field for ingenious persons to discourse philosophically upon, when they shall bend their minds to the searching out of truth, rather than riches.

Another and earlier mention of guano occurs in the translation of the Spanish Jesuit, Joseph de Acosta's *Historia natural y moral de las Indias*, published in the year 1604, by E. G., the initials, it is supposed, of Edward Grimestone, under the title of the *Naturall and Morall Historie of the East and West Indies*.

Acosta had resided seventeen years in Peru, and his work was first printed at Seville in 1590. The extract (at p. 311) is as follows :—

There are other birdes at the Indies, contrarie to these, of so rich feathers, the which (besides that they are ill-favoured) serve to no other use but for dung; and yet perchance they are of no lesse profite. I have considered this, wondering at the providence of the Creator, who hath so appointed that all creatures should serve man. In some islands or *phares*, which are joyning to the coast of Peru, wee see the toppes of the mountaines all white, and to sight you would take it for snow, or for some white land; but they are heapes of dung of sea fowle, which go continually thither; and there is so great abundance as it riseth many elles, yea, many launces in height, which seemes but a fable. They go with boates to these ilands, onely for the dung, for there is no other profit in them. And this dung is so commodious and profitable, as it makes the earth yeelde great aboundance of fruite. They cal this dung *guano*, whereof the valley hath taken the name, which they call Limaguana,* in the valleys of Peru, where they use this dung, and it is the most fertile of all that countre. The quinces, poungranets, and other fruites there, exceede all other in bountie and greatnes: and they say the reason is, for that the water wherewith they water it passeth by a land compassed with this dung, which causeth the beautie of this fruite. So as these birds have not only the flesh to serve for meate, their singing for recreation, their feathers for ornament and beautie, but also their dung serves to fatten the ground. The which hath bin so appointed by the soveraigne Creator for the service of man, that he might remember to acknowledge and be loyall to Him from whom all good proceedes.

PHONETIC SPELLING.

In Howell's *Familiar Letters*, on what would be, if it were paged, p. 256 (edit. 8vo. London, 1650), is an address "To the Intelligent *Reader*," from which we learn that an attempt to introduce a phonetic spelling of the English language was then made by the author. He did not, however, project so great a change as the more recent professors of the phonetic art, the editor of *The Phonetic News* for example, the first number of which paper, published 6th January, 1849, is now before me. In this paper the phonetic alphabet is made to consist "of forty letters and two auxiliary signs," with several additional letters to express "foreign sounds which do not occur in English." How-

* *Lunaguana* in the original.

ell, however, is content to remove such letters as appear to him redundant. He speaks on this wise :—

Amongst other reasons which make the *English* Language of so small extent, and put strangers out of conceit to learn it, one is, that we do not pronounce as we write, which proceeds from divers superfluous letters, that occur in many of our words, which adds to the difficulty of the language : Therefore the *Author* hath taken pains to retrench such redundant, unnecessary letters in this work (though the *Printer* hath not bin so carefull as he should have bin), as amongst multitudes of other words may appear in these few, *done, some, come ;* which though wee, to whom the speech is *connaturall,* pronounce as monosyllables, yet when strangers com to read them, they are apt to make them dissillabls, as *do-ne, so-me, co-me,* therefore such an *e* is superfluous.

Amongst the changes which the author advocates, many agree with our present orthography, as *physic*, *favor*, *war*, *pity*, not *physique*, *favour*, *warre*, *pitie ;* but in others he differs greatly from the received mode, as he proposes *peeple*, *tresure*, *toung*, *parlement*, &c., for *people*, *treasure*, *tongue*, *parliament*, &c. He adds :—

The new Academy of Wits call'd *L'Académie de beaux esprits,* which the late Cardinal *de Richelieu* founded in *Paris,* is now in hand to reform the *French* language in this particular, and to weed it of all superfluous Letters, which makes the *Toung* differ so much from the *Pen* that they have expos'd themselves to this contumelious Proverb, *The Frenchman doth neither pronounce as he writes, nor speak as he thinks, nor sing as he pricks.*

And he quotes a "topic axiom" of Aristotle as applicable to phonetics, "Frustra fit per plura, quod fieri potest per pauciora."

HOGARTH'S PORTRAIT OF GARRICK.

Hogarth and Garrick sitting together after dinner, Hogarth was lamenting there was no portrait of Fielding, when Garrick said, "I think I can make his face." "Pray, try, my dear Davy," said the other. Garrick then made the attempt, and so well did he succeed, that Hogarth immediately caught the likeness, and exclaimed with exultation, "Now I have him : keep still, my dear Davy!" To work he went with pen and ink, and the likeness was finished by their mutual recollections. This sketch has been engraved from the original drawing, and is preserved among several original drawings and prints in the *illustrated* copy of Lyson's *Environs*, vol. i. p. 544, in the King's Library, British Museum.

UNPUBLISHED LETTER OF BOSWELL.

EDINBURGH, 11*th April*, 1774.

DEAR SIR:—

When Mr. Johnson and I arrived at Inveraray after our expedition to the Hebrides, and there for the first time *after many days* renewed our enjoyment of the luxuries of civilized life, one of the most elegant that I could wish to find was lying for me, a letter from Mr. Garrick. It was a pineapple of the finest flavor, which had a high zest indeed amongst the heath-covered mountains of Scotia. That I have not thanked you for it long ere now, is one of those strange facts for which it is so difficult to account, that I shall not attempt it. The *Idler* has strongly expressed many of the wonderful effects of the *vis inertiæ* of the human mind. But it is hardly credible that a man should have the warmest regard for his friend, a constant desire to show it, and a keen ambition for a frequent epistolary intercourse with him, and yet should let months roll on without having resolution, or activity, or power, or whatever it be, to write a few lines. A man in such a situation is somewhat like Tantalus reversed. He recedes, he knows not how, from what he loves, which is full as provoking as when what he loves recedes from him. That my complaint is not a peculiar fancy, but deep in human nature, I appeal to the authority of St. Paul, who, though he had not been exalted to the dignity of an apostle, would have stood high in fame as a philosopher and orator, "*What I would that do I not.*" You need be under no concern as to your debt to me for the book which I purchased for you. It was long ago discharged; for, believe me, I intended the book as a present. Or if you rather chuse that it should be held as an exchange with the epitaphs which you sent me, I have no objection. Dr. Goldsmith's death would affect all the club much. I have not been so much affected with any event that has happened of a long time. I wish you would give me, who am at a distance, and who cannot get to London this spring, some particulars with regard to his last appearances. Dr. Young has a fine thought to this purpose, that every friend who goes before us to the other side of the river of death, makes the passage to us the easier. Were our club all removed to a future world but one or two, *they*, one should think, would incline to follow. By all means let me be on your list of subscribers to Mr. Morrell's *Prometheus.* You have enlivened the town, I see, with a musical piece. The prologue is admirably fancied *arripere populum tributim;* though, to be sure, Foote's remark applies to it, that your prologues have a culinary turn, and that therefore the motto to your collection of them should be, *Animus jamdudum in Patinis.* A player upon words might answer him, "Any Patinis rather than your Piety in Pattens." I wonder the wags have not been quoting upon you, "Whose erudition is a *Christmas tale.*" But Mr. Johnson is ready to bruise any one who calls in question your classical knowledge and your happy application of it. I hope Mr. Johnson has given you an entertaining account of his Northern Tour. He is certainly to favor the world with some of his remarks. Pray do not fail to quicken him by word as I do by letter. Posterity will be the more obliged to his friends the more that they can prevail with him to write. With best compliments to Mrs. Garrick, and hoping that you will not punish me by being long silent, I remain faithfully yours, JAMES BOSWELL.

To David Garrick, Esq., Adelphi, London.

SIR ROBERT AYTOUN.

The following verses are from the *Poems of Sir Robert Aytoun*, edited by Charles Roger : Edinburgh, 1844. The volume contains a memoir of the author, and a genealogical tree of the family. He was the second son of Andrew Aytoun, proprietor of Kinaldie in Fifeshire, and was born in 1570. He was, according to Dempster, (who gives an account of him in his *Historia Ecclesiastica Gentis Scotorum,*) a writer of Greek and French, as well as of Latin and English verses. He was acquainted with many of his learned and poetical cotemporaries. Ben Jonson made it his boast, that " Sir Robert Aytoun loved him dearly." He was a member of the royal household of King James I., and afterwards became secretary to Henrietta Maria, Queen of Charles I., and enjoyed the favor of that monarch till his death, which took place in the palace of Whitehall, in March, 1638. His remains were consigned to Westminster Abbey. A monument, with bust, was erected to his memory by his nephew Sir John Aytoun. They are still in good preservation.

In a note to the poem the editor says :—

This poem is reprinted from Watson's collection, where it appears anonymous, as well as in many others of our earlier collections of English poetry. From its similarity to Aytoun's other productions, it has been often ascribed to him, and little doubt can be entertained as to its authenticity. It is undoubtedly one of Aytoun's best productions: and it so attracted the notice of the poet Burns that he made an attempt " to improve the simplicity of the sentiments, by giving them a Scottish dress." Burns' alteration, however, was a complete failure.

I do confess thou'rt smooth and fair,
And I might have gone near to love thee,
Had I not found the slightest prayer
That lips can speak had power to move thee ;
But I can let thee now alone,
As worthy to be loved by none.

I do confess thee sweet, but find
Thee such an unthrift of thy sweets;
Thy favors are but like the wind,
That kisseth every thing it meets:
And since thou canst with more than one,
Thou'rt worthy to be kiss'd by none.

The morning rose that untouch'd stands,
Arm'd with her briers, doth sweetly smell,
But pluck'd and strain'd through ruder hands
Her sweets no longer with her dwell,
But scent and beauty both are gone,
And leaves fall from her one by one.

Such fate ere long will thee betide,
When thou hast handled been awhile—
Like sere flowers to be thrown aside;
And I shall sigh, while some will smile,
To see thy love to every one,
Hath caused thee to be loved by none.

FALSE SPELLINGS ARISING OUT OF SOUND.

A curious list might be compiled of English words conveying in their present form meanings totally in discordance with their derivatives. The sound of such words has given birth to a new idea, and this new idea has become confirmed by a corresponding, but of course erroneous, mode of spelling. Such are the following, some of which have been already noticed by Dr. Lathom in his large grammar:—

Buffetiers has been transformed into *Beef-eaters.*

Dent de lion has been corrupted to *dandylion,* from an idea of the bold and flaunting aspect of the flower, whereas its name has reference to the root.

Contre-danse is spelled *country-dance,* as implying rural or common life pastime, instead of the position of the dancers.

Shamefastness, altered by our *modern* printers of the authorized version of the New Testament to *shamefacedness,* though the connection of the passage shows it to have reference to the attire and not to the countenance. Query, has not Miss Strickland, in her life of Mary of Lorraine, fallen into the same error, in a quotation which states that while the court ladies were dressing gaily on one occasion, the princess (afterwards queen) Elizabeth preferred keeping to her own *shamefacedness?* This must surely be an alteration from *shamefastness.*

Cap-à-pie, armed from head to foot: this has given rise to the homely term of *apple-pie* order.

Folio-capo (Italian), first size sheet, suggestive of *foolscap.*

Asparagus, popularized into *sparrow-grass.* Lathom.

Chateau-vert hill, near Oxford, well known as *Shotover* hill. Lathom.

Girasole artichoke, *Jerusalem artichoke.* Lathom.

Farced-meat balls. The notion of their containing essence artificially concentrated has occasioned the spelling *forced*, whereas the meaning is simply *chopped.* French, *farcée.*

Spar-hawk (or rock-hawk), *sparrow-hawk.*

Satyr and Bacchanals, a public-house sign, *Satan and the Bag of Nails.*

Double-doré, *double-gilt;* from his bright yellow spot, the bee called in the west of England the *dumbledoor*, still further softened into *humble-bee.*

Gut-cord, *cat-gut.*

Engleford, or the Englishman's ford, modernized into *Hungerford;* but the corruption in the names of places is a very wide field.

Laak (Ang.-Sax.), play, has been turned into *lark*, and even tortured into *sky-lark.* Lathom.

Sambuca, altered (through a French medium), though certainly not euphonized, into *sackbut*, treated by Miss Strickland in the work above mentioned as a Scottish bagpipe. Her version is not positively disputed, but merely the doubt raised whether or not the original chronicler intended to suggest the mode of inflation. Furthermore, is it likely that, as Miss Strickland surmises, the bagpipe was used at church? The meanings of ancient musical terms are doubtless very obscure. In some parts of England the *sackbut* is even identified with the *trombone.*

Massaniello is universally recognized as the name of the celebrated Neapolitan insurrectionist, who at one time nearly overturned the government of that kingdom. How few who use the word are aware that "Mas-Aniello" is but a corruption of *Thomas Aniello*, so pronounced by his vulgar companions, and now raised to the dignity of an historical name.

Hougoumont is a conspicuous feature of the great field of Waterloo, and a name familiarly used in speaking of the famous battle; in course of time it will be forgotten that this is a mere mistake, said to have originated with the great general who achieved the victory, catching up from the peasantry around, the sound of *Chateau Goumont*, and the real name of the little rural demesne in question. Nobody doubts, however, the right of the "Great Duke" to call a place he has made so famous by any name he might please to apply, and so *Hougoumont* it will remain while history lasts.

HAMPDEN'S DEATH.

On the 21st of July, 1828, the corpse of John Hampden was disinterred by the late Lord Nugent for the purpose of settling the disputed point of history as to the manner in which the patriot received his death-wound. The examination seems to have been conducted after a somewhat bungling fashion for a scientific object, and the facts disclosed were these:—"On lifting up the right arm we found that it was dispossessed of its hand. We might therefore naturally conjecture that it had been amputated, as the bone presented a perfectly flat appearance, as if sawn off by some sharp instrument. On searching under the cloths, to our no small astonishment we found the hand, or rather a number of small bones, inclosed in a separate cloth. For about six inches up the arm the flesh had wasted away, being evidently smaller than the lower part of the left arm, to which the hand was very firmly united, and which presented no symptoms of decay further than the two bones of the fore-finger loose. Even the nails remained entire, of which we saw no appearance in the cloth containing the remains of the right hand. . . . The clavicle of the right shoulder was firmly united to the scapula, nor did there appear any contusion or indentation that evinced symptoms of any wound ever having been inflicted. The left shoulder, on the contrary, was smaller and sunken in, as if the clavicle had been displaced. To remove all doubts, it was adjudged necessary to remove the arms, which were amputated with a pen-knife (!). The socket of the left (*sic*) arm was perfectly white and healthy, and the clavicle firmly united to the scapula, nor was there the least appearance of contusion or wound. The socket of the right (*sic*) shoulder, on the contrary, was of a brownish cast, and the clavicle being found quite loose and disunited from the scapula, proved that dislocation had taken place. The bones, however, were quite perfect." These appearances indicated that injuries had been received both in the hand and shoulder, the former justifying the belief in Sir Robert Pye's statement to the Harleys, that the pistol which had been presented to him by Sir Robert, his son-in-law, had burst and shattered his hand in a terrible manner at the action of Chalgrave Field; the latter indicating that he had either been wounded in the shoulder by a spent ball, or had received an injury there by falling from his horse after his hand was shattered. Of these wounds he died three or four days after, according to Sir Philip Warwick. According to Clarendon, "three weeks after being shot into the shoulder with a brace of bullets, which broke the bone." The bone, however, was not found broken, and the "brace of bullets" is equally imaginary.

This account is from a newspaper cutting of *The News*, August 3, 1828.

TEACHING A DOG FRENCH.

The original of the following curiosity is in the Lansdowne MS. (114, No. 8), in the British Museum; and the fact of its being in Lord Burleigh's papers, shows that the occurrence mentioned in it took place between 1571 and 1598, the respective dates of his appointment as "l tresurer" and his death. The supposition that D. Julio was some obnoxious Frenchman, protected by the government, seems necessary to account for the "teachyng a dogg frenche," in front of his door, constituting such a dire offence.

D. JULIO'S ABSTRACT OF THE DEPOSICŌNS OF YE WITNESSES SWORNE TOUCHING YE SPECHES OF JOHN PAGET.

To proue that one William (sic) Paget, on the vth day of this present moneth, being Fryday, betwixt VIII and IX of the clocke at nyght, went vp and down teachyng a dogg frenche.

1. Mris Karter, a jentilwoman borne, sayeth, that about the same tym, she did hear the said Paget, that he wold teache his dogg to speak frenche.
2. Mris Anne Coot, a jentilwoman, affirmeth the same.
3. One William Poyser, yeoman, sayeth, that he harde Paget saye that he wold make his dogg speake as good frenche as any of them.
4. James Hudson sayeth, that standing at his maister's doore he did hear Paget speake to his dogg in a straunge language, but what language he knew not.
5. Edward, a grosser, is to be deposed that he harde Paget say, I will teache my dogg to speake frenche, and was talking with his dogg in frenche.

To proue that the sayd Paget did say, Shortlye will come vnto the realme frenche dogges, I hope I shall see thame all rootted out.

1. M^ris Karter sayeth, she harde Paget say, Shortlie wil come vnto the realme frenche dogges, I hope I shall see thame all rootted out.

2. M^ris Anne Coot affirmeth the same.

3. William Poyser sayeth, he harde Paget say, Within this week or two, there will come a great many frenche dogges.

4. M^ris Eleonore Borgourneci vppon her othe affirmeth the same.

5. The l maior writteth in his lre to my l tresurer that Paget affirmeth before him that he wold the realme were ryd of all yll straungers, adding this qualification. [Qualification not given.]

To proue the great assembly that was with Paget, before D. Julio came home to his howse.

1. John Polton saieth, when his maister came home there was about a hundreth persone of men, women, and chyldren, vp and downe there.

2. James Hudson sayeth, that he thinketh there was about IIII people assembled in the streett before this examinăt his maister came home.

3. Richard Preston sayeth, that there was in his iudgement aboue a hundred people in the streett before this deponēts maister came home, and after his m^r came home the nomber of the people were greater.

To proue that the sayd Paget did resiste to the constable when he came to apprehend him.

1. William Poyser sayeth, when the constable came to apprehende the sayd Paget he kept the constable out with force, and sayd he should not enter on him.

2. James Hudson sayeth, Paget wold not suffer the constable to entere vnto his howse, but sayd if any man will entere vnto this howse, yf it were not f^r felony or treason to apprehend him, he wold kill hym, yf he could, f^r he sayd his howse was his castell.

3. Richard Preston sayeth, when the constable came to apprehend Paget, he hauing a bill or halberd in his hand, did keepe him out of his howse, and sayd, he should not enter except it were f^r feloney or treason, or that he brought my l maior's warrant.

"OLD FOGY."

In the kindred Teutonic tongues the word runs through the various forms of *vogt*, *fogat*, *phogat*, *voget*, *voogde*, *fogde*, *foged*, *fogeti*, with the meaning of bailiff, steward, preses, watchman, guard or protector, tutor, overseer, judge, mayor, policeman; and doubtless *fogie* belongs to the same family, though it has lost its tail. Words frequently degenerate in meaning, falling from the noblest to the basest, from the purest to the most obscene. Is there then any thing improbable in supposing that a word once applied to the governor or chief keeper of a castle, came at last to be applied to all, even the meanest of his subordinates? Dr. Jamieson asserts that the word *fogde* in the Su.-G. has actually had that fate. Dr. Jamieson, in his Scottish Dictionary, defines the word "foggie or fogie," to be first, "an invalid, or garrison soldier," secondly, "a person advanced in life;" and derives it from "Su.G-*fogde*, formerly one who had the charge of a garrison."

It was a well-known name a century ago in Dublin, being applied to the old men in the Royal Hospital. In Edinburgh Castle, in the latter part of the last and beginning of the present centuries, there were a peculiar body of men called the *Fogies*. They were an invalid company, being old men, dressed in red coats with apple-green facings, and cocked hats. In a word, it would appear that the word "fogie, in its most general acceptation, means by itself, without the "old," an old soldier; and that "old fogie" is only a tautological form, arising from ignorance of its meaning.

SONNET BY BLANCO WHITE.

This sonnet first appeared in *The Bijou*, an annual published by Pickering in 1828.

NIGHT AND DEATH.

A Sonnet: dedicated to S. T. Coleridge, Esq., by his sincere friend Joseph Blanco White.

Mysterious night, when the first man but knew
Thee by report, unseen, and heard thy name,
Did he not tremble for this lovely frame,
This glorious canopy of light and blue?
Yet 'neath a curtain of translucent dew,
Bathed in the rays of the great setting flame,
Hesperus, with the host of heaven, came,
And lo! creation widen'd on his view.
Who could have thought what darkness lay concealed
Within thy beams, O Sun? Or who could find,
Whilst fly, and leaf, and insect stood reveal'd,
That to such endless orbs thou mad'st us blind?
Weak man! Why to shun death this anxious strife?
If *light* can thus deceive, wherefore not *life*?

In a letter from Coleridge to White, dated Nov. 28, 1827, he thus speaks of it:—

I have now before me two fragments of letters *begun*, the one in acknowledgment of the finest and most graceful sonnet in our language (at least, it is only in Milton's and Wordsworth's sonnets that I recollect any rival, and this is not my judgment alone, but that of the man *κατ' ἐξοχὴν φιλόκαλον*, John Hookham Frere), the second on the receipt of your "Letter to Charles Butler," &c.

In a subsequent letter, without date, Coleridge thus again reverts to the circumstance of its having been published without his or White's sanction:—

But first of your sonnet. On reading the sentences in your letter respecting it, I stood staring vacantly on the paper, in a state of feeling not unlike that which I have too often experienced in a dream: when I have found myself in chains, or in rags, shunned, or passed by, with looks of horror blended with sadness, by friends and acquaintance; and convinced that, in some alienation of mind, I must have perpetrated some crime, which I strove in vain to recollect. I then ran down to Mrs. Gillman, to learn whether she or Mr. Gillman could throw any light on the subject. Neither Mr. nor Mrs. Gillman could account for it. I have repeated the sonnet often, but, to the best of my recollection, never either gave a copy to any one, or permitted any one to transcribe it; and as to publishing it without your consent, you must allow me to say the truth: I had felt myself so much flattered by your having addressed it to me, that I should have been half afraid that it would appear to be asking to have my vanity tickled, if I had thought of applying to you for permission to publish it. Where and when did it appear? If you will be so good as to inform me, I may perhaps trace it out: for it annoys me to imagine myself capable of such a breach of confidence and of delicacy.

In his Journal, October 16 [1838 ?], Blanco White says:—

In copying out my "Sonnet on Night and Death" for a friend, I have made some corrections. It is now as follows:—

Mysterious Night! when our first parent knew
Thee from report divine, and heard thy name,
Did he not tremble for this lovely frame,
This glorious canopy of light and blue?
Yet 'neath a curtain of translucent dew,
Bathed in the rays of the great setting flame,
Hesperus with the host of heaven came,
And lo! creation widen'd in man's view.
Who could have thought such darkness lay conceal'd
Within thy beams, O Sun! or who could find,
Whilst fly, and leaf, and insect stood reveal'd,
That to such countless orbs thou mad'st us blind!
Why do we then shun death, with anxious strife?
If light can thus deceive, wherefore not life?

THE OMENS OF SNEEZING.

In the Odyssey, xvii. 54–57, we have, imitating the Hexameters, the following passage:—

Thus Penelope spoke. Then quickly Telemachus *sneez'd* aloud,
Sounding around all the building; his mother with smiles at her son, said,
Swiftly addressing her rapid and high-toned words to Eumæus,
"Go then directly, Eumæus, and call to my presence the strange guest.
See'st thou not that my son, *ev'ry word I have spoken hath sneez'd at?*
Thus portentous, betok'ning the fate of my hateful suitors,
All whom death and destruction await by a doom irreversive."

Dionysius Halicarnassus, on Homer's poetry (s. 24), says, sneezing was considered by that poet as a good sign (σύμβολον ἀγαθόν); and from the *Anthology* (lib. ii.) the words οὐδὲ λέγει, Ζεῦ σῶσον, ἐὰν πταρῇ, show that it was proper to exclaim "God bless you!" when any one sneezed.

Aristotle, in the Problems (xxxiii. 7), inquires why sneezing is reckoned a God (διὰ τί τὸν μὲν πταρμὸν, θεὸν ἡγούμεθα εἶναι); to which he suggests that it may be because it comes from the head, the most divine part about us (θειοτάτου τῶν περὶ ἡμᾶς).

Athenæus, says Potter in his *Archæologia Græca*, proves that the head was esteemed holy, because it was customary to swear by it, and adore as holy the sneezes that proceeded from it.

> Oscitatio in nixu letalis est, sicut
> Sternuisse a coitu abortivum.
> Quoted from Pliny by Aulus Gellius,
> *Noct. Att.* III. xvi. 24.

Persons having the inclination, but not the power to sneeze, should look at the sun, for reasons he assigns in Problems (xxxiii. 4).

Plutarch, on the Dæmon of Socrates (s. 11), states the opinion which some persons had formed, that Socrates' dæmon was nothing else than the sneezing either of himself or others. Thus, if any one sneezed at his right hand, either before or behind him, he pursued any step he had begun; but sneezing at his left hand caused him to desist from his formed purpose. He adds something as to different kinds of sneezing. To sneeze twice was usual in Aristotle's time; but once, or more than twice, was uncommon (Prob. xxxiii. 3).

Petronius (*Satyr.* c. 98) notices the "blessing" in the following passage:—

> Giton collectione spiritus plenus, *ter* continuo ita sternutavit, ut grabatum concuteret. Ad quem motum Eumolpus conversus, *salvere* Gitona *jubet.*

> Et n'esternuay point regardant le soleil.
> And did not sneeze as he looked upon the sun.
>
> Ronsard, tom. v. p. 158, quoted in Southey's *Common Place Book*, 3d series, p. 303.

Here, not to sneeze appears to be looked on as an ill omen.

Ammianus has an epigram upon one whose nose was so long that he never heard it sneeze, and therefore never said Ζεῦ σῶσον, God bless.—*Notes on the Variorum Plautus* (ed. Gronov., Lugd. Bat.), p. 720.

Erasmus, in his *Colloquies*, bids one say to him who sneezes, "Sit faustum ac felix," or "Servet te Deus," or "Sit salutiferum," or "Bene vertat Deus."

> Quare homines sternutant?
> Respondetur, ut virtus expulsiva et visiva, per hoc purgetur, et cerebrum a sua superfluitate purgetur, etc. Etiam qui sternutat frequenter, dicitur habere forte cerebrum.—*Aristotelis Problemata:* Amstelodami, anno 1690.

Query whether from some such idea of the beneficial effect of sneezing, arose the practice of calling for the divine blessing on the sneezer?

When Themistocles was offering sacrifice, it happened that three beautiful captives were brought him, and at the same time the fire burnt clear and bright, and a sneeze happened on the right hand. Hereupon Euphrantides the soothsayer, embracing him, predicted the memorable victory which was afterwards obtained by him, &c.

Sneezing was not always a lucky omen, but varied according to the alteration of circumstances—"Τῶν πταρμῶν οἱ μὲν εἰσὶν ὠφέλιμοι, οἱ δὲ βλαβεροί," "Some sneezes are profitable, others prejudicial"—according to the scholiast upon the following passage of Theocritus, wherein he makes the sneezing of the Cupids to have been an unfortunate omen to a certain lover:—

> Σιμιχίδα μὲν ἔρωτες ἐπέπταρον.

If any person sneezed between midnight and the following noontide it was fortunate, but from noontide till midnight it was unfortunate.

If a man sneezed at the table while they were taking away, or if another happened to sneeze upon his left hand, it was unlucky; if on the right hand, fortunate.

If, in the undertaking any business, two or four sneezes happened, it was a lucky omen, and gave encouragement to proceed; if more than four, the omen was neither good nor bad; if one or three, it was unlucky, and dehorted them from proceeding in what they had designed. If two men were deliberating about any business, and both of them chanced to sneeze together, it was a prosperous omen.—*Archæol. Græc.* (5th ed.). pp. 339, 340.

Strada, in his Prolusions, Book III. Prol. 4, replies at some length, and not unamusingly, to the query, "Why are sneezers saluted?" It seems to have arisen out of an occurrence which had recently taken place at Rome, that a certain *Pistor Suburranus*, after having sneezed twenty-three times consecutively, had expired at the twenty-fourth sneeze: and his object is to prove that Sigonius was mistaken in supposing that the custom of saluting a sneezer had only dated from the days of Gregory the Great, when many had died of the plague in the act of sneezing. In opposition to this notion, he adduces passages from Apuleius and Petronius Arbiter, besides those from Ammianus, Athenæus, Aristotle, and Homer, already quoted. He then proceeds to give five causes from which the custom may have sprung, and classifies them as religious, medical, facetious, poetical, and augural.

Under the first head, he argues that the salutation given to sneezers is not a mere expression of good wishes, but a kind of veneration; "for," says he, "we rise to a person sneezing, and humbly uncover our heads, and deal reverently with him." In proof of this position, he tells us that in Ethiopia, when the emperor sneezed, the salutations of his adoring gentlemen of the privy chamber were so loudly uttered as to be heard and re-echoed by the whole of his court; and thence repeated in the streets, so that the whole city was in simultaneous commotion.

The other heads are then pursued with considerable learning, and some humor; and, under the last, he refers us to St. Augustin, *De Doctr. Christ*, ii. 20, as recording that—

When the ancients were getting up in the morning, if they chanced to sneeze whilst putting on their shoes, they immediately went back to bed again, in order that they might get up more auspiciously, and escape the misfortunes which were likely to occur on that day.

It is a curious circumstance that if any one should sneeze in company in North Germany, those present will say, "Your good health;" in Vienna, gentlemen in a *café* will take off their hats, and say, "God be with you;" and in Ireland Paddy will say, "God bless your honor," or "Long life to your honor." In Italy and Spain similar expressions are used. The custom is also very common in Russia. The phrases the Russians use on these occasions are—"To your good health!" or "How do you do?" It is said that in Bengal the natives make a "salam" on these occasions. One of the salutations, by which a sneezer is greeted amongst the lower class of Romans at the present day is, *Figli maschi*, "May you have male children!"

The *Athenæum*, in a review of M. Nisard's curious though ill-executed work on the popular literature of France, remarks that the following passage contains evidence of the almost universal practice of salutation after sneezing:—

If you sneeze in the presence of another person, you should take off your hat, turn aside; put your hat, your handkerchief, hand, or napkin before him; and as soon as the paroxysm is past, you ought to salute those who have saluted, or ought to have saluted you, although they may not have said any thing.

At different stages of social progress, such instructions may be found occupying positions in the social scale correspondingly various, and helping accordingly to mark the point reached by different nations. In France the above extract, at the middle of the nineteenth century, occupies a page in a chap-book destined for the classes at the bottom of the social pyramid. In Italy is found the following in a child's primer, issued authoritatively in 1553, and stated in the title-page to be "enriched with new and moral maxims adapted to form the hearts of children." Among "the duties of man to society" are enumerated those of—

> Abstaining from scratching your head, putting your fingers in your mouth, crossing one knee over the other in sitting . . . and being prompt in saluting any one who may sneeze, and returning thanks to any who, on such an occasion, may have wished you well.

It is a commonly current statement, that the practice in question had its origin at the time of a wide-spread epidemic, of which sneezing was supposed to be a premonitory symptom.

Another of the maxims, in the same little book, supposed by its author to be "adapted for the formation of the juvenile heart," is characteristic and noteworthy. "One ought never," it is taught, "to introduce any conversation on topics unseasonable or *contrary to current opinions.*"

A less morally questionable, though more inconvenient precept, is, that you are never to blow your nose in the presence of any one!

CORPULENCE A CRIME.

Mr. Bruce has written, in his *Classic and Historic Portraits* that the ancient Spartan paid as much attention to the rearing of men as the cattle-dealers in modern England do to the breeding of cattle. They took charge of firmness and looseness of men's flesh; and regulated the degree of fatness to which it was lawful, in a free state, for any citizen to extend his body. Those who dared to grow too fat, or too soft for military exercise and the service of Sparta, were soundly whipped. In one particular instance, that of Nauclis, the son of Polytus, the offender was brought before the Euphori, and a meeting of the whole people of Sparta, at which his unlawful fatness was publicly exposed; and he was threatened with perpetual banishment if he did not bring his body within the regular Spartan compass, and give up his culpable mode of living; which was declared to be more worthy of an Ionian than a son of Lacedæmon.

THE STARS AND STRIPES.

The American Congress, on the 14th of June, 1777, "Resolved that the flag of the thirteen United States be thirteen stripes, alternately red and white; that the Union be thirteen stars, white in a blue field, representing a new constellation." As to the origin of the combination, and who first suggested the idea, some have supposed that it might have been derived from the arms of General Washington, which contains three stars in the upper portion, and three bars running across the escutcheon. There is no means of knowing at this day whether this conjecture is correct, but the coincidence is rather striking. There were several flags used before the striped flag by the Americans. In March, 1775, "a union flag with a red field" was hoisted at New York upon the liberty pole, bearing the inscription "George Rex and the liberties of America," and upon the reverse, "No Popery." On the 18th of July, 1778, Gen. Putnam raised, at Prospect Hill, a flag bearing on one side the Massachusetts motto, "*Qui transtulit sustinet*," on the other "An appeal to Heaven." In October of the same year the floating batteries at Boston had a flag with the latter motto, the field white with a pine-tree upon it. This was the Massachusetts emblem. Another flag, used during 1775 in some of the colonies, had upon it a rattlesnake coiled as if about to strike, with the motto "Don't tread on me." The grand union flag of thirteen stripes was raised on the heights near Boston, January 2, 1776. Letters from there say that the regulars in Boston did not understand it; and as the king's speech had just been sent to the Americans, they thought the new flag was a token of submission. The *British Annual Register* of 1776 says:—"They burnt the king's speech, and changed their colors from a plain red ground, which they had hitherto used, to a flag with thirteen stripes, as a symbol of the number and union of the colonies." A letter from Boston about the same time, published in the *Penna Gazette*, for January, 1776, says:—"The grand union flag was raised on the 2d, in compliment to the united colonies." The idea of making each stripe for a State was adopted from the first; and the fact goes far to negative the supposition that the private arms of General Washington had any thing to do with the subject. The pine tree, rattlesnake, and striped flag were used indiscriminately until July, 1777, when the blue union with the stars was added to the stripes, and the flag established by law. Formerly a new stripe was added for each new State admitted to the Union, until the flag became too large, when by act of Congress the stripes were reduced to the old thirteen; and now a star is added to the union at the accession of each new State.

ANTIQUARIAN DISCOVERY.

A few weeks ago, in clearing out the ruins of an old chapel at Nuncham Regis in Warwickshire, which had been pulled down (all but the belfry tower) about forty years since, we thought it necessary to trench the whole space, that we might more certainly mark out the boundaries of the building, as we wished to restore it in some measure to its former state; it had been used as a stackyard, and a depository of rubbish by the tenants of the farm on which it was, ever since its dilapidation. We began to trench at the west end, and came on a great many bones and skeletons, from which the coffins had crumbled away, till, finding the earth had been moved, we went deeper, and discovered a leaden coffin quite perfect, but without date or inscription of any kind; there had been an outer wooden coffin which was decayed, but quantities of the black rotted wood were all round it. We cut the lead and folded back the top so as not to destroy it; beneath was a wooden coffin in good preservation, and also without any inscription. As soon as the leaden top was rolled back, a most overpowering aromatic smell diffused itself all over the place; we then unfastened the inner coffin, and found the body of a man embalmed with great care, and heaps of rosemary and aromatic leaves piled over him. On examining the body more closely, we found it had been beheaded, the head was separately wrapped up in linen, and the linen shirt that covered the body was drawn quite over the neck where the head had been cut off; the head was laid straight with the body, and where the joining of the neck and head should have been, it was tied round with a broad black ribbon. His hands were crossed on his breast, the wrists were tied with black ribbon, and the thumbs were tied together with black ribbon. He had a peaked beard, and a quantity of long brown hair curled and clotted with blood round his neck: the only mark on any thing about him was on the linen on his chest, just above where his hands were crossed; on it were the letters T. B. worked in black silk. On trenching towards the chancel we came on four leaden coffins laid side by side, with inscriptions on each: one contained the body of Francis, Earl of Chichester and Lord Dunsmure, 1653; the next the body of Audrey, Countess of Chichester, 1652; another the body of Lady Audrey Leigh, their daughter, 1640; and the fourth, the body of Sir John Anderson, son of Lady Chichester, by her first husband. We opened the coffin of Lady Audrey Leigh, and found her perfectly embalmed and in entire preservation, her flesh quite plump, as if she were alive, her face very beautiful, her hands exceedingly small and not wasted; she was dressed in fine linen, trimmed all over with old point lace, and two rows of lace were laid flat across her forehead. She looked exactly as if she were lying asleep, and seemed not more than sixteen or seventeen years old; her beauty was very great; even her eyelashes and eyebrows were quite perfect, and her eyes were closed; no part of her face or figure was at all fallen in. We also opened Lady Chichester's coffin, but with her the embalming had apparently failed; she was a skeleton, though the coffin was half full of aromatic leaves: her hair, however, was as fresh as if she lived; it was long, thick, and as soft and glossy as that of a child, and of a perfect auburn color. In trenching on one side of where the altar had been, we found another leaden coffin with an inscription. It contained the body of a Dame Marie Browne, daughter of one of the Leighs, and of Lady Marie, daughter to Lord Chancellor Brackley. This body was also quite perfect, and embalmed principally with a very small coffee-colored seed, with which the coffin was nearly filled, and it also had so powerful a perfume that it filled the whole place. The linen, ribbon, &c., were quite strong and good in all these instances, and remained so after exposure to the air: we kept a piece out of each coffin, and had it washed without its being at all destroyed. Young Lady Audrey had earrings in her ears, black enamelled serpents. The perfume of the herbs and gums used in embalming them was so sickening, that we were all ill after inhaling it, and most of the men employed in digging up the coffins were ill also. The chapel is on the estate of Lord John Scott, who inherited it from his paternal grandmother the Duchess of Buccleuch, daughter of the Duke of Montagu, into whose family Nuneham Regis and other possessions in Warwickshire came by the marriage of his grandfather with the daughter of Lord Dunsmure, Earl of Chichester.

STERNE IN PARIS.

The following is a copy of an autograph letter of Sterne's, written when at Paris. It is very interesting, and is not contained among his published letters. Some few words are illegible, and several of the proper names may be inaccurately copied.

PARIS, *March* 15, 1762.

MY DEAR:—Having an opportunity of writing by a physician, who is posting off for London to-day, I would not omit doing it, though you will possibly receive a letter (which is gone from hence last post) at the very same time. I send to Mr. Foley's every mail-day, to inquire for a letter from you; and if I do not get one in a post or two, I shall be greatly surprised and disappointed. A terrible fire happened here last night, the whole fair of St. Germain's burned to the ground in a few hours; and hundreds of unhappy people are now going crying along the streets, ruined totally by it. This fair of St. Germain's is built upon a spot of ground covered and tiled, as large as the Minster Yard, entirely of wood, divided into shops, and formed into little streets, like a town in miniature. All the artisans in the kingdom come with their wares—jewellers, silversmiths—and have free leave from all parts of the world to profit by a general licence from the Carnival to Easter. They compute the loss at six millions of livres, which these poor creatures have sustained, not one of which have saved a single shilling, and many fled out in their shirts, and have not only lost their goods and merchandise, but all the money they have been taking these six weeks. *Oh! ces moments de malheur sont terribles,* said my barber to me, as he was shaving me this morning; and the good-natured fellow uttered it with so moving an accent, that I could have found in my heart to have cried over the perishable and uncertain tenure of every good in this life.

I have been three mornings together to hear a celebrated pulpit orator near me, one Père Clement, who delights me much; the parish pays him 600 livres for a dozen sermons this Lent; he is K. Stanislas's preacher—most excellent indeed! his matter solid, and to the purpose; his manner, more than theatrical, and greater, both in his action and delivery, than Madame Clairon, who, you must know, is the Garrick of the stage here; he has infinite variety, and keeps up the attention by it wonderfully; his pulpit, oblong, with three seats in it, into which he occasionally casts himself; goes on, then rises, by a gradation of four steps, each of which he profits by, as his discourse inclines him: in short, 'tis a stage, and the variety of his tones would make you imagine there were no less than five or six actors on it together.

I was last night at Baron de Bagg's concert; it was very fine, both music and company; and to-night I go to the Prince of Conti's. There is a Monsieur Popignière, who lives here like a sovereign prince; keeps a company of musicians always in his house, and a full set of players; and gives concerts and plays alternately to the grandees of this metropolis; he is the richest of all the farmer . . . . .; he did me the honor last night to send me an invitation to his house, while I stayed here—that is, to his music and table.

I suppose you had terrible snows in Yorkshire, from the accounts I read in the London papers. There has been no snow here, but the weather has been sharp; and was I to be all the day in my room, I could not keep myself warm for a shilling a day. This is an expensive article to great houses here—'tis most pleasant and most healthy firing; I shall never bear coals I fear again; and if I can get wood at Coswold, I will always have a little. I hope Lydia is better, and not worse, and that I shall hear the same account of you. I hope my Lydia goes on with her French; I speak it fast and fluent, but incorrect both in accent and phrase; but the French tell me I speak it most surprisingly well for the time. In six weeks I shall get over all difficulties, having got over one of the worst, which is to understand what is said by others, which I own I found much trouble in at first.

My love to my Lyd——. I have got a color into my face now, though I came with no more than there is in a dishclout.

I am your affectionate

L. Sterne.

For Mrs. Sterne at York.

GERMAN SATIRE.

There is a work which a German critic has attributed to Tieck, entitled *Comedia Divina, mit drei Vorreden von Peter Hammer, Jean Paul, und dem Herausgeber*, 1808. The absence of publisher's name and the place of publication leaves little doubt that the name, W. G. H. Gotthardt, and the date, "Basel, Mai 1, 1808," are both fictitious. No one who has read this can suppose it was written by Tieck. The Catholic-romantic school, of which he was the most distinguished member, furnishes the chief objects of the author's ridicule. Novalis, Görres, and F.

Schlegel are the most prominent; but at p. 128 is an absurd sonnet "on Tieck."

The Comedia Divina is a very clever and somewhat profane satire, such as Voltaire might have written had he been a German of the nineteenth century. It opens with Jupiter complaining to Mercury of ennui (*eine langweilige existenz*), and that he is not what he was when he was young. Mercury advises a trip to Leipzic Fair, where he may get good medical advice for his gout, and certainly will see something new. They go, and hear various dealers sing the catalogues of their goods.

They visit the garret of Herr Novalis Octavianus Hornwunder, a maker of books to order upon every subject: they learn the mysteries of the manufacture. The scene is clever, but much of the wit is unappreciable as directed against productions which have not survived. Jupiter, in compassion to Hornwunder, changes him to a goose, immediately after which a bookseller enters, and, mistaking the gods for authors, makes them an offer of six dollars and twelve groschen the octavo volume, besides something for the kitchen. Jupiter, enraged, changes him to a fox, which forthwith eats the goose, "feathers and all."

They then go to see the play of the Fall of Man (*Der Sündenfall*). The subject is treated after the manner of Hans Sachs, but with this difference, that the simple-minded old Nuremburger saw nothing incongruous in making Cain and Abel say their catechism, and Cain go away from the examination to fight with the low boys in the street; whereas the author of *Der Sünderfall* is advisedly irreverent. Another proof, if one were wanted, that he was not Tieck.

FROZEN WORDS.

Dickens, in his Old Curiosity Shop, has made a very felicitous use of the idea (to be found in Baron Munchausen and elsewhere) of words being congealed at the time they were spoken, and afterwards sounding when thawed :—

"Don't be frightened, mistress," said Quilp, after a pause. "Your son knows me: I don't eat babies: I don't like 'em. It will be as well to stop that young screamer though, in case I should be tempted to do him a mischief. Holloa, Sir! will you be quiet?" *Little Jacob stemmed the course of two tears which he was squeezing out of his eyes, and instantly subsided into a silent horror.* . . . . *The moment their* [Quilp and Swiveller] *backs were turned, little Jacob thawed, and resumed his crying from the point where Quilp had frozen him.*—Vol. i. pp. 207–9.

BYRONIANA.

In Lady Blessington's *Conversations with Lord Byron*, pages 176, 177, the poet is represented as stating that the lines—

While Memory, with more than Egypt's art,
Embalming all the sorrows of the heart,
Sits at the altar which she raised to woe,
And feeds the source whence tears eternal flow!"

suggested to his mind, "by an unaccountable and incomprehensible power of association," the thought—

Memory, the mirror which affliction dashes to the earth, and, looking down upon the fragments, only beholds the reflection multiplied;

afterwards apparently embodied in *Childe Harold*, iii. 33.

Even as a broken mirror, which the glass
In every fragment multiplies; and makes
A thousand images of one that was,
The same, and still the more, the more it breaks.

Now, Byron was, by his own showing, *an ardent admirer* of Burton's *Anatomy of Melancholy*. See Moore's *Life of Byron*, vol. i. page 144. Notices of the year 1807.

Turn to Burton, and you will find the following passage :—

And, as Praxiteles did by his glass, when he saw a scurvy face in it, brake it to pieces, but for that one, he saw many more as ba in a moment.—Part 2, sect. 3, mem. 7.

Dant les premières passions les femmes aiment l'amant; dans les autres elles aiment l'amour.—La Rochefoucauld, *Max.* 494.

In her first passion woman loves her lover,
In all the others all she loves is love,
Which grows a habit she can ne'er get over,
And fits her loosely—like an easy glove, &c.
Don Juan, canto iii. st. iii.

There is no note on *this* passage; but, on the concluding lines of the *very next* stanza,—

Although, no doubt, her first of love affairs
Is that to which her heart is wholly granted!
Yet there are some, they say, who have had *none*,
But those who have ne'er end with only *one*,

we have the following editorial comment: "These two lines are a versification of a saying of Montaigne." (!!!) The saying is *not* by Montaigne, but by La Rochefoucauld:—

On peut trouver des femmes qui n'ont jamais eu de galanterie; mais il est rare d'en trouver qui n'en aient jamais eu qu'une.—*Max.* 73.

Byron borrows the same idea again:—

Writing grows a habit, like a woman's gallantry. There are women who have had no intrigue, but few who have had but one only; so there are millions of men who have never written a book, but few who have written only one.—*Observations upon an Article in Blackwood's Magazine; Byron's Works*, vol. xv. p. 87, Moore's Edition, 17 vols. duod. London, 1833.

Mrs. Radcliffe (who was never out of England) is describing in her *Mysteries of Udolpho*, chap. xvi., the appearance of Venice: "Its terraces, crowded with airy yet majestic fabrics, touched as they now were with the splendor of the setting sun, appeared as if they had been *called up from the ocean by the wand of an enchanter.*"

In the first stanza of the fourth canto of *Childe Harold* we have the well-known lines—

> I stood in Venice on the Bridge of Sighs,
> A palace and a prison on each hand:
> I saw from out the wave her structures rise
> As from the stroke of an enchanter's wand.

In one of his letters Lord Byron tells us of his fondness for the above novel.

Again, in Kirke White's *Christiad*—

> The lyre which I in early days have strung,
> And now my spirits faint, and I have hung
> The spell that solaced me in saddest hour
> On the dark cypress—

may be compared with the last stanza but one of the fourth canto.

AMONTILLADO SHERRY.

The wines of Xérès consist of two kinds, viz., sweet and dry, each of which is again subdivided into two other varieties. Amontillado sherry, or simply Amontillado, belongs to the latter class, the other description produced from the dry wines being sherry, properly so called, that which passes in this country generally by that name. These two wines, although differing from each other in the peculiarities of color, smell, and flavor, are produced from the same grape, and in precisely a similar manner; indeed, it frequently happens that of two or more *botas*, or large casks, filled with the same *moût* (wort or sweet wine), and subjected to the same manipulation, the one becomes Amontillado, and the other natural sherry. This mysterious transformation takes place ordinarily during the first, but sometimes even during the second year, and in a manner that has hitherto baffled the attempts of the most attentive observer to discover. The peculiar flavor is caused by a process of fermentation, over which the growers have no control, and for which they cannot account Sometimes only one or two butts in a vintage will be affected, and in other years none at all. Those which some mysterious influence designs for Amontillado, produce a kind of vegetable weed after having been put in the cask; it is long and stringy, like some of our fresh-water weeds, but with very fine fibres, and bears a very inute white mflower. Immediately after shedding these flowers, the whole plant dies away, and never again appears, but it leaves that peculiar flavor. This description has been positively stated and verified by those who have visited the Spanish wine districts. Natural sherry has a peculiar aromatic flavor, somewhat richer than that of its brother, the Amontillado, and partakes of three different colors, viz., pale or straw, golden, and deep golden, the latter being the description denominated by us brown sherry. The Amontillado is of a straw color only, more or less shaded according to the age it possesses. Its flavor is drier and more delicate than that of natural sherry, recalling in a slight degree the taste of nuts and almonds. The word "Amontillado" signifies like or similar to Montilla, *i. e.* the wine manufactured at that place. Montilla is situated in Upper Andalusia, in the neighborhood of Cordouc, and produces an excellent description of wine, but which, from the want of roads and communication with the principal commercial towns of Spain, is almost entirely unknown.

Amontillado sherry was first imported into England about the year 1811, and the supply was so small that the entire quantity was only sufficient for the table of three consumers, who speedily became attached to it, and thenceforward drank no other sherry. One of these was the late Duke of Kent.

The two sweet wines of Xérès are the "Paxarite," or "Pedro Ximenès," and the "Muscatel." The first-named is made from a species of grape called "Pedro Ximenès," sweeter in quality than that which produces the dry sherry, and which, moreover, is exposed much longer to the action of the sun previous to the process of manufacture; its condition when subjected to the action of the pressers resembling very nearly that of a raisin. Fermentation is in this case much more rapid on account of the saccharine nature of the *moût* or wort. In flavor it is similar to the fruit called "Pedro Ximenès," the color being the same as that of natural sherry. Muscate wine is made from the grape of that name, and in a manner precisely similar to the Paxarite. The wine produced from this grape is still sweeter than the Pedro Ximenès, its taste being absolutely that of the Muscat grape. In color also it is deeper; but the color of both, like that of the two dry wines, increases in proportion to their age, a circumstance exactly the reverse of that which takes place in French wines. German sherry wines are capable of preservation both in bottles and casks for an indefinite period. In one of the *bodegas* or cellars belonging to the firm of M. P. Domecq, at Xérès, are to be seen five or six casks of immense size and antiquity (some of them, it is said, exceeding a century). Each of them bears the name of some distinguished hero of the age in which it was produced, Wellington and Napoleon figuring conspicuously amongst others: the former is preserved exclusively for the taste of Englishmen.

The history of sherry dates, in a commercial point of view, from about the year 1720 only. Before this period it is uncertain whether it possessed any existence at all: at all events, it appears to have been unknown beyond the immediate neighborhood in which it was produced. It would be difficult, perhaps, to say by whom it was first imported; all that can be affirmed with any degree of certainty is, that a Frenchman, by name Pierre Domecq, the founder of the house before mentioned, was among the earliest to recognize its capabilities, and to bring it to the high state of perfection which it has since attained. In appreciation of the good service thus rendered to his country, Ferdinand VII. conferred upon this house the right exclusively to bear upon their casks the royal arms of Spain. This wine, from being at first cultivated only in small quantities, has long since grown into one of the staple productions of the country. In the neighborhood of Xérès there are at present under cultivation from ten thousand to twelve thousand *arpents* of vines; these produce annually from thirty thousand to thirty-five thousand *botas*, equal to seventy thousand or seventy-five thousand hogsheads. In gathering the fruit, the ripest is invariably selected for wines of the best quality. The wines of Xérès, like all those of the peninsula, require the necessary body or strength to enable them to sustain the fatigue of exportation. Previous, therefore, to shipment (none being sold under four to five years of age), a little *eau de vie* (between the fiftieth and the sixtieth part) is added, a quantity in itself so small, that few would imagine it to be the cause of the slight alcoholic taste which nearly all sherries possess.

In consequence of the high price of the delicious wines, numerous imitations, or inferior sherries, are manufactured, and sold in immense quantities. Of these the best are to be met with at the following places: San Lucar, Porto, Santa Maria, and even Malaga itself. The spurious sherry of the first-named place is consumed in larger quantities, especially in France, than the genuine wine itself. One reason for this may be, that few vessels go to take cargoes at Cadiz, whilst many are in the habit of doing so to Malaga for dry fruits, and to Seville for the fine wool of Estremadura. San Lucar is situated at the mouth of the Guadalquiver.

RHYMES ON PLACES.

Roger Gale, in a letter dated August 17, 1739, states that he saw the following lines in a window at Belford (between Newcastle and Berwick) :—

Cain, in disgrace with heaven, retired to Nod,
A place, undoubtedly, as far from God
As Cain could wish; which makes some think he went
As far as Scotland, ere he pitch'd his tent;
And there a city built of ancient fame,
Which he, from Eden, Edinburgh did name.

Reliquiæ Galeanæ, 67.

Charles Mathews, in a letter directed to his son at Mold, N. W., dated 4th November [1825], says:—

Lord Deerhurst, who franked this letter, laughed at the idea of your being condemned to be at Mold, and told me an impromptu of Sheridan's, upon being compelled to spend a day or two there:—

Were I to curse the man I hate
From youth till I grow old,
Oh, might he be condemned by fate
To waste his days in Mold!

Memoirs of Charles Mathews, v. 504.

THE ELECTRIC TELEGRAPH.

In one of the early numbers of *The Spectator*, is a paper by Addison, in which he introduces in his excellent and playful manner a quotation from Strada, a learned Italian Jesuit, in one of his *Prolusiones Academicæ;* and though, it is true, the story aims at nothing further than a chimerical supposition of the *instantaneous transmission of thoughts and words* between two individuals, over an indefinite space, and which, when Strada wrote and Addison quoted, never entered into the minds of either as to its *almost ultimate realization;* yet, as perhaps there may be some persons who may not have particularly noticed this *apparently prophetic forewarning*, the story is worth recording for the benefit of those who have never seen or thought on the subject. It should be observed that Strada tells this story about 250 years ago, and Addison relates it 140 years afterwards.

Addison tells us, in the 241st number of *The Spectator*, that—

> Strada, in one of his *Prolusions*, gives an account of a chimerical correspondence between two friends by the help of a *certain loadstone*, which had such virtue in it, that if it touched two several needles, when one of the needles so touched began to move, the other, though at never so great a distance, moved at the same time and in the same manner. He tells us that the two friends being each of them possessed of one of these needles, made a kind of *dial* plate, inscribing it with the four-and-twenty letters, in the same manner as the hours of the day are marked upon the ordinary dial plate. They then fixed one of the needles on each of these plates in such a manner that it could move round without impediment, so as to touch any of the four-and-twenty letters. Upon their separating from one another into distant countries, they agreed to withdraw themselves punctually into their closets at a certain hour of the day, and to converse with one another by means of this their invention. Accordingly, when they were some hundred miles asunder, each of them shut himself up in his closet at the time appointed, and immediately cast his eye upon his dial plate; if he had a mind to write any thing to his friend, he directed his needle to every letter that formed the words which he had occasion for, making a little pause at the end of every word or sentence, to avoid confusion. The friend in the meanwhile saw his own sympathetic needle moving of itself to every letter which that of his correspondent pointed at. By this means they talked together *across a whole continent*, and conveyed their thoughts to one another *in an instant over cities or mountains, seas or deserts.*

Addison goes on to say—

> That in the mean while, if ever this invention should be revived or put in practice, I would propose that upon the lover's dial-plate there should be written not only the four-and-twenty letters, but several entire words, which have always a place in passionate epistles, as *flames*, *darts*, *die*, *language*, *absence*, *Cupid*, *heart*, *eyes*, *hang*, *drown*, and the like. This would very much abridge the lover's pains in this way of writing a letter, as it would enable him to express the most useful and significant words with a single touch of the needle.

There is a passage in the *Pseudodoxia Epidemica* of Sir Thomas Browne, wherein this invention is foreshadowed in terms more remarkable and significant, if less imaginative and beautiful, than that from *The Spectator*, which, perhaps, may have been written, with this particular example of the "received tenets and commonly presumed truths" of the learned physician's day, distinctly present to the mind of Addison. The passage referred to is as follows :—

There is another conceit of better notice, and *whispered thorow the world* with some attention; credulous and vulgar auditors readily believing it, and more judicious and distinctive heads not altogether rejecting it. The conceit is excellent, and, if the effect would follow, somewhat divine: whereby we might communicate like spirits, and confer on earth with Menippus in the moon. And this is pretended from the sympathy of two needles touched with the same loadstone, and placed in the centre of two abecedary circles, or rings with letters described round about them, one friend keeping one, and another the other, and agreeing upon the hour wherein they will communicate. For then, *saith tradition*, at what distance of place soever, when one needle shall be removed unto any letter, the other, by a wonderful sympathy, will move unto the same.—Book II. chap. ii., 4to., 1669, p. 77.

It would appear that the principle of the electric telegraph and its *modus operandi*, almost identically as at present, were known and described upwards of a century ago. In the *Scots Magazine*, vol. XV. p. 73, is a letter initialed C. M., dated Renfrew, Feb. 15, 1753, in which the writer not only suggests electricity as a medium for conveying messages and signals, but details with singular minuteness the method of opening and maintaining lingual communication between remote points, a method which, with only a few improvements, has now been so eminently successful.

THE NAPOLEON FAMILY.

The names of the male crowned heads of the extinct Napoleon dynasty form a remarkable acrostic :—

N-apoleon, Emperor of the French.
I-oseph, King of Spain.
H-ieronymus, King of Westphalia.
I-oachim, King of Naples.
L-ouis, King of Holland.

CURLL TOSSED IN A BLANKET.

Curll, the bookseller, it is well known, was tossed in a blanket by the scholars of Westminster: upon this occasion there appeared a small poetical tract, called *Neck or Nothing;* a consolatory letter from Mr. D-nt-n (Dunton) to Mr. C. C-rll (Curll), upon his being Tost in a Blanket, &c. Sold by Charles King in Westminster Hall, 1716.

The following is an extract from it:—

"Come, hold him fair; we'll make him know
What 'tis to deal with scholars." "Oh!"
Quoth *Edmund.* "Now, without disguise,
Confess," quo' they, "thy rogueries.
What makes you keep in garret high
Poor bards ty'd up to poetry?"
"I'm forced to load them with a clog,
To make them study." "Here's a rogue
Affronts the school; we'll make thee rue it."
"Indeed I never meant to do it!"
"No? Didst thou not th' oration print
Imperfect, with false Latin in't?"
"O, pardon!" "No, sir; have a care;
False Latin's never pardon'd here!"
"Indeed I'll ne'er do so again;
Pray handle me like gentlemen."

. . . . .

Oh! how th' unlucky urchins laugh'd,
To think they'd maul'd thee fore and aft:
'Tis such a sensible affront!
Why, *Pope* will write an Epick on't!
Bernard will chuckle at thy moan,
And all the booksellers in town,
From *Tonson* down to *Boddington,*
Fleet Street and *Temple Bar* around,
The *Strand* and *Holborn,* this shall sound:

For ever this shall grate thine ear,
Which is the way to *Westminster?*

For further information regarding Dunton and Curll, see Pope's *Dunciad*, and notes to same.

GIBBON'S LIBRARY.

The following quotation is from Cyrus Redding's "Recollections of the Author of Vathek" (*New Monthly Magazine*, vol. lxxi. p. 308) :—

"I bought it (says Beckford) to have something to read when I passed through Lausanne. I have not been there since. I shut myself up for six weeks, from early in the morning until night, only now and then taking a ride. The people thought me mad. I read myself nearly blind."

I inquired if the books were rare or curious. He replied in the negative. There were excellent editions of the principal historical writers, and an extensive collection of travels. The most valuable work was an edition of *Eustathius;* there was also a MS. or two. All the books were in excellent condition; in number, considerably above six thousand, near seven perhaps. He should have read himself mad if there had been novelty enough, and he had stayed much longer.

"I broke away, and dashed among the mountains. There is excellent reading there, too, equally to my taste. Did you ever travel alone among mountains?"

I replied that I had, and been fully sensible of their mighty impressions. "Do you retain Gibbon's library?"

"It is now dispersed, I believe. I made it a present to my excellent physician, Dr. Schall or Scholl (I am not certain of the name). I never saw it after turning hermit there."

DESCENDANTS OF JUDAS ISCARIOT.

In Southey's *Omniana* is the following :—

It was believed in Pier della Valle's time, that the descendants of Judas still existed in Corfu, though the persons who suffered this imputation stoutly denied the truth of the genealogy.

POPE AND THE DUNCES.

In Pope's "Letter to the Honorable James Craggs," dated June 15, 1711, after making some observations on Dennis's remarks on the *Essay on Criticism*, he says :—

> Yet, to give this man his due, he has objected to one or two lines with reason; and I will alter them in case of another edition: I will make my enemy do me a kindness where he meant an injury, and so serve instead of a friend.

An interesting paper might be drawn up from the instances, for they are rather numerous, in which Pope followed out this sensible rule. One of the heroes of the *Dunciad*, Thomas Cooke, the translator of Hesiod, was the editor of a periodical published in monthly numbers, in 8vo., of which nine only appeared, under the title of *The Comedian, or Philosophical Inquirer*, the first number being for April, and last for December, 1732. It contains some curious matter, and amongst other papers is, in No. 2, "A Letter in Prose to Mr. Alexander Pope, occasioned by his Epistle in Verse to the Earl of Burlington." It is very abusive, and was most probably written either by Cooke or Theobald. After quoting the following lines as they then stood :—

> He buys for Topham drawings and designs,
> For Fountain statues, and for Curio coins,
> Rare monkish manuscripts for Hearne alone,
> And books for Mead, and rarities for Sloane,—

the letter-writer thus unceremoniously addresses himself to the author :—

> Rarities! how could'st thou be so silly as not to be particular in the rarities of Sloane, as in those of the other five persons? What knowledge, what meaning is conveyed in the word *rarities?* Are not some drawings, some statues, some coins, all monkish manuscripts, and some books, *rarities?* Could'st thou not find a trisyllable to express some parts of nature for a col-

lection of which that learned and worthy physician is eminent? Fy, fy! correct and write:—

Rare monkish manuscripts for Hearne alone,
And books for Mead, and butterflies for Sloane.

Sir Hans Sloane is known to have the finest collection of butterflies in England, and perhaps in the world; and if rare monkish manuscripts are for Hearne only, how can rarities be for Sloane, unless thou specifyest what sort of rarities? O thou numskull!—No. 2, pp. 15–16.

The correction was evidently an improvement, and therefore Pope wisely accepted the benefit, and was the channel through which it was conveyed; and the passage accordingly now stands as altered by the letter-writer.

ORIGIN OF VARIOUS BOOKS.

The incidents and thoughts which have induced various authors to commence their works are, in many cases, somewhat interesting.

Thus, Milton's *Comus* was suggested by the circumstance of Lady Egerton losing herself in a wood. The origin of *Paradise Lost* has been ascribed by one to the poet having read Andreini's drama of *L'Adamo Sacra Representatione*, Milan, 1633; by another, to his perusal of Theramo's *Das Buch Belial, &c.*, 1472. Dunster says that the *prima stamina* of *Paradise Lost* is to be found in Sylvester's translation of Du Bartas's *Divine Weekes and Workes.* It is said that Milton himself owned that he owed much of his work to Phineas Fletcher's *Locusts or Appolyonists. Paradise Regained* is attributable to the poet having been asked by Elwood the Quaker what he could say on the subject. Gower's *Confessio Amantis* was written at the command of Richard II., who, meeting Gower rowing on the Thames, invited him into the royal barge, and after much conversation, requested him to "book some new thing." Chaucer, it is generally agreed, intended, in his *Canterbury Tales*, to imitate the *Decameron* of

Boccaccio. When Cowper was forty-five he was induced by Mrs. Unwin to write a poem, that lady giving him for a subject *The Progress of Error.* The author of *The Castle of Otranto* says in a letter, now in the British Museum, that it was suggested to him by a dream, in which he thought himself in an ancient castle, and that he saw a gigantic hand in armor on the uppermost banister of the great staircase. Defoe is supposed to have obtained his idea of *Robinson Crusoe* by reading Captain Rogers' *Account of Alexander Selkirk in Juan Fernandez.* Dr. Beddoes' *Alexander's Expedition down the Hydaspes and the Indus to the Ocean* originated in a conversation in which it was contended that Darwin could not be imitated. Dr. Beddoes, some time afterwards, produced the MS. of the above poem as Darwin's, and completely succeeded in the deception.

EPITAPHIANA.

The following is a *real* epitaph. It was written by Dr. Greenwood on his wife, who died in childbed, and it is in all probability still to be seen, where it was originally set up, in Solyhull churchyard, Warwickshire. The most amusing point in it is, that the author seriously intended the lines to rhyme. There is wonderful merit in the couplet where he celebrated her courage and magnanimity in preferring him to a lord or judge:—

Which heroic action, join'd to all the rest,
Made her to be esteem'd the Phœnix of her sex!

Go, cruel Death, thou hast cut down
The fairest Greenwood in all this kingdom!
Her virtues and her good qualities were such
That surely she deserved a lord or judge:
But her piety and great humility
Made her prefer me, a Doctor in Divinity;

Which heroic action, join'd to all the rest,
Made her to be esteem'd the Phœnix of her sex;
And like that bird a young she did create,
To comfort those her loss had made disconsolate.
My grief for her was so sore
That I can only utter two lines more.
For this and all other good woman's sake,
Never let blisters be applied to a lying-in woman's back.

The following lines may be seen on a gravestone in the churchyard at Kinver, Staffordshire:—

Tired with wand'ring thro' a world of sin,
Hither we came to *Nature's common Inn*,
To rest our wearied bodys for a night,
In hopes to rise that Christ may give us light.

A Leicestershire poet has recorded, in the churchyard of Melton Mowbray, a very different conception of our "*earthly Inn.*" He says:—

This world's an Inn, and I her guest:
I've eat and drank and took my rest
With her awhile, and now I pay
Her lavish bill, and go my way.

This is in the churchyard of Crayford, Kent:—

To the memory of PETER IZOD, who was thirty-five years clerk of this parish, and always proved himself a pious and mirthful man.

The life of this clerk was just three score and ten,
During half of which time he had sung out Amen.
He married when young, like other young men;
His wife died one day, so he chaunted Amen.
A second he took, she departed,—what then?
He married, and buried a third with Amen.
Thus his joys and his sorrows were treble, but then

His voice was deep bass, as he chaunted Amen.
On the horn he could blow as well as most men,
But his horn was exalted in blowing Amen.
He lost all his wind after threescore and ten,
And here with three wives he waits till again
The trumpet shall rouse him to sing out Amen.

Tradition reports these verses to have been composed by some curate of the parish.

The following inscription is on the tombstone of one Margaret Scott, who died in the town of Dalkeith, February 9, 1738, aged one hundred and twenty-five years:—

Stop, passenger, until my life you read;
The living may get knowledge by the dead.
Five times five years I lived a virgin's life;
Ten times five years I was a virtuous wife;
Ten times five years I lived a widow chaste;
Now, weary'd of this mortal life, I rest.
Between my cradle and my grave have been
Eight mighty kings of Scotland and a queen.
Four times five years the Commonwealth I saw;
Ten times the subjects rose against the law.
Twice did I see old Prelacy pull'd down;
And twice the cloak was humbled by the gown.
An end of Stuart's race I saw; nay, more!
My native country sold for English ore,
Such desolations in my life have been,
I have an end of all perfection seen.

The following is very beautiful. It is copied from an inscription in All Saints Church, Cambridge:—

In Obitum Mri. Johannis Hammond Oenopolæ Epitaphium.

Spiritus ascendit generosi Nectaris astra,
  Juxta Altare Calix hic jacet ecce sacrum.
Corporũ αναστασει cũ fit Communia magna
  Unio tunc fuerit Nectaris et Calicis.

The following very beautiful epitaph is inscribed on a tablet in the parish church of Bardsey, near Leeds:—

Hic Jacet
Carolus Lister in utraque
Acad: Med: Stud: Qui ipse, paulo
Ante mortem, suam cecinit
Cygnæam cantionem.

1 *Cor.* xv. 55.	*Phil.* i. 23.
Ubi mors aculeus tuus, &c.	Cupio dissolvi, &c.
Grata venis, mors,	Mens mea mundum,
Grata venis, nec	Vanaque vitæ
Me tua terrent	Somnia et umbras
Spicula quæ nunc	Læta relinquit,
Sentio in ægro	Et cupit alis
Corpore fixa.	Nixa duabus
Mors etenim agni	Speque, fideque,
In cruce cæsi	Scandere summas
(O amor ingens!)	Ætheris oras,
Undique mentem	Merset ubi se
Munit, et illam	Flumine puri
Servat ab omni	Gaudii, Jesu,
Vulnere tutam.	Teque fruatur
	Omnia in æva.

Obiit die 5 Aug. Æt. 23, Sal. 1684.

The following epitaph may be found on an old gravestone in the burying-ground of the parish church of Brighton:—

In Memory of
PHŒBE HESSEL,
who was born at Stepney
in the year 1713.
She served for many years as a private
Soldier in the 5th Regiment of foot
in different parts of Europe,
and in the year 1745 fought under
the command of the

Duke of Cumberland
at the battle of Fontenoy, where she received a bayonet wound in her arm. Her long life, which commenced in the time of Queen Anne, extended to the reign of George IV., by whose munificence she received comfort and support in her latter years.

She died at Brighton, where she had
long resided, Dec. 12th, 1821.
Aged 108 years.

In the churchyard of St. Edmund's, at Salisbury, is the following epitaph, written by a Swedenborgian of the name of Maton, on his children:—

Innocence embellishes divinely complete
To prescience co-egent now sublimely great
In the benign, perfecting, vivifying state.
So heav'nly guardian occupy the skies
The pre-existent God, omnipotent, all-wise;
He shall surpassingly immortalise thy theme
And permanent thy bliss, celestial supreme.
When gracious repulgene bids the grave resign,
The Creator's nursing protection be thine;
Then each perspiring ether shall joyfully rise
Transcendently good, supereminently wise.

Here is an inscription on a tablet in Limerick Cathedral:—

Mementi Mory.

Here lieth Littele Samuell Barinton, that great Under Taker, of Famious Cittis Clock and Chime Maker; He made his one Time goe Early and Latter, But now He is returned to God his Creator.

The 19 of November Then He Seest, And for His Memory this Here is Pleast, By His Son Ben 1693.

PULPIT HOUR-GLASSES.

It is said that the ancient fathers preached, as the old Greek and Roman orators declaimed, by this instrument; but were the sermons of the ancient fathers an hour long? Many of those in St. Augustine's ten volumes might be delivered with distinctness in seven or eight minutes; and some of those of Latimer and his contemporaries in about the same time. But, query, are not the *printed* sermons of these divines merely outlines to be filled up by the preachor *extempore?* Dyos, in a sermon preached at Paul's Cross, in 1570, speaking of the walking and profane talking in the church at sermon time, also laments how they grudged the preacher his customary *hour.* So that an hour seems to have been the practice at the Reformation.

The hour-glass was used equally by the Catholics and Protestants. In an account of the fall of the house in Blackfriars, where a party of Romanists were assembled to hear one of their preachers, in 1623, the preacher is described as—

> Having on a surplice, girt about his middle with a linnen girdle, and a tippet of scarlet on both his shoulders. He was attended by a man that brought after him his book and *hour-glass.*—See *The Fatal Vespers,* by Samuel Clark, London, 1657.

In the Preface to the Bishops' *Bible*, printed, by John Day, in 1569, Archbishop Parker is represented with an *hour-glass* at his right hand. And in a work by Franchinus Gaffurius, entitled *Angelicum ac Divinum opus Musice*, printed at Milan in 1508, is a curious representation of the author seated in a pulpit, with a book in his hand; an *hour-glass* on one side, and a bottle on the other; lecturing to an audience of twelve persons. This woodcut is engraved in the second volume of Hawkins' *History of Music*, p. 333.

Hour-glasses were often very elegantly formed, and of rich

materials. Shaw, in his *Dresses and Decorations of the Middle Ages,* has given an engraving of one of the cabinet of M. Debrugé at Paris. It is richly enamelled, and set with jewels. In the churchwardens' accounts of Lambeth Church are two entries respecting the hour-glass: the first is in 1579, when 1*s.* 4*d.* was "payed to Yorke for the frame in which the *hower* standeth;" and the second in 1615, when 6*s.* 8*d.* was "payd for an iron for the *hour-glasse.*" In an inventory of the goods and implements belonging to the church of All Saints, Newcastle-upon-Tyne, taken about 1632, mention is made of "one *whole* hour-glasse," and of "one *halfe* hour-glasse." (See Brand's *Newcastle,* vol. i. p. 370.)

Fosbroke says, "Preaching by the *hour-glass* was put an end to by the Puritans" (*Ency. of Antiq.*, vol. i. pp. 273, 307). But the account given by a correspondent of the *Gentleman's Magazine* (1804, p. 201), is probably more correct:—

> Hour-glasses, in the puritanical days of Cromwell, were made use of by the preachers; who, on first getting into the pulpit, and naming the text, turned up the glass; and if the sermon did not hold till the glass was out, it was said by the congregation that the preacher was lazy: and if he continued to preach much longer, they would yawn and stretch, and by these signs signify to the preacher that they began to be weary of his discourse, and wanted to be dismissed.

Butler speaks of "gifted brethren preaching by a carnal *hour-glass*" (*Hudibras,* Part 1., canto III., v. 1061). And in the frontispiece of Dr. Young's book, entitled *England's Shame, or a Relation of the Life and Death of Hugh Peters,* London, 1663, Peters is represented preaching, and holding an *hour-glass* in his left hand, in the act of saying:—"I know you are good fellows, so let's have another *glass.*" The same words, or something very similar, are attributed to the Nonconformist minister, Daniel Burgess. Mr. Maidment, in a note to "The New Litany," printed in his *Third Book of Scottish Pasquils* (Edin., 1828, p. 49), also gives the following version of the same :—

A humorous story has been preserved of one of the Earls of Airly, who entertained at his table a clergyman, who was to preach before the Commissioner next day. The glass circulated, perhaps too freely; and whenever the divine attempted to rise, his Lordship prevented him, saying, "Another glass, and then." After "flooring" (if the expression may be allowed) his Lordship, the guest went home. He next day selected a text: "The wicked shall be punished, and that RIGHT EARLY." Inspired by the subject, he was by no means sparing of his oratory, and the hour-glass was disregarded, although repeatedly warned by the precentor; who, in common with Lord Airly, thought the discourse rather lengthy. The latter soon knew why he was thus punished by the reverend gentleman, when reminded, always exclaiming, *not* sotto voce, "Another glass, and then."

Macaulay, speaking of Gilbert Burnet, Bishop of Salisbury, says :—

He was often interrupted by the deep hum of his audience; and when, after preaching out the hour-glass, which in those days was part of the furniture of the pulpit, he held it in his hand, the congregation clamorously encouraged him to go on till the sand had run off once more.—Macaulay's *History*, vol. ii. p. 177, edit. 3, with a reference in a foot-note to Speaker Onslow's Note on *Burnet*, i. 596; Johnson's *Life of Sprat*.

Gay, in his *Pastorals*, writes :—

He said that Heaven would take her soul no doubt,
And spoke the *hour-glass* in her praise quite out.

Zacharie Boyd says, in *The Last Battell of the Sovle in Death*, 1629, reprinted Glasgow, 1831, at p. 469 :—

Now after his Battell ended hee hath surrendered the spirit, *Clepsydra effluxit*, his *houre-glasse* is now runne out, and his soule is come to its wished home, where it is free from the fetters of flesh.

This divine was minister of the barony parish of Glasgow, the church for which was then in the crypt of the cathedral. I have no doubt the hour-glass was there used from which he draws his simile. To judge from the contents of "Mr. Zacharie's" MS. sermons still preserved in the library of the College of Glasgow, each, at the rate of ordinary speaking, must have occupied at least an hour and a half in delivery. When he had become infirm and near his end, and had found it necessary to shorten his sermons, his "kirk session" was offended, as—

Feb. 13, 1651. Some are to speak to Mr. Z. Boyd about the soon skailing (dismissing) of the Baronie Kirk on Sunday afternoon.

Though sermons are now generally restricted to from three quarters to an hour's delivery, the practice of long preaching in the olden times in the west of Scotland had much prevailed. Early among a few classes of the first Dissenters, on "Sacramental occasions" as they are yet called, the services lasted altogether (not unfrequently) continuously from ten o'clock on Sabbath forenoon, to three and four o'clock the following morning.

Among Dr. Rawlinson's manuscripts in the Bodleian Library, No. 941 contains a collection of *Miscellaneous Discourses*, by Mr. Lewis of Margate, in Kent, whence the following extract has been made :—

It appears that these hour-glasses were coeval with our Reformation. In a fine frontispiece, prefixed to the Holy Bible of the bishops' translation, printed in 4to. by John Day, 1569, Archbishop Parker is represented in the pulpit with an hour-glass standing on his right hand; ours, here, stood on the left without any frame. It was proper that some time should be prescribed for the length of the sermon, and clocks and watches were not then so common as they are now. This time of an hour continued till the Revolution, as appears by Bishop Sanderson's, Tillotson's, Stillingfleet's, Dr. Barrow's, and others' sermons, printed during that time.

The writer of this article was informed in 1811, by the Rev. Mr. Burder, who had the curacy of St. Dunstan's, Fleet Street, that the large silver hour-glass formerly used in that Church, was melted down into two staff-heads for the parish beadles.

An hour-glass frame of iron, fixed in the wall by the side of the pulpit, was remaining in 1797 in the church of North Moor, in Oxfordshire.

Hogarth, in his "Sleeping Congregation," has introduced an hour-glass on the left side of the preacher; and Mr. Ireland observes, in his description of this plate, that they are "still placed on some of the pulpits in the provinces." The stands are still to be found in many churches in England; but it has been said that there are only three hour-glass stands where any portion of the glass is remaining.

PORSON.

The following passage is from the *Facetiæ Cantabrigiensis*, p. 95. (London, Charles Mason, 1836):—

Porson observing that he could pun on any subject, a person present defied him to do so on the Latin gerunds, which, however, he immediately did in the following admirable couplet:—

> When Dido found Æneas would not come,
> She mourned in silence, and was DI-DO-DUM.

The late Professor Porson's own account of his academic visits to the Continent:—

> I went to Frankfort, and got drunk
> With that most learn'd professor—Brunck:
> I went to Worts, and got more drunken,
> With that more learned professor—Ruhncken.

EARLY PHILADELPHIA DIRECTORIES.

The first Philadelphia Directories were published in the year 1785, when two appeared: White's and M'Pherson's. The latter is a duodecimo volume of 164 pages, and contains some things worth making a note of.

Some persons do not seem to have comprehended the object of the inquiries made of the inhabitants as to their names and occupations; supposing, perhaps, that they had some connection with taxation. The answers given by such are put down in the *Directory* as the *names* of the respondents. Thus :—

"I won't tell you," 3 Maiden's Lane.
"I won't tell it," 15 Sugar Alley.
"I won't tell you my name," 160 New Market Street.
"I won't have it numbered," 478 Green Street.
"I won't tell my name," 185 St. John's Street.
"I shall not give you my name," 43 Stamper's Alley.
"What you please," 49 Market Street.

In the *errata* are the following :—

For Cross Woman read Cross Widow.
For Cox Cats read Cox Cato.

The alphabetical arrangement of a *Directory* is as great a leveller as the grave. In the *Directory* for 1798, after—

Dennis, Mr., *Taylor*, Pewter Platter Alley,

appears the following :—

Dorleans, Messrs., *Merchants*, near 100 South Fourth Street.

These were Louis Philippe and one of his brothers, who lived at the north-west corner of Fourth and Princes Streets, in a house still standing, and now numbered 110.

Talleyrand and Volney lived for some time in Philadelphia; but, not being housekeepers, their names do not appear in any of the Directories.

LETTERS OF SWIFT.

The following are two hitherto unedited letters of Swift. They were written in his sixty-fifth year, and are obviously addressed to Frances Lady Worsley, only daughter of Thomas Lord Viscount Weymouth, and wife of Sir Robert Worsley, Baronet, and the mother of Lady Carteret. In Sir Walter Scott's edition of Swift's *Works* (vol. xvii. p. 302) will be found one letter from the Dean of St. Patrick to Lady Worsley; and in vol. xviii. p. 26, is the letter from that lady to the Dean which accompanied the escritoire alluded to in the second of the two letters which we now print. This appears from Swift's endorsement of it—"Lady Worsley, with a present of a writing-box japanned by herself."

Madam,—It is now three years and a half since I had the Honor to see Your Ladyship, and I take it very ill that You have not finished my Box above a Month. But this is allways the way that You Ladyes treat your adorers in their absence. However upon Mrs. Barber's account I will pardon You, because she tells me it is the handsomest piece of work she ever saw: and because you have accepted the honor to be one of her protectors, and are determined to be one of her principall recommenders and encouragers. I am in some doubt whether envy had not a great share in your work, for you were I suppose informed that my Lady Carteret had made for me with her own hands the finest box in Ireland; upon which you grew jealous, and resolved to outdo her by making for me the finest box in England; for so Mrs. Barber assures me. In short, I am quite overloaden with favors from Your Ladyship and your Daughter; and what is worse, those loads will lye upon my Shoulders as long as I live. But I confess my self a little ungrateful, because I cannot deny Your Ladyship to have been the most constant of all my Goddesses, as I am the most constant of all your Worshippers. I hope the Carterets and the Worsleys are all happy and in health, and You are obliged to let Sir Robert Worsley know that I am his most humble Servant; but You need say nothing of my being so long his Rival. I hear my friend Harry is returning from the fiery Zone, I hope with more money than he knows what to do with; but whether his vagabond Spirit will ever fix is a question. I beg your Ladyship will prevail on S[r] Robert Worsley to give me a Vicarage in the Isle of Wight; for I am weary of living at such a distance from You. It need not be above forty pounds a year.

As to Mrs. Barber, I can assure you she is but one of four Poetesses in this town, and all Citizens' wives; but she has the vogue of being the best: yet one of them is a Scholar, and hath published a new edition of Tacitus, with a Latin dedication to My Lord Carteret.

I require that Your Ladyship shall still preserve me some little corner in your memory: and do not think to put me off onely with a Box, which I can assure you will not contribute in the least to* . . . my esteem and regard for Your Ladyship . . . I have been always, and shall ever remain,

Madam,

Your Lady . . .

Obedient and . .

humble .

JON[N] . . . .

Dublin, May 1[re], 1731.

As Lady Worsley's letter serves to explain several allusions in Swift's letters, and is obviously the one to which the second letter is the reply, it is inserted:—

August 6th, 1732.

Sir,—I flatter myself, that if you had received my last letter, you would have favoured me with an answer; therefore I take it for granted it is lost.

I was so proud of your commands, and so fearful of being supplanted by my daughter, that I went to work immediately, that her box might not keep her in your remembrance, while there was nothing to put you in mind of an old friend and humble servant. But Mrs. Barber's long stay here (who promised me to convey it to you) has made me appear very negligent. I doubt not but you think me unworthy of the share (you once told me) I had in your heart. I am yet vain enough to think I deserve it better than all those flirting girls you coquet with. I will not yield (even) to *dirty Patty*, whom I was the most jealous of when you were last here. What if I am a great-grandmother, I can still distinguish your merit from all the rest of the world; but it is not consistent with your good-breeding to put one in mind of it, therefore I am determined not to use my interest with Sir Robert for a living in the Isle of Wight,† though nothing else could reconcile me to the place. But if I could make you Archbishop of Canterbury, I should forget my resentments, for the sake of the flock, who very much want a careful shepherd. Are we to have the honour of seeing you, or not? I have fresh hopes given me; but I dare not please myself too much with them, lest I should be again disappointed. If I had it as much in my power as my inclination to serve Mrs. Barber, she should not be kept thus long attending; but I hope her next voyage may prove more successful. She is just come in, and tells me you have sprained your foot, which will prevent your journey till next summer; but

* A small portion of the original letter has been lost.

† Where her husband, Sir Robert Worsley, possessed the estate of Appuldercombe.

assure yourself the Bath is the only infallible cure for such an accident. If you have any regard remaining for me, you will shew it by taking my advice; if not, I will endeavour to forget you, if I can. But, till that doubt is cleared, I am as much as ever, the Dean's

Obedient humble Servant,

F. Worsley.

Madam,—I will never tell, but I will always remember how many years have run out since I had first the honor and happiness to be known to Your Ladyship, which however I have a thousand times wished to have never happened, since it was followed by the misfortune of being banished from You for ever. I believe you are the onely Lady in England that for a thousand years past hath so long remembered a useless friend in absence, which is too great a load of favor for me and all my gratitude to support.

I can faithfully assure your Ladyship that I never received from You more than one letter since I saw you last; and that I sent you a long answer. I often forget what I did yesterday, or what passed half an hour ago; and yet I can well remember a hundred particulars in Your Ladyship's company. This is the memory of those who grow old. I have no room left for new Ideas. I am offended with one passage in Your Ladyship's letter; but I will forgive You, because I do not believe the fact, and all my acquaintance here joyn with me in my unbelief. You make excuses for not sooner sending me the most agreeable present that ever was made, whereas it is agreed by all the curious and skilfull of both sexes among us, that such a piece of work could not be performed by the most dextrous pair of hands and finest eyes in Christendom, in less than a year and a half, at twelve hours a day. Yet Mrs. Barber, corrupted by the obligations she hath to you, would pretend that I over reckon six months, and six hours a day. Be that as it will, our best virtuosi are unanimous that the Invention exceeds, if possible, the work itself. But to all these praises I coldly answer, that although what they say be perfectly true, or indeed below the truth, yet if they had ever seen or conversed with Your Ladyship, as I have done, they would have thought this escritoire a very poor performance from such hands, such eyes, and such an imagination. To speak my own thoughts, the work itself does not delight me more than the little cares you were pleased to descend to in contriving ways to have it conveyed so far without damage, whereof it received not the least from without; what there was came from within; for one of the little rings that lifts a drawer for wax, hath touched a part of one of the Pictures, and made a mark as large as the head of a small pin; but it touches onely an end of a cloud;

and yet I have been carefull to twist a small thread of silk round that wicked ring, who promiseth to do so no more.

Your Ladyship wrongs me in saying that I twitted you with being a great-grandmother. I was too prudent and carefull of my own credit to offer the least hint upon that head, while I was conscious that I might have been great-grandfather to you.

I beg you, Madam, that there may be no quarrells of jealousy between Your Ladyship and My Lady Carteret: I set her at work by the authority I claymed over her as your daughter. The young woman showed her ready-nesse, and performed very well for a new beginner, and deserves encourage-ment. Besides, she filled the Chest with Tea, whereas you did not send me a single pen, a stick of wax, or a drop of Ink; for all which I must bear the charge out of my own pocket. And after all if Your Ladyship were not by I would say that My Lady Carteret's Box (as you disdainfully call it instead of a Tea-chest) is a most beautiful piece of work, and is oftener used than yours, because it is brought down for tea after dinner among Ladyes, whereas my escritoire never stirrs out of my closet, but when it is brought for a sight. Therefore I again desire there may be no family quarrells upon my account.

As to Patty Blount, you wrong her very much. She was a neighbor's child, a good Catholick, an honest Girl, and a tolerable Courtier at Richmond. I deny she was dirty, but a little careless, and sometimes wore a ragged gown, when she and I took long walks. She saved her money in summer onely to keep a Chair at London in winter: this is the worst you can say; and she might have a whole coat to her back if her good nature did not make her a fool to her mother and sanctifyed sister Teresa. And she was the onely Girl I coquetted in the whole half year that I lived with Mr. Pope in Twitenham, whatever evil tongues might have informed your Ladyship, in hopes to set you against me. And after this usage, if I accept the Archbishoprick of Canter-bury from your Ladyship's hands, I think you ought to acknowledge it as a favor.

Are you not weary, Madam? Have you patience to read all this? I am bringing back past times; I imagine myself talking with you as I used to do; but on a sudden I recollect where I am sitting, banished to a country of slaves and beggars; my blood soured, my spirits sunk, fighting with Beasts like St. Paul, not at Ephesus, but in Ireland.

I am not of your opinion, that the flocks (in either Kingdom) want better Shepherds; for, as the French say, "à tels brebis tel pasteur:" and God be thanked that I have no flock at all, so that I neither can corrupt nor be cor-rupted.

I never saw any person so full of acknowledgment as Mrs. Barber is for Your Ladyship's continued favors to her, nor have I known any person of a more humble and gratefull spirit than her, or who knows better how to distinguish the Persons by whom she is favored. But I will not honor myself so far, or dishonor you so much, as to think I can add the least weight to your own naturall goodness and generosity.

You must, as occasion serves, Present my humble respects to My Lord and Lady Carteret, and my Lady Dysert, and to S[r] Robert Worsley.

I am, and shall be ever, with the truest respect, esteem, and gratitude,

Madam,

Your Ladyship's most obedient
and most humble Servant,

JONATH. SWIFT.

Dublin, Nov. 4[re], 1732.

I know not where my old friend Harry Worsley is, but I am his most humble servant.

On the back of the letter is the following postscript:—

Madam,—I writ this Letter two months ago, and was to send it by Mrs. Barber; but she falling ill of the gout, and I deferring from day to day, expecting her to mend, I was at last out of patience. I have sent it among others by a private hand.

I wish your Ladyship and all your family many happy new years.

Jan. 8[e], 1732.

THE EATING OF OLD.

The food of the people must always be regarded as an important element in estimating the degree of civilization of a nation, and its position in the social scale. Mr. Macaulay, in his masterly picture of the state of England at the period of the accession of James II., has not failed to notice this subject as illustrative of the condition of the working classes of that day. He tells us that meat, viewed relatively with wages, was "so dear that hundreds of thousands of families scarcely knew the taste of it. . . . . . The great majority of the nation lived almost entirely on rye, barley, and oats." (*Hist. Eng.* vol. i. p. 418, 4th ed.)

Pepys, who was unquestionably a lover of good living, and never tired of recording his feastings off "brave venison pasty," or "turkey pye," has given in his *Diary* many curious notices of the most approved dishes of his day. The following "Bills of fare" of the period referred to speak, however, directly to the point; they are taken from a work entitled, *The accomplisht Lady's Delight, in Preserving, Physick, Beautifying, and Cookery.* London, printed for B. Harris, 1683.

A BILL OF FARE FOR A GENTLEMAN'S HOUSE ABOUT CANDLEMAS.

1. A Pottage with a Hen. 2. A *Chatham*-pudding. 3. A Fricacie of Chickens. 4. A leg of mutton with a Sallet. Garnish your dishes with Barberries.

Second Course. 1. A chine of Mutton. 2. A chine of Veal. 3. Lark-pye. 4. A couple of Pullets, one larded. Garnished with orange slices.

Third Course. 1. A dish of Woodcocks. 2. A couple of Rabbits. 3. A dish of Asparagus. 4. A Westphalia Gammon.

Last Course. 1. Two orange tarts, one with herbs. 2. A Bacon Tart. 3. An apple Tart. 4. A dish of Bon-chriteen Pears. 5. A dish of Pippins. 6. A dish of Pearmains.

A BANQUET FOR THE SAME SEASON.

1. A dish of Apricots. 2. A dish of marmalade of Pippins. 3. A dish of preserved Cherries. 4. A whole red Quince. 5. A dish of dryed sweetmeats.

A BILL OF FARE UPON AN EXTRAORDINARY OCCASION.

1. A collar of brawn. 2. A couple of Pullets boyled. 3. A bisk of Fish. 4. A dish of Carps. 5. A grand boyled Meat. 6. A grand Sallet. 7. A venison pasty. 8. A roasted Turkey. 9. A fat pig. 10. A powdered Goose. 11. A haunch of Venison roasted. 12. A Neats-tongue and Udder roasted. 13. A Westphalia Ham boyled. 14. A Joll of Salmon. 15. Mince pyes. 16. A Surloyn of roast beef. 17. Cold baked Meats. 18. A dish of Custards

Second Course. 1. Jellies of all sorts. 2. A dish of Pheasants. 3. A Pike boyled. 4. An oyster pye. 5. A dish of Plovers. 6. A dish of larks. 7. A Joll of Sturgeon. 8. A couple of Lobsters. 9. A lumber pye. 10. A couple of Capons. 11. A dish of Partridges. 12. A fricacy of Fowls. 13.

A dish of Wild Ducks. 14. A dish of cram'd chickens. 15. A dish of stewed oysters. 16. A Marchpane. 17. A dish of Fruits. 18. An umble pye.

The fare suggested for "Fish days" is no less various and abundant; twelve dishes are enumerated for the first course, and sixteen for the second. Looking at the character of these viands, some of which would not discredit the genius of a Soyer or a Mrs. Glasse, it seems pretty evident that in the article of food the laboring classes have been the greatest gainers since 1687.

The following morsel is copied from a small MS. volume of a very miscellaneous character, consisting of poetical extracts, epigrams, receipts, and family memoranda:—

A Bill of ffare at the Christning of Mr Constable's Child, Rector of Cockley Cley in Norfolk, Jan. 2, 1682.

1. A whole hog's head, souc'd, with carrotts in the mouth and pendants in the ears, with guilded oranges thick sett.
2. 2 ox.'s cheekes stewed, with 6 marrow bones.
3. A leg of veal larded, with 6 pullets.
4. A leg of mutton, with 6 rabbits.
5. A chine of bief, a chine of venison, chine of mutton, chine of veal, chine of pork, supported by 4 men.
6. A venison pasty.
7. A great minced pye, with 12 small ones about it.
8. A gelt fat turkey, with 6 capons.
9. A bustard, with 6 pluver.
10. A pheasant, with 6 woodcocks.
11. A great dish of tarts made all of sweetmeats.
12. A Westphalia hamm, with 6 tongues.
13. A jowle of sturgeon.
14. A great charg[r] of all sorts of sweetmeats, with wine and all sorts of liquors answerable.

The child, a girle; godfather, Mr. Green, a clergyman; godmothers, Mis Beddingfield of Sherson, and a sister-in-law of Mr. Constable's.

The guests, Mr. Green, Mr. Bagg and his daughter, and the godmothers.

The parish[rs] entertained at another house with rost and boil'd bief, geese, and turkeys. Soon after the child dy'd, and the funerall expences came to 6*d.*

The following curious memorandum of the last century, appears to be a bill of fare for the entertainment of a party, upon the "flitch of bacon" being decreed to a happy couple. It is at Harrowgate, and not at Dunmow, which would lead us to believe that this custom was not confined to one county. The feast itself is almost as remarkable, as regards its component parts, as that produced by Mr. Thackarey, in his delightful "Lectures," as characteristic of polite feeling in Queen Anne's reign :—

JUNE 25.—MR. AND MRS. LIDDALL'S DINNER AT GREEN DRAGON, HARROWGATE, ON TAKING FFLITCH BACON OATH.

Bill Fare.

Beans and bacon.
Cabbage, colliflower.
Three doz. chickens.
Two shoulders mutton, cowcumbers.
Two turbets.
Rump beef, &c., &c.
Goose and plumbpudding.
Quarter lamb, sallad.
Tarts, jellies, strawberries, cream.
Cherrys, syllabubs, and blomonge.
Leg lamb, spinnage.
Crawfish, pickled salmon.
Fryd tripe, calves' heads.
Gravy and pease soup.
Two piggs.
Breast veal, ragoud.
Ice cream, pine apple.
Surloin beaf.
Pidgeons, green peas.
Lobsters, crabs.
Twelve red herrings, twenty-two dobils.

EPIGRAM BY SOUTHEY.

On Queen Elizabeth's dining on board Sir Francis Drake's ship, on his return from circumnavigating the globe :—

Oh, Nature! to old England still
  Continue these mistakes;
Give us for all our *Kings* such *Queens*,
  And for our *Dux* such *Drakes*.

SONG BY THOMAS OTWAY.

In turning over a quantity of miscellaneous papers in MS. (some originals and some copies) of the latter half of the seventeenth century, the following song, by the unfortunate author of *Venice Preserved*, turned up. It may, possibly, have been printed in one or more of the numerous volumes of "miscellany poems" which teemed from the press at the end of the seventeenth and beginning of the following century; but it is not to be found after looking over a tolerable assemblage of these volumes of the time. The MS. does not appear to be an original, although the handwriting is of the author's period. The punctuation is as I found it:—

Health breeds care; love, hope and fear;
What does love or bus'ness here?
While Bacchus merry does appear,
  Fight on and fear no sinking:
Charge it briskly to the brim,
Till the flying topsails swim:
We owe the great discovery to him
  Of this new world of drinking.

Grave cabals that states refine,
Mingle their debates with wine;
Ceres and the god o' th' vine
  Makes ev'ry great commander.
Let sober sots small-beer subdue,
The wise and valiant vine does woe;
That *Stagyrite* had the honour to
  Be drunk with *Alexander*.

Stand to your arms, and now advance,
A health to the *English* King of France ;
On to the next, a *bon speranze*,
  By Bacchus and Apollo.
Thus in state I lead the van,
Fall in your place by your right-hand man;
Beat drum! now march! dub a dub, ran dan;
  He's a Whigg that will not follow. T. OTWAY.

That poor Otway was a lover of the "juice of the grape," is too well known; and it seems from his biography in Cibber's *Lives of the Poets*, that he was for some time a soldier, and served in Flanders. The half-bacchanalian, half-military character of this song, seems to identify it with the poet. The popular story, that Otway died for want at an ale-house on Tower Hill, is, it is to be hoped, not strictly true. Dennis, the critic (as he is called), tells us that—

Otway had an intimate friend (one Blackstone), who was shot; the murderer fled towards Dover, and Otway pursued him. In his return he drank water when violently heated, and so got a fever, which was the death of him.

This story is creditable to the warmth of Otway's friendship, and one should be glad to meet with any additional authority to give it confirmation.

REMARKABLE IMPRINTS.

The horrors of the Star Chamber and the Ecclesiastical Courts produced many extraordinary imprints, particularly to those seditious books of the Puritans, better known as the *Marprelate Family;* works which were printed by ambulatory presses, and circulated by unseen hands, now under the walls of Archiepiscopal Lambeth, and *presto!* (when the spy would lay his hands upon them) sprite-like, Martin reappeared in the provinces! This game at hide and seek between the brave old Nonconformists and the Church, went on for years without detection:

but the readers of "N. & Q." do not require from me the history of the Marprelate Faction, so well told already in the *Miscellanies of Literature* and elsewhere; the *animus* of these towards the hierarchy will be sufficiently exhibited for my purpose in a few of their imprints. *An Almond for a Parrot*, for example, purports to be—

Imprynted at a place not farre from a place; by the Assignes of Signior Some-body, and are to be soulde at his shoppe in Trouble-Knave Street.

Again, *Oh read ouer D. John Bridges, for it is a worthy work*, is

Printed ouer sea, in Europe, within two forlongs of a Bouncing Priest, at the Cost and Charges of Martin Marprelate, Gent, 1589.

The Return of the renowned Cavaliero Pasquill has the following extraordinary imprint:—

If my breath be so hote that I burne my mothe, I suppose I was printed by Pepper Allie, 1589.

The original "Marprelate" was John Penri, who at last fell into the hands of his enemies, and was executed under circumstances of great barbarity in Elizabeth's reign. "Martin Junior," however, sprung up, and *The Counter-Cuffe* to him is—

Printed between the Skye and the Grounde, wythin a Myle of an Oake, and not many Fields off from the unpriuileged Presse of the Ass-ignes of Martin Junior, 1589.

The virulency of this theological warfare died away in James's reign, but only to be renewed with equal rancor in that of Charles, when Marprelatism was again called into activity by the high-church freaks of Archbishop Laud. *Vox Borealis, or a Northerne Discoverie by way of Dialogue between Jamie and Willie*, is an example of these later attacks upon the overbearing of the mitre, and affords the imprint—

Amidst the Babylonians. Printed by Margery Marprelate, in Thwack-Coat Lane, at the Signe of the Crab-Tree Cudgell, without any privilege of the Cater-Caps, 1641.

Others of this stamp will occur to your readers: this time the Puritans had the best of the struggle, and ceased not to push their advantage until they brought their enemy to the block.

When the liberty of the press was imperfectly understood, the political satirist had to tread warily; consequently we find that class of writers protecting themselves by jocular or patriotic imprints. A satirical pamphlet upon the late *Sicke Commons* is "Printed in the Happie Year 1641." *A Letter from Nobody in the City to Nobody in the Country* is "Printed by Somebody, 1679." *Somebody's Answer* is "Printed for Anybody." These were likely of such a tendency as would have rendered both author and printer amenable to *somebody*, say Judge Jeffries. During the administration of Sir Robert Walpole, there were many skirmishing satirists supported by both ministry and people, such as James Miller, whose pamphlet, *contra*, *Are these things so?* is "Printed for the perusal of all Lovers of their Country, 1740." This was answered by the ministers' champion, James Dance, *alias* Love, in *Yes, they are!* alike addressed to the "Lovers of their Country." *What of That?* was the next of the series, being Miller's reply, who intimated this time that it was "Printed, and to be had of all True Hearts and Sound Bottoms."

When there was a movement for an augmentation of the poor stipends of the Scots Clergy in 1750, there came out a pamphlet under the title of *The Presbyterian Clergy seasonably detected*, 1751, which exceeds in scurrility, if possible, the famous, or infamous, *Scotch Presbyterian Eloquence Displayed;* both author and printer, however, had so much sense as to remain in the background, and the *thing* purported to be "Printed for Mess John in Fleet Street." Under the title of *The Comical History* *of the Marriage betwixt Heptarchus and Fergusia*, 1706,* the Scots figured the union of the Lord Heptarchus, or England, with the independent, but coerced, damsel Fergusia, or Scotland; the discontented church of the latter finding that the former broke faith with her, could not help giving way to occasional murmurings, and these found vent in (among others) a poetical Presbyterian tract, entitled *Melancholy Sonnets, or Fergusia's Complaint upon Heptarchus*, in which the author reduced to rhyme the aforesaid *Comical History*, adding thereto all the evils this ill-starred union had entailed upon the land after thirty-five years' experience. This curious production was "Printed at Elguze? for Pedaneous, and sold by Circumferaneous, below the Zenith, 1741." Charles II., when crowned at Scone, took the solemn league and covenant; but not finding it convenient to carry out that part of his coronation oath, left the Presbyterians at the Restoration in the hands of their enemies. To mark their sense of this breach of faith, there was published a little book † describing the inauguration of the *young profligate*, which expressively purports to be "Printed at Edinburgh in the Year of Covenant-breaking." The Scots folk had such a horror of any thing of a deistical tendency, that John Goldie had to publish his *Essays, or an attempt to distinguish true from false Religion* (popularly called "Goldie's Bible"), at Glasgow, "Printed for the Author, and sold by him at Kilmarnock, 1779;" neither printer nor bookseller would, apparently, be identified with the *unclean thing*. Both churchmen and dissenters convey their exultations, or denouncements, upon political changes, through the

* G. Chalmers ascribed this to one "Balantyne." In Lockhart's *Memoirs*, Lond. 1714, Mr. John Balantyne, the minister of Lanark, is noticed as the most uncompromising opponent of the Union.

† *A Phœnix, or the Solemn League and Covenant, &c.*, 12mo. pp. 168, with a frontispiece representing Charles burning the book of the Solemn League and Covenant, above the flames from which hovers a phœnix.

medium of imprints; and your correspondents who have been discussing that matter, will see in some of these that the "Good Old Cause" may be "all round the compass," as Captain Cuttle would say, depending wholly upon the party spectacles through which you view it. *Legal Fundamental Liberty*, in an epistle from Selburne to Lentnal, is "Reprinted in the Year of Hypocritical and Abominable Dissimulation, 1649;" on the other hand, *The Little Bible* of that militant soldier, Captain Butler, is "Printed in the First Year of England's Liberty, 1649." *The Last Will and Testament of Sir John Presbyter* is "Printed in the Year of Jubilee, 1647." *A New Meeting of Ghosts at Tyburn*, in which Oliver, Bradshaw, and Peters figure, exhibits its royal tendency, being "Printed in the Year of the Rebellious Phanatick's Downfall, 1660." "Printed at N., with Licence," is the cautious imprint of a republication of *Doleman's Conference* in 1681. *A proper Project to Startle Fools*, is "Printed in a Land where Self's cry'd up, and Zeal's cry'd down, 1699." *The Impartial Accountant, wherein it is demonstratively made known how to pay the National Debt, and that without a New Tax, or any Inconveniency to the People*, is "Printed for a Proper Person," and, I may add, can be had of a *certain person*, if Mr. Gladstone will come down with an adequate consideration for the secret! These accountants are all mysterious—you would think they were plotting to empty the treasury rather than to fill it; another says his *Essay upon National Credit* is "Printed by A. R., in Bond's Stables!" Thomas Scott, the English minister at Utrecht, published, among other oddities, *Vox Cœlis; or, Newes from Heaven, being Imaginary Conversations there between Henry VIII. (!), Edward VI., Prince Henrie, and others*, "Printed in Elysium, 1624." Edward Raban, an Englishman, who set up a press in the far north, published an edition of Lady Culros' *Godlie Dreame*, and finding that no title commanded such respect among the canny Scots as that of *Laird*, announced the book to be "Imprinted at Aberdene, by E. R., Laird of Letters, 1644." *The Instructive Library*, containing a list of apocryphal books, and a satire upon some theological authors of that day, is "Printed for the Man in the Moon, 1710." *The Oxford Sermon Versified*, by Jacob Gingle, Esq., is "Printed by Tim. Atkins at Dr. Sacheverell's Head, near St. Paul's, 1729." "Printed, and to be had at the Pamphlett Shops of London and Westminster," was a common way of circulating productions of questionable morals or loyalty. The Chapmen, or Flying-Stationers, had many curious dodges of this kind to give a relish to their literary wares: *The Secret History of Queen Elizabeth and the Earl of Essex* derived additional interest in the eyes of their country customers by its being "Printed at Cologne for Will-with-the-Wisp, at the Sign of the Moon in the Ecliptic, 1767." The *Poems* of that hard-hearted Jacobite, Alexander Robertson, of Struan, are "Printed at Edinburgh for Charles Alexander, and sold at his house in Geddes Close, where Subscribers may call for their Copies, circa 1750." *The New Dialogues of the Dead* are "Printed for D. Y., at the foot of Parnassus Hill, 1684." Professor Tenant's poem of *Papistry Stormed*, imitates the old typographers, it being "Imprentit at Edinbrogh be Oliver and Boyd, anno 1827." A rare old book is Goddard's *Mastiffe Whelpe*, "Imprinted amongst the Antipodes, and are to be sould where they are to be bought." Another, by the same author, is a *Satirical Dialogue*, "Imprinted in the Low Countreyes for all such Gentlemen as are not altogether idle, nor yet well occupyed." These were both, I believe, libels upon the fair sex. John Stewart, otherwise *Walking Stewart*, was in the habit of dating his extraordinary publications "In the year of Man's Retrospective Knowledge, by Astronomical Calculation, 5000;" "In the 7000 year of Astronomical History in the Chinese Tables;" and "In the Fifth Year of Intellectual Existence." "Mulberry Hill, Printed at Crazy Castle," is an imprint of J. H. Stevenson.

The Button Makers' Jests, by Geo. King of St. James', is "Printed for Henry Frederick, near St. James' Square;" a coarse squib upon royalty. One Fisher entitled his play *Thou shalt not Steal; the School of Ingratitude*. Thinking the managers of Drury Lane had communicated his performance, under the latter name, to Reynolds the dramatist, and then rejected it, he published it thus: "Printed for the curious and literary—shall we say? Coincidence! refused by the Managers, and made use of in the farce of 'Good Living,'" published by Reynolds in 1797. *Harlequin Premier, as it is daily acted*, is a hit at the ministry of the period, "Printed at Brentafordia, Capital of Barataria, and sold by all the Booksellers in the Province, 1769." "Printed Merrily, and may be read Unhappily, betwixt Hawke and Buzzard, 1641," is the *satisfactory* imprint of *The Downefall of temporising Poets, unlicensed Printers, upstart Booksellers, tooting Mercuries, and bawling Hawkers*. Books have sometimes been published for behoof of particular individuals; old Daniel Rogers, in his *Matrimonial Honovr*, announces "A Part of the Impression to be vended for the use and benefit of Ed. Minsheu, Gent., 1650."

"CHERRY RIPE."

There is a quaint grace in this lyric, perfect in its kind, characteristic of the song-writing of the time. It is from a work entitled *An Hour's Recreation in Music*, by Richard Alison, published in 1606:—

There is a garden in her face,
  Where roses and white lilies grow;
A heavenly Paradise is that place,
  Wherein all pleasant fruits do flow.
There cherries grow, that none may buy,
Till cherry ripe themselves do cry.

These cherries fairly do inclose
  Of orient pearl a double row;
Which, when her lovely laughter shows,
  They look like rosebuds fill'd with snow,
Yet there no peer nor prince may buy,
Till cherry ripe themselves do cry.

Her eyes, like angels, watch them still:
  Her brows like bended bows do stand,
Threatening with piercing frowns to kill
  All that approach with eye or hand,
Those sacred cherries to come nigh,
Till cherry ripe themselves do cry.

PASQUINADES.

The following admirable epigram was written, it is said, by one of the most accomplished scholars of the university of Oxford:—

Cum Sapiente Pius nostras juravit in aras:
Impius heu Sapiens, desipiensque Pius.

Thus translated:—

The wise man and the Pius have laid us under bann,
Oh Pious man unwise! oh impious Wise-man!"
1850.

In May, 1851, these verses were placed upon Pasquin's statue in Rome, translated into Italian:—

Quando Papa o' Cardinale
Chies' Inglese tratta male,
Quel che chiamo quella gente
Pio? No-no, *se* sapiente.

Pope Leo XII. was reported, whether truly or not, to have been the reverse of scrupulous in the earlier part of his life, but was remarkably strict after he became Pope, and was much disliked at Rome, perhaps because, by his maintenance of strict discipline, he abridged the amusements and questionable indulgences of the people. On account of his death, which took place just before the time of the carnival in 1829, the usual festivities were omitted, which gave occasion to the following pasquinade, which was much, though privately, circulated :—

Tre cose mal fecesti, O Padre santo ;
Accettar il papato,
Viver tanto,
Morir di Carnivale
Per destar pianto.

On the decease of Pope Clement IX. in 1669, Cardinal Bona was named amongst those worthy of the tiara, when a French Jesuit (Père Dangières), in reply to a line inscribed, as usual upon those occasions, on the statue of Pasquin, " Papa Bona sarebbe un solecisma," made the following epigram :—

Grammaticæ leges plerumque Ecclesia spernit :
Forte erit ut liceat dicere Papa Bona.
Vana solæcismi ne te conturbat imago :
Esset Papa bonus, si Bona Papa erit.

The successful candidate, however, was Cardinal Emilio Altieri, who assumed the name of Clement X., in April, 1670: Bona (Giov.) died in October, 1674.

These two epigrams were affixed to the statue of Pasquin at Rome, in the year 1820, upon two Cardinals who were candidates for the Popedom :—

PASQUINALIA.

Sit bonus, et fortasse pius—sed semper ineptus—
Vult, meditatur, agit, *plurima, pauca, nihil.*

IN ALTERUM.

Promittit, promissa negat, ploratque negata,
Hæc tria si junges, quis neget esse Petrum.

APULEIUS ON MESMERISM.

The following passage in Apuleius seems to be an allusion to Mesmerism :—

Quin et illud mecum reputo, posse animum humanum, præsertim puerilem et simplicem, seu carminum avocamento, sive odorum delenimento, soporari, et ad oblivionem præsentium externari; et paulisper remota corporis memoriâ, redigi ac redire ad naturam suam, quæ est immortalis scilicet et divina; atque ita, veluti quodam sopore, futura rerum præsagire.—Apuleius, *Apol.* 475. Delph. ed.

BABBLING.

In his *Aggravations of Vain Babbling*, speaking of gossips, Baxter says :—

If I had one to send to school that were sick of the talking evil—the *morbus loquendi*—I would give (as Isocrates required) a double pay to the schoolmaster willingly; one part for teaching him to hold his tongue, and the other half for teaching him to speak. I should think many such men and women half cured if they were half as weary of speaking as I am of hearing them. *He that lets such twattling swallows build in his chimney may look to have his pottage savour of their dung.*

PROVERBIAL EXPRESSIONS.

Smelling of the Lamp.—Plutarch *vit. Demosth.*, c. 8, attributes to Pytheas the expression ἐλλυχνίων ὄζειν, to smell of the lamp-wick.

The Nine of Diamonds.—Why the nine of diamonds is called the curse of Scotland is thus explained in Grose's Dictionary of the Vulgar Tongue :—

Diamonds imply royalty, being ornaments to the imperial crown, and every ninth King of Scotland has been observed for many ages to be a tyrant, and a curse to that country.

The Two Kings of Brentford.—These celebrated worthies

made their first appearance in the farce of The Rehearsal, written by Villiers, Duke of Buckingham, with the assistance of Butler, Sprat, and others. Dryden is satirized in it under the name of Bayes.

A little Bird told me.—The origin of this phrase is doubtless to be found in *Ecclesiastes*, x. 20:—

Curse not the king, no, not in thy thought; and curse not the rich in thy bed-chamber: for a bird of the air shall carry the voice, and that which hath wings shall tell the matter.

By Hook or Crook.—This saying is probably derived from a forest custom. Persons entitled to fuel wood in the king's forest, were only authorized to take it of the dead wood or branches of trees in the forest, "with a cart, a hook, and a crook."

To Eat Humble Pie.—The *humble pie* of former times was a pie made out of the "umbles" or entrails of the deer, a dish of the second table, inferior, of course, to the venison pasty which smoked upon the dais, and therefore not inexpressive of that humiliation which the term "eating humble pie" now painfully describes. The "umbles" of the deer are constantly the perquisites of the gamekeeper.

Grin like a Chesire Cat.—Some years since Chesire cheeses were sold moulded into the shape of a cat, bristles being inserted to represent the whiskers. This may possibly have originated the saying. Charles Lamb's ingenious theory that Chesire was a county Palatine, and that the cats, when they think of it, are so tickled that they cannot help grinning, is not entirely satisfactory

"*The Wise Men of Gotham.*"—In Thoroton's Nottinghamshire, vol. i. pp. 42, 43, the origin of the general opinion about the wisdom of these worthies is thus given, as handed down by tradition:—

King John intending to pass through Gotham towards Nottingham, was prevented by the inhabitants, they apprehending that the ground over which a king passed was for ever after to become a public road. The king, incensed at their proceedings, sent from his court, soon afterwards, some of his servants to inquire of them the reason of their incivility and ill-treatment, that he might punish them. The villagers hearing of the approach of the king's servants, thought of an expedient to turn away his majesty's displeasure from them. When the messengers arrived at Gotham, they found some of the inhabitants engaged in endeavouring to drown an eel in a pool of water; some were employed in dragging carts upon a large barn, to shade the wood from the sun: and others were engaged in hedging a cuckoo, which had perched itself upon an old bush. In short, they were all employed upon some foolish way or other, which convinced the king's servants that it was a village of fools.

"*God tempers the wind to the shorn lamb.*"—This saying is from Sterne's Sentimental Journey. He, however, takes it from the French: "*A brebis tondue, Dieu mesure le vent.*" It appears to be of some antiquity, as it is to be found in somewhat different versions in a collection of proverbs published in 1594—"Dieu mesure le froid à la brebis tondue, Dieu donne le froid selon la robbe."

Cæsar's wife must be above suspicion.—The origin of this proverb may be found in Plutarch (Julius Cæsar, cap. 10), or in the following passage from Suetonius (Jul. Cæs. 74):—

The name of Pompeia, the wife of Julius Cæsar, having been mixed up with an accusation against P. Clodius, her husband divorced her; not, as he said, because he believed the charge against her, but because he would have those belonging to him as free from suspicion as from crime.

SONG BY SIR JOHN SUCKLING.

The following verses are contained in a small quarto MS. Collection of English Poetry, in the handwriting of the time of Charles I. They are much in Suckling's manner, and in the MS are described as—

Sir John Suckling's Verses.

I am confirm'd a woman can
Love this, or that, or any other man:
This day she's melting hot,
To-morrow swears she knows you not;
If she but a new object find,
Then straight she's of another mind;
  Then hang me, Ladies, at your door,
  If e'er I doat upon you more.

Yet still I'll love the fairsome (why?—
For nothing but to please my eye);
And so the fat and soft-skinned dame
I'll flatter to appease my flame;
For she that's musical I'll long,
When I am sad, to sing a song;
  Then hang me, Ladies, at your door,
  If e'er I doat upon you more.

I'll give my fancy leave to range
Through every where to find out change;
The black, the brown, the fair shall be
But objects of variety.
I'll court you all to serve my turn,
But with such flames as shall not burn;
  Then hang me, Ladies, at your door,
  If e'er I doat upon you more.

DISCOVERY OF AMERICA.

In reference to the discovery of America by Madoc, Seneca shadows forth such a discovery:—

Venient annis sæcula seris
Quibus Oceanus vincula rerum
Laxet, et ingens pateat tellus,
Ichthysque novos deteget orbes;
Nec sit terris ultima Thule.

Medea, act ii. ad finem, v. 375.

"A vaticination," says the commentator, "of the Spanish discovery of America."

The probability of a short western passage to India is mentioned in *Aristotle de Cœlo*, ii., near the end.

AN OLD-WORLD VILLAGE.

Years hence, in the time of Mr. Macaulay's New Zealander, when the great Holyhead Road is good pasture, and Cary has sensitive commentators, I don't imagine that the precise locality of Newton Prodgers will be settled without inkshed. It is the very height of improbability that any reader of "N. & Q.," unless he is a taxman, ever went there; still less, having done so once, that he would be desirous of enjoying the felicity twice, for the road to Newton Prodgers is not only not the road to any other place whatsoever, but is moreover the true and only genuine site of the stupendous adventure of the Manchester Bagman, which the Yankees have appropriated with characteristic coolness, and pitched somewhere or other down in Alabama. The thing itself actually occurred to a respectable farmer of our village, no way connected with the public press, who set to work one fine morning to dig out a riding whip, the tip of which he saw sprouting out of the middle of the road. After an hour's hard digging he came to a hat, and under that, to his intense horror, was a head belonging to a body in a state of advanced suffocation. Assistance was procured, and after several hours of unremitting exertion, worthy of Agassiz or Owen, the entire organism of a bagman was developed. "Now, gentlemen," said the exhumed commercial to his perspiring diggers, who of course concluded their labors finished, "now, gentlemen, you've saved my life; and now, for God's sake, lend a hand to get out my mare!" I am aware that at first sight this anecdote appears to tell against our village; but then everybody knows it is the business of the Little Pudgington folks to mend these roads, and not ours. We never have repaired them, and it is not very likely we shall begin now, for we have a religious antipathy to all innovation, especially when it is likely to touch the rates. In M'Adam's time, when the aforesaid Little Pudgington folks were going to bring the branch turnpike through a corner of Newton Prodgers, we rose as one man, called a public meeting, and passed a resolution expressing strong abhorrence of French principles; and we have not degenerated, for it is only the other day since we thrashed the surveyors of the "Great Amalgamated Central." Search the whole county, and I doubt if you find such another respectable old-fashioned place. When I get out at the Gingham Station, and mount for Newton, after an absence in town, I feel I am stepping back two centuries, and am quite disappointed next morning that the postman don't deliver a Mercurius Politicus with the latest intelligence of his Majesty's forces in the north, and the last declaration of his Majesty's affectionate Parliament. It is true we have no resident clergyman or squire either since the last Prodgers was cleaned out at Crockford's; but then, by way of set-off, we haven't a school or a sanitary law in the parish; no spelling-books to put improper notions into the people's heads; and as for pig legislation, I should just like to see them try it on at Newton Prodgers, that's all.

Our village is not one of those rural paradises which the adventurous explorer might discover among the properties at the Adelphi, nor one of Mr. James's receptacles for benighted horsemen, not even one of Miss Mitford's charming villages—all gables and acacia—nor any thing, in short, but a plain average parish of the Bedford Level, still in a state of refreshing pastoral simplicity, or, as our radical paper perversely has it, "frightfully neglected condition." We have a church, green, and stocks in tolerable repair. A green is always the germ of the Saxon thorpe, no matter where found—Schleswig, Kent, Massachusetts, Australia, or New Zealand. In our village, as in most others of our country side, it is called the Cross Hill, and there are yet the steps and part of the shaft of the cross, which no doubt stood there long before the church was thought of, and formed the nucleus of the village. On the left of the cross is the well, the "town well," so called to distinguish it from the "holy well," which is nearer the church, and probably supplied the piscina and font. Opposite the stocks there, with the portentous effigy of an owl *in extremis*, is the Red Eagle, much noted for superlative October; and farther on, at the corner, is the less aristocratic Chequers, where they brew beer very small indeed, which, as I once heard a *habitué* plaintively asseverate, "wets where it goes" and no farther. Three roads branch out of the Cross Hill, one to the church, and two to outlying homesteads. And now the reader knows as much of Newton Prodgers as I do.

When I first knew Newton Prodgers, old John Gibbs was the great man for burning Guys and keeping up the old Christmas customs. He was the OLDBUCK of Newton—the OLDBUCK without the *Prætorium*—the fogie without the ghastly tie. On working days Jack was not to be distinguished from his laborers; but on Sundays, when he donned his black velvet smalls and leather leggings all tied in true-lovers' knots, he looked a "warm" man every inch of him. It was a treat to see him lead his dame up the aisle of the church, and to watch his demeanor during the sermon, trying to look as though he understood it. John was by no means partial to literature, and his reading was wholly confined to the Family Bible, and the enlivening feats of the "Seven Champions," of which honest John swallowed every morsel—the dragon included. Upon scientific subjects generally, Master Gibbs was very considerably behind the age. His notions of cosmogony and planetary affairs were opposed to those of Humboldt and Herschel, presenting indeed many points of remarkable similarity to the Ptolemeian doctrines of my friend Moravanjee, who lately filled with so much credit the astronomical chair at Benares, modified, however, to some extent, by the theories of the late Dr. Francis Moore, as yearly perpetuated by the Worshipful Company of Stationers. In politics Jack was a thorough-going Church and King man, and stoutly swore to the last day of his life that tea and pantaloons had ruined England, and worked between them the fall of the corn laws. A more honest, thick-headed, open-hearted, and prejudiced old booby never drew breath. He was the last man for miles round our place who kept open house to all comers; and, I regret to add, he was the identical old rascal who set the bells ringing when the lamented news of the death of the late Sir Robert Peel reached Newton Prodgers. If you took a peep into his stone-floored house-room on Christmas Eve, you would see Misrule *redivivus.* Hodge senior smokes long pipes, plays at cards, and looks on. Adolescent Agriculture dances quaint old country dances not found in the *Ball-room Monitor*, and sings rough old songs in rough old measure that would scandalize Sims Reeves; while the younger fry are wild and dripping at duck-apple, snap-apple, and half a score of other equally intellectual amusements. But the mumming is the great fun of the night. With us this consists of a kind of rude drama, which formerly represented the adventures of St. George and the Dragon; but of late years St. George has given place to George III., and the Dragon been supplanted by Napoleon. In the last scene the emperor indulges in such strong vituperation against Mr. Pitt, and insinuates such unpleasant things about Mr. Pitt's mamma, as to induce that placid gentleman to give him a blow on the nose; whereupon a fight ensues, in which the pilot gets decidedly the worst of it, and is about to receive the *coup-de-grâce*, when up comes George III. with a cocked-hat and broadsword, and the royal asseveration—

As sure as I am England's king, I'll break your neck.

—a threat which, after a severe encounter, he manages to accomplish, and the Corsican tyrant is finally carried off by Beelzebub, who, I should say, is a leading member of the company. He was a bold genius, whoever he was, who conceived the idea of making George III. a hero. The fool, whose principal duty is to blow flour into the emperor's eyes, is a relic of the older drama, and carries a stick with a bladder tied to it by way of bauble. He still performs the old legerdemain tricks described by Ben Jonson. When the fun was at its height, the Christmas block used to be brought in and put on the fire, to be taken off again when only half burnt, and preserved in the cellar or some other safe place till next year. This precious piece of charred wood old Jack used to look upon as a sovereign amulet against fire during the ensuing year, and as safe as a fire policy. And this is still the usual custom in our neighborhood.

It is a grand old superstition that, which represents the powers of darkness as more than usually active on the anniversary of the last day of Pagandom—dim echo through the ages of that first Nativity which silenced the oracles and drove the nymphs from their ancient haunts. Old Smudgers, the rat-catcher, was quite Miltonic, although he didn't know it, when he told me "No good Christian would even turn a dog out" on Christmas Eve. All our ghosts have holiday on that night, and we have lots of ghosts of all grades at Newton Prodgers; from that old-established aristocratic old ghost, Sir Miles Prodgers, who drives about the lanes in the same old coach that took him to St. Paul's after Ramillies, down to Mary Potts, who drowned herself in Sludgepond, and is a mere *parvenu* ghost—a spirit of no pretensions whatever. It is the Walpurgis of the witches and demons on the wold and in the woods. Ghosts of suicides hold high carnival at dreary crossroads, and he who has courage enough to watch in the churchyard with an ash stick in his hand, will see the fetches of those who are to die during the next year. Sometimes, also, the wayfarer sees lights and hears solemn music in lonely churches—another fine old idea which has haunted man's mind ever since Reginald of Durham's friend, the Yorkshire monk, fell asleep and dreamed of the ghostly mass at Farne. But all this *diablerie* terminates at the first sound of the midnight bells; and the spirit or demon, wherever he is, must hie him back instanter. Old Smudgers, who knows more legends than the brothers Grimm, and has killed incomparably more rats, tells a tale of a dissipated young fellow who, loveworn and morose, wandered out one Christmas eve instead of joining the carol singers—how, full of evil thoughts, he sauntered through the common field, and was accosted by the enemy in the guise of (probably his nearest prototype) a Yorkshire horsedealer, who tried all manner of ways to get hold of him, by engaging him in some game of chance, but all without success; till he offered to drink him for a "bag of gold," which our thirsty rustic could not find it in his heart to refuse, and proposed an instantaneous adjournment to the "Red Eagle." "No time like the present," said the old gentleman, drawing out a bottle and a couple of horns; and so they sat down on the hill-side, and drank as though for their lives. Dick held out manfully for some time, but felt the liquor gradually stealing away his senses. He sees his adversary's eyes glaring with triumph, and feels a burning grasp at his throat, when suddenly, borne by the breeze over the hills and fens, comes the merry sound of the midnight chimes—ringing out from every tower and steeple down the country side. With a shriek that woke every one up at Mud Wallingham, twenty-one miles off, the Yorkshireman abandoned his prey; and next morning Dick was found with his gold at the bottom of the hill. But the ill-gotten riches never made Dick thrive. His favorite son left him alone in his old age, and he became a miser, and barred himself up in the old house near the church—still called the "Miser's House." One wintry Christmas eve, when all was wind and storm without, there was a knock, and a supplication for relief at his door; but all the beggar got was a curse. Next morning the body of his long-lost son was found frozen on the step, and that day the old man died—but not to rest: for, at a certain hour on Christmas eve, the wretched old miser unbars the window with his bony hands, and showers down, from between the old stanchions, coins of a date and coinage long passed away: of late years, probably because of the unhappy scarcity of specie, he has been less liberal; but Smudgers watched once, a long time ago, and picked up a penny, which he has still carefully wrapped up in silver paper, beneath the false bottom of his old chest.

N. B.—Smudgers is indisputably the biggest liar in our village.

WHIPPING-BOYS OF PRINCES.

An allusion to the practice of whipping a young prince by proxy, when he did not know his lessons, is to be found in a very scarce old play, in which the whipping-boy was knighted, entitled *When You see Mee You know Mee*, as it was played by the High and Mighty Prince of Wales his Servants, by Samuel Rowley, London, 1632:—

Prince. (Ed. VI.) Why, how now, Browne; what's the matter?

Browne. Your Grace loyters, and will not plye your booke, and your tutors have whipt me for it.

Prince. Alas, poore Ned! I am sorrie for it. I'll take the more paines, and entreate my tutors for thee; yet, in troth, the lectures they read me last night out of Virgil and Ovid I am perfect in, onely I confesse I am behind in my Greeke authors.

Will (Summers). And for that speech they have declined it uppon his breech, &c.—Pages 48–53.

The subject is also noticed by Sir Walter Scott, *Fortunes of Nigel*, ch. vi. p. 114, vol. xxvi. of Waverley Novels, Edinburgh, 1833, 8vo.; and also by Burnet in *The History of his own Time*. The latter, in speaking of Elizabeth, Countess of Dysart, whom he describes as an *intrigante*, and who afterwards became Duchess of Lauderdale, says her father, *William Murray*, had been page and *whipping-boy* to Charles I. We hear nothing of such office being held by any one in the household of Prince Henry, the elder brother of Charles I.; nor, if we can believe Cornwallis and others, can we suppose that "incomparable and heroique" prince infringed the rules of discipline, in any respect, to justify any castigation. It does not appear that it was the practice to have such a *substitute* in France; for Louis XIV., who was contemporary with our Charles I., on one occasion, when he was sensible of his want of education, exclaimed, "Est-ce qu'il n'y avait point de verges dans mon royaume pour me forcer à étudier?" And Mr. Prince (*Parallel History*, 2d edition in 3 vols. 8vo., London, 1842–3, at p. 262, vol. iii.) states, that George III., when Dr. Markham inquired "how his Majesty would wish to have the princes treated?"—"Like the sons of any private English gentleman," was the sensible reply; "if they deserve it, let them be flogged: do as you used to do at Westminster." This is very like the characteristic and judicious language of the honest monarch.

EPIGRAM.

This beautiful epigram was written by Jerome Amaltheus, who died in 1574. The subjects of it are uncertain, although it is supposed that by Venus was intended the Duchess of Eboli, mistress of Philip II. of Spain:—

DE GEMELLIS FRATRE ET SONORE LUSCIS.

Lumine Acon, dextro, capta est Leonilla sinistro,
Et potis est forma vincere uterque Deos.
Blande puer, lumen, quod habes concede *puellæ*,
Sic tu cæcus Amor, sic erit illa Venus.

It has been thus translated:—

One eye is closed to each in rayless night,
  Yet each has beauty fit the gods to move,
Give, Acon, give to Leonill *thy* light,
  She will be Venus, and thou sightless Love

SPIRITUAL RAPPINGS.

Rushton Hall, near Kettering in Northamptonshire, was long the residence of the ancient and distinguished family of Treshams. In the reign of Queen Elizabeth, the mansion was occupied by Sir Thomas Tresham, who was a pedant and a fanatic; but who was an important character in his time by reason of his great wealth and powerful connections. There is a lodge at Rushton, situate about half a mile from the old hall, now in ruins, but covered all over, within and without, with emblems of the Trinity. This lodge is known to have been built by Sir Thomas Tresham; but his precise motive for selecting this mode of illustrating his favorite doctrine was unknown until it appeared from a letter written by himself about the year 1584, and discovered in a bundle of books and papers inclosed, since 1605, in a wall in the old mansion, and brought to light about twenty years ago. The following relation of a "rapping" or "knocking" is extracted from this letter :—

> If it be demanded why I labour so much in the Trinity and Passion of Christ to depaint in this chamber, this is the principal instance thereof: That at my last being hither committed,* and I usually having my servants here allowed me, to read nightly an hour to me after supper, it fortuned that Fulcis, my then servant, reading in the *Christian Resolution*, in the treatise of *Proof that there is a God, &c.*, there was upon a wainscot table at that instant three loud knocks (as if it had been with an iron hammer) given; to the great amazing of me and my two servants, Fulcis and Milkton.

In Glanvill's *Blow at Modern Sadducism*, in his account of the "Dæmon of Tedworth," who was supposed to haunt the

* This refers to his commitments for recusancy, which had been frequent.

house of Mr. Mompesson, and who was the original of Addison's "drummer," it is stated that on the 5th November, 1662, "in the sight and presence of the company, the chairs walked about the room," p. 124.

Defoe, in his veracious *History of Mr. Duncan Campbell* (2d ed., p. 107), quotes a story of spirit-knocking from "the renowned and famous" Mr. Baxter's *History of Apparitions*, prefacing it thus:—

What in nature can be more trivial than for a spirit to employ himself in knocking on a morning at the wainscot by the bed's head of a man who got drunk over night, according to the way that such things are ordinarily explained? And yet I shall give you such a relation of this, that not even the most devout and precise *Presbyterian* will offer to call in question.

He then gives the following extract from *The certainty of the Worlds of Spirits fully evinced by the Unquestionable Histories of Apparitions, &c.*, by Richard Baxter, London, 1691:—

Mr. Baxter, in his *Historical Discourse of Apparitions*, writes thus: "There is now in London an understanding, sober, pious man, oft one of my hearers, who has an elder brother, a gentleman of considerable rank, who having formerly seemed pious, of late years does often fall into the sin of drunkenness; he often lodges long together here in his brother's house, and whensoever he is drunk and has slept himself sober, something knocks at his bed's-head, as if one knocked on a wainscot. When they remove his bed it follows him. Besides other loud noises on other parts where he is, that all the house hears, they have often watched him, and kept his hands lest he should do it himself. His brother has often told it me, and brought his wife, a discreet woman, to attest it, who avers moreover, that as she watched him, she has seen his shoes under the bed taken up, and nothing visible to touch them. They brought the man himself to me, and when we asked him how he dare sin again after such a warning, he had no excuse. But being persons of quality, for some special reason of worldly interest I must not name him."—Defoe's *Life of Duncan Campbell*, 2d ed. p. 107.

There is a curious criminal process on record, manuscript 1770, noticed by Voltaire as in the library of the King of France, which was founded upon a remarkable set of visions said to have occurred to the monks of Orleans.

The illustrious house of St. Memin had been very liberal to the convent, and had their family vault under the church. The wife of a Lord of St. Memin, Provost of Orleans, died, and was buried. The husband, thinking that his ancestors had given more than enough to the convent, sent the monks a present, which they thought too small. They formed a plan to have her body disinterred, and to force the widower to pay a second fee for depositing it again in holy ground.

The soul of the lady first appeared to two of the brethren, and said to them, "I am damned, like Judas, because my husband has not given sufficient." They hoped to extort money for the repose of her soul. But the husband said, "If she is really damned, all the money in the world won't save her," and gave them nothing. Perceiving their mistake, they declared she appeared again, saying she was in *Purgatory*, and demanding to be disinterred. But this seemed a curious request, and excited suspicion, for it was not likely that a soul in purgatory would ask to have the body removed from holy ground, neither had any in purgatory ever been known to desire to be exhumed.

The soul after this did not try *speaking* any more, but haunted everybody in the convent and church. Brother Peter of Arras adopted a very awkward manner of conjuring it. He said to it, "If thou art the soul of the late Madame de St. Memin, strike four knocks," and the four knocks were struck. "If thou art damned, strike six knocks," and the six knocks were struck. "If thou art still tormented in hell, because thy body is buried in holy ground, knock six more times," and the six knocks were heard still more distinctly. "If we disinter thy body, wilt thou be less damned, certify to us by five knocks," and the soul so certified. This statement was signed by twenty-two cordeliers. The father provincial asked the same questions and received the same answers. The Lord of St. Memin prosecuted the father cordeliers. Judges were appointed. The general of the commission required that they should be burned; but the sentence only condemned them to make the "amende honorable," with a torch in their bosom, and to be banished.

This sentence is of the 18th of February, 1535. Vide Abbé Langlet's *History of Apparitions*.

In Ammianus Marcellinus, lib. xxix. cap. i. p. 552 of a Paris edition, 1681, two persons, Patricius and Hilarius, charged with disseminating prophecies injurious to the Emperor Valens, were brought before a court of justice, and a tripod, which they were charged with using, was also produced. Hilarius then made the following acknowledgment :—

Construximus, magnifici judices, ad cortinæ similitudinem Delphicæ, diris auspiciis, de laureis virgulis infaustam hanc mensulam quam videtis; et imprecationibus carminum secretorum choragiisque multis ac diuturnis ritualiter consecratam movimus tandem; movendi autem, quoties super rebus arcanis consulebatur, erat institutio talis. Collocabatur in medio domûs emaculatæ odoribus Arabicis undique, lance rotunda pure superposita, ex diversis metallicis materiis fabrefacta; cujus in ambitu rotunditatis extremo elementorum viginti quatuor scriptiles formæ incisæ perite, dijungebantur spatiis examinate dimensis. Hac linteis quidam indumentis amictus, calciatusque itidem linteis soccis, torulo capiti circumflexo, verbenas felicis arboris gestans, litato conceptis carminibus numine præscitionum auctore, cærimoniali scientia perstitit; cortinulis pensilem anulum librans, sartum ex carpathio filo perquam levi, mysticis disciplinis initiatum: qui per intervalla distincta retinentibus singulis litteris incidens saltuatim, heroos efficit versus interrogationibus consonos, ad numeros et modos plene conclusos; quales leguntur Pythici, vel ex oraculis editi Branchidarum. Ibi tum quærentibus nobis, qui præsenti succedet imperio, quoniam omni parte expolitus fore memorabatur et adsiliens anulus duas perstrinxerat syllabas, ΘΕΟ cum adjectione litteræ postrema, exclamavit præsentium quidem, Theodorum præscribente fatali necessitate portendi.

In lib. xxxi. cap. ii. p. 621 of same edition, a method of prognostication by the Alami is described; but there is no mention of tables there. The historian only says :—

Rectiores virgas vimineas colligentes, easque cum incantamentis quibusdam secretis præstituto tempore discernentes, aperte quid portendatur norunt.

The following curious passage is from the *Apologeticus* of Tertullian, cap. xxiii :—

Porro si et magi phantasmata edunt et jam defunctorum infamant animas; si pueros in eloquium oraculi elidunt; si multa miracula circulatoriis præstigiis ludunt; si et somnia immittunt habentes semel invitatorum angelorum et dæmonum assistentem sibi potestatem, *per quos* et capræ et *mensæ divinare consueverunt;* quanto magis, &c.

Here table divination by means of angels and demons seems distinctly alluded to.

PARALLELS.

Macaulay's *Hist. of England* (1st ed.), ii. 476 :—

But the iron stoicism of William never gave way: and he stood among his weeping friends calm and austere, as if he had been about to leave them only for a short visit to his hunting-grounds at Loo.

. . . . non alitèr tamen
Dimovit obstantes propinquos,
Et populum reditus morantem,
Quàm si clientum longa negotia
Dijudicatâ lite relinqueret,
Tendens Venafranos in agros,
Aut Lacedæmonium Tarentum.
Hor. *Od.* iii. v. 50–56.

Princes are like to heavenly bodies, which cause good or evil times, and *which have much veneration, but no rest.*—Bacon, *Essay* 20, "Of Empire."

Kings are like stars—they rise and set—*they have*
The worship of the world, but no repose.
Shelley, *Hellas.*

How when the Fancy, lab'ring for a birth,
With unfelt Throws brings its rude issue forth:
How after, when imperfect, shapeless thought
Is by the judgment into Fashion wrought.
When at first search I traverse o'er my mind,
Nought but a dark and empty void I find:
Some little hints at length like sparks break thence,
And glimmering thoughts just dawning into sense:
Confus'd awhile the mixt ideas lie,
With nought of mark to be discover'd by,
Like colours undistinguish'd in the night,
Till the dusk images, moved to the light,
Teach the discerning Faculty to choose
Which it had best adopt and which refuse.
"Some New Pieces" in Oldham's Works,
pp. 126–27, 1684.

Dryden, alluding to his work :—

When it was only a confused mass of thoughts *tumbling* over one another in the dark; when the fancy was yet in its *first work*, moving the *sleeping images of things* towards the light, there to be distinguished, and there either to be *chosen* or rejected by the *judgment*.—Dedication to the *Rival Ladies*, 1664.

Lord Byron's appropriation of the same idea :—

—— As yet 'tis but a chaos
Of darkly brooding thoughts: my fancy is
In her *first work*, more nearly to the light
Holding the sleeping images of things
For the selection of the pausing judgment.

Doge of Venice

There is an acre sown with royal seed, the copy of the greatest change from rich to naked, from cieled roofs to arched coffins, from *living like gods to die like men*.—Jeremy Taylor's *Holy Dying*, chap. i. sect. 1, p. 272, ed. Edin.

Here's an acre sown indeed
With the richest *royalest seeds*,
That the earth did e'er suck in,
Since the first man dyed for sin:
Here the bones of birth have cried,
Though *gods they were, as men they died.*

F. Beaumont.

Coleridge. *The Nightingale. A conversation poem.*

The nightingale—
'Most musical, most melancholy' bird!
A melancholy bird! Oh! idle thought!
In nature there is nothing melancholy.
But some night-wandering man whose heart was pierced
With the remembrance of a grievous wrong,
. . . . he, and such as he,
First named these notes a melancholy strain.

Plato Phædo, § 77 (p. 85, Steph.) :—

Men, because they fear death themselves, slander the swans, and say that they sing from pain lamenting their death, and do not consider that no bird sings when hungry, or cold, or suffering any other pain; no, not even the nightingale, and the swallow, and the hoopoe, which you know are said to sing for grief, &c.

Campbell's famous line,

> Like angels visits, few and far between,

has been clearly shown by a correspondent in another paper, to be all but copied from Blair:—

> ———————— like an ill-used ghost
> Not to return;—or if it did, its visits,
> *Like those of angels, short and far between.*
> Blair's *Grave.*

But the same phrase, though put differently, occurs in a religious poem of Norris, of Bemerton, who died in 1711:—

> But those who soonest take their flight,
> Are the most exquisite and strong,
> *Like angels visits, short* and bright,
> Mortality's too weak to bear them long.

In Norris's *Miscellanies*, in a poem "To the Memory of my dear Neece, M. C." (Stanza A, p. 10, ed. 1692), are the following lines:—

> No wonder such a noble mind
> Her way to heaven so soon could find:
> Angels, as 'tis but seldom they appear,
> So neither do they make long stay;
> They do but visit, and away.

There is a strange inclination to attribute similarity of sentiment to plagiarism; as if it were almost impossible for two men of genius to hit upon the same notions, independently of each other. In Propertius (II. i. 3, 4), we find:—

> Non hæc Calliope, non hæc mihi cantat Apollo,
> Ingenium nobis ipsa puella facit.

In Burns we read :—

O, were I on Parnassus' hill!
Or had of Helicon my fill;
That I might catch poetic skill,
To sing how dear I love thee.
But Nith maun be my Muse's well,
My Muse maun be thy bonnie sel'.

Had Burns been much of a Latin scholar, he would probably have been accused of stealing from Propertius.

Again, few persons are unacquainted with Burns's lines—

Her 'prentice han' she tried on man,
An' then she made, &c.

In an old play, *Cupid's Whirligig* (4to. 1607), we read :—

Man was made when Nature was but an apprentice, but woman when she was a skilful mistress of her art.

Pliny, in his *Natural History*, has the pretty notion that—

Nature, in learning to form a lily, turned out a convolvulus.

LIFTING EXPERIMENT.

A living man, lying on a bench, extended as a corpse, can be lifted with ease by the *forefingers* of two persons standing on each side, provided the lifters inhale at the moment the effort is being made. This curious fact was recorded by Pepys, who, in his *Diary*, under the date 31st July, 1665 (vol. iii. p. 60), writes as follows :—

This evening with Mr. Brisband, speaking of enchantments and spells, I telling him some of my charmes; he told me this of his own knowledge, at Bourdeaux, in France.

The words were these :—

"Voyci un̄ Corps mort.
Royde com̄e un Baston,
Froid comme Martre,
Leger com̄e un Esprit,
Levons te au nom de Jesus Christ."

He saw four little girls, very young ones, all kneeling each of them, upon one knee; and one begun the first line, whispering in the eare of the next, and the second to the third, and the third to the fourth, and she to the first.

Then the first begun the second line, and so round quite through; and putting each one finger only to a boy that lay flat upon his back on the ground, as if he was dead: at the end of the words, they did with their four fingers raise this boy as high as they could reach. And Mr. Brisband, being there, and wondering at it, as also being afraid to see it, for they would have had him to have bore a part in saying the words, in the room of one of the little girls that was so young that they could hardly make her learn to repeat the words, did, for fear there might be same slight used in it by the boy, or that the boy might be light, call the cook of the house, a very lusty fellow, as Sir G. Carteret's cook, who is very big: and they did raise him just in the same manner. This is one of the strangest things I ever heard, but he tells it me of his own knowledge, and I do heartily believe it to be true. I inquired of him whether they were Protestant or Catholique girls; and he told me they were Protestant, which made it the more strange to me.

In illustration of this passage, Lord Braybrooke adds, at vol. v. p. 245, the following note, which we insert, as it serves to bring before our readers evidence of this, at present, inexplicable fact on the authority of one of the most accomplished philosophers of our day :—

The secret is now well known, and is described by Sir David Brewster, in his *Natural Magic*, p. 256. One of the most remarkable and inexplicable experiments relative to the strength of the human frame is that in which a heavy man is raised up the instant that his own lungs, and those of the persons who raise him, are inflated with air. This experiment was, I believe, first shown in England a few years ago by Major H., who saw it performed in a large party at Venice, under the direction of an officer of the American navy. As Major H. performed it more than once in my presence, I shall describe as nearly as possible the method which he prescribed. The heaviest person in the company lies down upon two chairs, his legs being supported by the one, and his back by the other. Four persons, one at eash leg, and one at each shoulder, then try to raise him; and they find his dead weight to be very great, from the difficulty they experience in supporting him. When he is replaced in the chair, each of the four persons take hold of the body as before; and the person to be lifted gives two signals, by clapping his hands.

At the first signal, he himself, and the four lifters, begin to draw a long, full breath; and when the inhalation is completed, or the lungs filled, the second signal is given for raising the person from the chair. To his own surprise, and that of his bearers, he rises with the greatest facility, as if he were no heavier than a feather. On several occasions, I have observed, that when one of the bearers performs his part ill by making the inhalation out of time, the part of the body which he tries to raise is left as it were behind. As you have repeatedly seen this experiment, and performed the part both of the load and of the bearer, you can testify how remarkable the effect appears to all parties, and how complete is the conviction, either that the load has been lightened, or the bearer strengthened, by the prescribed process. At Venice the experiment was performed in a much more imposing manner. The heaviest man in the party was raised and sustained upon the points of the forefingers of six persons. Major H. declared that the experiment would not succeed, if the person lifted were placed upon a board, and the strength of the individuals applied to the board. He conceived it necessary that the bearers should communicate directly with the body to be raised.

I have not had an opportunity of making any experiments relative to these curious facts; but whether the general effect is an illusion, or the result of known principles, the subject merits a careful investigation.

The inhalation of the lifters the moment the effort is made is doubtless essential, and for this reason :—When we make a great effort, either in pulling or lifting, we always fill the chest with air previous to the effort; and when the inhalation is completed, we close the *rima glottidis* to keep the air in the lungs. The chest being thus kept expanded, the pulling or lifting muscles have received, as it were, a fulcrum round which their power is exerted, and we can thus lift the greatest weight which the muscles are capable of doing. When the chest collapses by the escape of the air, the lifters lose their muscular power. The inhalation of air by the lifter can certainly add nothing to the power of the lifters, or diminish his own weight, which is only increased by the weight of the air which he inhales.

In the *Zoist* for January, is an article entitled, "A suggestion to explain certain Phenomena of Levity," in which the subject of his Query is discussed. The writer throws out a hint that a clue may be found to the hitherto inexplicable experiment, in the Odic fluid of Baron Reichenbach, suspending or neutralizing the law of gravitation, in a way similar to that of magnetism in the instance of the iron rod in the electro-magnetic helix. The subject is certainly one which, as Sir David Brewster, who testifies to the reality of the fact, remarks, *merits a careful investigation.*

CHARADE ON A GAMING-TABLE.

The following charade was written by Mrs. Piozzi :—

A place I here describe, how gay the scene!
Fresh, bright, and vivid with perpetual green,
Verdure attractive to the ravish'd sight,
Perennial joys, and ever new delight,
Charming at noon, more charming still at night.
Fair pools where fish in forms pellucid play ;
Smooth lies the lawn, swift glide the hours away.
No mean dependence here on summer skies,
This spot rough winter's roughest blast defies.
Yet here the government is curs'd with change,
Knaves openly on either party range,
Assault their monarch, and avow the deed,
While honour fails, and tricks alone succeed ;
For bold decemvirs here usurp the sway ;
Now all some single demagogue obey,
False lights prefer, and hate the intruding day.
Oh, shun the tempting shore, the dangerous coast,
Youth, fame, and fortune, stranded here, are lost!

There have several charades been written on the same subject, evidently in imitation of this. The following has been attributed to Sheridan :—

There is a spot, say, Traveller, where it lies,
And mark the clime, the limits, and the size,
Where grows no grass, nor springs the yellow grain,
Nor hill nor dale diversify the plain ;

Perpetual green, without the farmer's toil,
Through all the seasons clothes the favor'd soil,
Fair pools, in which the finny race abound,
By human art prepar'd, enrich the ground.
Not India's lands produce a richer store,
Pearl, ivory, gold and silver ore.
Yet, Britons, envy not those boasted climes,
Incessant war distracts, and endless crimes
Pollute the soil :—Pale Avarice triumphs there,
Hate, Envy, Rage, and heart-corroding Care,
With Fraud and Fear, and comfortless Despair.
There government not long remains the same,
Nor they, like us, revere a monarch's name.
Britons, beware ! Let avarice tempt no more ;
Spite of the wealth, avoid the tempting shore ;
The daily bread which Providence has given,
Eat with content, and leave the rest to heaven.

HOUSE OF COMMONS, TEMP. ELIZABETH AND JAMES.

On running over the pages of the Commons' Journals, many a little characteristic incident turns up.

Coughing down a Member.—"Whosoever hisseth or disturbeth any speech hereafter, shall be called to the bar. Growing upon Sir Lewis Lewknor's speech"—that is, the practice gained strength during his speech (2 James I., June 20).

Absenteeism.—This was most rigorously denied, except by special leave for attending Assizes or other public matters. The following permission being accompanied by a stipulated *honorarium*, suggests that the cause of absence was regarded by the House as frivolous: "Sir Rob Wroth hath leave to absent himself for a se'nnight, upon the king's hunting in the forest; hath leave, paying a brick to Mr. Speaker (June 12, 2 James I).

A Lawyer outvoted by a Jackdaw.—This was in a case for a "bill for costs in a prohibition," which was dashed in the division of the House ; for a jackdaw flew in at the window, during his (Mr. Fuller's) speech, which was called *omen* to the bill (May 31).

Bill against costly Apparel.—Mr. Brook's speech for this bill (18 Jac. I) is a prose version of the *New Courtiers' Alteration*, or second part of what is now called the *Old Country Gentleman*. He attributes to extravagance in dress, decay of the public treasure, the ceasing of old-fashioned hospitality, the debts of the knights and gentlemen; and what he terms the inequality of trade, importation and exportation (only think of); "£18 a year by a great courtier for shoe strings!" Now-a-days, roses worn by members of this House on their shoes, cost more than did their fathers' apparel; and he concludes by observing, that gilding and lace are clothing neither for winter nor summer. Scripture teaching us that man's first covering, even by gift of heaven, was nothing but skins.

Quoting Latin.—The trick so common among the members at that time, of dragging in Latin upon all occasions, was a fashion strengthened, if not set on foot, by the king's pedantry. It was all very well in Sir Francis Bacon and such as he, but must have been insufferable when Sir Roger Owen could not allude to a straight line without adding, "Brevissima extensio a puncto ad punctum." The greatest array of Latinisms occurs in the numerous debates about the union of Scotland and England, which, being a pet subject of James', would of course attract his eye. But (independently of the quackery here referred to) it is worth adding that if the disjointed jottings-down of these brief but energetic debates touching Scotland were judiciously linked into continuous dialogue, they would bring out an array of facts and arguments more instructive than chapters of formal history-writing.

Fulsome Homage towards the King.—This, it must be confessed, showed itself more in words than in deeds; but the words are often inexcusably extravagant, and James is perpetually referred to as guided by maxims and influenced by a motive power unknown to common men. Sir George Moore said, "They could not follow a better guide than his Majesty; though, like Peter, afar off" (March 19, 21 James I). A more glaring instance of abject homage could hardly be furnished than by the examination of Edward Floyd, Esq., for speaking jeeringly of the Queen of Bohemia, James' daughter. One member after another starts up and proposes some cruel or grotesque form of punishment, such as boring the tongue, pillory, fining, flogging, riding backwards on horseback with his beads and friar's girdle about him. Sir George Goring moved for "twelve rides on an ass, at every stage to swallow a bead, and twelve jerks to make him." "As he laughed at the loss of Prague, therefore let him cry by whipping." Sir Edward Wardbur: "As many lashes as the Prince and Princess are old." Mr. Angell: "A gag in his mouth to keep him from crying and procuring pity." Sir Francis Seymour of Marlborough delivered his judgment as follows; "To go from Westminster at a cart's tail, with his doublet off, to the Tower, the beads about his neck, and to receive as many lashes by the way as he had beads." It is satisfactory to add, that the merciful part of the House prevailed, and though the riding backwards and fining were inflicted, there was "no blood." James, in one of his messages to the Commons, tells them that "he was infinite, and his occasions infinite" (vol. i. p. 946); but the House, without presuming to question this modest attribute, do appear to have considered it necessary to promise a corresponding "subsidy."

The Long-bow versus the Gun.—An act, in 1621, for the preservation of game, is based on the now "inordinate shooting in pieces," but it was opposed as absurd, the long-bow being now an obsolete weapon, and "guns being the service of the State;" meaning thereby that the practice of gun-shooting was valuable, however acquired. Yet, though the long-bow is declared obsolete at the period here mentioned, it is certain that at the commencement of the civil wars, twenty years later, it was an arm by no means neglected by the Parliament. It may also be remembered that Sir W. Scott has introduced its use into the *Legend of Montrose* in 1643, greatly to the contempt of Dugald Dalgetty.

Purity of Elections.—Mr. Noy, on this point, tells the House a story of Lord Bruce of Bremberghe, for only uttering the word *reminiscar* by way of threat to one Roger, a Baron of the Exchequer, being adjudged: To go up and down Westminster Hall, in his hose and doublet, without his hat; to go to all the Courts, and then to go to the Tower. "And fit it were," he then adds, "that these men (divers Yorkshire constables) for forstalling freedom of election, and terrifying the men with as much as *reminiscar*, should go to the Tower." Then, as to the qualification of voters, there is abundant evidence that electors in boroughs always lose their right by non-residence; and it was not till the 13th Elizabeth that an attempt was made by a bill to give "validity to burgesses *non resiant*"—the term *burgesses* here meaning representatives. And the independence of cities and towns is illustrated by the unchallenged assertion of a member, in 1604, that the interference of a sheriff would be tantamount to the "disinherison of any corporation."

Plan for keeping Members to their Seats.—"Ordered: That if after the reading of the first bill, any of the House depart before the rising of Mr. Speaker, to pay to the poor men's box four pence" (Nov. 9, 9 Elizabeth).

QUEEN ELIZABETH AND SIR PHILIP SIDNEY.

Among the objects of interest exhibited at the Museum of the Wilts Archæological Society, at Salisbury, was a lock of hair of Queen Elizabeth's, which was found some time since at Wilton House, between the leaves of a copy of *The Arcadia.*

The hair is light brown, approaching to auburn, certainly not red, although with a reddish tinge. Its authenticity is set forth in a paper in an early hand, which states:—

> This Lock of Queen Elizabeth's own Hair was presented to Sir Philip Sidney by Her Majesty's owne faire hands, on which He made these verses, and gave them to the Queen, on his bended knee. Anno Domini 1573.

And pinned to this is another paper, on which, written in a different hand, said to be Sidney's own, we have the verses,—

> Her inward worth all outward show transcends,
> Envy her merits with Regret commends;
> Like sparkling Gems her Virtues draw the Sight,
> And in her Conduct she is alwaies Bright.
> When She imparts her thoughts her words have force,
> And Sense and Wisdom flow in sweet discourse.

PUNCH.

The following extract has been taken from Fryer's *Travels to the East Indies*, 1672:—

> At Nerule (near Goa) is made the best arach, or *nepa die Goa*, with which the English on this coast make that enervating liquor called *paunch* (which is Indostan for five), from five ingredients, as the physicians name this composition *diapente;* or from four things, *diatesseron.*

OLDEST CHURCH IN THE UNITED STATES.

The oldest Church in America is one in the State of Virginia, and built of timber imported from England during the reign of Charles I.

HOPE.

The Rev. R. A Willmott, in his agreeable and tasteful little volume, *A Journal of Summer Time in the Country*, speaking of Prior, says:—

His Solomon, though rough and deficient in variety of interest, is sown with thoughts and images of pensive grace that dwell in the memory:—

Vex'd with the present moment's heavy gloom,
Why seek we brightness from the years to come?
Disturb'd and broken, like a sick man's sleep,
Our troubled thoughts to distant prospects leap,
Desirous still what flies us to o'ertake;
For hope is but the dream of those that wake.

"The last line," adds Mr. Willmott, "is scarcely excelled by Pope's description of 'Faith, our early immortality.'"

Dr. Johnson observed of Prior that "his stories, and even his points, may be traced," and the line here quoted with just admiration of its beauty by Mr. Willmott, furnishes a remarkable instance in point.

The sentiment occurs in that very beautiful letter of Basil (Bishop of Cæsarea about 370 A.D.) to his friend Gregory of Nazianzum, which is quoted and accompanied with some judicious and admirable observations, in the Cosmos of A. Von Humboldt (Sabine's *Translation*, vol. ii. p. 26):—

For the hopes of men have been justly called waking dreams.

The simile appears here not to have been original with Basil, but its beauty did not escape his poetical tone of mind. Now Basil was one of the Greek Fathers, and we may expect to find it, if anywhere, in a Greek classic. Accordingly we do find it as one of the profound and admirable sayings attributed to Aristotle, in the *Life of Aristotle*, by Diogenes Laertius. On one occasion the question was put to him, what hope is? and his answer was, "The dream of a waking man." An English translation of this work was published in 1696, and whence Prior probably took it, for he is said to have been a reader of various literature, and not particular in acknowledging his sources.

PENNY SIGHTS IN THE REIGN OF JAMES I.

The following curious list is to be found among the host of panegyrical verses prefixed to Master Tom Coryate's *Crudities*, published in 1611. Even in those days it will be admitted that the English were rather fond of such things, and glorious Will himself bears testimony to the fact (See *Tempest*, Act II. Sc. 2). The hexameter verses are anonymous. Drake's ship was broken up, and a chair made from the wood, which is now to be seen at the Bodleian Library, Oxford.

Why doe the rude vulgar so hastily post in a madnesse
To gaze at trifles, and toyes not worthy the viewing?
And thinke them happy, when may be shew'd for a penny
The Fleet-streete Mandrakes, that heavenly motion of Eltham,
Westminster Monuments, and Guildhall huge Corinæus,
That horne of Windsor (of an Unicorne very likely),
The cave of Merlin, the skirts of Old Tom a Lincolne,
King John's sword at Linne, with the cup the Fraternity drinke in,
The tombe of Beauchampe, and sword of Sir Guy a Warwicke,
The great long Dutchman, and roaring Marget a Barwicke,
The mummied Princes, and Cæsar's wine yet i' Dover,
Saint James his ginney-hens, the Cassawarway* moreover,

* An East Indian bird at Saint James, in the keeping of Mr. Walker, that will carry no coales, but eate them as whot as you will.

The Beaver i' the Parke (strange Beast as e'er any man saw),
Downe-shearing Willowes with teeth as sharp as a hand-saw,
The lance of John a Gaunt, and Brandon's still i' the Tower,
The fall of Ninive, with Norwich built in an hower.
King Henries slip-shoes, the sword of valiant Edward,
The Coventry Boares-shield, and fire-workes seen but to bedward,
Drake's ship at Detford, King Richard's bed-sted i' Leyster,
The White Hall Whale-bones, the silver Bason i' Chester;
The live-caught Dog-fish, the Wolfe, and Harry the Lyon,
Hunks of the Beare Garden to be feared, if he be nigh on.
All these are nothing, were a thousand more to be scanned,
(Coryate) unto thy shoes so artificially tanned.

In explanation of the last line, Tom went no less than nine hundred miles on one pair of soles, and on his return he hung up these remarkable shoes for a memorial in Odcombe Church, Somersetshire, where they remained till 1702.

Another "penny" sight was a trip to the top of St. Paul's. (See Dekker's *Gul's Horne Book*, 1609.)

SIGNS.

The Romans had signs; and at Pompeii a pig over the door represents a wine-shop within. The Middle Ages adopted a bush. "Good wine needs no bush," &c., answering to the gilded grapes at a modern vintner's. The bush is still a common sign. At Charles I.'s death, a cavalier landlord painted his bush black. Then came the modern square sign, formerly common to all trades. Old signs are generally heraldric, and represent royal bearings, or the blazonings of great families. The White Hart was peculiar to Richard II.; the White Swan of Henry IV. and Edward III.; the Blue Boar of Richard III.; the Red Dragon came in with the Tudors, and also the Rose and Fleur de Lys; the Bull, the Falcon, and Plume of Feathers commemorated Edward IV.; the Swan and Antelope were the Arms of Henry V.; the Greyhound and Green Dragon, of Henry VII.; the Castle, the Spread Eagle, and the Globe (Alphonso's), were probably adopted from the arms of Spain, Germany, and Portugal, by inns which were the resort of merchants from those countries. Then we have the Bear and Ragged Staff of Leicester, &c. Monograms are common; as Bolt and Tun for *Bolton;* Hare and Tun for *Harrington.* The Three Suns is the favorite bearing of Edward IV.; and all Roses, white or red (as at Tewkesbury), are indications of political predilection. Other signs commemorate historical events; as the Bull and Mouth, Bull and Gate (the Boulogne engagement in Henry VIII.'s time, and alluded to by Shakspeare). The Pilgrim, Cross Keys, Salutation, Catharine Wheel, Angel, Three Kings, Seven Stars, St. Francis, &c., are mediæval signs. Many are curiously corrupted; as the Cœur Doré (Golden Heart) to the Queer Door; Bacchanals (the Bag of Nails); Pig and Whistle (Peg and Wassail Bowl); the Swan and Two Necks (literally Two *Nicks*); Goat and Compasses (God encompasseth us); the Bell Savage (La Belle Sauvage, or Isabel Savage); the Goat in the Golden Boots (from the Dutch, Goed in der Gooden Boote), Mercury, or the God in the Golden Boots; the Cat and Fiddle (the Caton Fidele). The Swan with Two Nicks represented the Thames Swans, so marked on their bills under the "Conservatory" of the Goldsmiths' Company. The Coach and Horses remind us of the times when the Superior Inns were the only posting-houses, in distinction to such as bore the sign of the Pack-horse. The Fox and Goose denoted the games played within; the Country Inn, the Hare and Hounds, the vicinity of a sporting Squire. The Puritans altered many of the monastic signs; as the Angel and Lady, to the Soldier and Citizen. In signs we may read every phase of ministerial popularity, and all the ebbs and flows of war in the Sir Home Popham, Rodney, Shovel, Duke of York, Wellington's Head, &c. At Chelsea, a sign called the "Snow Shoes," still indicates the excitement of the American war.

A century ago, when the houses in streets were unnumbered, they were distinguished by sign-boards. The chemist had the dragon (some astrological device); the pawnbroker the three golden pills, the arms of the Medici and Lombardy, as the descendant of the ancient bankers of England; the barber-chirurgeon the pole for the wig, and the parti-colored ribands to bind up the patient's wounds after blood-letting; the haberdasher and wool-draper the golden fleece; the tobacconist the snuff-taking Highlander; the vintner the bunch of grapes and ivy-bush; and the Church and State bookseller the Bible and crown. The Crusaders brought in the signs of the Saracen's Head, the Turk's Head, and the Golden Cross. Near the church were found the Lamb and Flag, the Bell, the Cock of St. Peter, the Maiden's Head, and the Salutation of St. Mary.

KHOND FABLE.

The following is a free version of a fable current among the Khonds of Oriosa, of whom a very interesting account is given by Captain Macpherson in the *Journal of the Royal Asiatic Society* for 1852:—

A mosquito was seated on the horn of a bull, and fearing that his weight might be oppressive to the quadruped, he politely accosted him, begging that, if he felt any inconvenience, he would mention it, and professing himself ready, in that case, to remove to some other position. The bull replied, "O mosquito, so far are you from oppressing me with your weight, that I was not even aware of your existence."

This fable is clearly from Lokman, of which the following is Hélot's translation:—

,ne moustique se posa un jour sur la corne d'un taureau, et, pensant qu'elle pouvait être trop lourde pour lui, elle lui dit: "Si je te suis à charge, fais-le-moi savoir afin que je m'envolé." Le taureau lui résponditt: "Je ne t'ai point sentie au moment où tu es descendue, je ne saurai pas davantage quand tu t'envoleras." Cette fable regarde celui qui cherche à s'atribuer de l'honneur et de la gloire tandis qu'il est faible et méprisable.

The sense of the bull's reply in Arabic seems to be—

O you, whatever you are [*Ya hadi*]. I did not know when you descended, nor shall I know when you take yourself off [*Taterin*].

A pointed reply, leaving the mosquito on one horn of the dilemma.

The following fable by Prior somewhat resembles the other :—

" Say, sire of insects, mighty Sol ! "
A fly on the chariot pole cried out,
" What blue-bottle alive
Did ever with such fury drive ? "

" Tell, Beelzebub, great father, tell ! "
Says t'other, perch'd upon the wheel,
Did ever any mortal fly
Raise such a cloud of dust as I ? "

MORAL.

My judgment turn'd the whole debate !
My valour saved the sinking state !

OLD EPIGRAM.

The emperor and king of the following epigram, found among some old papers, are Leopold I. and Louis XIV. :—

EPIGRAM BY THE EMPEROR, 1666, AND THE KING OF FRANCE.

Bella fugis, sequeris bellas, pugnæque repugnas,
Et bellatori sunt tibi bella tori.
Imbelles imbellis amas, totusque videris
Mars ad opus Veneris, Martis ad arma Venus.

PARISH REGISTERS.

Those who have had opportunities of looking over parish registers have doubtless often been amused at reading many of the entries which are to be found therein, not a few of which are calculated to throw a light on the customs, manners, and habits of the good people in the olden times, which are interesting, not only to antiquarians and those who are admirers of venerable antiquity, but also to the general reader; it is as it were looking through Time's telescope, and viewing through the vista long-past events, which are brought out in full review before the eye, like objects in a panorama. The following extracts, compiled from authentic sources, part of which have been transcribed from the originals, will serve to illustrate the foregoing remarks. The first on the list relates principally to the town of Braintree.

Anno 1580.—April 2 was baptized Joseph Mann, son of Joseph Mann. Mem. That the said Joseph Mann the son, in the year 1631, did lay open the street called New Street, and also built the New Cross, at his own proper costs and charges, and afterwards sold the same to the Right Hon. Robert Earl of Warwick, for the sum of 600*l.*, being then bailiff to the said Earl of the town of Brayntree.—23 Hen. VIII., Robert Pucklow gave a crown for a light before St. Nicholas; Richard Norfolk the like before St. Catharine; John Tomkin the like before St. Michael; and Henry Evet the like before Trinity.—A drinking in Lent, towards which, besides what private persons paid, was given by Rayne, 4*s.*; Cressing, 3*s.*; Black Notley, 3*s.* 8*d.*; Bocking, 3*s.*; and Braintree, 5*s.*

These were in Popish times. There was a canon against these drinkings; but Whitsun ales, which were similar things, were allowed in King James's *Book of Sunday Sports*. Images in churches do not appear to have been entirely removed until 1588 (1 Eliz.), when the churchwardens received for three images, 26*s.* 8*d.*

1574. Received for six almanvyvets, 22*s.* (Qy. German music-books?

which seem to have been superseded by the more solemn music adapted to such psalmody as that of Sternhold and Hopkins)—Received for the organ pipes. . . . .

The almanvyvets and organ pipes seem to have fallen before the Puritanic spirit which was at this time prevailing.

1581. Payd for ryngiug on crowenation-day, 2*s.* 6*d.*; layd out for yenk and paper [ink and paper], 1*d.*; payd the hie constable for Cataway Bridge, 10*s.*; payd to Father Wod, for helling [healing] of Widow Matthews, 20*s.*

Father Wod was most likely a Popish priest, but that "occupation gone," he practised physic. It is well known that at the present period, in Roman Catholic countries, the priests, actuated by a kind and benevolent feeling, study in some degree the healing art, in order that they may be enabled to prescribe remedies in cases of sudden illness among the poorer members of their flock, when medical aid through a surgeon, from distance or other causes, is not attainable.

1585. Payd for discharging Father Andrew howt of the Cowrte, being cited for reading the servyce, 16*d.*

This, probably, was another Popish clergyman, who had committed himself by performing some duty contrary to the Reformed doctrines and laws.

1586. Payd to Persom for rushes and flaskes gathering when the byshope was here [to strew the church with], 12*d.*

Strewing churches, and even private houses, with rushes, was at this time a common practice.

1593. Received from "The Hart," 24 quarts of wyne, at 8*d.*, 15*s.* 4*d.*; and 11 quarts of muskydine, at 11*d.*, 10*s.* 1*d.*; and 8 quarts of wyne, at 9*d.*, 6*s.* Item, received from the coke [cook] 27 quarts of wyne, at 8*d.*, 18*s.*; and 23 quarts of wyne, at 9*d.*, 17*s.* 3*d.*; and 1 quart of sack, 12*d.* Payd for bread, 3*s.* 2*d.*

That is, 94 quarts of wine (nearly 8 dozen) in one year for the Communion, in a town with a population of about 2,000; but this was at a period when almost every adult communicated; and there are some intimations that at this period our ancestors drank *deep* on those occasions, in order to evince their sincerity. For instance, it is said of "Rare Ben Jonson," that he was twelve years a Papist, but was afterwards reconciled to the Church of England, and that at his first communion, in token of his true reconciliation, he drank the full cup of wine. The quantities and the prices charged do not in several instances agree : but our ancestors were in general very bad arithmeticians.

1625. It is agreed that Hugh Wises's wife shall have some barley allowed her, at the best hand, to bake bread.

Poor persons at the present time would not evince much gratitude for such a gift as this.

1635. J. M. hath payd to Mr. W. 5*s.* 6*d.*, which he layed out to send Burnham with a letter to my Lord of Warwick, in London [distance 40 miles].—1637. It is agreed that J. M. shall have 2*s.* for his journey to Heddingham, about ship-money.

The levying "ship-money" at this time was one of the principal causes which led to the civil war.

1662. In an inventory of the goods belonging to the parish is enumerated a sheet for harlots to do penance in. It appears as if the parish authorities at Braintree, at this period, were desirous of establishing a high standard of morality in their town. Whether the article in question was frequently called into use or otherwise, we are not informed.

1719. Ordered, to allow John Wilkinson's wife 9*s.* to redeem a piece of gold touched by the king.

This was a relic of the ancient practice of touching for the king's evil. The practice had been discontinued some time, but the pieces of money used on those occasions were supposed to retain their virtue. In the next article we hardly know which is most remarkable, the apparent knavery of the parties or the attempted legal formalities of the scribe.

1745. This witnesseth an agreement by and between the parishioners below mentioned, on behalf of themselves and the whole parish, and David Stearns, that he the said David Stearns, for and in consideration of a crown bowl of punch, this day paid by him, shall be excused for the future from paying all parish rates, of what name or description soever they be, for the house he dwells in, *the king's tax only excepted.* Signed by David Stearns and eight other parishioners, and witnessed by the vestry clerk.

If the parties in the above agreement had any misgivings as to the legality or honesty of the course they were adopting, we may suppose that, in the words of the old ballad, "they drowned them in the bowl." Being, however, loyal subjects, they desired that the king's taxes should be paid.

The following extracts were transcribed *verbatim* from an old rate-book belonging to the parish of Elmstood, near Colchester :—

April 28, 1704. Paid for the berrill of Jane Hicks, 4*s.*—April 2, 1707. Paid for two payer of britches and a neck of moten, 4*s.*

This is an amusing item; "two pair of breeches and a neck of mutton:" food and clothing jumbled together in a rather incongruous manner, and all for the small sum of four shillings. Breeches as well as mutton must have been marvellously cheap in those days. It reminds one of Shakspeare's saying of King Stephen :—

King Stephen was a worthy peer,
His breeches cost him but a crown;
He held them sixpence all too dear,
With that he called the tailor—lown.

By the way, this quotation aptly illustrates Burke's remark, that "there is but one step from the sublime to the ridiculous." Thus, for instance, the first line conveys to the mind the idea of a grand and magnificent monarch arrayed in all the pomp of regal splendor; in the next line his majesty's nether garment is exhibited in a ridiculous light, in the same manner that Hogarth's "Simon Gripe, pawnbroker," holds up that necessary article of dress, to satisfy himself that it is neither threadbare nor moth-eaten. And when at the conclusion we find his royal majesty haggling with his tailor about sixpence in a pair of crown breeches, we come to the conclusion that he was any thing but a liberal monarch. But to return: the next entry we have to notice is under the date of

Oct. 26, 1707. Paid Mr. Phillips for catching a fox, 5*s.*

It is evident that Mr. Phillips was no fox-hunter, nor the parish officer who paid him this sum, and that, too, out of the poor-rates. It appears as if the parishioners were resolved to protect the poultry from reynard's depredations, and therefore set a price upon his head. We may suppose, at the present day, that if any fox-hunter saw an item of this kind in the parish accounts, little hesitation would be felt in drawing a pen across it.

Nov. 19, 1710. Paid at Sidney's, for bear at Goodey Inman's berrill, 1*s.*—Paid for a wascote for Cramphorne's boy, and bleeding and a purg, 3*s.*

The overseer who ordered this was probably a humane personage. It appears that after this poor lad Cramphorne had been well bled and physicked, it being in the dreary month of November, the parish officer generously gave him a waistcoat to keep out the cold. We may say of him, in the words of honest Tom Dibdin—

Prized be such hearts; aloft they shall go,
Who always are ready compassion to show.

May 6, 1711. Paid for a cofen for Goodey Keebl, 6*s.*—Paid to the minister and clerk for berren Goodey Keebl, 5*s.*—April 4, 1743. It is agreed this day that any townsman that has a yearly servant that shall have any bone or bones broken, to be allowed by the parish the charge thereof. As witness our hands . . . *If the person cannot pay it himself.*

The concluding proviso shows that the parish officers wished to guard against the imputation of being *too liberal* in expending their funds.

April 11, 1748. An agreement between the townsmen of the parish and Robert Freeman, to take the boy Isaac Hunt for nine years, and to release him double suited, and to give him five shillings in his pocket.

There are various entries in the book similar to the above. It appears to have been thought a great favor to possess two suits of clothes and five shillings in money after nine years' servitude. The probable inference is, that these were poor, friendless lads, whom the parishioners thus allotted out amongst themselves according to their own will and pleasure. There is nothing to show that the boys were consenting parties to these arrangements.

Memoranda. I promise, upon being released from the town rates, to bury all, gratis, that are concerned with the parish officer, and don't pay scot and lot.—Allington Harrison, vicar.

This clergyman was probably a quiet, easy, good-natured man, who did not wish to keep a debtor and creditor account with his parishioners, and so this plan was adopted to save trouble.

The following is extracted from Lord Braybrooke's *History of Audley End,* in which there are various interesting particulars relating to the town of Saffron Walden. Amongst the extracts which are given from the parish registers, we find the following :—

1611, May 12. Martha Warde, a young mayd coming from Chelmesford on a carte, was overwhelmed and smothered with certayn clothes which were in the carte, and was buried here.—1623, Sept. 4. Buryed a poore man brought by the Little Chesterford constables, to be examined by the justice ; the justice being a hunting, the poore man died before his coming home from hunting.

Perhaps the squire had a longer run than usual with the hounds on this occasion.

1716, Nov. 18. The oulde girle from the workhouse was buried.

The corporation accounts contain some singular items. We have entries of money paid for saffron given to the "queen's (Elizabeth) attorney," and of 2*s.* "to my Lord Staffourd's players;" a large *honorarium* of 10*s.* having been paid for the mediation of the Earl of Suffolk's secretary; and the sum of 1*l.* 9*s.* 3*d.* for "setting uppe the cucking-stole." Bailey designates this

A machine formerly used for the punishment of scolds and brawling women, in which they were placed and lowered into a river or pond, until they were almost choked with water.

Happily for scolds, this ancient method of "taming the shrew" has long been abolished. Mrs. Caudle, so graphically described in *Punch*, would have been a good subject for this sort of discipline.

Paid 4*d.* for nailing up the Quakers' door twice; and received 10*s.* for rent of the mountebank.

The following are extracts from an old parish book belonging to St. Giles's, London:—

1641. Received of the vintner, at "The Cat" in Queen Street, for permitting of tippling on the Lord's Day, 1*l.* 10*s.*—Received of three poore men for drinking on the Sabbath daie at Tottenham Court, 4*s.*—1645. Received of John Seagood, constable, which he had of a Frenchman for swearing three oaths, 3*s.*—Received of Mrs. Sunder, by the hands of Francis Potter, for her being drunk and swearing seven oaths, 12*s.*—1646. Received of Mr. Hooker for brewing on a fast-day, 2*s.* 6*d.*—Payd and given to Lyn and two watchmen, in consideration of their pains, and the breaking of two halberts, in taking the two drunkards and swearers that paid, 1*l.* 4*s.*—Received of fairmen travelling on the fast-day, 1*s.*—1648. Received of Isabella Johnson, at the Cole Yard, for drinking on the Sabbath day, 4*s.*

This was the year previous to that in which King Charles I. was beheaded. It appears that there were persons at that period who could "strain at a gnat and swallow a camel." These turbulent subjects could put their sovereign to death apparently without much remorse; but to brew on a fast-day, or to be found travelling on those days or on the Sabbath, were enormities that they would by no means tolerate. With respect to their zeal against tippling and swearing, in that they are to be commended.

1652. Received of Mr. Huxley and Mr. Morris, who were riding out of town during sermon time on a fast-day, 11*s*.—1654. Received of William Glover in Queen Street, and of Isaac Thomas, a barber, for trimming of beards on the Lord's day [the sum not stated].—1655. Received of a mayd taken in Mr. Johnson's ale-house on the Sabbath day, 5*s*.—Received of a Scotchman for drinking at Robert Owen's on the Sabbath, 2*s*.—1658. Received of Joseph Piers for refusing to open his doores to have his house searched on the Lord's daie, 10*s*.

1659. There is an entry of "one Brookes's goods, sold for a breach of the Sabbath," but the produce is not set down.

The following memorandum is copied from an old register in the parish of Great Easton :—

Matthew Tomlinson, curate of this parish, left Feb. 1, 1730.

To my Parishioners.

Farewell, dear flock, my last kind wish receive,
The only tribute that I now can give.
May my past labours claim a just regard,
Great is the prize, and glorious the reward;
Transcendent joys, surpassing human thought,
To meet in heaven whom I on earth had taught.

In concluding this account of parish registers, it may be mentioned that, many years since, there was a good old-fashioned farmer, James Biddell by name, who lived at Bradfield St. George, near Bury, who, when he served the office of overseer, used to close his account by putting down, "For bustling about, 10*s*." The parishioners used to smile at this item in the worthy old gentleman's account, but they all agreed in thinking that it was a very moderate charge for "bustling about" for so long a period on parish business.

CHINESE PROVERBS.

Chinese proverbs which were in the Great Exhibition of 1851:—

Let every man sweep the snow from before his own door, and not busy himself about the frost on his neighbour's tiles.

Great wealth comes by destiny; moderate wealth by industry.

The ripest fruit will not fall into your mouth.

The pleasure of doing good is the only one which does not wear out.

Dig a well before you are thirsty.

Water does not remain on the mountain, nor vengeance in a great mind.

GLASS IN WINDOWS.

It is impossible to determine at what period the use of glass utensils for domestic purposes was first introduced into this country; but being manufactured by the Egyptians and Phœnicians, we may very probably owe the introduction of it to them. Window glass appears to have been used in the churches of France as early as the sixth century; and, according to Bede, artificers skilled in the art of glass-making were invited into England by Abbot Benedict in the seventh century; and the churches or monasteries of Wearmouth and Garrow were glazed and adorned by his care. Wilfrid, Bishop of Worcester, about the same time took similar steps for substituting glass in lieu of the heavy shutters which were then in use; and great astonishment was excited, and supernatural agency suspected, when the moon and stars were seen through a material which excluded the inclemency of the weather. York Cathedral was glazed about the same time; and in the eleventh and twelfth centuries, when a great stimulus was given to the erection of religious edifices, glass was generally employed in the windows. It appears to have been used in domestic architecture but very sparingly, till a much later period, when it came to be gradually adopted in the residences of the wealthy.

As late as the middle of the sixteenth century it was recommended, in a survey of the Duke of Northumberland's estates, that the glass in the windows should be taken down, and laid by in safety during the absence of the Duke and his family, and be replaced on his return; as this would be attended with smaller cost than the repair rendered necessary by damage or decay. In Brooke's *Abridgment*, tit. "Chatteles," it appears that in the 21st Hen. VII., A.D. 1505, it was held that though the framework of the windows belonged to the heir, the *glass* was the property of the executors, and might therefore be removed by them, "*quar le meason est perfite sauns le glasse.*" In A.D. 1599 Lord Coke informs us it was in the Common Pleas "resolved *per totam curiam*, that glass annexed to windows by nails, or in any other manner, could not be removed; for without glass it is no perfect house."

In Ray's *Itinerary* it is mentioned that in Scotland, even in 1661, the windows of ordinary houses were not glazed, and those only of the principal chambers of the King's palaces had glass; the lower ones being supplied with shutters, to admit light and air at pleasure.

Plate glass for mirrors and coach windows was introduced into England by the second Duke of Buckingham, who brought over workmen from Venice, and established a manufactory at Lambeth, where the works were carried on successfully according to the process in use at Venice.

The first manufactory for cast plate glass, according to the process invented by Abraham Thevart, was established in 1773, at Prescot in Lancashire, by a society of gentlemen, to whom a royal charter was granted under the name of the "British Plate Glass Company."

WAGERS.

The celebrated epistolographer, James Howell, after dilating, in a letter to a friend, upon the wondrous medicinal and other properties of the then novelty, tobacco, observes :—

If one would try a petty conclusion how much smoke there is in a pound of tobacco, the ashes will tell him ; for let a pound be exactly weighed, and the ashes kept charily and weighed afterwards, what wants of a pound weight in the ashes, cannot be denyed to have been smoke which evaporated into air. I have been told that Sir *W. Rawleigh* won a wager of Queen *Elizabeth* upon this nicety.—*Epistolæ Ho-Elianæ*, 9th ed. p. 418.

The learned Menage appears to have been not unfriendly to this mode of deciding a dispute :—

Nous sommes (says he) de grands parieurs à Angers. Je dis souvent, *Il faut parier ou se taire*, et c'est une façon de parler commune parmi nous. Je disais un jour à M. le premier Président de Lamoignon, ces paroles de Marc Aurèle, &c.

He then proceeds to narrate how he made and won a wager with the President as to the correctness of his quotation. (*Menagiana*, tom. ii. p. 362.)

Popular tradition has long associated the assumption of the Ulster badge—the bloody hand— by the Holte family of Aston, with a barbarous murder, committed at the commencement of the seventeenth century, by Sir Thomas Holte upon his cook, by splitting open his head with a cleaver. It need not be said that the assumption of the badge has no connection whatever with this circumstance, which may, or may not, have occurred :—

"The most probable tradition," says Mr. Atkinson, the historian of the family, "of the cause of the commission of the crime is, that Sir Thomas, when returning from hunting, in the course of conversation, laid a wager to some amount, as to the punctuality of his cook, who, most unfortunately, for once was behind time. Enraged at the jeers of his companions, he hastened into the kitchen, and seizing the first article at hand, avenged himself on his domestic."—*History of the Holtes of Aston*, Birmingham, 1854, p. 25.

Wagers to an immense amount were laid at the latter end of last century, as to the sex of that epicene notoriety, the Chevalier D'Eon. One of these became the subject of judicial decision. The cause came on, 1st July, 1777, in the Court of King's Bench, before Lord Mansfield and a special jury at Guildhall. It appeared that the plaintiff had paid the defendant one hundred guineas, for which the defendant had signed a policy of insurance to pay the plaintiff seven hundred guineas whenever he could prove that the Chevalier D'Eon was a female. After hearing the evidence, which was "too indelicate to be mentioned," Lord Mansfield, after expressing his abhorrence of the transaction, and a wish that it had been in his power, in concurrence with the jury, to make both parties lose, stated, that as the wager was laid, and wagers were not expressly prohibited by law, the question before them was, *Who had won?* His lordship farther observed that the indecency of the proceeding arose more from the unnecessary questions asked, than from the case itself; that the witnesses had declared that they perfectly knew the Chevalier to be a woman; that if she is not so they are certainly perjured; that there was no need of inquiring how, and by what method, they knew it; and finally, that he was of opinion that the jury must find a verdict for the plaintiff. The jury, without going out of court, after consulting about two minutes, gave a verdict for the plaintiff of seven hundred pounds and forty shillings. Besides this, the plaintiff, Mr. Hayes, recovered three thousand pounds on other policies, and it was asserted that immense sums depended on the decision in the suit.

Burnet, speaking of the Peace of Ryswick, says:—

The Military men in France did generally complain of the Peace as dishonourable and base: The Jacobites among us were the more confounded at the News of it, because the Court of France did, to the last minute, assure King

James, that they would never abandon his Interests: And his Queen sent over assurances to their Party here, that England would be left out of the Treaty, and put to maintain the War alone: Of which they were so confident, that they entered into deep Wagers upon it; a practice little known among us before the War, but it was carried on, in the progress of it, to a very extravagant degree; so that they were ruined in their fortunes, as well as sunk in their Expectations by the Peace.—*Own Time*, Bk. 6, 1697.

By an act of Parliament (stat. 7 Anne, cap. 17) all wagers laid upon a contingency relating to the war with France were declared to be void.

A PAPER OF TOBACCO.

Pipes.—It is worthy of remark, that although the common clay pipe is entirely different in material and form from the original American pipe, it was used in nearly its present shape at the first introduction of tobacco, as though before approved for a similar use. Clay pipes, supposed to be of a date anterior to this period, have occasionally been found in the Irish bogs. An engraving of a *dudheen*, which was dug up at Brannockstown, county Kildare, sticking between the teeth of a human skull, will be found in the *Anthologia Hibernica* (vol. i. p. 352), together with a paper, which, on the authority of Herodotus (lib. i. sec. 36), Strabo (lib. vii. 296), Pomponius Mela (2), and Solinus (c. 15), would prove that the northern nations of Europe, long before the discovery of America, were acquainted with tobacco, or an herb of similar properties, and that they smoked it through small tubes. (See note to Croker's *Legends and Traditions of the South of Ireland.*)

That the clay pipe was the original smoking apparatus in England is evident from the following lines in Skelton's *Eleanor Rummin.* After lamenting the knavery of that age compared with King Harry's time, he continues:—

Nor did that time know,
To puff and to blow,
In a peece of white clay,
As you do at this day,
With fier and coale,
And a leafe in a hole, &c.

These lines are from an edition of 1624, printed in the *Harl. Misc.*, i. 45. Skelton died in 1529.

Dr. Whitaker, in his *Loidis and Elmete*, tells us that after the tower of Kirkstall Abbey was blown down, Jan. 27, 1779, he discovered several little *tobacco-pipes* embedded in the mortar of the fallen fragments, similar in shape to those used in the reign of James I. This tower was completed in the reign of Henry VII. Not many years ago an old house, built not later than Henry VIII.'s time, was standing at Seacroft, near Leeds; on demolishing it, several small clay pipes were found *beneath* the foundations; they were similar in pattern to those of the seventeenth century. Great numbers of tobacco-pipe heads are found about Leeds, but these date no further back than 1749, being doubtless relics of General Wade's encampment. About the roots of some elms cut down at Sheepscar were found scores of these pipe-heads, but only one entire specimen. They have been picked up, too, in the fields bordering on Marston Moor; indeed, they are common enough in all the districts through which the soldiery of the great civil war may have marched. The country people call them "fairy pipes," simply from their small size. The pipe and pipe-mould occur on Yorkshire tokens of the seventeenth century, and the little figure our tobacconists still hang out, a negro with a pipe in his mouth, and a roll of "pigtail" under one arm, also occurs on another. A common remark often made when one person manages to ruffle the temper of another is, "he has got his pipe put out," a local phrase synonymous with "drawing his peg," but perhaps more obscure in its origin. Pipe-bowls of English manufacture have been found *beneath* the encaustic pavement of Buildway Abbey, in Shropshire. The pipes found in such abundance in the bed of the Thames, and everywhere in and about London, are of Dutch manufacture; they are identical with those which Teniers and Ostade put into the mouths of their boors, and have for the most part a small pointed heel, a well-defined milled ring around the lip, and bear no mark or name of the maker. The English pipes, on the contrary, have a very broad and flat heel, on which they may rest in an upright position, so that the ashes might not fall out prematurely; and on this heel the potter's name or device is usually stamped, generally in raised characters, though sometimes they are incised. Occasionally the mark is to be found on the side of the bowl.

The *Inverness Courier* says, that in one of the ancient chimney-pieces in Cawdor Castle there is a rude carving in stone of a fox smoking a tobacco-pipe, with the date 1510. The fox holds the fragrant tube in his mouth, exactly as it is held by its human admirers; and the instrument is such as may be seen every day with those who patronize the cutty pipe.

Aubrey, speaking of the fashion of using tobacco, says:—

> They first had silver pipes, but the ordinary sort made use of a walnut shell and a strawe. I have heard my grandfather say, that one pipe was handed from man to man round the table. Within these 35 years (written about 1680) 'twas scandalous for a divine to take tobacco. It was then sold for its wayte in silver. I have heard some of our old yeomen neighbours say, that when they went to market they culled out their biggest shillings to lay in the scale against the tobacco. Now the customes of it are the greatest His Majestie hath.

Cutty Pipes.—The term is Scotch, *cutty* being a word which means little or short. Thus, a little girl is called a *cutty;* there are *cutty pipes* and *cutty spoons;* and the readers of Burns need not be reminded of the scantily-draped lady who is styled *cutty-sark.*

Smoking.—It seems certain that a habit of smoking had been acquired in England long before the days of Sir Walter Raleigh, and yet we seem to be left in the dark respecting what ingredient was chiefly consumed before the "Indian weed" was introduced; if smoking had been indulged in to any extent before this, it would doubtless be many years ere tobacco would become universal. It is a somewhat singular fact, and would seem to support the theory that *something* was smoked before the introduction of the tobacco plant, that, in spite of the suppressive edict of Queen Elizabeth, and the *Counterblaste* of James, the Society of Tobacco-pipe Makers, in the seventeenth year of the reign of the latter, had become so very numerous and considerable a body, that they were incorporated by royal charter, and bore on their shield a tobacco plant in full blossom. It would seem strange, unless the process of "smoking something" had been familiar to our ancestors, that the custom of "taking tobacco" in public places should have become so extensively prevalent at so short a period after its introduction. Malone (*History of the English Stage*) quotes from the *Skialethia* a collection of epigrams and satires, 1598, and an epigram by Sir John Davis of the same date, to show that the playgoers of the time of Shakspeare were wont to be attended at the theatres by pages, who furnished them with pipes and tobacco, which were smoked not only on the stage, where spectators were then allowed to sit, but in other parts of the house. Paul Hentzner, the author of *Itinerarium Germaniæ, Galliæ, Angliæ, Italiæ, scriptum a Paulo Hentznero, J. C.*, published in Nuremberg, A. D. 1612, was struck with the prevalence of this custom in England, which, however, was evidently new to him. The author visited England in 1598, and relates, among many other things, how one of his friends had his pocket picked in London, whilst present at the civic ceremonies and pastimes of St. Bartholomew's Day. He afterwards describes the sort of theatre used for bull and bear baiting, and in this place is found the notice of tobacco-smoking and clay pipes:—

Utuntur in hisce spectaculis sicut et alibi, ubicunque locorum sint Angli, *herba* Nicotiana quam Americano idiomate *Tabacam* nuncupant (*Pætum* alii dicunt) hoc modo frequentissimè; Fistulæ in hunc finem ex argillâ factæ, orificio posteriori, dictam herbam probe exiccatam, ita ut in pulverem facilè redigi possit, immittunt, et igne admoto accendunt, unde fumus ab anteriori parte ore attrahitur, qui per nares rursum, tanquam per infurnibulum exit, et phlegma ac capitis defluxiones magnâ copiâ secum educit.—pp. 132, 133.

Here, and everywhere else, the English are constantly smoking of tobacco, and in this manner: they have pipes on purpose made of clay, into the further end of which they put the herb, so dry that it may be rubbed into powder; and putting fire to it, they draw the smoke into their mouths, which they puff out again through their nostrils, like funnels, along with it plenty of phlegm, and defluxion of the head.

We must not forget, however, that James I., in his *Counterblaste*, asks his subjects to consider what "honours or policy can move them to *imitate* the manners of such wild, godlesse, and slavish people?" and proceeds to say, "It is not long since the first entry of this abuse amongst us here (as this present age can very well remember both the first author and forms of its introduction)." It would seem, too, that the phenomenon (so aptly described by Virgil, who deserved to be a smoker,—

Faucibus ingentem fumum, mirabile dictu,
Evomit, involvitque domum caligine cæcâ,)

which struck such terror into the mind of Sir Walter Raleigh's servant, who thought his master to be on fire, must have been altogether new to that individual; though now so universal that, as is pleasantly remarked by Dr. Maginn (*apud* Frazer, vol. iv., p. 435), "The mode of explifflicating the smoke out of one's mouth is at present, as it were, a shibboleth demonstrative of an English gentleman."

There is no doubt that a curious chapter might be written on the history and literature of this subject. Every body has heard of James I.'s *Counterblaste to Tobacco*, in which he inveighs right royally against a habit already widely and fondly cherished. Pope Urban VIII. (1623–1644) issued a bull against the use of tobacco in *churches*. The third Mexican synod, and the third synod of Lima, as well as a synod in the Canary Islands, also expressly condemned it under similar circumstances, as appears from the *Sacerdos Christianus* of Abelly (ed. 1737, pp. 562–4). Jacobus Balde, a Jesuit, the author of sundry Latin poems (cir. 1625), has one (*Satyra* 19), with this title, *Medici cujusdam longe clarissimi, Tabacophilia et fatum.* Among the *Lusus Westmonasterienses* (ed. 1740, p. 25,) is one with the motto—

Disce tubo genitos haurire et reddere fumos."

Nor are we likely to forget the lucubrations on tobacco, appended by the Rev. R. Erskine to his *Gospel Sonnets!* To these many additions may be made, especially from prose writers, as Salmasius, who, in his ludicrous character of the Independents, given in the *Defensio Regia* (ed. 1649, p. 354) amusingly says of their ecclesiastical assemblies :—

Quidam interim, hausti fistula tabaci fumos in angulo revomunt!

In a list of *Rates of Merchandises*, printed in 1642, under the head of Tobacco, is the following. (The sums are the duties payable) :—

Tobacco *vocat.** Spanish, and Brazeil tobacco, or any not English plant, the l., 3*l.*

* Note, that this sort of tobacco until the ninth of September, 1642, is to pay after the rate of 2*l.*, and afterwards according to the rate of 3*l.*

Spanish or Brazeil tobac. in pudding or roull, the l., 3*l.*

So much for European smoking; when or how did the nations of the East become acquainted with this grand source of physical solace? What did they *do* before they smoked? are they indebted to Europe for this "bright occidental star," or is tobacco indigenous to the coasts of Syria and the hills of Laodicea, where the choicest in the world is now produced? When we consider how entirely the *chibouque* in Turkey, the *hookah* in India, the *sheesha* in Egypt, and the *nargilly* in Persia, is part and parcel of the orientalist, when we take into consideration his superstitious reverence for custom, and his contempt for novelty and innovation, we are almost led to suppose that his use of tobacco is of immemorial antiquity. This would seem, however, not to be the case, if we are justified in drawing such an inference from an observation of old Sandys, who complains of the badness of the tobacco in the Levant, which he ascribes to the circumstance that Turkey is supplied with the refuse of the European markets:—

They also, says he, delight in tobacco, which they take thorow reeds, which have joyned unto them great heads of wood to contain it. I doubt not but lately taught them, as taught them by the *English;* and were it not sometimes lookt into (for *Morat Bassa* not long since commanded a pipe to be thrust thorow the nose of a *Turk*, and so to be led in derision thorow the city), no question but it would prove a principal commodity. Nevertheless they will take it in corners, and are so ignorant therein, that that which in England is not saleable, doth pass here amongst them for most excellent."—Sandys' *Travels*, &c., folio, 1673, p. 52.

M. Ampère, in the *Revue des Deux Mondes* for August, 1853, states that in the *Arabian Nights Entertainments*, which are said to be such faithful pictures of oriental manners, there is no mention of the pipe. Neither is coffee to be met with in those tales, so delightful to all ages.

Java is said to have possessed it before 1496. Dr. Ruschenberg says:—

We are informed the Portuguese met with it on their first visit to Java. —*Voy. of U. S. S. Peacock*, vol. ii. p. 456, Lond. ed. 8vo. 1838.

Edmund Scott, factor for the East India Company at Bantam, thus describes the luxuries of the Javans :—

> They are very great eaters—and they haue a certaine hearbe called *bettaile* which they vsually have carryed with them wheresoeuer they goe, in boxes, or wrapped vp in cloath like a suger loafe : and also a nutt called *pinange*, which are both in operation very hott, and they eate them continually to warme them within, and keepe them from the fluxe. They doe likewise take much *tabacco*, and also *opium*.—*An exact discovrse*, etc., *of the East Indians*, London, 1606. 4o. Sig. N. 2.

Crauford dates its introduction into Java, 1601, but admits that the natives had traditions of having possessed it long before. (*Indian Archipelago*, vol. i. pp. 104, 409, 410. 8vo.) Rumphius, in the latter part of the seventeenth century, found it universal even where the Portuguese and Spaniards had never been.

Savary, in his *Parfait Négociant*, states that the Persians have used tobacco 400 years, and probably received it from Egypt. (See *Med. Chir. Review*, 1840, p. 335.)

Olearius found it fully established in Persia, 1637, only about fifty years after its arrival in England. (Lond. 1662, in fol. p. 322.)

Sir John Chardin, who was in Persia about the year 1670, relates in his Travels, that the Persians smoked long before the discovery of America, and that tobacco had been cultivated there from time immemorial.

> Coffee without tobacco is meat without salt.—Persian Proverb, Sale's *Koran*, Preliminary Discourse, 169. ed. 8vo.

In Persia smoking was prohibited by Shah Abbas. There were two princes of this name. The first began his reign 1585 A. D., died 1628 : the second began 1641, died 1666. The proclamation against smoking was probably issued by the first, in 1634.

Ledyard says, the Tartars have smoked from remote antiquity (*Travels*, 326). Du Halde speaks of tobacco as one of the natural productions of Formosa, whence it was largely imported by the Chinese (p. 173. Lond. ed. 8vo. 1741).

"Honest John Bell" (of Antermony), who travelled in China about 1720, asserts that it is reported the Chinese have had the use of tobacco for many ages. Mr. Lane, on the other hand, speaks of the "introduction of tobacco into the East, in the beginning of the seventeenth century of our era."—(*Arabian Nights*, Note 22, cap. iii.)

In 1634 Olearius found the Russians so addicted to tobacco that they would spend their money on it rather than bread. (See edit. above quoted, lib. iii. p. 83.)

Snuff.—In a "Natural History of Tobacco," in the *Harleian Misc.*, 535, we are told that,—

The Virginians were observed to have pipes of clay before ever the English came there; and from those barbarians we Europeans have borrowed our mode and fashion of smoking. * * * * *The Irishmen do most commonly powder their tobacco, and snuff it up their nostrils*, which some of our Englishmen do, who often chew and swallow it.

Howell, in a letter on Tobacco, says:—

The Spaniards and Irish take it most in powder or smutchin, and it mightily refreshes the brain, and I believe there's as much taken in this way in Ireland, as ther is pipes in England; one shall commonly see the serving-maid upon the washing-block, and the swain upon the plowshare, when they are overtir'd with labour, take out their boxes of smutchin and draw it into their nostrils with a quill, and it will beget new spirits in them, with a fresh orjour to fall to their work again.—*Epistolæ Ho-Elianæ*, Jan. 1st, 1646.

Cowper and Smoking.—The following genial and characteristic letter from Cowper is taken from a scarce and ephemeral *brochure*, entitled, *Convivialia et Saltatoria, or a few Thoughts upon Feasting and Dancing*, a poem, in two parts, &c., by G. Orchestikos: London, printed for the author, 1800, pp. 62. At page 39 will be found

Nicotiana: a Poetical Epistle, in praise of Tobacco; intended as a refutation of the ill-founded remarks of William Cowper, Esq., respecting this plant, in his elegant poem on Conversation. By Phil. Nicot.

The man I pity who abhors the fume
Of fine *Virginia* floating in his room;
For, truly may Tobacco be defined,
A Plant preserving Health and Peace of mind.
1800.

Next follows the poem, dedicated "To the Tobacconists in general of England and its colonies," and consisting of some 350 lines, concluding with the following .—

Now by way of a Postscript, for I cannot conclude
Without *once more* entreating, that you'll be so good
As to favour me with an Epistle, and soon
Which in *my* estimation will be such a boon
That I'll *carefully* keep it; and dying, take care
To enjoin like Respect from my Son or my Heir;
And lest He should forget its great Value to ask,
Shall say,
It was wrote by the Hand, that first wrote out the Task:
No more I need mention, its Worth will appear,
And be kept as a Relic I *justly* hold dear.

Next comes the poet's kindly response:—

Dear Sir,

It is not in my power to send you an epistle that will entitle itself to any of the *honours* which you are so good as to promise to one from me. My time is not my own, but is partly engaged in attendance on a dear friend, who has long been in a very helpless state, and partly to the performance of what I owe to the public, a new edition of my Homer, and also of the poetical works of Milton.

With these labours in hand, together with the common avocations incident to everybody, it is hardly possible that I should have opportunities for writing letters. In fact, I am in debt to most of my friends, and to many of them have been long in debt, whose claims upon me are founded in friendship of long standing. To this cause you will be so good as to ascribe it, that I have not sooner thanked you for your humorous and pleasant contest with me on the subject of TOBACCO; a contest in which I have not, at present, leisure to exercise myself, otherwise I am hardy enough to flatter myself, that I could take off the force of some of your arguments.

"Should you execute your design of publishing what you have favoured me with a sight of, I heartily wish success to your muse militant, and that your reward may be—many a pleasant pipe supplied by the profits of your labours.

Being in haste, I can add no more, except that I am, with respect, and a due sense of the honour you do me,

Your obliged, &c.,

Weston Underwood, WILLIAM COWPER.
Oct. 4, 1793.

The Virtues of Tobacco.—It is refreshing to followers of the "Indian weed," in these modern days of "British Anti-Tobacco" Societies, to read the following celebration of its virtues by an early votary—James Howell—who writes thus in a letter already quoted from :—

January 1, 1646.

SIR, to usher in again old Janus, I send you a parcel of Indian perfume, which the Spaniard calls the holy herb, in regard of various virtues it hath, but we call it Tobacco. I will not say it grew under the King of Spain's window, but I am told that it was gathered near his gold mines of Potosi, (where they report, that in som places ther is more of that oar than earth) therefore it needs must be precious stuff. If moderately and seasonably taken, (as I find you always do,) 'tis good for many things, it helps digestion taken a while after meat, it makes to voi d rheume, break wind, and keeps the body open. A leaf or two being steept ore night in a little white wine is a vomit that never fails in its operation. It is a good companion to him that converseth with dead men, for if one hath bin long upon a book, or is toil'd with the pen, and stupified with study, it quicketh him, and dispels those clouds that usual o'refer (?) the brain. The smoak of it is one of the wholsomest sents that is against all contagious airs, for it o'remasters all other smells, as king James they say found true, when being once a hunting, a showr of rain drove him into a pigsty for shelter; wher he caus'd a pipe full to be taken of purpose. It cannot endure a spider or a Flea, with such like vermin, and if your hawk be troubled with any such, being blown into his feathers it frees him; It is good to fortifie and preserve the sight, the smoak being let in round about the balls of the eyes once a week and frees them from all rhemes, driving them back by way of repercussion; being taken backward 'tis excellent against the colick, and taken into the stomach 'twill beat and cleanse it; for I could istance in a great Lord (my Lord of Sunderland, President of York) who told me that he taking it downward into his stomach, it made him cast up an imposthume, bag and all, which had bin a long time engendered out of a bruise he had received at football, and so preserved his life for many years. Now to descend from the substance of the smoak, to the ashes, 'twis well known that the medcinal qualities thereof are very many; but they are so common that I will spare the inserting of them here. But if one would try a pretty conclusion how much smoak ther is in a pound of tobacco, the ashes will tell him; for let a pound be exactly weighed, and the ashes kept charily and weighed afterwards, what wants of a pound weight in the ashes cannot be denied to have bin smoak, which evaporated into air; I have bin told that Sir Walter Rawleigh won a wager of Queen Elizabeth upon this nicety.

In Barbary and other parts of Africa tis wonderful what a small pill of tobacco will do; for those who use to ride post through the sandy desarts, wher they meet not with anything thats potable or edible, sometimes three days together, they use to carry small balls or pills of tobacco, which being put under the toung, it affords them a perpetual moysture, and takes off the edge of appetit for som dayes.

Do you desire to read with pleasure all the Virtues of this modern Herb, you must read Doctor *Thorius Potologis*, an accurate piece couched in a strenuous Heroic Verse full of matter, and continuing its strength from first to last; insomuch, that for the bigness, it may be compared to any piece of Antiquity, and in my opinion, is beyond βατρακομιομαχία or γαλεωνομαχία.

So I conclude these rambling notions, presuming you will accept this small argument of my great respect unto you: If you want paper to light your pipe, this letter may serve the turn; and if it be true what the poets frequently sing, that *Affection* is *Fire*, you shall need no other than the clear Flames of the Donor's Love to make ignition, which is comprehended in this Distich

Ignis Amor si sit, Tobaccum accendere nostrum
Nulla petetœnda tibi fax nisi dantis Amor.

If *Love* be *Fire*, to light this Indian Weed,
The Donor's *Love* of Fire may stand instead.

So I wish you as to myself a most happy New Year; may the beginning be good, the middle better, and the end best of all.

Your most faithful and truly affectionate servant, J. H.

Tobacco and Health.—Mr. W. H. Wills, of Bristol, one of the largest tobacco manufacturers of England, writes:—

For some years past I have noticed the freedom of our work-people from epidemic attacks. There are upwards of five hundred persons in Bristol engaged in the manufacture of tobacco, many of whom are living in some of the worst localities, in a sanitary point of view, that the city can exhibit; yet, during the severe visitations of the cholera in 1849 and 1852, only one person out of this number was fatally attacked. Among our own hands, numbering upwards of ninety, we had not a single case. I am satisfied too, that, apart from acute disease, the business is not injurious to the duration of life, as I can enumerate nearly twenty persons who have worked in our manufactory for terms varying from twenty-five to fifty years, and who have always enjoyed excellent health.

N. Simeon, in a report presented by him to the Minister of Public Works, and communicated to the *Annales d'Hygiène Publique*, October, 1843, states that at that time the French government, which has the monopoly of tobacco, employed more than five thousand workmen in its manufacture; who were found, as a body, to enjoy a remarkable exemption from prevailing epidemics. This was especially the case at Lyons, where those so employed escaped to a man the typhoid fever of 1842, and at Toulouse, when the influenza attacked four per cent. of the inhabitants, while of those employed in the manufacture of tobacco, but two out of 286 were affected. With regard to phthisis, this exemption is still more remarkable. It is true that the workmen are subject to catarrhs, which are, however, slight, and easily removed. Phthisis is also of rare occurrence among the workmen at Bordeaux; at Hâvre, where this disease makes fearful ravages, the tobacco manufacturers are exempt; and at Strasburg, Morlaix, and Lille, it is less frequent among this class than those engaged in other occupations. These facts are attributed by M. Simeon to the narcotic properties of the tobacco; but he invites the attention of the profession to the subject.

In 1836, M. Maurice Ruef, of Strasbourg, published a paper on the health of the workmen in the Royal Manufactorie, in which he asserted that—"Pulmonary consumption is rare among the workmen who are engaged from their youth in the manipulation of tobacco; moreover, this disease makes much less rapid progress than it does usually in those who may happen to have the germ of it already developed when they enter the workshop."

Six years afterwards, (May 31, 1842,) this gentleman wrote a letter to the editor of the *Gazette Médicale*, affirming that his experience during the interval had amply confirmed the accuracy of his statements.

In 1849, which was a terrible year to New Orleans, and the towns on the Mississippi River, there were some spots comparatively safe from the epidemic, and these were the tobacco manufactories.

But the term tobacco manufacturer is, perhaps, too exclusive as a principal one in so interesting an inquiry. For practical purposes, it would be well to know how far man's connexion with tobacco exempts him from various complaints.

Besides cigar rollers, cut-and-dry choppers, and snuff makers, there are those engaged in planting, attending, curing, packing, warehousing, and loading—all being brought in different degrees of contact with the 'weed.' On plantations, the negro and overseer are alike subject to the cholera, and indeed to the same complaints as the neighboring cotton grower. In curing and drying houses, the men are partially safe from epidemics, and invariably free from lung complaints. But it is to the factory we must go to learn the full extent of this singular preservative. Not until the leaf has been cured for some time, or at all events passed through the hogshead, do these neutralizing qualities show themselves; and it must be brought into continual contact with the men, and in a room or workshop of some kind, for them to be the subjects of its preservation.

In London, the great tobacco *quartier* is Goodman's Fields. The manufacturers there—mostly Jews—describe their men as being remarkably free from lung complaints, skin diseases, and affections of the liver; although there are a few instances where torpidity of the latter organ is complained of. Many of these men use oil as a part of their diet, agreeably to the custom of their race, and enjoy health superior still to those who do not take any.

One thing, however, is observable in all cigar and tobacco factories, the men neither are nor look cheerful; they rarely enjoy those bright animal spirits which other occupations induce.

A tobacco manufacturer is seldom high, he is seldom low; he appears to have entered that middle state of existence which some think the most enviable. His trot may be called the "jog trot." He rarely figures as a declaimer, rarely gets drunk and alarms the neighborhood of his residence. What he invariably does, is to live contentedly, and without grumbling; and consents to undergo a pickling in tobacco, to perhaps the slight deadening of his nerves, the undoubted weakening of his mind and strength of will, for the sake of preserving his skin, liver, and lungs from frequent epidemics.

Another peculiarity still more remarkable is this—the ordinary nervous distrust which smoking induces is seldom experienced by those engaged in manipulating tobacco. It has been remarked, indeed, that where a man could not indulge in three pipes a day without feeling symptoms of indigestion, he could double the number after he became employed by a tobacconist, and feel none of the old symptoms.

Smoking before drinking impure river water will prevent the diarrhea. In certain unmentionable skin disorders, the washing of the parts with water having tobacco steeped in it will drive it away. These, and similar recipes, are common in the Mississippi Valley.

Raleigh's Snuff-box.—Sir Walter Raleigh's snuff-box, out of which he took a pinch on the scaffold, was in constant use by the late Duke of Sussex, and was knocked down at his sale for £6.

Tobacco-takers.—Dr. Caldwell says that there are but three animals that can abide tobacco, namely: the African rock goat —the most loathsome creature on earth—the foul tobacco worm —and the rational creature, man!

Tobacco Literature.—As an illustration of the precedence which Englishmen took of foreigners in their propensity for smoking, Mons. Misson, in his *Memoirs of his Travels over England*, written in 1697, notices the very general use of tobacco; and in Devon, (Raleigh's native county,) and Cornwall, among the women. Misson attributes to their much smoking not only the thoughtfulness, taciturnity, and melancholy of the English, but also their excellence as theologians; for, he says:—

Tobacco not only breeds profound theologists, but also begets moral philosophers; witness the following *sonnet* to a pipe:

Doux charme de ma solitude
Brulante pipe, ardent fourneau!
Qui purges d'humeur mon cerveau,
Et mon esprit d'inquietude.

Tabac! dont mon ame est ravie,
Lorsque je te voi te perdre en l'air,
Aussi promptement q'un éclair,
Je vois l'image de ma vie:

Tu demets dans mon souvenir,
Ce q'un jour je dois devenir,
N'étant q'une cendre animée;
Et tout d'un coup je m'aperçois;
Que courant apres ta fumée
Je pape de même que toi.

Mr. Ozell, who did Misson's Travels into English, has somewhat shorn the sonnet of its just proportions, thus:—

Sweet smoking pipe, bright glowing stove,
Companion still of my retreat,
Thou dost my gloomy thoughts remove,
And purge my brain with gentle heat.

Tobacco, charmer of my mind,
When, like the meteor's transient gleam,
Thy substance gone to air, I find,
I think, alas! my life's the same.

What else but lighted dust am I?
Thou show'st me what my fate will be;
And when my sinking ashes die,
I learn that I must end like thee.

The author of this sonnet was Esprit de Raymond, Comte de Modène, putative father of Armande Béjart, wife of Moliere. He is also the author of some pleasant verses: "La Peinture du Pays d'Adioussias, c'-est-à-dire de l'état d'Avignon; an epistle to a young person about to take the veil; a set of monorhymes in *if*, addressed to "Inizul;" and a sonnet on the crucifixion. While on the subject of Misson, allow me to recommend the perusal of Ozell's Preface or Dedication; it is the. finest gem of snobbery in the language.

There is a *Hymnus Tabaci*, a poem in two books, written in Latin verse, in imitation of Lucretius by Raphael Thorius, a Dutch (French?) bard, entitled '*De Paeto seu Tabaco.*' A *resumè* of this poem is given in Horae Nicotianae, (vol. v. p. 47, etc., of *Blackwood's Magazine.*)

Thorius was a notorious bon vivant, and once took advantage of the learned Peirex, whose powers as a wine bibber by no means equalled his own, to pledge him in an enormous beaker of wine; nor would he accept any of Peirex's excuses for getting off. But when the other, having challenged Thorius in turn, filled the beaker with water, it cost our poet many a qualm to swallow the whole of such an unwonted draught. Bayle says:—

Je pense qu'il ne doutoit guère de la maxime, que les buveurs d'eau ne sauvoient faire de bon vers. De sa vie, peut-être, il ne se trouva plus embarrassé que quand M. de Peirex l'obliga de boire boire un grand verre d'eau: le roi Jacques souhaita qu'on lui fit ce conte qui est fort visible.—*Dict. Critiq.*, tom. iii. p. 2875.

See, too, Gapendus, *in vit.* Periesk ad *ann* 1606. Thorius was long a favorite about the Court of James I., and died in London of the plague in 1629.

Nothing, says the writer in *Blackwood*, can be finer than the commencement, in which he invokes (*Pieridum loco*) a certain celebrated smoking knight of Amsterdam, by name Paddæus, or Van Paddy.

> Innocuus calices et amicam, Vatibus herbam
> Vinque datam foli, et laeti miracula fumi
> Aggredior. Tu, qui censu decoratus Equestri
> Virtutem titulis, titulos virtutibus ornas,
> Antiquum et Phœbi nato promitteis honorem,
> Tu, Paddæe, fave.

This poem was translated into English verse by Henry Player, who appended the original in 1716, dedicating his version to Mrs. Mary Owen, who appears to have been a learned lady and a snuff-taker, and the latter to Solomon Lowe, her tutor.

Player has brought out his author with all the paraphernalia of *testimonia auctorum*, lists of his works, of editions of this on tobacco, (the *editio princep* of which appears to have appeared anterior to 1625), *Judicia Virorum Doctorum*, etc.

An earlier translation into English had appeared with the following title :

> Hymnus Tabaci, a poem in Honour of Tobacco, Heroically composed by Raphäel Thorius, made English by Peter Hausted, Master of Arts, Cambridge, London, 1651, 8vo.

Dr. Aldrich, Dean of Christ Church, Oxford, a liberal patron of the weed (and indeed of all good things) has, also, moralized smoking, as the following declares :—

> Aldricius nobis nomen memorabile, paeti
> Omnia qui novit commoda, sic cecinit,
> Paetum mane viget, marescit nocte, cadit,
> Ut redit in cineres incensum ; mortuus omnis

Sic redit in cineres, fitque quod ante fuit.
Quis non è tubulis discat nunc reddere fumos,
Vivere cum doceant et benè posse mori.

And in a similar strain is this song:—

Tobacco is an Indian weed,
Grows green at morn, cut down at eve;
It shows our decay, we are but clay.
Think on this when you smoak Tobacco.

The pipe that is so lily-white,
Wherein so many take delight,
Is broke with a touch: Man's life is such.
Think on this when you smoak Tobacco.

The pipe that is so foul within,
Shows how man's soul is stained with sin.
It does require to be purg'd with fire.
Think on this when you smoak Tobacco.

The ashes that are left behind
Do serve to put us all in mind
That unto dust return we must.
Think on this when you smoak Tobacco.

The smoke that does so high ascend,
Shows that man's life must have an end;
The vapour's gone: Man's life is done.
Think on this when you smoak Tobacoo.

The author and date of this song are uncertain. There are several versions of it. The following, the earliest yet discovered, is from a MS. of the early part of the seventeenth century, in the possession of J. Payne Collier. It has the initials "G. W." (*i. e.*, George Withers?) at the end. Like Milton, Withers is said to have indulged in the luxury of smoking; and many of his evenings in Newgate (during his long imprisonment), when weary of numbering his steps, or telling the panes of glass, were solaced with "meditations over a pipe," not without a grateful acknowledgment of God's mercy in thus wrapping up "a blessing in a weed."

Why should we so much despise,
So good and wholesome an exercise,
As early and late to meditate:
Thus think, and drink tobacco.

The earthen pipe so lily-white,
Shows that thou art a mortal wight,
Even such, and gone with a touch:
Thus think, and drink tobacco.

And when the smoke ascends on high,
Think on the worldly vanity
Of worldly stuff 'tis gone with a puff:
Thus think, and drink tobacco.

And when the pipe is foul within,
Think how the soul's defiled with sin,
To purge with fire it doth require:
Thus think, and drink tobacco.

Lastly, the ashes left behind,
May daily show to move the mind
That to ashes and dust return we must:
Thus think, and drink tobacco.

Drinking tobacco was another term for smoking it:—

The smoke of tobacco (the which Dodoneus called rightly Henbane of Peru) *drunke* and *drawen* by a pipe, filleth the membranes of the brain, and astonisheth and filleth many persons with such joy and pleasure, and sweet loss of senses, that they can by no means be without it.—*The Perfuming of Tobacco and the great Abuse committed in it,* 1611.

The following riddle, headed "Tobacco," is taken from the "Cambridge University MS.," D. D. V. 75, and, as the dates of other pieces in the volume prove, was written between 1580 and 1600:—

A foole or a phisicion, I know not whether
His penner hath and inck horn all in one;

Kept in an eeles skin, or in a case of leather,
   And made of clay converted to a stone:
His cotton is of dark deroied grene,
   His matter all within his nose is pend,
And in the strangest guise y^{t} may be seene
   He drawes his incke out of a candel's end.
Herewith his missives round about he sendes,
   Till breath and beard and all the house do stink:
He wrings his neck and giueth to his freindes,
   "Hold galantes here, and to Galenus drink."

THE END.

www.ingramcontent.com/pod-product-compliance
Lightning Source LLC
LaVergne TN
LVHW021144110826
845150LV00005B/1121

* 9 7 8 1 4 2 5 5 4 7 8 3 7 *